Praise for *Lights, Camera, Witchcraft*

"This book is a must-read for anyone interested in US history, film studies, anthropology, psychology, literature, folklore, practicing witches, and for people who like movies. It is a meticulously researched and scholarly, yet highly readable, humorous, and entertaining analysis of the role of the figure of the witch in American culture."

—Candace C. Kant, PhD, academic dean of Cherry Hill Seminary

"Heather Greene's comprehensive and lively survey of witches in US film and television deftly digs into the inherent tension within this fascinating recurring figure—one that can offer thrilling spectacle and feminist liberation while contending with the forces of folklore and Hollywood patriarchy."

—Dr. Jonathan Lupo, associate professor of communication,
English department, Saint Anselm College

"Witches are the curious stuff of dual dimensions: real-world religious practitioners, and horror and fantasy characters of the entertainment industry. These expressions often overlap, and then inform each other, at least in the assumptions of many genre consumers. In this volume Heather Greene provides a helpful discussion of this phenomenon that is both entertaining and informative."

—John W. Morehead, creator of www.TheoFantastique.com
and coeditor of *The Journal of Gods and Monsters*

"Heather Greene talks of revenge and redemption in an artful socio-cultural exploration of the cinematic texts we have known all our lives. *Lights, Camera, Witchcraft* is a comprehensive look at some of the rarer and more revealing witch tropes on film. The book discusses racism, female agency, and more, while artfully depicting film's obsession with the witch in all its wild and wonderful glory. I loved it."

—Lilith Dorsey, author of *Water Magic* and *Orishas,
Goddesses and Voodoo Queens*

"Heather Greene's beautiful compendium of TV and movie witches is a rich source of information on the times in the US and the witch figures that embody the zeitgeist of each."

—H. Byron Ballard, author of *Roots, Branches & Spirits*

"American cinema has greatly impacted how both the public sees witchcraft and how witches see themselves. That fascinating history has never been told before now. This book is a 'must-read' for anyone interested in the history of modern witchcraft."

—Jason Mankey, author of *Transformative Witchcraft*

"A definitive guide to the subject of witchcraft in American television and film… Greene expertly maps out the archetype of the witch and the witch's evolution as

portrayed by the media, both positive and negative lights … The book is informative, intelligent, and entertaining."

—Mat Auryn, bestselling author of Psychic Witch

"A perceptive, nuanced, and comprehensive overview of the witch figure in American film and television, from the late 1800s to the present day. Based on solid scholarship, yet user-friendly and entertaining, this book will appeal to anyone interested in film and media history, representations of women and magic, and feminist analysis. Highly recommended for all libraries."

—Sabina Magliocco, professor of anthropology
and chair, program in the Study of Religion at
University of British Columbia, Vancouver

"Heather Greene offers a thorough and well-written historical overview … Greene contextualizes these depictions amid broader social developments, including the Satanic Panic and the emergence of new religions like Wicca and LaVeyan Satanism whose practitioners called themselves 'witches.'"

—Dr. Ethan Doyle White, author of Wicca: History, Belief,
and Community in Modern Pagan Witchcraft and
coeditor of Magic and Witchery in the Modern West

"Heather Greene has conjured a comprehensive compendium of witch films from the very earliest silent reels right up to the present … This is an invaluable handbook which follows themes threading through the whole history of movies."

—Dr. K.A. Laity, author and tenured professor of film,
gender studies, and popular culture

"If you've been hunting for a thorough—and thoroughly enjoyable—tome about witches in pop occulture, look no further! Heather Greene has written the definitive book on the subject. Lights, Camera, Witchcraft is a smart and spellbinding excursion into the history of bewitching storytelling for the screen. Read it and be dazzled."

—Pam Grossman, author of Waking the Witch
and host of The Witch Wave podcast

"Scholarly yet accessible, Greene provides a masterful visual and symbolic taxonomy of the witch, framed expertly within the context of American film and media history. Greene holds up the magic mirror to American culture, showing us how the cinematic witch is a thinly veiled metaphor for the reinforcement of women's social roles."

—Amy Hale, PhD, anthropologist and folklorist, writing
about the occult, culture, art, women, and Cornwall

LIGHTS, CAMERA, WITCHCRAFT

© Sandra Flores Photography

About the Author

Heather Greene is a freelance writer, journalist, and editor. She received a BA in film at Wesleyan University and an MA in film studies from Emory University. She also studied film and theater at Cornell University and the University of Paris. She has written for Religion News Service, Turner Classic Movies, *The Wild Hunt*, *Circle Magazine*, Patheos.com, and other outlets. She is a member of Circle Sanctuary, Covenant of the Goddess, and the Religion Newswriters Association.

A Critical History of Witches in American Film and Television

LIGHTS, CAMERA
WITCHCRAFT

HEATHER GREENE
Foreword by Peg Aloi

Llewellyn Publications
Woodbury, Minnesota

First Edition: *Bell, Book, and Camera: A Critical History of Witches in American Film and Television* © Heather Greene, McFarland & Company, 2018.

Second Edition, Expanded and Revised

Art credit list on page 419
Book design by Samantha Peterson
Cover design by Shannon McKuhen
Cover illustration by Dominick Finelle

Llewellyn Publishing is a registered trademark of Llewellyn Worldwide Ltd.

Library of Congress Cataloging-in-Publication Data (Pending)
ISBN: 978-0-7387-6853-3

Llewellyn Publications
A Division of Llewellyn Worldwide Ltd.
2143 Wooddale Drive
Woodbury, MN 55125-2989
www.llewellyn.com

Printed in the United States of America

Magic is creating what you dream.
Don't ever stop dreaming.

*This book is dedicated to my parents, who
taught me to always believe in magic.
To my partner "in all things"
and to my wonderfully eclectic children.*

Contents

Acknowledgments

There have been many people who have supported this project and allowed me the time to walk through this magical journey of cinematic witchcraft. I'd like to thank, first and foremost, my family who left me alone to watch endless hours of movies and endured my nonstop chatter on the subject. Their unconditional support and love are inspiring and can never be repaid.

I also want to acknowledge a few people who took time for personal correspondence to clarify and assist with various topics, including Bill Krause, Hanna Grimson, and the entire team at Llewellyn Worldwide, Thomas Doherty, Philip Heselton, Steven Intermill, Dr. Emerson Baker, Ashley Mortimer, Rev. Selena Fox, Jason Mankey, Eric Stedman, Adam Simon, Chika Oduah, Michael Henry, Jerry Murbach, Bob Sennett, Emily Uhrin, Anna Biller, Tomas Zurek, Sean Bridgeman, Geraldine Beskin, and Jeff Miller.

I'm sure there are others. It has been a long road, and projects like this cannot be done without a team of excellent people pushing them along.

Foreword

Witches seem to be everywhere in twenty-first century America: at the movies, on television, in comics, cartoons, literature, music, video games, and advertising. Indeed, witches are so pervasive in popular culture that we barely notice them anymore, and it seems barely a month goes by without a new witchy series, film, comic, or video game arriving on the scene. We've seen this before in the occult revival of the 1960s and '70s, in the New Age witchcraft of the 1980s, and in the Hollywood-fueled witchcraft obsession of the 1990s. Since the late 1990s, witches have also invaded the internet, and in more recent years, our newest form of media: social media. Witchcraft is now not only a subject for entertaining fiction but a widely disseminated form of self-care and social engagement. It's hard to say how we got here, but there's no question that the witches of film and television have been with us for the entire journey.

Beginning with her introduction, Heather Greene reminds us that the figure of the witch is nothing if not complex and contradictory: "The witch archetype," she says, "exists in two modes: one of oppression and one of empowerment." As well, the witch is someone who changes and adapts to the times she inhabits: our view of witches historically is difficult to separate from our contemporary view of them. This is one reason why *Lights, Camera, Witchcraft* is such a valuable contribution to scholarship: it has such a specific focus on the historical and cultural context of witches in entertainment media. The historical evolution of the witch, it turns out, is a significant factor in how she is portrayed in both historical and contemporary narratives; for example, what we now know about the witch craze in medieval Europe or the North American witchcraft persecutions shifts frequently as more scholars pursue research in the social sciences, archaeology, and other fields.

Clearly a contemporary witch in 1939 (such as the Wicked Witch of the West, played by Margaret Hamilton in *The Wizard of Oz*), arriving in the midst of war and economic strife, has a completely different cultural context compared to the witch who appears in 1987 (like the trio of women in the film adaptation of John Updike's novel *The Witches of Eastwick*), at a time when the nation is experiencing economic growth and the decadence and inequity that often accompanies it. Seeing witches inhabit our modes of entertainment through the decades of the twentieth century and beyond, we begin to see she has always been with us, bewitching us on the silver screen, beckoning us to keep watching from the couch late into the night. The witch pervades the horror genre too, and no exploration of horror would be complete without considering the witch's role.

But beyond horror, the witch is also a figure that has gifted us with comedy, romance, and social commentary. She may be scary at times, but she is also seductive, strong, and occasionally silly. It's all here, in this comprehensive guide to the witch's presence in film and television, from the early days of silent pictures to the latest series on Netflix. Guiding the reader with specific cultural signposts within and around the film and television industries, Greene's expert survey includes witchcraft on-screen and also the magic occurring behind the scenes as film and television become more inventive, sophisticated, and influential over the years. The level of historical detail is fascinating and often reveals surprising insights.

I hope all readers interested in any aspect of witchcraft will appreciate the enormous impact that film and television representations have had on our understanding and reception of the witch and the culture, communities, and stories that surround her. Greene's deeply thoughtful history of the witch in American film and television is also on some level a powerful and loving examination of American history itself. This book shows us all the wondrous things the witch—whose presence has imbued American culture for centuries with magic and knowledge, power and wisdom, fear and fantasy—can ultimately teach us about ourselves.

Peg Aloi
Film and TV critic
Media studies scholar

A Woman Unleashed:
An Introduction

The word "witch" and what it evokes is complicated, but yet it seems so simple. The witch is a woman with a black hat, green skin, and a broom. She is a deviant mistress of the dark arts. She understands how to work with herbs and roots, and she eats children for supper. The witch owns crystals, books, beads, and a black cat. She dances under the moon and cackles while stirring her brew. She is the seducer of husbands and the consort of Satan. She worships the great goddess and loves nature. She wears a lace bonnet to church, breaks glass with her mind, and serves mousse with tannis root. We know who she is. We recognize her.

As a child, I adored the Metro-Goldwyn-Mayer (MGM) classic film *The Wizard of Oz* (1939). I looked forward to watching it each year when CBS aired the movie on Halloween. I was particularly fascinated with and simultaneously terrified by Margaret Hamilton's portrayal of the Wicked Witch of the West. I loved her loud cackle and how her cape flew as she spun dramatically in the orange-colored smoke. Over the years, as I became increasingly interested in the occult and reality-based Witchcraft, I never abandoned my childhood love of that film. To this day, after years of film scholarship and occult study, I still credit *The Wizard of Oz* as my favorite movie of all time. While the film as a whole is undoubtedly one of Hollywood's gems, it is the Wicked Witch who ultimately stood out for me. She triggered something that I understood on a deeper level—something inspirational. Although clearly the antagonist, this green-skinned woman in her jet-black dress depicts someone who commands her own power. She is a woman unleashed, a nonconformist, and a rebel.

Within fictional narratives, the witch is, at her most basic, a woman who lives in the space society has chosen to abandon. She practices the crafts that her community marks as unacceptable or that religion defines as sinful. She is the adolescent girl discovering her sexuality, the woman who commands it, and the crone who no longer needs it but still understands it. That is the witch; she is all of those things and more. At her very essence, she is the woman who knows too much—about society, about life, and about herself. She is both the oppressed and the empowered.

In the introduction of her book *The Witch in History*, Diane Purkiss writes, "I argue that the witch is not solely or simply the creation of patriarchy, but that women also invested heavily in the figure as a fantasy which allowed them to express and manage otherwise unspeakable fears and desires, centering on the question of motherhood and children." [1] Purkiss's statement hits on one of the central reasons I began this study. The witch archetype exists in two modes: one of oppression and one of empowerment. How is it possible that one single cultural construct can contain two strikingly different and seemingly opposed central meanings? Moreover, when and how does this meaning shift and how does it affect narrative presentations?

In her book *A Skin for Dancing In: Possession, Witchcraft and Voodoo in Film*, Tanya Krzywinska observes the same point, saying:

> The figure of the female witch has commonly been seen in critical works on the horror film as a product of male fantasies … little consideration has been given to the idea that the cinematic witch is likely to appeal to a different set of fantasies specific to women. [2]

As noted by Purkiss and Krzywinska, Western manifestations of what we know as a witch are far more complicated as the curtain is pulled back. While it would seem that her construction is wholly driven by patriarchal concepts and a very specific religious bias, the story is far more intricate. Upon closer observation, it appears that the witch archetype is not only dependent upon traditional religious or political views stemming from a male-centered eye, but she is also dependent on shifting social contexts with regard to gender politics, sexuality, demographics of reception, and even modes of storytelling, which in this discussion would be limited to cinema and television.

The witch as a narrative character construction within Western culture is not as fixed in meaning as one might first think. Centuries of influence are woven into a

---

1. Diane Purkiss, *The Witch in History: Early Modern and Twentieth-Century Representations* (London: Routledge 1996), 2.

2. Tanya Krzywinska, *A Skin for Dancing In: Possession, Witchcraft and Voodoo in Film* (Trowbridge, Wiltshire: Flicks Books, 2000), 117.

very weighted and tangled mess of iconography and symbolic value that has modulated through belief systems, time, and cultural experience. As a result, the witch archetype exists in a type of liminal space where she has been used and used again as both a tool of oppression and an inspiration for self-making. The Wicked Witch, for example, was for me both a source of fear and one of empowerment. I understood that she was bad but also indulged in her decisiveness and strength.

Before going forward, it is important to note that Hollywood did not "re-create the wheel," so to speak. The witch archetype was already a recognizable, fully functioning cultural icon prior to the birth of the American film industry. She came to Hollywood already loaded with a depth of meaning derived predominantly from European and American colonial origins, but also partly from African Tradition Religions such as Vodun. More specifically, the dominant and most recognizable iconography found within the construction of the American narrative cinematic witch is primarily from fairy tales or folklore (e.g., Charles Perrault, the Grimm Brothers, Hans Christian Andersen), classic literature (e.g., Shakespeare, Nathaniel Hawthorne), visual art (e.g., Francisco Goya's *Witches' Sabbath*, 1798), American history (e.g., Salem's witch trials), or Catholic-based religious documents, including the infamous *Malleus Maleficarum* written in 1486.

Considering that legacy, the witch archetype easily found its way into the language of the fledgling American film industry through the cinematic adaption of known and beloved fairytales, mythologies, history, and literature. Over time, as the industry grew and responded to shifts in society, the witch's construction also changed, expanding her reach and her role. Based on this early anecdotal observation and other similar studies done in the past, I wondered if the changes in the witch's narrative, visual, or character construction over time would illustrate a relationship between this symbolic figure and American society. Would the changes in the character reflect society's relationship with or negotiation of gender roles, expressions of femininity, religiosity, content censorship, and more?

The Wicked Witch of the West is clearly different from Nancy in *The Craft* (1996) and both are different still from Samantha of the television series *Bewitched* (1964–1972). When does the witch change and why? If her most typical presentation is defined by its relationship to the patriarchy, how did changing social attitudes toward women affect fictional witch construction? Similarly, how did the modern Witchcraft movement affect the representation of fictional witches? What iconography lasted? What didn't? When is she popular and why?

To explore these questions, I had to limit my study to American productions. The US film and television industries are businesses as well as art forms that function within a definitive socioeconomic system for consumption first, if not wholly, by

American viewers. By limiting the study to that creative environment, it is easier to see the uniquely American construction of the witch and how she transforms within that unique social context. As a figure from the edges of society, the symbolic witch can potentially act as a mirror cast back inward, shedding light on the limitations imposed by American societal structures.

These observations and related questions are only a few examples of what I sought to explore through observing the extensive number of American witch films and television shows that span American cultural history. Some questions were answered quite clearly and some required speculation. Overall, the study demonstrates the continued love affair that Americans have with the witch and the story of a woman on the edge. It also demonstrates the contemporary evolution of a well-embedded and powerful cultural construct—one that has survived in Western society for centuries. In addition, the study shows how industry events and changing social dynamics can influence the makeup of our shared iconography, affecting how we see things beyond the silver screen. As such, the story of the Hollywood witch is a uniquely American tale, illustrating the industry's dance with censorship, sexual expression, gender negotiations, religious piety, and the overall transgressive social experience. In this way, the Hollywood witch is telling not only her own story, but rather a larger one about American society.

Understanding the Research

The first step in building this study was to delineate the different historical periods, each of which corresponds to a chapter in the book. The beginning and ending markers are informed either by trends in production, industry-based changes, or larger, socially relevant events. The journey begins in the 1800s with the very beginnings of the American film industry. Hollywood's actual birthdate is somewhat arbitrary due to parallel productions and inventions going on during the 1880s and 1890s. However, in 1898, the first American film containing a witch was produced and released: *The Cavalier's Dream* by the Edison Manufacturing Company.

Both chapters 1 and 2 explore the silent era from 1898–1920. During this time, the American film industry expanded from peep shows and novelty fun to viable narrative entertainment for mass audiences. The industry's center moved from its East Coast home to the West, emerging into the behemoth known as Hollywood. In these early days, filmmakers had free rein with regard to artistic experimentation and little censorship. They moved increasingly away from recording live events and plays to producing medium-driven art and entertainment. Witch characters were found predominantly in fantasies, literary adaptations, and historical works—all popular silent-era genres.

Chapters 3 and 4 explore a period of technological and industry change as Hollywood moved into what is called its Golden Age. From 1921–1939, filmmakers saw the coming of sound, color, and animation. In 1934, as the Great Depression took hold of the country, the film industry began to enforce a self-censorship code, which sought to maintain strict standards in cinematic content. By 1939, the industry introduced two of the most famous American witch characters: Disney's Wicked Queen (1937) and MGM's Wicked Witch of the West (1939).

Chapter 5 explores the war era and its influence on Hollywood output, including the production of films containing witches. Due to the call to support the cause, films increasingly became combat-focused, patriotic in nature, and centered on a certain amount of realism. Witch-related films, although not common, followed suit with narratives depicting the importance of maintaining a status quo. It was during this era that the film *I Married a Witch* (1942) was produced.

The year 1951 saw the coming of a conservative post-war consumerist America and the dawn of television. The new entertainment technology increasingly infiltrated American households and TV broadcasting reigned king; the film industry was forced to shift again. Chapter 6 begins in that year as television entered its own Golden Age and Hollywood found new ways to reach its audiences. Then, as detailed in chapter seven, the famed studio system went into decline. During the 1960s, the entertainment industry as a whole was forced to adapt to the progressive changes occurring in American society. Together, these two periods saw the production of one of Hollywood's most famous witch films: *Bell, Book and Candle* (1958), and the birth of three of the most famous American television witches: Sabrina, Samantha, and Morticia.

By 1968, the Production Code Administration and its tight censorship gave way to the MPAA rating system, opening a new chapter in American entertainment history and the American narrative witch's story. Consequently, chapter 8, which runs from 1968–1977, sees an explosive burst of activity in terms of witch productions. During this time, American society was changing fast as people were pushing cultural boundaries, challenging standards of behavior, and redefining roles and limitations with regard to sexuality, race, politics, gender, religion, and so on. In film specifically, the removal of the Production Code acted as a dam bursting, allowing filmmakers to depict subject matter never seen before this time. The fictional witch could not help but be affected, and the era saw the true birth of the Satanic horror witch and the release of two famous American witch films: *Rosemary's Baby* (1968) and *Carrie* (1976).

Before going forward, it is important to note that, due to the increase in output and the lack of a closed and censored studio system, I had to change the method of study and presentation. Rather than looking closely at a few films or episodes that fit the study's criteria, I had to focus on trends in production. With that change in methodology, it became obvious that the witch underwent a shift in her overall role within American narrative entertainment. From 1968 forward, her popularity came in waves about every twenty years.

In earlier decades, it was not the witch herself that was popular but rather the re-telling of certain narratives that happened to already include a witch figure such as the fairy tale or historical drama. In those early films, the witch rarely propelled the narrative. She merely existed as a symbolic or defining element within a plot. In later decades, the witch comes into her own as a powerful cultural icon of influence. She garners her own popularity through her own embedded meanings, which include social deviance, expressive sexuality, femininity, empowerment, and enchantment. Her popularity is driven by either social fear or by viewers aligning with the oft-marginalized female character. In each of the three popularity waves, there is a specific "season of the witch," including a growth in her popularity, a peak, and a decline.

With that said, chapter 9 begins in 1978 after the first witch popularity wave ended and a sociopolitical conservatism gripped the nation. Then, in the late 1980s, a second popularity wave began in reaction to a rising moral panic. Chapter 10 examines the ramifications of the so-called Satanic Panic, a conservative moral movement that started in 1983 and lasted well into the 1990s. Over these two decades, the US population became simultaneously obsessed with and terrified of Satanic-related crimes and stories. Chapter 10 closes in 1998 as the moral panic dissipated and the second witch popularity wave was ending. These two periods produced popular films such as *The Witches of Eastwick* (1987) and *The Craft* (1996) as well as the popular television shows *Sabrina, the Teenage Witch* (1996–2003) and *Charmed* (1998–2006).

The final two chapters run from 1999 to 2020. During these two periods, digital media changed the way entertainment was produced, distributed, and consumed. For the witches, the indie market allowed for an increase in replication of popular themes, such as the ghost witch and other paranormal topics. As such, the number of productions skyrocketed. In addition, as shown in chapter 11, the emergence of the Witchcraft movement directly influenced the language of witch productions. However, it wasn't until 2010 that a third wave of witch popularity began. As the interest in epic fantasy gave way to dark fantasy, the witch began to take center stage once again. By this period, horror had become a viral infection infiltrating other genres and flipping well-known stories on their heads, bringing an entirely new focus to the witch archetype. Maybe she was right all along and it was the world that was wrong.

Defining the "Witch Film"

Outside of marking the periods, the other challenge was to define the witch film or show. There is no prescribed "witch" genre, nor are there any other easily delineated lines in character construction. Is *Carrie* (1976) a witch film? If not, is Carrie a witch? These questions needed to be considered before moving forward with the study.

As my focus was on American film and television witches, the first easy elimination was any productions made outside the US. While that seems obvious, there are a number of popular films with witches that are not American (e.g., *The Wicker Man*, 1973). Additionally, after 1980, there was an increasing number of jointly made projects, including the famed Harry Potter film franchise. If my study was going to focus on the influence of American sociopolitical or film industry changes on the witch to derive a uniquely American archetype, all foreign productions would prove problematic and had to be left aside. In some cases, these jointly produced films and shows will be mentioned or considered to a degree when their influence merits such a mention.

More difficult was the selection of the films and shows themselves. With no pre-designated genre and no clear picture on how Hollywood specifically defines its narrative witch, I had to loosely create boundaries that would determine what productions would be included and what would not be. Magical figures abound in Hollywood film from wizards and mages to fairies and sorceresses. Witches are a particular type of magical figure in that canon. They are predominantly, but not always, women, and carry with them certain expectations, cultural baggage, narratives, iconography, and other accoutrements. The fairy or troll, magical nanny, fairy godmother, gypsy, Voodoo priestess, and even the sorceress is not necessarily the witch, although there are intersections. Similarly, the wizard, the mad scientist, the Voodoo priest, and the mage are also not necessarily witches. While these figures are all deviations of the fictional magical persona, they do not play the same iconic role or contain the same social implications with regard to gender and female sexuality.

As such, I determined that a production would be included only if there was a specific character called a witch. The narrative has to, at some point, define a key character as a witch in a clear recognizable form. This resulted in a body of films and shows that could be defined best by concentric circles based on character roles.

The smallest ring contains all productions that are about witchcraft with a main character who is a witch (e.g., *I Married a Witch*, 1942; *Bewitched*, 1964–1972; *The Witches of Eastwick*, 1987). The next circle out is made up of productions in which an important secondary character or antagonist is labeled a witch. The stories are not necessarily focused on witchcraft, but magic does play a role. (e.g., *The Wizard of Oz*,

1939; *Sleeping Beauty*, 1959; *Buffy the Vampire Slayer*, 1997–2003). The third ring includes productions that contain a minor witch character, typically a store owner, tarot card reader, or an old witch in the woods. This background character is often used as a plot device, a looming threat, comic relief, or moral compass (e.g., *Comin' Round the Mountain*, 1951; *Pumpkinhead*, 1988; *The Witch*, 2015).

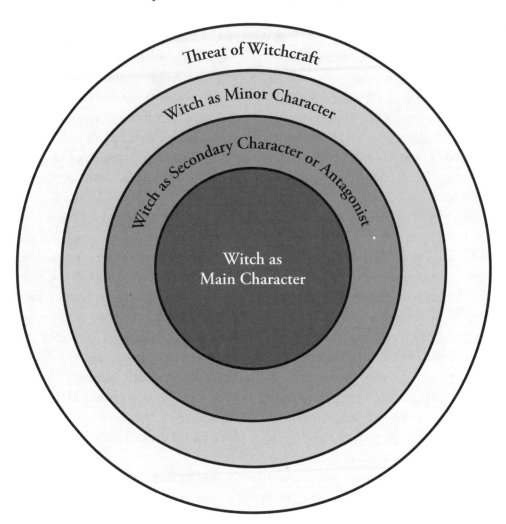

Witch Film Graphic Concentric Rings Diagram

The last circle contains films or shows that harbor the threat of a witch and witchcraft but no true witch. This threat can be posed by an actual physical character with supernatural ability (e.g., *Carrie*, 1976) or a ghost of a murdered woman labeled a witch (e.g., *The Blair Witch Project*, 1999). These productions are sometimes designated as witch films due to the suggestion of a magical or supernatural woman. However, there is no fully identified central witch character. For example, Carrie is only called "witch" one time in the entire film. Witchcraft exists in these stories only as a threat to the safety of the narrative's constructed world or a character's reality.

Floating on the outskirts of the graph are other types of witches who appear on a limited basis. These include warlocks, wizards, or other male witches as well as female witches defined specifically as having non-European origins. All of these witch constructions are discussed periodically when they intersect with other witch constructions or play a significant role in defining cinematic witchcraft.

Typecasting the Witch

Through the entire book I use several terms to categorize the witches themselves. The three main designations are "the accused woman," "the wild woman," and "the fantasy witch," each of which has its own number of subcategories. In addition, there are two minor witch constructions, including the magical other and the magical man. While these classifications do not always have hard lines of division, they do follow through over the entire history. As such, they provide a solid basis for understanding the trajectory and movements in American cinematic witch construction.

The "accused woman" is not a magical practitioner in any form, nor is she purposefully deviant. The "accused woman" generally functions within the established status quo; however, due to something that she did by accident or through the manipulation of others, she is labeled a witch. (e.g., *Maid of Salem*, 1937; *The Crucible*, 1996). The accused woman is most typically found in Salem-based stories or similar historically influenced narratives of abuse and persecution. Some of the ghost witches who appear in later films are defined through a back story as an "accused woman," who transforms after death into the second category: the "wild woman" (e.g., *Para-Norman*, 2012).

The "wild woman" is defined as a woman on the edge. She has knowledge beyond her social station, powers beyond the natural, or skills beyond acceptability (e.g., *Spitfire*, 1934; *Carrie*, 1976; *Witchcraft II*, 1989; *The Love Witch*, 2016). These witches live in a world constructed as real, not fantasy. Consequently, their magic, perceived or real, must be sourced whether its origin is divine, Satanic, nature-based, mental instability, or something else. The wild woman's power must have a *raison d'être*. The wild woman construction appears in a number of forms based predominately on age and genre. The subcategories include the wild child or teen (e.g., *Carrie*), the vamp (e.g., *Witchcraft II*), the elderly folk witch (e.g., *Pumpkinhead*), and the ghost witch (e.g., *Blair Witch*, 2016).

The third category, the "fantasy witch," is the largest of the three and contains some of the most well-known characters. It carries with it the greatest amount of cultural iconography from green faces to broomsticks. It is important to note that the fantasy witch category is not defined by the fantasy genre but rather a fantastical narrative premise defining the character construction. The fantasy witch can be found in productions that are pure fantasy (e.g., *The Wizard of Oz*), as well as comedies or dramas (e.g., *Bewitched*). The defining factor of a fantasy witch is found in her use of magic. Unlike the wild woman, her power does not need to be sourced or defined in moral, theological, or cultural terms. Fantasy is enough to justify her existence. Magic just is.

Like the wild woman, the fantasy witch contains a number of subcategories based on age and genre: the teen or child witch (e.g., *Sabrina, the Teenage Witch,* 1996–2003), the vamp (e.g., *Maleficent,* 2014), the fantasy crone (e.g., *Snow White and the Seven Dwarfs,* 1937), the clown witch (e.g., *The Wonderful Wizard of Oz,* 1910), and the Halloween witch (e.g., Witch Hazel in Warner Bros. *Looney Tunes* series, 1930–1969). There are other minor variations that appear as well.

The final two categories are the magical other and the magical man; both appear periodically over time. The magical other is defined by a marked ethnic, racial, or cultural difference from the main characters. Just as most witches are women, most American cinematic witches are racially white and constructed based on European historical and cultural trends. Magical practitioners outside of that specific context are often framed by an otherness, defined by accent or skin color, and carry with them their own language and presumptions as informed by mainstream society. Examples of this type of magic figure include the indigenous folk witch, Voodoo priestess, the gypsy fortune-tellers, and the witch doctor. It is important to note that while many of these characters do practice some form of magic or esoteric spiritual work, they are not always considered witches, and they do not qualify for the study unless they fit into the framework as designated earlier (e.g., *Maid of Salem,* 1937).

Similarly, the magical man appears just as infrequently because the witch is traditionally defined as a woman, and the themes surrounding the character are focused on female agency. However, male witches do appear on occasion. The character can be further broken down into the occultist, male clown witch, fantasy magician, the boy witch, the elderly wizard, and the warlock. As with the magical other, these various figures are not always defined as witches, and they only qualify for the study when the internal film structure posits them specifically as a witch (e.g., *Simon, King of the Witches,* 1971).

The delineations between these character constructions are not always perfect, especially as time goes on and filmmakers become increasingly interested in challenging their viewers by pitting film expectations against them to elicit reaction. In the early years, the genre-based use of witch characters makes their construction clear and the characters fit neatly into the various categories. The accused woman appears in westerns and historical dramas, and fantasy witches are in fairy tale adaptations. However, as time goes on, these lines are blurred. For example, the 1987 film *Witches of Eastwick* has its wild women flirt dangerously close to a fantasy realm, and in the 2014 film *Maleficent*, Disney reconstructs its famous fantasy witch character with the backstory of the accused woman who is forced to become wild.

Main Types of American Cinematic Witches

- The accused woman
- The wild woman (e.g., wild child or teen, vamp, folk witch, the modern clown witch)
- The fantasy witch (e.g., Victorian clown witch, Halloween witch, fantasy crone, child or teen witch, vamp, magical mom, good fairy)
- Other witches (e.g., the magical man, the magical other)

It is also important to note that the definitions above are formed solely by the structure of the films themselves and what is presented within the limitations of their own worlds and not by external analysis or influence. In other words, one could say that all magic, as witchcraft, is sourced because it is culturally defined by overarching theological assumptions. Witchcraft is evil. This suggestion is readily apparent in fantasy and horror films in which only the evil characters, specifically women, use magic. While this important sociocultural observation is addressed within the context of each period and within trends of witch construction, it does not define the study's categories. For example, "Hansel and Gretel" adaptations typically contain an evil witch, and the fairy tale has been used to promote that point. However, within the narrative itself, the witch's magical ability is not defined by theology or the like. In other words, it isn't sourced. She just is, because, in the fantasy realm, magic exists as a working part of the universe.

Another good example is found in categorizing the witches in *The Wiz* (1978). While the three figures are all played by Black Americans, none of them can be designated as magical others. Within the film's own universe, the narrative does not "other" these witches in any way outside of them just being magical women. The entire cast is made up of Black Americans and the adaptation is presented as a uniquely and recognizable American story. The witches belong in that world. *The Wiz* is a fantasy film, and the witches fall into the fantasy category of witch construction. As demonstrated with sourcing, it is the film's internal universe that informs the study's categorization of the witch, not its relationship to an external subjective influence.

Thematic and Narrative Repetition

There are a number of themes and narratives that consistently follow the witch through her journey across the decades in American film and television. Many of these are a result of beloved stories being told and retold; others are a function of general themes that surround femininity within Western society, and still others are theologically or historically based.

The most common literary adaptations are Shakespeare's *Macbeth*, the German fairy tales *Hansel and Gretel* and *Snow White and the Seven Dwarfs* both collected by the Brothers Grimm, L. Frank Baum's *The Wonderful Wizard of Oz*, and *Feathertop*, a moral tale written by novelist Nathanial Hawthorne. These well-loved and well-known literary stories are consistently sourced, adapted, re-adapted and reworked over Hollywood's entire history, producing subtle variations on their classic witches. The repetition helps to perpetuate the common mythology we tell of these characters.

Two other consistently reproduced stories are the legendary histories of Joan of Arc and Salem, Massachusetts. While there are few productions that retell the stories as a whole (e.g., *Joan the Woman*, 1916; *Three Sovereigns for Sarah*, 1985), the two histories act as inspiration. Salem or "a small town in New England" exists as a backdrop or proscenium for many witch sagas. For example, productions like *Love at Stake* (1987), *Bewitched*, and *ParaNorman* (2012) use the Salem motif to set the stage for the antics or horror involving their witches. Similarly, Joan gets referenced in stories regarding witch trials or the victimization of women (e.g., *Frozen*, 2013).

Many recurring themes and witch iconography stem from these literary and historical sources, including magical sisterhoods, evil mothers, dead witches, psychic ability, magical bargains, love potions, and the ethical message "Be careful what you wish for." There is a language surrounding the witch and her stories that ebbs and flows as her narrative changes. Names also repeat, such as Sarah, Margaret, Maggie or Mags, Velma, Thelma, Zelma, and Hazel. These are typical witch names found across genres and narratives. These character and narrative trends, even within the limits of Hollywood itself, build on each other and help to create a definitive and distinct central witch archetype within the American pop cultural mindset.

Let's Get Started

Over the years, much has been written about cinematic witches or witches in general. As mentioned earlier, Purkiss explored the subject in her comprehensive book *The Witch in History*. In that study, Purkiss looks at various constructions across cultural content and meanings, not only those found in film and television. Other books, such as Emily Edwards's *Metaphysical Media: The Occult Experience in Popular Culture* include a single chapter devoted to what are defined as witch films. While Edwards used a sociological methodology to break down the elements of construction, her study includes films from different national industries as well as nonnarrative productions.

Tanya Krzywinska's *A Skin for Dancing In* is a comprehensive theoretical approach to the subject of witches in film. However, like Edwards, she also incorporates works from multiple national industries. In addition, her study is broader, exploring a variety of magical personas within fictional worlds. Krzywinska's focus is theoretical and not historical.

My purpose is not to replace the work done above or others like it, but rather add to it. There has yet to be a focused study on witches over time within an American film and television framework and with consideration of historical, sociocultural, or industry contexts, including the consideration of modern Witchcraft practice. One important note on that context concerns language and the use of the word "witch" and "witchcraft" in this study. To denote the genuine practice of magic by people who identify as practitioners in contemporary society, the letter *W* will always be capitalized, as one would do with any religious practice. Witchcraft or Wicca is practiced by Witches or Wiccans. On the other hand, when speaking of fictional characters and magic in a fiction setting, the words will always be used with a lowercase *w*. The witch in *Snow White and the Seven Dwarfs* practices witchcraft. This is an important distinction that becomes vital in the later decades as the Pagan movement begins to influence mainstream film.

While my study is comprehensive, it is impossible to capture and discuss every film or show containing a witch. The witch's existence is prolific throughout American entertainment. Undoubtedly, there are productions and characters that are not mentioned. At the end of each chapter, I have included a list of all films and shows central to the discussions, as well as noting a few others that were reviewed but not mentioned.

Additionally, it is important to note that the study is by no means conclusive in terms of defining the cinematic witch. The key component of the character as a symbolic icon, as mentioned earlier, is that she is at her essence a woman unleashed. She is malleable and changeable, always appearing in the space that society has forgotten or deemed horrific. As culture shifts, she shifts, and therefore who she is or how she looks will ultimately change as well. In addition, her definitions change according to the viewers' own perspective, which is what allows for subversive readings as was mine with the Wicked Witch.

Although I was able to identify markers and methods in witch construction, I propose, ultimately, that it is only by our personal standards of normalcy that we know when we are looking at the female rebel. How this persona makes us feel and how we interpret her symbolic meaning is largely dependent upon our own relationship with culture, religion, gender, and what we define as progressive. The witch is as much defined by who we are as who she is. As a result, the witch will always be someone who is elusive, just beyond our grasp, or perhaps even ahead of our time.

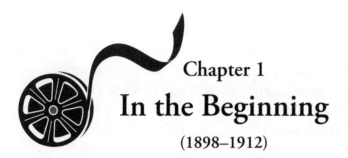

Chapter 1
In the Beginning
(1898–1912)

The study of the Hollywood cinematic witch begins in earnest with the first recorded witch character in an American film. That honor goes to the fantasy short *The Cavalier's Dream*, which is an Edison film released in December 1898. Directed by J. Stuart Blackton, the film tells the story of a young cavalier who falls asleep and dreams of various fantastical characters, including demons, ghosts, and a witch. Appearing only briefly, the cloaked witch is the first American cinematic presentation of the classic magical crone. Four years after the release of *The Cavalier's Dream*, the Edison Manufacturing Company produced another fantasy short called *The Devil's Prison* (1902) that also contained a similar robed witch who visits a sleeping hero.

While both silent films include light storytelling, neither contains a fully invested film narrative. That was not their purpose. Most early silent films were simply recordings of live events or theatrical performances, or they showcased the new visual technology. In her book *Babel and Babylon*, film historian Miriam Hansen explains that "the basic conception of early filmmaking is one of display, of demonstration, [or] of showmanship."[3] Viewers were invited into the film's quasi-realistic world to witness events as voyeurs. In the case of Edison's two witch shorts, the goal was to show off the technology. In Hansen's terms, they were films "of demonstration." The filmmakers

---

3. Miriam Hansen, *Babel and Babylon: Spectatorship in American Silent Film* (Cambridge: Harvard University Press, 1991), 33.

used cutting techniques to make the witch and the other supernatural creatures appear and disappear from the screen.

It wasn't until 1903 with the release of Edwin S. Porter's *The Great Train Robbery* that Hollywood began to shift into classic narrative filmmaking. Porter's film, a milestone in cinematic history, is still considered the first American narrative film. While France's Georges Méliès earns the title of the world's first narrative film director, it was Porter and *The Great Robbery* that brought this mode of filmmaking to the forefront of the fledgling American industry. After this important shift, the next witch-related production and the first narrative film to contain a witch is Vitagraph's short, aptly named *The Witch*. It was released in 1908 and is loosely based on Sir Walter Scott's 1819 historical novel *Ivanhoe*.

Retelling Old Stories

Before examining the films and their respective witch characters, it is important to take a brief look at US cinematic history over this period as it pertains to the choice of productions and stories told. As noted, films made prior to 1900 were mostly considered sideshow novelties. The attraction was simply to see a photograph move—to see a so-called "movie." Film historian William K. Everson observes that movement was enough to entertain viewers; there was no need, at first, to explore the art form further or "exploit comic or dramatic materials."[4] Filmmakers were content to be exhibitionists inviting spectators to engage in a type of public voyeurism. In the beginning, the majority of films were live recordings or reenactments of current and historical events, or recordings of live theatrical performances.

As time progressed, the industry began to organize, consolidate, and increase its output. In 1908, the Motion Picture Patents Company (MPPC) was formed to protect the production rights of its members as more production companies opened their doors. Then, in 1910, the entire industry began moving its operations from its East Coast home in New Jersey to Southern California. Not only was the West Coast's weather less likely to interfere with outdoor shooting schedules, but the region also provided independent filmmakers the sought-after freedom from the demands of the East-Coast-based MPPC.

In addition, film technology itself was expanding and, as a result, filmmakers were inspired to experiment with the medium itself. Film length increased as did the number of narrative fictional works. Films went from one-reel shorts in the 1800s to two- or three-reel features by 1912. The stories being told became more complex and productions more elaborate. There is a marked difference between *The Cavalier's*

4. William K. Everson, *American Silent Film* (New York: Da Capo Press, 1998), 21.

Dream (1898) and *The Wonderful Wizard of Oz* (1910), and still more difference as the silent era moves past 1912.

Despite all this expansion and change, filmmakers remained tied to the retelling of popular stories and historically based events such as *Hansel and Gretel* (1909) or *In the Days of Witchcraft* (1909). Witch films were no different. Of all the early silent witch films examined in this period and beyond, the majority are adaptations of literature classics or are historical dramas. The remaining few exist as showcases for popular cinematic trends, such as the demonstration of elaborate on-screen movement (e.g., *The Witch*, 1908), film cutting (e.g., *The Cavalier's Dream*, 1898), and the display of classic American topography (e.g., *Blackened Hills*, 1912).

The Films

It is important to know that many early silent films, witch-related or not, are lost in whole or in part. Of the films considered in this period, only three have survived: *The Cavalier's Dream* (1898), *Rose O' Salem-Town* (1910), and *The Wonderful Wizard of Oz* (1910). Consequently, assessing the visual and narrative construction of the films' witch characters had to be based largely on academic studies and period texts, such as reviews, stills, and any other surviving studio documentation. Unfortunately, this limits the ability to address any nuances of expression. All interpretations must come through a reaction by another person: a reviewer, publicist, or historian. This is a reality with lost film texts. While the nuance of character construction may be lost, the general concept of a witch's visual construction and narrative role can still be ascertained.

Of the films examined between 1898–1912, witches appear in three genres. These include the historical drama (e.g., *Rose O' Salem-Town*, 1910), the western adventure (e.g., *Blackened Hills*, 1912), and the fantasy film (e.g., *Hansel and Gretel*, 1909). Breaking it down further, the fantasy genre contains several subcategories due to the variety of films and the different fantasy witch constructions that appear within them. These subcategories include the classic fairytale (e.g., *Hansel and Gretel*, 1909), the literary adaptation (e.g., *The Wonderful Wizard of Oz*, 1910), and the studio original (e.g., *The Cavalier's Dream*, 1898).

Within each of these early silent genres and subgenres, the witch plays a unique and specific narrative role. For example, in the historical drama, she is a young, accused woman. In the western adventure, she is an elderly wild woman. In the fantasy genre, the witch takes her most iconic role as the magical fantasy crone with a broomstick and bubbling cauldron. In each case, the witch is a woman who exists just slightly outside of the dominant social structure as defined by the film's specific moral code—a code that is presumably constructed by contemporary American society at the turn of the century.

It is important to note that these roles were not invented by the period's film-makers. They are direct copies of already established witch constructions that appear through the repeated adaptation of popular fiction and histories. These figures do not offer innovative ways of understanding witches or witchcraft. Whether they are accused, wild, or fantastic, these characters are iconic, recognizable, and comfortably resident in their specific genres. Their presence, even when minor, lays the groundwork of symbolic and narrative meaning that will follow cinematic witches through the decades.

The Accused Woman in the Historical Drama

As noted, Vitagraph's short called *The Witch* is the first Hollywood narrative film to contain a witch character or theme. Released October 24, 1908, the short is a historically based fictional witch trial drama set in medieval Europe. According to surviving details, the film was loosely based on the novel *Ivanhoe*. In a 1908 review, *The New York Dramatic Mirror* described the film's plot as a "young hero fights with the templar Brian du Bois Guilbert to prove by trial of combat that Rebecca, the Jewess, is not a witch." The article goes on to call the film "interesting" and "instructive."[5]

The Witch is classified as a historical drama, which was a common genre to the silent era. Considering filmmakers regularly showcased cinema's novelty by offering depictions of events or well-established stories, it is not surprising that historical dramas would be popular. Even as producers moved from narrative shorts into more complex and longer films, historical events continued to provide source material for the fledgling industry. Audiences were consistently drawn to these well-known stories and, as a result, they were good for business.[6] For the witch, that meant only one thing: the witchcraft trial.

Salem in Silent Film

While *The Witch* (1908) is set in Europe due to its literary origins, the setting for most silent historical dramas is New England. From 1898–1912, there were four such films produced including *In the Days of Witchcraft* (1909), *Rose O' Salem-Town* (1910), *The House of the Seven Gables* (1910), and *The Trials of Faith* (1912). These films are not reenactments of historical fact, but rather they are loose retellings of a known history or they are fictional stories set within a historical framework. Three have original scripts (i.e., *In the Days of Witchcraft, Rose O' Salem-Town, The Trials of Faith*) and

---

5. "Reviews of New Films: *The Witch*," *The New York Dramatic Mirror*. October 31, 1908, 6.

6. Kristin Thompson and David Bordwell, *Film History: An Introduction* (Boston: McGraw Hill, 2003), 28–41.

the third is a literary adaptation of Nathaniel Hawthorne's popular 1851 novel of the same name, *The House of the Seven Gables*.

In an email, historian Dr. Emerson Baker explained that the city of Salem, which was the center of the infamous American witch panic of the 1690s, became "a metaphor of persecution, scapegoats and rushing to judgment—well before [the publication of Arthur Miller's 1953 play] *The Crucible*."[7] That fact is evident alone in the work of American novelist and Salem resident Nathaniel Hawthorne. In the mid-1800s, Hawthorne was writing and publishing stories about the dangers of a moral panic and chronicling the city's history. Due to the popularity of his works, Hawthorne's influence on witch films is significant, first affecting the silent historical drama, the fantasy film (e.g., *Feathertop*, 1912) and eventually, in later decades, the horror film (e.g., *Pumpkinhead*, 1988).

Through known history and the writings of authors like Hawthorne, Salem became an integral part of a uniquely American mythology on superstition and religious fanaticism, and the area's historical narrative found its way into the earliest silent witch films. Despite this public attention, the city itself refused to acknowledge its painful legacy, Dr. Emerson said, and it had yet to embrace its unique place within American culture or accept its universal designation as "America's Witch City."[8] This would not happen in full until the 1970s.

Despite resistance, Salem citizens still defended the town's history. As noted in a 1910 *Moving Picture World* review, "Salem Theater patrons thoroughly enjoy the motion picture portion of the daily performances there fully as much as the vaudeville, but when scenes supposed to be founded on local history are presented they are disposed to be critical."[9] The reporter was writing about the 1910 adaption of Hawthorne's novel *The House of the Seven Gables*. Filmmakers had the witch burned at the stake, and as the reviewer notes, nobody was burned in that city. The accused were all hung.

The continued fascination with Salem provided silent filmmakers with the fodder it needed to produce narrative films that appealed to American audiences. In fact, the silent era as a whole produced the largest number of historical dramas based specifically on witchcraft trials, most of which are, in fact, set in Salem or, at the least, an unnamed small town in New England. The uniquely American motif enabled contemporary audiences to easily connect with the film's story through a common heritage. Film became the new way to tell our collective stories.

---

7. Emerson W. Baker, email to author, January 14, 2015.

8. Baker, email to author, January 14, 2015.

9. J. P. Chalmers and Thomas Bedding F.R.P.S., eds. "Blunder in the Moving Pictures," *The Moving Picture World* 7, no. 22 (November 26, 1910): 1242.

In a review of *In the Days of Witchcraft* (1909), the writer comments, "It is hard to think that such scenes as this were almost daily enacted in Massachusetts not so very long ago and to have it brought before one so vividly is interesting." [10] In a review of D. W. Griffith's *Rose O' Salem-Town*, the writer notes, "Biograph, revivifies history in commendable style, showing Salem Mass., in the old puritan days. It reveals our forefathers in no admirable light, but as they thoroughly disgraced themselves during their spells of witchcraft fanaticism…" [11] While the silent era produced the greatest number of Salem-based films, the subject of the trials never fully recedes from America's collective memory or interest. The city's legacy eventually fades into the background, becoming a powerful character marker, an iconic landscape detail, or a cue to set up the coming of any witchcraft-themed film. (e.g., *Witches of Eastwick*, 1987; *Devonsville Terror*, 1983).

The Accused Woman's Narrative

Despite differences in setting, the period's four historical dramas are all typical trial films, during which accusations of witchcraft are used as personal weapons of revenge. Three of the films tell the story of a young woman who is charged with the practice of witchcraft after being accused of social disobedience. In the film *In Days of Witchcraft*, the hero, Nancy, is labeled a witch after she would not kiss the villain, Lord Craven.[12] In *The Trials of Faith*, the heroine is an herbal healer who is loved by another woman's betrothed.[13] In *Rose O' Salem-Town*, the young heroine, Rose, not only lives outside the city limits with only her mother, but she also rejects the sexual advances of a prominent Puritan deacon. As for *The Witch*, it is difficult to know what characterizations were included. If the short remained faithful to the novel, the heroine, Rebecca, was accused of witchcraft due to being Jewish after rejecting the advances of a powerful man.

---

10. J. P. Chalmers and Thomas Bedding F.R.P.S., eds. "*In the Days of Witchcraft*," *Moving Picture World*, 4, no. 17 (April 24, 1909): 517.

11. "*Rose O' Salem-Town*," *The Nickelodeon* 4, no. 7 (October 1, 1910): 201.

12. J. P. Chalmers, ed. "Review of *In the Days of Witchcraft*," *Moving Picture World* 4, no. 15 (April 10, 1909): 449.

13. "*Trials of Faith*," *The Moving Picture World* 14, no. 7 (November 16, 1912): 665.

*Town leaders arrive at Rose's home to arrest her (Dorothy West) and her mother
(Clara T. Bracy) for the practice of witchcraft.* Rose O' Salem Town *(1910).
[Source: Screengrab. Copyright: Public Domain]*

These four films offer prototypes of the accused woman. She is labeled as an outsider by her social status, whether defined by religion or living location. She is then
accused as a witch due to that status along with a social misstep. Most typically, the
misstep is, for the young women, the rejection of sexual advances perpetrated by a
powerful male figure. In the case of Rose's mother, who is an older accused woman,
the misstep is simply supporting her daughter's rejection of the deacon. It is important to remember that none of these female witch characters actually practice any
form of occult magic. What these films contain is a woman who is or does something
that is outside the bounds of defined social acceptability.

Redemption and Rescue

While each of these films does define witchcraft accusations as baseless, the accused
woman still has transgressed even if only accidentally. In that way, the film essentially
blames the woman for the villain's advances and her own victimization. For example,
unlike the other townswomen, Rose wears a long white gown and her hair flows freely.
She exists as a temptation to men and that alone is a transgression that requires redemption.

In all cases, the young, accused woman is granted redemption and saved from
death by a man who is, more often than not, a romantic interest. It is the proverbial
white knight rescue. In the 1909 version of *In the Days of Witchcraft*, Nancy is "saved
by her sweetheart" just as the torch is being applied.[14] In a *Moving Picture World*
review of *Rose O' Salem-Town*, the writer notes, "[Rose's] sweetheart has gotten his
Mohawk friends and is rushing to the rescue, arriving just as the torch is put to the
brushwood piled up around the girl." [15] After this daring rescue, the victimized young

---

14. Review of *In the Days of Witchcraft*, *Tyrone Daily Herald*, April 21, 1909, 4.

15. J. P. Chalmers and Thomas Bedding, F.R.P.S., eds. "*Rose O' Salem-Town*," *The Moving Picture World*
    7, no. 14 (October 1, 1910): 760.

woman will presumably become a wife and mother and never transgress again. This is the beginning of a specific gender dynamic found in witch films that continues into the future.

However, this redemption through rescue is only available to the young, accused woman. An elderly woman accused of witchcraft does not fare so well. In this period, there is only one such figure: Rose's mother. Like her daughter, she is an outsider who lives alone and practices herbal healing. She is visually constructed similarly to the wild elderly folk witch who is often found in the period's western adventures. Her short, stooped frame is costumed in dark clothing and her head is covered in a dark scarf.

Despite the mother's classic crone appearance, the film does not label her a witch until her daughter rejects the deacon. Before that point, she is an accepted member of society, even if she is an outsider. She is warm, hugs her daughter, and is kind to children. It is only after the rejection that she is accused of witchcraft, seized, and burned at the stake while her daughter watches from a jail cell. In these narratives, the old, accused woman is basically expendable, no longer useful as a wife or mother. Instead of being offered redemption through a heroic rescue, the character is used as a plot device to pressure the young woman into submission and to compel the narrative forward.

The Male Accused Witch

There is one anomaly worth mentioning in this group of films. It fits the theme but has a unique twist. Edison's short adaptation of *The House of the Seven Gables* (1910) contains a witch trial, but the victim is a man. The two-reel short is an adaption of Hawthorne's novel of the same name. The original book was published shortly after the author had gained notoriety for his novel *The Scarlet Letter*, which also tackles issues of moral panic. *The House of the Seven Gables*, both novel and film, are set in historic Salem at the home of an actual mansion that has since been preserved as a historic site in the Massachusetts city.

As with most witch trial stories, regardless of the victim's gender, the narrative centers around a local resident who is subjected to social tyranny. In this case, Maule, the male head of a household, is killed because he won't submit to another man's power over him. While the narrative has no gender play, the story centers on similar concepts such as irrationality, moral panic, social domination, and revenge. Where a man's power over a woman is depicted as sexual, a man's power over another man is depicted as ownership of property, business, and even life.

The House of the Seven Gables received mixed reviews with a few complaints about its poor rendering of the novel's thematic complexities.[16] A Salem-based reviewer writing for *Moving Picture World* said that the film was excellent, but then noted that the filmmakers made the "usual inexcusable blunder of burning at the stake a prisoner accused of witchcraft."[17] As noted earlier, the Salem witches were hung. While the Edison short was not popular, it is worth pointing out that the accused witch, Maule, is one of the first male witches to appear in American cinema and the first ghost witch to haunt his accuser's descendants.

Superstition and the Rational

With the dominance of Salem's history in these early historical dramas, it is not surprising that these films provide a narrative forum for the ongoing social discourse about and the tensions between rational science, superstition, and religious belief. Early twentieth century American culture placed a higher value on rationality, moderate displays of religiosity and science over anything defined as extreme religious zealotry or superstition. This was a time of industrial invention and scientific expansions. In fact, the value placed on science overall is one reason why witchcraft itself was classified as a relic of a bygone medieval era and the occult was considered silly or a passing fancy. These early historical films, similar to Arthur Miller's famous play, work as allegories upholding the American cultural ideal of rationalism and, thereby, demonstrating what happens when irrationality triumphs over rationality.

In an advertisement for the film *Rose O' Salem-Town*, producers write, "Reliable authority states that nine million human lives were sacrificed through the zeal of fanatical reformers during the Christian epoch. Religious fanaticism was in most cases the cause … this Biograph subject shows how easily such a crime can be perpetrated."[18] While the early silents do not capture the complexity of such a dialog, which can be found in later films on the subject (e.g., *Maid of Salem*, 1937; *The Crucible*, 1996), they all champion the path of reason over superstition as symbolized in part by the heroic rescues, which champion male power over female power. This underlying gendered narrative theme serves to accentuate the film's directive and create a more riveting film.

---

16. "The House of Seven Gables," *The Nickelodeon* 4, no. 9 (November 1, 1910): 251.

17. Chalmers and Bedding, eds., "Blunder in the Moving Pictures," 1242.

18. J. P. Chalmers and Thomas Bedding, F.R.P.S., eds., "Biograph Films, Released September 26th, 1910, *Rose O' Salem-Town*, A Story of Puritan Witchcraft," *The Moving Picture World* 7, no. 14 (October 1, 1910): 761.

For example, in three of the historical dramas, the young adolescent woman is accused simply for fending off a man. She exists symbolically as a temptation that tears men away from the rational world of being and, therefore, she is a danger that must be contained through a heterosexual marriage. In her naivete, the young heroine is cast in the role of the witch. A reviewer for *Moving Picture World* was unhappy with this undercurrent in Griffith's *Rose O' Salem-Town* saying, "It really seems that the fact of the witchcraft martyrs has been used as an excuse upon which to build an unhealthy love tragedy in a way that is not honest." [19]

As the silent era progresses, these narrative tensions begin to penetrate deeply into most witchcraft-based subthemes of rationality versus religion and of youth versus age. In other words, the noted gender dynamic evolved quickly beyond what the reviewer called an excuse for a "revolting love plot." [20] Later films are more than simple romance plots and yet the characterization of the irrational woman as witch becomes the standard.

Wild Women and the Western Adventure

During this period, witches make their first appearance in the western adventure film—a genre still very much in its nascent form. Early western filmmakers were predominantly interested in capturing the mythology and iconography of America's wild past. The nineteenth-century Wild West travelling shows provided a wealth of content for early filmmakers, and this narrative backdrop eventually became a key component in the industry as it attempted to capture Americana for its eager audiences. This point is illustrated in a *Moving Picture World* review of *The Witch of the Ranch* (1911) in which the writer specially comments on the "superb 'American' photography." [21] Film historian William K. Everson notes "The Westerners, sad to see their way of life giving way to progress, must have been overjoyed at the new lease on that life provided by Hollywood." [22]

In addition, the subjects and themes common to the western story adapted very easily to the early filmmaking process—one that relied heavily on outdoor settings and fast action. From 1898–1912, there were six notable westerns that contained a witch. These include: *The Witches' Cavern* (1909), *The Witch of the Ranch* (1911), *The Witch of the Everglades* (1911), *The Witch of the Range* (1911), *The Wise Witch of Fairyland* (1912), and *Blackened Hills* (1912). With the exception of one, these films

---

19. "*Rose O' Salem-Town*," 813.

20. "*Rose O' Salem-Town*," 813.

21. "*The Witch of the Ranch*," *The Moving Picture World*, June 3, 1911, 1261.

22. Everson, *American Silent Film*, 223–244.

were produced by either Selig Polyscope or the American Film Manufacturing Company, also known as Flying "A" Studios. These were two of the first studios to relocate operations to southern California. The west coast setting provided the perfect backdrop for the western.

Genre popularity is always a major factor and driving force behind the appearance and disappearance of witch-themed films during the studio-driven periods of Hollywood's history. Therefore, it is not surprising that the only period that rivals the silent era with respect to witches in westerns is late 1950s television programming (e.g., *Bonanza*, "Dark Star," 1960; *Wanted: Dead or Alive*, "The Healing Woman," 1959). However, it is important to note that those later shows are classic cowboy westerns, which is distinctly different from those westerns found in the silent era.

The early films teeter between melodrama and attempts to depict life on the frontier. For this reason, they are frequently labeled western adventures or sometimes even western dramas. Rather than focusing on fighting bandits or so-called "Indians" as is common to the cowboy western, the western adventure's primary subject matter is more typically interpersonal relationships. In all cases, the western seeks to explore the junction at which the wild world, defined by nature, meets structure and civilization. It is at this thematic junction that the wild woman or witch comes into play.

As with the historical drama, the western adventures use the term "witch" to define a woman who has transgressed boundaries and expectations. In the historical drama, the label was a weapon thrown most typically at a young woman who refused to submit to the advances of a powerful man. In the western, the wild woman as witch can be of any age and her transgression is defined by a conscious decision to live an unrefined, "wild" lifestyle connected to the natural world. Unlike the accused woman, the wild woman is not a fully accepted member of society and her defiance is a conscious expression of agency. Although in future decades there are a variety of wild woman constructions, in this era there are only two: the young wild mother and the old woman in the woods. It is the latter that dominates.

The Wild Woman as Elderly Folk Witch

The construction of the iconic elderly folk witch is born from a long legacy left by Western literature and culture that, narratively speaking, posits the old woman as useless, inconsequential, or simply in the way. Both feared and revered, she is derived from characters like the three hags of Shakespeare's *Macbeth* and the *Baba Yaga* of Russian folklore. In her study "Weird Sisters and Wild Women," film scholar Daphne Lawless writes, "it was the most marginalised members of the community—old women, ugly and deformed, incapable of making an independent living and thus forced to rely on begging—who were imagined by a resentful community to be the enemy of the very social order itself." [23]

In a genre that relies heavily on themes of confrontation between society and the wild, it is not surprising to find this type of witch. *The Witches' Cavern* (1909), *The Blackened Hills* (1912), *The Witch of the Ranch* (1911), and *The Witch of the Range* (1911) are four of the earliest films to introduce the elderly folk witch. A 1912 review of *Blackened Hills* demonstrates the essence of the character construction: "Alone in one of the wildest canyons of the mountains lived an old woman, reputed, to be a witch, who was shunned by the superstitious mountain folk and feared because of her supposed supernatural powers." [24] In 1911, *Motography* describes the crone character in *The Witch of the Range* as "an old gypsy with witch-like characteristics, who is seen wandering through picturesque mountain scenery." [25] In Selig Polyscope's short *The Witches' Cavern*, *Moving Picture World* reports that the hero and heroine take a hunting trip to the far west where they encounter a wild man and his mother, the old witch of the valley. [26]

As noted earlier, Rose's mother in the historical drama *Rose O' Salem-Town* was visually constructed as an elderly folk witch. She wears dark rags, practices herbal healing, and lives alone by the seaside. These are visual and narrative markers of the elderly folk witch. However, there is one important distinction between Rose's mother, who is an accused woman, and the western's old wild woman: that is their relationship to the narrative. In the historical drama, the accused woman begins as an accepted member of society and the viewer witnesses the transgressive act that leads to her accusation. In the western, the film opens with the female character already playing the role of witch; she is already the symbolic wild element and remains so. Western adventures are not stories of persecution and victimization with court scenes and hangings; they are redemption stories for transgressive women who have already lost their way or, in the case of the elderly folk witch, know too much.

Just as Rose's mother visually resembles the elderly folk witch of the western adventure, the elderly folk witch is also remarkably close in construction to the fantasy crone. Both she and the fantasy crone are designed, visually and narratively, after a long cultural legacy of witches in fairy tales, literature, and mythology. They both embody the feared, isolated woman who lives alone in a wooded or other abandoned

---

23. Daphne Lawless, "Weird Sisters and Wild Women: The Changing Depiction of Witches in Literature, from Shakespeare to Science Fiction" (masters diss, Victoria University of Wellington, 1999), 27.

24. "*Blackened Hills*," *The Moving Picture World* 14, no. 12 (Oct–Dec 1912): 1232.

25. "*The Witch of the Range*," *Motography* 5, no. 6 (June 1911): 149.

26. J. P. Chalmers and Thomas Bedding, F.R.P.S., eds., "*The Witches' Cavern*," *The Moving Picture World* 5, no. 20 (November 13, 1909): 695.

location. Both are said to have powers that are often employed in exchange for money or goods.

However, the western's elderly folk witch cannot be the fantasy crone because she lives in what is defined as the real world and, as such, she is constructed as a potential real figure in the viewer's world. Due to this undercurrent of realism, she is prevented from stepping over any boundaries into fantasy. Her witchcraft must be explained by scientific, religious, or other reality-based terms. The magic must be sourced. For example, *The Blackened Hills* witch has "supernatural powers" as assumed by the superstitious mountain folk. While her magic lives only in the imagination of the unenlightened villagers, it is still sourced.

Despite any perceived dangers that the elderly folk witch might pose to the social order, she is mostly left alone because she does not live within the boundaries of community. In other words, unlike the elderly accused woman who is part of the established social order, the elderly folk witch has been discarded into a state of liminality, marked by her wild existence, and does not need to be assimilated, killed, or exorcised, so to speak, of her magical ways. She has been discarded, not through death but through isolation.

The Role of Elderly Folk Witch

The main narrative role of the elderly folk witch in these early western adventures is most typically as a foil or plot device. She engages with characters either to scare them or to exchange magic for money. In *The Witches' Cavern*, the mother scares the main characters and disrupts the narrative; thereby pushing the entire sequence of events forward. In *The Blackened Hills*, Martha, the heroine, gives the witch food, and in return, the witch rescues the imprisoned hero so he can then save Martha. In *The Witch of the Range*, "better members of the community" save the witch from a lynching.[27] In return, she warns the hero and heroine of coming dangers. In these films, the elderly folk witch is not necessarily defined by any prescribed markers of good or evil. She exists on the edge of ethics and morality. Paralleling her wild lifestyle is this moral state of liminality in which she is simultaneously feared and needed.

While the elderly folk witch does appear in other genres over time, she is most at home in the western or the western-inspired story where she can exist symbolically as an antagonist to encroaching civilization, the counterpoint to modern medicine, and the embodiment of patriarchal defiance. Even after the western genre shifts its

---

27. "*The Witch of the Range*," 149.

focus to gun fights and cowboys, and then even after the genre's popularity wanes entirely, the archetype of the elderly folk witch, who sees her beginnings in these western adventures, persists within other genres (e.g., *Pumpkinhead*, 1988).

The Wild Woman as Young Mother

While most of the silent western adventures do indeed take place in the literal American West, the wild setting was not always limited to that specific region of the country, particularly since many of these films were produced on the East Coast. *The Witch of the Everglades* is a perfect example. The wild setting in this film is the Florida swamp lands.

Not only does the film's setting distinguish it from the others, so does its witch. During this period, *The Witch of the Everglades* is the only one to define its witch as a young wild woman. Her construction and narrative journey are quite different from the elderly folk witch. Unlike the crone, the young woman must be reincorporated back into civilization to take her place as wife and mother. She is still considered socially useful, similar to the young, accused woman.

In *The Witch of the Everglades*, Dora is a young mother who, prior to the film's start, was driven insane after her husband was murdered and baby taken. When the film begins, she is already living alone in the swamps and as a result is already considered a witch. As described in the official movie flier, "[Dora] is … an object of superstitious terror to the Indians." [28] Like an accused woman, Dora is a victim. However, unlike the accused woman, the accusations are not sparked by something she does within society, but rather by her wild existence outside the very literal boundaries of the social order. While she did not choose the death of her husband, she did choose to take up residence alone in the Everglades and, as a result, became the witch. Like all wild women, Dora begins the film in that liminal and wild state.

---

28. "*Witch of the Everglades*," promotional flier, 1915; source: Margaret Herrick Library, Academy of Motion Picture Arts and Sciences, Beverly Hills, California.

*After years alone in the Everglades, Dora (Kathlyn Williams) is brought to
her senses and reunited with her daughter in* The Witch of the Everglades *(1911).
[Source: William Selig Papers, Margaret Herrick Library, Academy
of Motion Pictures Arts & Sciences. Copyright: Public Domain]*

However, the young witch cannot be left in that state of liminality like the elderly folk witch. She must be reincorporated to resume her place in proper, rational society. As described in the film's flier, Dora is finally "wounded in the head and the bullet restores her to reason."[29] Like the accused woman, the wild woman is offered redemption through a white knight rescue. In this case, the rescue is accomplished by a classic western symbol of masculinity—the bullet and the gun. She is saved from her wild existence, reunited with her lost daughter, and returned to her proper place as mother. She is rescued from irrationality and chaos by a rational man, and in doing so, she moves from her designation as wild witch to mother and wife, taking her proper place in society.

29. "*Witch of the Everglades,*" promotional flier, 1915.

Othering and the Indigenous Folk Witch

Two of the western adventure films have another unique element that becomes increasingly important in the development of the cinematic witch in general and acts as another indicator of the witch's relationship to magical practice. In both *The Witch of the Range* and *The Wise Witch of Fairyland*, the western's wild woman is narratively depicted as an elderly folk witch who is something other than racially white and culturally American. In other words, she is not "us" as defined by the expected viewership. In *The Witch of the Range*, the elderly folk witch is defined as a gypsy. In *The Wise Witch of Fairyland*, she is described as an "Indian." While they play the role of the elderly folk witch, they are contemporary examples of the magical other.

It is important to note that, of all the western adventure films, *The Witch of the Range* and *The Wise Witch of Fairyland* are the only two that suggest that the witch actually practices some form of mysticism. A reviewer for *Motography* described the crone in *The Witch of the Range* as "muttering incantations and casting dark spells over nature."[30] A *Moving Picture World* review calls her magic simply "second sight" and notes that she reads tarot.[31] In *The Wise Witch of Fairyland*, the witch is described as creating a love potion for the main characters and a poison potion for the villain.[32] These reviews all suggest that genuine spellwork is being performed. This is an important distinction when it comes to the representation of magical practice.

As is the case with any wild woman, the source of these two witches' magical ability must be explained in a way that is viable in the viewer's real world. For example, herbalism or superstition are credible sources, and as time goes on, satanic pacts and religion become equally as valid. For these two witches, the source of their power is simply their otherness. In other words, the ability of these two witches to make potions or have second sight is explained chiefly through their ethnic heritage.

The cinematic cue linking race and ethnicity to mysticism is a function of deeply embedded prejudice and racism within American society. It is a product of a colonialist attitude that posits American culture as more advanced, rational, and enlightened than any other. In a 1910 review of *Rose O' Salem-Town*, a writer calls out the deeply problematic nature of these cinematic depictions, saying, "Motion pictures have villainized the Indian for so long that they have thereby added another burden to the load of injustice already borne by that unfortunate race."[33] While the gypsy or "Indian" folk witches are not villainized in *The Witch of the Range* and *The Wise Witch*

---

30. "*The Witch of the Range*," 149.

31. "*The Witch of the Range*," *The Moving Picture World* 8, no. 23 (June 10, 1911): 1326–1327.

32. "*The Wise Witch of Fairyland*," *The Moving Picture World* 11, no. 7 (February 17, 1912): 622.

33. "*Rose O' Salem-Town*," 201.

of Fairyland, they are othered through the diminished value placed on their cultures as defined by their belief in and practice of genuine magic. The films remind the audience that these indigenous women are not "us." And, as long as they remain at a distance, they and their magic do not pose a threat to the established social order and are therefore left alone, just as any elderly witch might be.

During the silent era, the majority of characters that are defined as magical others are described as either "Indian" or gypsy. By Hollywood's golden era, this character construction shifts from depictions of Native Americans entirely and focuses on indigenous people from outside the US, including various African nations, Haiti, and the South Seas. While discussions of embedded racism and bigotry within cinema go far beyond the scope of this study, it is essential to note when and where these characters appear in witch films and why. In doing so, another story develops entirely—one that demonstrates how themes of witchcraft and magic have relied on common cues of othering in the development and characterization of the witch as an outsider and have contributed to the demonization of nonwhite characters to the detriment of American society. In this early era, we witness the very beginnings of the trend through a turn-of-the-century mindset toward race and ethnicity.

The Fantasy Witch and Her Beginnings

From 1898–1912, the fantasy film is the most common genre for witch characters, a trend that continues into the future. Whether the setting is a mythical land (e.g., *The Wonderful Wizard of Oz*, 1910) or the real world (e.g., *Lord Feathertop*, 1908), the fantasy witch is fully developed as her own magical creature. Her mysticism is literally realized as witchcraft or magic and it does not need explanation. In the fantasy film, the witch is not a social victim wearing a derogatory label and her magic is not a product of a reality-based contagion, superstition, religious zealotry, otherness, second sight, or herbalism. While she harbors many of the markers of the wild woman and other associations inherited from European religious and popular culture, the fantasy witch is always caged or made safe by her unreality.

At this point in time, fantasy was the genre of choice for witches because the character was no longer considered real in any sense. Like werewolves or fairies, she was something out of childhood stories despite centuries of religious rhetoric stating otherwise. To the early twentieth-century American cultural mind, the witch was a symbol of a bygone era that was marked by religious zealotry and superstition, as noted earlier. Belief in witchcraft was the product of poor education, backward societies, female hysteria, or a child's fancy.

In *The Wonderful Wizard of Oz*, author L. Frank Baum demonstrates this idea very clearly. The Witch of the North says to Dorothy:

In the civilized countries I believe there are no witches left, nor wizards, no sorceresses, nor magicians. But, you see, the Land of Oz has never been civilized, for we are cut off from all the rest of the world. Therefore we still have witches and wizards among us.[34]

As demonstrated by Baum's words, the cultural renegotiation of witchcraft's meaning was not propelled by the newly created film industry; however, they are linked. An American culture that celebrated industrial invention, rationalism, and science helped to birth film technology itself and that same culture pushed the concept of real magic into the world of fantasy. As noted by film scholar Daphne Lawless:

> The conception of witchcraft as a pact with demonic powers, encouraged by the Church and held by a faction of the educated elite in early modern times, succumbed to the spread of Enlightenment ideas, and the "sceptical" discourse which considered the Witch nothing more than peasant superstition prevailed among the educated classes. Thus, by the nineteenth century the figure of the Witch was no longer taken seriously in elite circles, and the "demonological" discourse of Witchcraft became regarded, outside of the Church, as a superstition in itself.[35]

Since the witch had lost most of its ties to any iconic theological elements that might horrify a viewer, it is not surprising that the innocuous and spirited genre of fantasy, not horror, became the first and primary home for the American cinematic witch. In that respect, Hollywood deviated significantly from other national cinemas. Many foreign filmmakers were actively engaging in the subject of witchcraft within a religious framework during the silent era (e.g., *Häxan*, 1922). This does not occur in mainstream American cinema in earnest until the 1950s.

Fairy Tales, Fantasy Shorts, and Literature

Fantasy witch films appear in the greatest concentration at the very beginning of the period when shorts were still simply sideshow novelties. These early films were predominantly original stories and not literary adaptations, such as *Devil's Prison* or *The Leprechawn* [sic]. As narrative films got longer and storytelling more complex, filmmakers increasingly turned to popular fairy tales and literature to attract the ever-

---

34. L. Frank Baum, *Oz: The Complete Collection Vol. 1* (New York: Aladdin, 2013), 12.

35. Lawless, "Weird Sisters and Wild Women," 28.

expanding audience, which included both adults and children. In 1917 William Fox, the founder of Fox Film Corporation, explained that fantasy films were not made only for children. He wrote, "We put this picture away and looked at it ourselves hundreds of times—with more enjoyment at each sitting, and we came to realize that these pictures were not only for children, but for grown-ups even more…we knew there was no end to what we could do."[36]

There were nine notable fantasy films with witches during this period. Thomas Edison's film company produced all of the early shorts including *The Cavalier's Dream* (1898), *Devil's Prison* (1902), *The Leprechawn [sic]* (1908), *Lord Feathertop* (1908), *Hansel and Gretel* (1909), and *The Mischievous Elf* (1909). Selig Polyscope produced *The Wonderful Wizard of Oz* (1910), Kalem released *The Little Old Men of the Woods* (1910), and Éclair American produced *Feathertop* (1912). Within this group, two important incarnations of the fantasy witch appear: the iconic fantasy crone (e.g., *The Cavalier's Dream*, 1898) and the whimsical Victorian clown witch (e.g., *The Wonderful Wizard of Oz*). The latter of the two is unique to this period and only appears again decades later but in modern form (e.g., *The Wiz*, 1978; *Hocus Pocus*, 1993). The fantasy crone is far more pervasive and appears in almost every decade going forward.

The Victorian Clown Witch

The period's clown witch is a leftover from a distinct Victorian children's aesthetic and is used most prominently in the Selig Polyscope short film *The Wonderful Wizard of Oz* (1910), which is the first adaptation of Baum's popular novel. Non-cinematic evidence of her existence is found in a variety of period illustrations from postcards to children's books. In fact, this aesthetic is not limited to witches or even women. One of the most recognizable places to find this stylized costuming is in the visual interpretations of Mother Goose. The fictional storyteller is typically depicted wearing a large, rounded collar, colorful clothing, and a pointy hat. In *The Wonderful Wizard of Oz*, a similar aesthetic informs the costumes designed for the Wicked Witch, the Munchkins, and some of the courtiers.

---

36. "The New Fox Pictures," *The Moving Picture World* 33, no. 5 (August 4, 1917): 804.

*The Wicked Witch of the West flies above the frightened
citizens of Oz in* The Wonderful Wizard of Oz *(1910).
[Source: Screengrab. Copyright: Public Domain]*

As for Momba the wicked witch, the whimsical style cages her villainy, making her devoid of true evil and incapable of anything but benign mischief. The Victorian clown witch is quite literally a clown, and in that way, she can exist as a villain in nursery stories without upsetting young children. This is particularly evident in L. Frank Baum's original 1899 printing of *The Wonderful Wizard of Oz*, which also used the clown design. Illustrator W. W. Denslow's drawings of both good witches and bad witches are examples of the Victorian clown aesthetic applied to witches.[37]

For the 1910 film adaptation, director Otis Turner mirrored Denslow's drawings to define his cinematic characters. This was strategic because Baum's novel had only been published ten years earlier and its popularity kept the story fresh in the minds of the American population. The drawings were a key to its success.

In 1903, prior to the film's release, Baum attempted to capitalize on the book's fame by staging his own musical theater adaptation called *The Wizard of Oz*. The book had been a best seller for over two years by that point. While the theater tour was marginally successful, Baum eventually found himself in financial difficulty due to his other ventures and was forced sell the rights to his early novels, including *The Wonderful Wizard of Oz*. Selig Polyscope bought the film rights and produced *The Wonderful Wizard of Oz* in 1910.

While the film witch's costume is not an exact replica of the original renderings, it does reflect the Victorian whimsical style found in the books. Momba is dressed in a large draping gown with puffy sleeves and a pointed hat. Her collar looms larger around her neck. Mirroring the clothing, her actions are limited to buffoonery and isolated mo-

---

37. Baum, *Oz: The Complete Collection Vol. 1*, 24, 140.

ments in which she flails her arms. She is a nonthreatening villain in a children's fantasy world.

The narrative attempts to declaw the Oz witches, both visually and narratively, go beyond Victorian clown costuming and character performance. *The Wonderful Wizard of Oz* filmmakers also renamed Glinda from the "Good Witch of the North," as specified in the original tales, to "Glinda the Good." Visually speaking, she resembles a fairy godmother, wearing a draping white gown and carrying a long thin staff rather than a wand or broomstick. In her scenes, she hovers gracefully in the air over the action without any aid.

*Glinda the Good descends from above to offer Dorothy advice
and magical help in* The Wonderful Wizard of Oz *(1910).
[Source: Screengrab. Copyright: Public Domain]*

With this construction, Glinda is not easily identifiable as a witch of any variety. She takes on an assumptive nonthreatening magical role, similar to an angel or fairy. Despite Baum labeling all four of his magical women as witches and Wenslow using Victorian witch whimsy to stylize their appearance, the 1910 film did not follow suit. Glinda's designation as a witch was removed by a name change and through her costuming. Baum's other two literary witches don't appear at all, leaving only Glinda the Good and Momba the Witch of the West. The presence of only two witches, good and bad, sets up a moral binary, although nonthreatening, within the narrative for easy viewer alignment. There is good and there is bad, and witches are bad.

The Fantasy Crone

The remaining fantasy films contain one of the most iconic of witches: the fantasy crone. Before looking at the construction, it is important to note that only one of these films has survived: *The Cavalier's Dream* and all character assumptions are taken from secondary sources. In some of these texts, the witch is labeled as old. For example, in a 1909 *Moving Picture World* review of *Hansel and Gretel*, the witch is described as "terrible" and "old." [38] However, more often than not, the witch is not described at all. While it is possible that these characters were clown witches, the non-whimsical nature of their stories and their literary legacy suggest that they were more likely fantasy crones.

As noted earlier, the fantasy crone is the most common archetype in Western culture. She is the feared hag who is sometimes referred to as the Baba Yaga. She is the cousin of the elderly folk witch and is far less comical than the clown witch. She is a caricature of the solitary old woman who lives in the deep dark woods practicing magic. Like the elderly folk witch, the fantasy crone's construction is derived predominantly from European folklore or fairy tales and Shakespeare's *Macbeth*. She is easily identifiable by her stooped posture, unkempt hair, and distorted facial features. Her clothes are generally dark and ragged, and she is often covered by a hooded cloak. Surrounding her are common witch-related icons such as cats, brooms, bats, cauldrons, and potions.

Narrative Role of the Fantasy Crone

Unlike the accused or wild woman, the fantasy crone has tangible magical powers that are explained simply by the film's genre being fantasy. In these early films, she plays the role of a morally ambiguous figure or the evil antagonist. She is never good. For example, in *Hansel and Gretel*, the witch is the primary antagonist, similar to the clown witch Momba in *The Wonderful Wizard of Oz*. While both witches are the main villains, they are not the only obstacle for the main characters, and their presence does not offer the same antagonistic pressure found in, for example, MGM's 1939 adaptation of Baum's classic. As explained by a 1909 review published in *Moving Picture World*, Edison's siblings, Hansel and Gretel, must overcome hunger, the sandman, and "strange, uncanny" faces in the trees before ever encountering the witch.[39] In both films, the witch is only the final challenge for hero and heroine. Although the witch is the primary villain, she is not frightening, and the narrative doesn't attempt to create an intense moral polarity. This typifies filmmaking interests at the time, as well as the cultural disinterest in depicting a witch as a monolithic, powerful threat.

In other cases, the silent fantasy crone's primary motivation and purpose cycle around her role as a straightforward magic-for-money businesswoman rather than a force of self-motivated, ideological evil. In other words, in these early fairy tale adaptations, the fantasy crone's motive is often one of personal profit, and magic is her

---

38. "Stories of the Films: *Hansel and Gretel*," *The Moving Picture World*, 5, no. 15 (October 9, 1909): 499, 501.

39. "Stories of the Films: *Hansel and Gretel*," 501.

business. Therefore, she is often neither bad nor good. She is morally ambiguous. In the short *The Leprechawn* (1908), several of the main characters ask a "witch-woman" for magical assistance. She reads fortunes and creates charms.[40] She assists the film's heroes and villain. Similarly, the hero in *The Mischievous Elf* turns to a witch for a bag of magic sand with which to trap the elf.[41]

Whether the witch is the film's main antagonist or simply a fantasy crone in the woods who is called upon for magical help, the fantasy witch exists in a place of liminality somewhere between good and evil or uncivilized and civilized, as expressed by Baum in his original stories. Just like the elderly folk witch, the fantasy crone's liminal existence is often symbolized by a cabin in the dark woods. The realms of wild nature are the realms of the witch, and over time, that visual and tangible cue helps to strengthen the narrative connection made between magic, nature, and the wild femininity.

Lost Literary Adaptations: *Feathertop*

One fantasy crone who was not discussed in the previous section is found in two adaptations of Nathaniel Hawthorne's 1852 short story "Feathertop." Hawthorne's "moralized legend," as he called it, is one of the most influential witch-related stories in American cinema, just behind *Macbeth*, *Hansel and Gretel*, and *The Wonderful Wizard of Oz*. Like Hawthorne's other works, "Feathertop" is set in small-town New England and tackles the darker aspects of civilized society with respect to ethics and morality. In this story, he tells the tale of an old witch in the woods who once had been wronged by society elites and, in order to get even, she brings a pumpkin-headed scarecrow to life.

This period saw two adaptations of the tale, both of which are lost: Edison's *Lord Feathertop* (1908) and Éclair American's *Feathertop* (1912). Once again, all assumptions on character construction, visual or otherwise, are taken from the original story, film plot synopses, and contemporary reviews. In all cases, the texts suggest that the two cinematic witches are devious and self-serving, but not villainous, similar to other fantasy witches of the period. A *Moving Picture World* review of the 1908 short *Lord Feathertop* simply calls Betty Grigsby "an old woman, credited with being a witch."[42] A printed synopsis of the 1912 adaptation, named *Feathertop*, labels the

---

40. "*The Leprechawn*," *The Moving Picture World* 3, no. 13 (September 26, 1908): 241.

41. "*The Mischievous Elf*," *The Moving Picture World*. December 25, 1909, 927.

42. "*Lord Feathertop*," *The Moving Picture World* 3, no. 23 (December 5, 1908): 458.

witch, Mother Rigby, as simply "old." [43] In both cases, the fantasy crone is an elderly woman who lives outside of society, tending her garden and performing real magic.

While the visual constructions are lost in time, the printed synopses do offer a look at the role the two witches play as morally ambiguous fantasy crones. The 1912 version sticks close to the original tale. Old Mother Rigby builds a scarecrow to sit in her garden but then decides to bring him to life in order to play a trick on a pretentious and morally devoid society. The 1909 version adds an element of revenge. Betsy Grigsby, as a youth, is scorned by a powerful man. Years later, in her old age, she enacts revenge by playing a trick with her pumpkin-headed scarecrow.

The witch defined as a woman scorned is a theme that often fuels wild woman narratives, particularly the ghost films of the 2000s. This character construction also fueled the plot of Hawthorne's other adapted work of the period, *The House of the Seven Gables*, with its male witch. The theme typically offers an avenue for viewer sympathy and aids in the development of the witch as a morally ambiguous figure rather than one of pure evil. Viewers may not agree with her actions, but they can understand her motivation. As noted, the trend becomes most prevalent in the 2000s as concepts of witchcraft lose their traditional binary moral distinctions and the witch is no longer trapped within strict character constructions. During this early era, the three Hawthorne adaptations evoke this theme for the first time, offering the witch a bit of moral relativism that does not come again in earnest for nearly a century.

Spiritualism in Early Silent Films

While Hawthorne's works do invite some conversations on religion, ethics, and spiritualty, most witchcraft-themed films in the silent era were devoid of any theological nuance. The silent fantasy witch, crone or clown, lives in a wild, magical space in the realm of unreality. The accused and wild women were only defined as witches through a misbehavior that flouted what was defined as civilized society. Religion, if present, is a marker of either the devout and rational man, the sinful deacon or minister, or in some cases, the extremist beliefs of local villagers. Religion is an addendum or unexplored descriptor.

More importantly, religion never defines a witch's beliefs or actions. In other words, magical practice is not depicted as a pact with the Devil, a belief in the occult, or the following of a legitimate spiritual practice. While there are a few subtle exceptions, witchcraft, at this point, was almost completely disengaged from its well-known Catholic ideology. To the turn-of-the-century mind, witches simply were not real.

---

43. "Éclair—*Feather Top,*" *The Pittsburgh Daily Post,* June 6, 1912, 36.

One exception is Edison's short *Devil's Prison*, which does contain a devil; however, the witch does not appear with him. They are not visually connected. Moreover, this short did not have a robust storyline so they don't have a narrative connection either. Interestingly, the Edison Manufacturing Company also produced an adaptation of the legendary story of Dr. Faust, who sells his soul for power and, in this case, renewed youth (i.e., *Faust*, 1909). While Dr. Faust is undoubtedly one of the most influential European-based archetypes for the male occultist, Edison's lost adaptation appears to focus solely on the pact, his transformation, and a romance, and does not contain any expressions of magical practice. As noted, the legitimate connection between magic and religion had largely been abandoned.

Although witchcraft was mostly devoid of traditional theological meaning, the turn-of-the-century ironically saw a distinct growing interest in the occult, ceremonial magic, Spiritualism, indigenous folk religions, and other forms of esoterica. This fascination began as early as the mid-1800s and continued into the early 1900s. In 1890, Sir James Frazer published his famous work *The Golden Bough*, documenting magical and religious world traditions and folklore. The Ouija Board, or the talking board as it was originally called, was born in its modern form at this time. And later, in 1909 the most commonly used and well-known tarot deck, the Rider-Waite Tarot, was first published.

More specifically, the Spiritualist movement was attracting writers, artists, and other luminaries, including Helena Petrovna Blavatsky, Marie Laveau, Marie Anne Lenormand, and William Butler Yeats. L. Frank Baum himself had occult community associations through his mother-in-law activist Matilda Gauge, who was a member of Blavatsky's Theosophist Society. In fact, the organization's journal published an article reporting that Baum and his wife became members themselves seven years after Gauge did. Baum's name is found in Register 1 on page 561, and his application is dated December 5, 1892.[44]

In the journal article, writer John Algeo adds that "[Baum's] son Frank admitted [to] the author's interest in Theosophy, but also reported that the elder Baum could not accept all its teachings."[45] In another Baum biography, author Katherine M. Rogers writes, "Baum's [newspaper] editorials also reflect his personal interest in non-traditional religion and opposition to the organized churches."[46] In the 1890s, Baum owned and edited the *Aberdeen Saturday Pioneer* in South Dakota, and according to

44. John Algeo, "Oz—A Notable Theosophist: L. Frank Baum," *American Theosophist* 74 (1986): 270–273. http://www.theosophical.org/publications.

45. Algeo, "Oz—A Notable Theosophist: L. Frank Baum," 270–273.

46. Katharine M. Rogers, *L. Frank Baum: Creator of Oz: A Biography* (Cambridge, MA: DaCapo Press, 2002), 33.

Rogers, his regular editorials promoted all of his causes, including women's suffrage and Theosophy.[47] In one editorial he celebrates Theosophy, claiming there is an "eager longing to penetrate the secrets of Nature."[48] As quoted by Rogers, Baum goes on to write:

> "Amongst the various sects so numerous in America today who find their fundamental basis in occultism, the Theosophists stand pre-eminent both in intelligence and in point of numbers ... Theosophy is not a religion. Its followers are simply 'searchers after Truth.'" They accept the truth in all religions, including Christianity, but believe that "the truth so earnestly sought is not yet found in its entirety ... They admit the existence of a God—not necessarily a personal God. To them God is Nature and Nature God.[49]

Baum's beliefs and his interest in the Spiritualist philosophy did influence his writing, and it can be safely speculated that his Theosophist beliefs were why he was able to distinguish the existence of both good and bad witches and depict the use of magic as a tool rather than a weapon of the Christian Devil. However, his unique perspective did not translate directly into the adaptation of any of his films. This is recognizable in *The Wonderful Wizard of Oz*'s expression of a binary morality, the elimination of several witches, and the removal of Glinda's title.

As noted earlier, Baum was not involved in this film's production. He sold the rights to *The Wonderful Wizard of Oz* in order to survive a bankruptcy. In fact, Baum was not involved in most Oz adaptations in the silent era and beyond. If Baum's unique literary witch constructions were a product of his Theosophist beliefs, this detail never made it to the screen, with possibly the exception of *The Wiz* (1978). In most cases, including the 1910 *The Wonderful Wizard of Oz*, the witches were created to fit the contemporary viewer's expectations and understanding of magic, witches, and witchcraft.

Conclusion

From 1892–1912, as the film industry was just beginning, the Hollywood witch established her place within American cinematic language. While fantasy shorts dominated the early years due to technical and storytelling limitations, filmmakers eventually

---

47. Rogers, *L. Frank Baum*, 29.
48. Rogers, *L. Frank Baum*, 33.
49. Rogers, *L. Frank Baum*, 33.

expanded their work to include more complex narratives. As that happened, witches began to appear more frequently in adaptations of beloved stories (e.g., *Hansel and Gretel*, *The Wonderful Wizard of Oz*, *Feathertop*), well-known histories (e.g., *In the Days of Witchcraft*, *Rose O' Salem-Town*), and tales of the Wild West (e.g., *The Witch of the Ranch*, *The Blackened Hills*).

During this early period of filmmaking, witch characters are merely derivatives of classic archetypes, whether it is the accused woman of Salem or the old crone in the woods. Hollywood did not create these iconic figures, nor did they deviate heavily from their origins. Filmmakers capitalized on their well-known fictional presence and repeated it over and over. Similarly, they used widely understood witchcraft iconography to easily communicate intention and character.

The only classic archetype missing from the era is the satanic witch, and that is largely due to the American cultural emphasis on reason and rationality. The witch's theological connection had been all but severed, and only remnants of a fantastical caricature remained. Ironically, there was growing cultural interest in the occult at this time. However, witchcraft was not connected to that movement, at least in mainstream circles. To the general public, the witch was still just fantasy, at best, or a derogatory label.

Chapter 1: Filmography

The Cavalier's Dream	1898	J. Stuart Blackton
Devil's Prison	1902	unknown
The Leprechawn (sic)	1908	Edwin S. Porter
Lord Feathertop	1908	Edwin S. Porter
The Witch	1908	Van Dyke Brooke
Hansel and Gretel	1909	J. Searle Dawley
In the Days of Witchcraft	1909	unknown
The Mischievous Elf	1909	unknown
The Witches' Cavern	1909	unknown
The House of the Seven Gables	1910	J. Searle Dawley
The Little Old Men of the Woods	1910	unknown
Rose O' Salem-Town	1910	D. W. Griffith
The Wonderful Wizard of Oz	1910	Otis Turner
The Witch of the Everglades	1911	Otis Turner
The Witch of the Ranch	1911	unknown
The Witch of the Range	1911	Allan Dwan
The Blackened Hills	1912	Allan Dwan
Feathertop	1912	unknown
The Trials of Faith	1912	unknown
The Wise Witch of Fairyland	1912	unknown

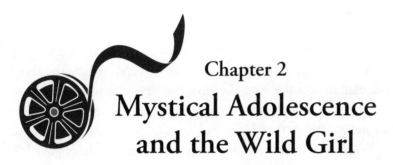

Chapter 2
Mystical Adolescence
and the Wild Girl
(1913–1920)

By the year 1913, the American film industry was quite literally on the move. Independent companies, such as Flying "A" Studios and Selig Polyscope had already established a West Coast presence and more studios followed. Southern California was quickly becoming the new center of American filmmaking, a move that would eventually give the industry its iconic name. By 1917, that geographic shift was complete, and by 1920, the industry was on its way to developing a system of production that would give way to its golden era. At the same time, Thomas Edison's regulatory organization, the Motion Picture Patents Company, was disbanded due to litigation over monopolistic practices. With the MPPC gone, new studios, innovators, and filmmakers easily emerged. Then in 1917, the entire industry saw a drop in revenue due to World War I and the closure of European markets. However, at the same time, the war limited the number of foreign films entering the country, providing an unexpected business opportunity for American filmmakers.

Despite these significant industry shifts, American producers continued to adapt well-known material in order to attract audiences. While audiences were indeed growing, the industry continued to struggle for respectability and still had to strive to separate their art from vaudeville and the nickelodeons. Historian Miriam Hansen notes that producers first tried to appeal to the upper class, but this move did not work. She writes, "The most effective strategy of legitimation, in the end, was the marketing of cinema as a 'democratic art,' the valorization of 'popular' culture." [50] Her observation points, once again, to one of the reasons behind the repeated use of recognizable stories and histories. Hansen writes, "Public interest was captured ... by the reproduction of scenes from people's everyday lives, the possibility of seeing oneself or someone familiar on the screen." [51] Producers gave people what they knew because that is what they wanted.

Throughout this period, there is a continuation and even expansion of the themes found in the earlier shorts, including displays of the Wild West and retellings of American history to the adaptation of well-known literature and stories. It was these popular themes, translated into genres, that proved profitable and pulled the industry out from the gutter into the spotlight. What this meant for the cinematic witch is more of the same. In one form or another, she continued to appear comfortably in the popular tales being told from witch trial stories and western adventures to the fantasy film.

However, at the same time, witch constructions did expand to include more nuanced expressions as narratives lengthened. Additionally, the elderly crone, either as a folk or fantasy witch, is no longer dominant. The young witch, in all forms, takes center stage. As such, a trend emerges, one that punctuates the entire period. The witch productions illustrate the contemporary cultural interest in the dynamic between female adolescence and mysticism. It is during this period, through repetition, increased output, and narrative complexity, that witchcraft representations first became a true model for expressions of femininity and female agency that go well beyond the appearance of the old woman in the woods.

The Films

As noted, the films of this period fall into the same general categories as the earlier era. Salem's legacy continued to attract filmmakers, which provided more retellings of the accused woman's story (e.g., *The Witch of Salem*, 1913; *Joan the Woman*, 1916). As studios moved to California, producers found increasing success with the western adventure, complete with the witch as a wild woman (e.g., *The Witch Girl*, 1914; *The Witch*, 1916). Finally, the fantasy witch, typically a crone, continued to dominate due to the popularity of fairy tale adaptations, a growing children's viewership, and the interest in elaborate fantasy spectacles (e.g., *A Daughter of the Gods*, 1916).

As with earlier films, few of these witch films have survived. Of those reviewed, only six are known to be viewable in full: *Ivanhoe* (1913), *Cinderella* (1914), *His Majesty, the Scarecrow of Oz* (1914), *The Story of the Blood Red Rose* (1914), *Fanchon the*

---

50. Hansen, *Babel and Babylon*, 64–65.

51. Hansen, *Babel and Babylon*, 31.

Cricket (1915), and *Joan the Woman* (1916). In addition, a 1915 film titled *The New Wizard of Oz* has also survived. However, it is simply a re-release of Oz film *His Majesty, the Scarecrow of Oz*. Despite the loss of these films, the growing film industry was fortunately followed closely by a growing media industry that was well-preserved and, to this day, provides ample data on many of these lost films.

Witch Trial Films and the Accused Woman

Witch trial films continued to fascinate American audiences through the later silent era, and filmmakers were happy to oblige. Trial films were produced by all the major film studios from Éclair American and Selig Polyscope to the fledgling Paramount Pictures. Most of these films were, as one might expect, set in Salem or New England, capitalizing on the public obsession with the city's history. Professor Gretchen Adams described it best when she wrote, "The specter of Salem witchcraft haunts the American imagination." [52] And that it did, finding expression in silent film after silent film into the 1920s. During this period, the Salem-based films include *The Witch of Salem* (1913), *In the Days of Witchcraft* (1913), *A Puritan Episode* (1913), *The Witch* (1913), *When Broadway Was a Trail* (1914), *A Witch of Salem Town* (1915), and *Witchcraft* (1916).

The attention being given to these shared cultural stories was noted and celebrated by contemporary reviewers. In a 1913 theater note in the *Indiana Gazette*, a writer described *The Witch of Salem* as "depicting the modes and customs of the early colonial days." [53] In the same year, *The Anaconda Standard* reviewer called *In the Days of Witchcraft* an interesting story, noting that "The atmosphere of Puritanism ... has been secured and maintained throughout." [54] In another review, a *Scranton Republican* writer noted "[*Witchcraft*'s] theme is the terrible witchcraft superstition that raged in Massachusetts in colonial days and during which so many innocent persons were burned at the stake." [55] All three writers remark on the films' engagement with American history and celebrate their attention to a shared heritage.

The American Allegory in European Settings

Two of the produced trial films were not set in Salem but rather in Europe. Both are adaptations of famous stories: *Ivanhoe* (1913) and *Joan the Woman* (1916). The former, *Ivanhoe*, is the third American cinematic adaptation of Scott's novel. Filmed

52. Gretchen A. Adams, *The Specter of Salem: Remembering the Witch Trials in Nineteenth-Century America* (Chicago: University of Chicago Press, 2008), 1.

53. "Grand Theater Tonight," *The Indiana Gazette*, December 22, 1913, 7.

54. "*In the Days of Witchcraft* Shown in American Films," *The Anaconda Standard*, August 14, 1913, 8.

55. "At the Strand," *The Scranton Republican*, November 15, 1916, 13.

partly on location in Scotland, *Ivanhoe* is far more complex than past adaptations as director Herbert Brenon attempted to faithfully render the original story. A review in *The Moving Picture News* reveals the film's epic scope by noting that "approximately 500 persons are involved in the various episodes."[56] However, like the earlier adaptations and the novel, *Ivanhoe*'s narrative focus is on warfare and the politics of men and not the persecution of the witch, Rebecca, whose story is embedded in a larger saga about male heroism. In this film, witchcraft is simply one plot point and not a thematic focus. While *Ivanhoe* is an anomaly with regard to trial locations, the film fits the industry's trend toward adapting popular literature.

Contrary to that is Cecil B. DeMille's spectacle *Joan the Woman*, which was released in December 1916. Unlike *Ivanhoe*, its narrative focus is the witch and her story, and it is the first and one of the few Joan of Arc films produced in the US. *Joan the Woman* is a full-length feature film. It is as complex and layered as any narrative story produced in the silent era. Although set in Europe, De Mille's film is an allegory for the American plight during World War I. *Joan the Woman* is a story about "us" masked in a famous European legend.

Geraldine Farrar stars as Joan of Arc in
Cecil B. DeMille's 1916 film Joan the Woman.
[Source: Library of Congress, Prints & Photographs.
Copyright: Public Domain]

---

56. "*Ivanhoe,*" *The Moving Picture News*, August 30, 1913, 12.

In her book *Visions of the Maid*, film historian Robin Blaetz calls DeMille's Joan a "quintessentially American figure."[57] By comparing *Joan the Woman*'s original American release to those versions released in France, Blaetz argues that DeMille's original film was primarily concerned with readying the country for war and depicting female heroism. Read as an allegorical text, the film loses its European otherness in order to connect with its American audience. While early silent shorts may have failed to offer such thematic and narrative complexities, *Joan the Woman* was produced toward the end of this period, after nearly a decade of experimentation and refinement. Therefore, it is not at all inconceivable that DeMille could generate that level of subtextual meaning into the work. Despite differences in setting, *Joan the Woman* is still a silent historical drama, and like most of the silent witch-related historical dramas, it tells a personal story of an accused woman set within what was, if only through allegory, a recognizable narrative setting.

Missteps, Accusations, and Burnings

Similar to the last period, these trial films tell stories of young women who misstep in some way, defying an accepted social order and, as a result, are accused of witchcraft. For example, in *Witchcraft* (1916), the heroine befriends an "old Indian" woman against "her cruel husband's wishes."[58] In *Ivanhoe* (1913), *In the Days of Witchcraft* (1913), and *A Witch of Salem Town* (1915), the heroine refuses to marry a powerful male figure. In *A Puritan Episode* (1913), the young woman is taken in by "Indians" after they kill her parents. The film's heroine either does something or knows something that offends the established social order.

As in the earlier films, the accused woman escapes death through a white knight rescue in which a rational man, often her lover, rides in just as the fires are being lit. In the 1916 film *Witchcraft*, the heroine's love interest intervenes in her case, which results in "the governor [issuing] an edict stopping the witchcraft persecutions."[59] The conclusion of *In the Days of Witchcraft*, as noted in *The Anaconda Standard*, has Governor Brent returning just "in time to prevent [the heroine's] mother from being burned at the stake," which ultimately saves the heroine as well.[60] Through these rescues, the rational man saves the young woman, allowing her to then marry or return to her father's care. In other words, she is both vindicated from the witchcraft accusations and offered redemption for her transgressions through a return to a proper woman's role in society as wife or daughter.

---

57. Robin Blaetz, *Visions of the Maid: Joan of Arc in American Film and Culture* (Charlottesville: The University of Virginia Press, 2001), 51.

58. "At the Strand," 13.

59. "At the Strand," 13.

60. "*In the Days of Witchcraft* Shown in American Films," 8.

However, in this era, not all the heroines are willing to accept redemption. Several women reject the traditional role, and as a result, they do not get rescued. In both *A Witch of Salem Town* and *Joan the Woman*, the heroines are burned. Neither woman opts to conform to the requests of society through any type of narrative salvation or thematic suggestion. According to a *Motography* synopsis, *A Witch of Salem Town* tells the story of young Desiré, an orphan who learns "herb-lore" through her elderly guardian Goody Martin. When Desiré refuses to submit to the romantic advances of the "old governor," she is accused of witchcraft. Up to that point, the story is typical. However, Desiré chooses her reclusive lifestyle over traditional redemption. In the end, she is "burned at the stake as a witch." [61]

A Closer Look: *Joan the Woman*

Joan of Arc also meets a tragic end for her own nonconformity. Her death is recorded history and, therefore, not surprising to anyone who knows the story. However, director Cecil B. DeMille took license in capturing Joan's mythology for allegorical purposes, as discussed earlier, and for intrigue. Most notably, DeMille introduced a love interest who attempts the classic white knight rescue. Despite this change and others, DeMille ultimately could not alter the story's resolution. The rescue must fail with Joan burned as a sorceress.

One might expect DeMille's *Joan the Woman* to differ thematically from most trial films due to its historical source and European origins. However, it does not. As noted earlier, DeMille employed the Joan of Arc mythology to craft a rallying cry for the American woman during wartime. He purposefully minimized the importance of Joan's imprisonment and her trial, choosing to focus on Joan simply as an average woman. Blaetz notes that doing so "attributes Joan's death not to her challenge to the institutions of her day but to the demented actions of a few personally motivated individuals who fear her as a witch." [62] The struggle is personal and not societal. It is noteworthy that a woman, Jeanie Macpherson was selected to write the screenplay.

As such, DeMille's *Joan the Woman* is a typical version of the contemporary witch trial film, pitting the rational against the irrational and encouraging women to maintain their proper social place. Accusations are led by personal vengeance rather than global structures. *Joan the Woman* doesn't attack or support religion as an institution, but rather criticizes the limitations and dangers of privately held, antiquated fears, irrationality, and hardened religious zealotry. In that way, it is a masked retelling of the Salem story and very relatable to American audiences obsessed by the specter of witchcraft. Moreover,

61. "*A Witch of Salem Town*," *Motography* 13, no. 22 (January–June 1915): 906.
62. Blaetz, *Visions of the Maid*, 62.

if DeMille had focused his Joan story on religious tension or her mystical visions, Joan would have been a different type of witch figure altogether—a wild woman with unexplained powers, similar to Carrie in Brian De Palma's famous 1976 film.

However, DeMille focused on her humanity and her victimization brought about by irrational thought. Therefore, Joan is constructed as a classic accused woman. The film is about the girl rather than the Catholic Saint. DeMille himself said that his goal was to capture the "humanness of this remarkable woman."[63] He focused so much on that fictional love story that, in the end, Joan's death becomes less about martyrdom for country and faith, as history explains, and more about the sacrifice of a nonconformist woman. Her death, then, becomes a means to enforce societal gender norms and perpetuate the culture of the "proper" woman. It is a warning to female viewers. The sacrifice of love for one's ideology is the young woman's undoing and death is her punishment.

Trial Films and the Crone

In all these films, the term "witch" is typically applied to characters like Joan: *young women* who step inadvertently outside the bounds of normalcy through birthright, education, call to action, or simply survival. This is similar to the last period. While elderly accused women do exist, such as in *A Witch of Salem Town* and *A Puritan Episode*, their purpose is more or less fused to the narrative plight of the heroine rather than being a driving force in their own storylines. The elderly accused woman is either the cause of the young woman's trouble as a teacher (e.g., *The Witch Girl*, 1914), or she is used as a tool to elicit the young girl's acquiescence (e.g., *A Puritan Episode*, 1913). In all cases, the narrative is focused on the young woman, and the elderly woman is simply collateral damage or completely ignored.

This concept is most readily seen in *A Witch of Salem Town*. Desiré is raised by an elderly herbalist who villagers leave alone until the young woman demonstrates an interest in her unconventional and nature-based science. It is at this point that "witch" is decried. As observed by a reviewer at the *Scranton Republican*, "The girl's friendship with an old Indian, suspected of being a witch, leads to suspicion falling on her …"[64] Similarly, in *A Puritan Episode*, the elderly accused woman is burned as a witch for her insanity and for taking refuge outside of Puritan society, whereas her granddaughter is offered redemption and a place in the village. As in the last period, these films make a clear distinction between adolescent femininity and aged femininity. One state is dangerous and the other is inconsequential or disposable.

---

63. J. P. Chalmers and Thomas Bedding F.R.P.S., eds. "Geraldine Farrar as Joan of Arc," *The Moving Picture World* 30, no. 13 (December 30, 1916): 1944.

64. "*At the Strand,*" 13.

Witchcraft and the "Child-Woman"

Over time, several themes begin to emerge relating to gender, age, and witchcraft. For example, the narratives pit heterosexual love and marriage against witchcraft and female agency, and this theme endures for decades as an underlying subtext in American witch films. (e.g., *I Married a Witch*, 1942; *Bell, Book and Candle*, 1958). When the witch accepts love and marriage, the woman symbolically apologizes for any misstep and thereby proves her desire to conform. In doing so, she relinquishes her personal power, represented by witchcraft, and enters the realm of true womanhood as defined by contemporary community standards.[65] Her choice is clear; she can be a wife or a witch. Never both.

Similarly, another theme posits that all things rational, including science, reasonable religion, education, and governance, belong to the domain of men while all things irrational, including witchcraft, religious zealotry, superstition, and wild nature, belong to women. As noted, cinematic witchcraft is presented as an outcropping of the ignorant or suspicious mind and is an epithet slung at a woman, not because she dabbles in the occult but because she has overstepped boundaries of acceptable behavior for women. In crossing the line, she enters the realm of the witch and the wild land of the mystical, whether real or imagined.

Finally, a third emerging theme links the mystical and irrational wild specifically to adolescence, and this merger is a direct reflection of the popularity of the adolescent girl in contemporary culture. Film historian Diana Anselmo-Sequeira explains, "American filmmakers recurrently depicted the girl as a mystical figure whose adolescent development was tied to concurrent supernatural and sexual awakenings" from which she had to be saved.[66] In the case of trial films, the symbolic "supernatural" is defined as the witchcraft accusation. In westerns, it might be an herbal healing practice, and in fantasy, it is predominantly signified by encounters with a fantasy crone.

In her essay on famous silent film actress Mary Pickford, film theorist Gaylyn Studlar makes a similar observation about adolescent female characters, although not specifically related to witchcraft. As Studlar notes, for a good portion of Pickford's career, she was largely portrayed as a "child-woman."[67] In witch films, Pickford plays Fanchon, the young heroine of *Fanchon the Cricket* (1915). Actresses Mary Fuller and Marguerite Clark, who appear in several witch films each, maintained a similar cultural profile to Pickford's.

---

65. Veronica Pravadelli, "Cinema and the Modern Woman," in *The Wiley-Blackwell History of American Film*, ed. Cynthia Lucia, Roy Grundmann, and Art Simon (New York: Blackwell Publishing, 2012), 4.

66. Diana Anselmo-Sequeira, "Apparitional Girlhood: Material Ephemerality and the Historiography of Female Adolescence in Early American Film," *Spectator* 33, no. 1 (Spring 2013): 25.

67. Gaylyn Studlar, "Oh, 'Doll Divine': Mary Pickford, Masquerade, and the Pedophilic Gaze," in *A Feminist Reader in Early Cinema*, ed. Jennifer M. Bean and Diane Negra (Durham: Duke University Press, 2002), 361.

*Actress Mary Pickford (center) pauses for a photo
on the set of* Fanchon the Cricket *(1915).*
*[Source: Mary Pickford Foundation and the Margaret Herrick Library,
Academy of Motion Pictures Arts & Sciences. Copyright: Public Domain]*

Studlar observes that Pickford was caught in a liminal state of femininity, between girlhood and womanhood, which fueled her popularity. She argues that "[Pickford] represented a dangerously attractive female whose masquerade of childishness appealed to adult men raised in the late Victorian period."[68] In witch films, the danger, as observed by Anselmo-Sequeira, is symbolically represented by "concurrent supernatural...awakenings" or witchcraft.

Studlar concludes that the popularity of this "child-woman" character was a backlash against shifting gender norms, particularly toward the end of the decade into the 1920s. She writes:

> Pickford's popularity drew on powerful cultural attitudes that sentimentalized the emergent sexuality of girls and adolescents at a time when women's more assertive and self-determined sexual desire was regarded as an intrusion into the traditional male domain of sexual subjectivity and a threat to the primacy of the family.[69]

In westerns and historical dramas, the young woman becomes the witch after a show of force, independence, or intelligence, or simply the rejection of a man's sexual advances.

Simultaneously, through these antics, the female viewer is also allowed to engage in a certain amount of voyeuristic pleasure. Studlar notes that in many of the period's "child-woman" films, female viewers "were invited to relive the pleasures and pains of girlhood and to identify with [the young heroine]" in her feisty, wild nature.[70] However, the films ultimately conclude with the containment of her dangerous mystical power through marriage, family, or death. She cannot be the witch and a wife; she cannot have power and be a working member of society. The conclusions restore the dominant social order and show women what they can and cannot be.

Western Dramas and the Witch

While not the most popular genre for witches during this later silent era, the western adventure gives way to what one might call the western drama. These narratives are similar to the early westerns in that they are set in a wilderness environment and thrive on the tensions between society and the wild. However, these later silent films are more character driven and focus solely on interpersonal relationships. Addition-

---

68. Gaylyn Studlar, "Oh, 'Doll Divine,'" 361.

69. Studlar, "Oh, 'Doll Divine,'" 368.

70. Studlar, "Oh, 'Doll Divine,'" 365.

ally, this period sees the dominance of the young wild woman, not the elderly folk witch. This reflects the public's general fascination with adolescent female heroines. This young wild woman, like her cousin in historical dramas, finds herself stuck in a battle between witchcraft and marriage, freedom, and conformity. The western dramas of this era include *The Mountain Witch* (1913), *The Witch Girl* (1914), *Fanchon the Cricket* (1915), *The Witch* (1916), and *The Witch Woman* (1918).

The Elderly Folk Witch

Although not common, several of the films do contain the classic elderly folk witch; however, she is typically a secondary character who simply serves to define the young woman as wild and a witch. For example, the elderly folk witch teaches herbalism (e.g., *The Witch Girl*, 1914) or raises children in the forest (e.g., *Fanchon the Cricket*). In this way, she actually grants the adolescent girl her personal power, allegorically speaking, through a connection to nature and, as a result, provides the tools by which the girl can choose to reject society or opt for redemption. The elderly folk witch essentially turns the young girl wild, something that can be read as both a blessing and curse. This dynamic, which pits old against young in relationship to the social order, plays out more vividly within later fairy tale adaptations (e.g., Disney's *Snow White and the Seven Dwarfs*, 1937) and horror films (*Witchcraft*, 1988). For now, the dynamic exists as a subtle undercurrent that reinforces contemporary biases with regard to age and gender.

It is important to note that several of the period's elderly witches are indigenous women, depicted as old "Indians." In these cases, it is not simply an isolation in the woods that defines her as a wild woman or witch, but rather it is also her ethnicity. As previously discussed, the indigenous folk witch is suspect because she is "not us," as defined by the viewer. Her ethnicity provides the narrative excuse for her nonconformist lifestyle, her wild behavior, and her belief in magic. In review of *A Puritan Episode*, the writer demonstrates the prevailing negative opinion held of indigenous cultures, explaining that the wild child is protected by the tribe because "Indians held an insane person sacred."[71] The comment typifies the film's racially based, coded cultural hierarchy through the suggestion that American culture upholds all that is rational and sane while "Indians" held sacred that which is irrational. Despite this problematic character construction, the indigenous folk witch serves the same purpose as any elderly folk witch: to teach herbalism, raise the wild child, and otherwise offer the heroine a path to power outside of expected norms.

---

71. "*A Puritan Episode,*" *The Moving Picture News*, September 13, 1913, 27.

The Young Wild Woman

Although the elderly folk witch is still present within these films, it is the young wild woman who takes center stage. In *Fanchon the Cricket* and *The Witch Girl*, the heroines are both living in the mountains with an elderly woman, practicing herbalism and living off the land. In *The Witch*, a suspicious young woman practices hypnotism, a skill taught to her by her late father. In *The Witch Woman*, a young girl lives alone in the woods after being cast out for having a sexual relationship with a prominent male figure. In *The Mountain Witch*, a newly arrived minister finds that his parishioners are fearful of a magical mountain woman who lives on the outskirts of their town.

When the western drama opens, the young wild woman is already designated a witch. She begins the film as the narrative's problem. In addition, her alleged magic must be explained by science or belief and can never be truly supernatural. In these five films, the witch's power turns out to be simply the product of suspicious minds. There is no mysticism or occult practice. The young women are feared because of their lifestyles, their knowledge of natural healing modalities, and their disinterest in acceptable socialization. For example, in *The Mountain Witch*, the young minister, Revell, discovers this very point when he meets Garrie, the wild witch, who is mistrusted due to her "peculiarities." He then works to convince his "ignorant" parishioners of their error and to resocialize Garrie.[72]

As with other films, the period's western dramas are predominantly redemption stories for the young woman who is defined as a type of monster, and as expected, the resolution is the same. The young woman, who is considered socially beneficial as a potential mother or wife, must be assimilated and the wildness exorcised from her spirit through a reengagement with her proper social position. In *The Mountain Witch*, Garrie is embraced and accepted by a helpful preacher. In *The Witch Girl*, Mary Fuller's "painfully innocent" wild character is assimilated back into society through marriage.[73]

The shift in the genre's character focus from the elderly folk witch to the young wild girl reinforces the observations made by historians Studlar and Anselmo-Sequeira. The cultural obsession with female adolescence was not limited in its expression to any one particular genre, and the term "witch" was no longer simply a symbolic cue for the uncivilized old woman. Just like the accused woman of the historical dramas, the young wild woman was often represented as a "child-woman" who lives in a liminal space between youth and adulthood. Adolescence is when the girl begins to discover her own sexuality and power, and when men or boys begin to notice her existence. For the young girl, this is a time filled with unknowns and self-making, and in that way, it is its own symbolic untamed wilderness. In a review

---

72. "*The Mountain Witch*," *Kalem Kalendar*, February 1, 1913, 15.

73. "*Witch Girl* Shows Mary Fuller at Best," *The Wilmington Morning Star*, November 8, 1914, 12.

of *The Witch Girl* in *The Wilmington Morning Star*, the writer celebrates actress Mary Fuller's youthful appeal and more specifically, describes her character's journey as a sexual "awakening" that is "something common to all women." [74]

A Closer Look: *Fanchon,* Family, Feminism

Based on George Sand's 1848 novel *La Petite Fadette*, the film *Fanchon the Cricket* contains both a young wild woman (Mary Pickford) and an elderly folk witch, who is also her biological grandmother. Many of Pickford's star vehicles were sourced from literature written by women containing strong-minded young female heroines. Studlar notes that these original stories "offered the adventures and triumphs of independent little girls whose behavior rebelled against expected norms of feminine refinement and morality," which framed Pickford's star persona.[75] *Fanchon the Cricket* does not stray terribly from Sand's novel in that respect and the characterization fits the genre model of the wild girl.

As a short, *Fanchon the Cricket* is unable to capture the depth of political or philosophical meaning or feminist expression implied in Sand's writing. It is also important to acknowledge that, while the original story was written by a woman, the film was produced by men. Therefore, any expressions of feminism or other similar themes were lost in translation. The adaptation, in fact, is traditional in terms of contemporary wild woman stories. The elderly folk witch exists simply to define the young heroine's character and to act as an obstacle to reintegration, which are both the standard narrative roles for this character construction at the time. The reviews describe Fanchon's own wildness chiefly as a function of her grandmother's disinterest in raising her by proper societal standards. It is only when the crone dies that Fanchon is able to resist her upbringing and accept redemption through marriage.

The film's familial connection between the elderly folk witch and the young wild woman is notable, because it is rare in American witch films. Parent-child witch relationships are more typically constructed between a daughter and father (e.g., *The Witch*, 1916; *I Married a Witch*, 1942) or, later, aunts, brothers, or cousins. If there is a mother-daughter pair, the older woman is either not typically magical (e.g., *A Puritan Episode*, 1913; *Teen Witch*, 1989) or one of the pair has rejected her magic (e.g., *Bewitched*, 1964–1972). In cases where an elderly folk witch does teach or consult a teenager, the relationship is found and is not familial (e.g., *Teen Witch*, 1989). It is not until the 1990s that positive familial mother-daughter witch pairings begin to show up regularly (e.g., *Practical Magic*, 1998). This indicates that *Fanchon the Cricket* did not entirely lose all feminist elements embedded in the original novel.

---

74. "*Witch Girl* Shows Mary Fuller at Best," 12.

75. Studlar, "Oh, 'Doll Divine,'" 356.

The Magic and Spectacle of Fantasy

While the western and historical dramas were popular, fantasy continued to be the primary genre for the witch. In a 1916 review of *A Daughter of the Gods*, writer W. Stephen Bush proclaims, "A Fairy Tale—this much I have concluded—is the screen's own favorite expression."[76] The genre not only lent itself to the retelling of popular stories, but it also provided fertile ground for the filmmakers' imaginations in a new and expanding art form. In addition, producers recognized the growing youth audience and wanted to offer a counterpoint to the violence found in other genres. In a 1929 interview, *The Star Prince* director, Madeline Brandeis, said, "I had written a fairy story, 'Twinkle, Twinkle, Little Star,' and thought I'd enjoy making it come to life on the screen—a souvenir for my grandchildren—if I ever had any."[77] Produced in 1918 as *The Star Prince*, the film was not broadly released until 1920 as *Twinkle Twinkle Little Star*. While not all the fantasies were aimed at young audiences, *The Star Prince*, directed by one of the first American woman film directors, was.

Within the period's fantasy films, witches were found in a variety of forms from the Victorian clown witch to the fantasy crone to a fantasy version of the indigenous folk witch. During this period, Hawthorne's short story "Feathertop" was retold twice as *Feathertop* (1913) and *The Woman Who Did Not Care* (1913), and Shakespeare's *Macbeth* saw its first full-length film adaptation. After the moderate success of Selig Polyscope's *The Wonderful Wizard of Oz* (1910), L. Frank Baum produced several cinematic adaptations of his works, including the film *His Majesty, the Scarecrow* (1914) that was later re-released as *The New Wizard of Oz* (1915). The Famous Players Film Company adapted classic fairy tales such as *Cinderella* (1914), *Snow White* (1916), and *The Seven Swans* (1917). Fox Film Corporation adapted classic tale *Hansel and Gretel*, titled *The Babes in the Woods* (1917). Finally, producers also released a number of original fantasy spectacles and serials including Fox Film Corporation's *A Daughter of the Gods* (1916), Universal Moving Pictures' *Neptune's Daughter* (1914), Selig Polyscope's *The Story of the Blood Red Rose* (1914), International Film Service's *The Mysteries of Myra* (1916), and Little Players' *The Star Prince* (1918).

The Last of the Victorian Clowns

After the release of *The Wonderful Wizard of Oz*, L. Frank Baum used what funds he could gather to start his own production company and adapt three of his own successful children's stories to which he still owned the rights. Not all of Baum's films contain

---

76. W. Stephen Bush, "A Daughter of the Gods," *The Moving Picture World* (November 4, 1916): 673.

77. Ruth M. Tildesley, "Filming Children for Children: The Delightful Pursuit of Madeline Brandeis" *National Board of Review Magazine* 4, no. 10 (December 1929): 5.

witches; in fact, only one does, and that one was the last, *His Majesty, the Scarecrow of Oz* (1914). Directed by J. Farrell McDonald, the film was often simply called *The Scarecrow of Oz* and, then in 1915, it was re-released, as already noted, with the title *The New Wizard of Oz*. The film's main antagonist is Old Mombi, the Witch of the North. She is a classic Victorian clown witch and one of the last of the silent era.

Dressed in a patchwork gown and constructed as a comedic fool, Mombi is the most striking example of this carnivalesque Victorian witch-style. Old Mombi's clothing is reminiscent of the original novel's illustrations by W. W. Denslow. She is clearly a comic figure whose stooped body lumbers along with a monkey-like shuffle. Instead of a broom, she brandishes an umbrella. Halfway through the film, the Tin Man lops off her head. With some movie magic, Old Mombi manages to put her head back on and she runs off. At the end of the film, she is literally canned with a sign that reads "preserved <u>sand</u>witches." The entire film maintains a fanciful, lighthearted approach to the Oz story. The witch is no exception.

Baum was not the only one to capitalize on the Victorian clown style. Famous Players Film Company and its director James Kirkwood used the readily identifiable construction in their adaptation of *Cinderella* (1914). Unlike the Oz films, *Cinderella* was geared at a more expansive audience, and the witch is not solely engaged in antagonistic buffoonery, despite her appearance. In addition, the use of the clown construction serves more than just an aesthetic purpose; it also serves to diminish the witch's threat from the viewer's perspective, allowing for greater empathy with the heroine. When *Cinderella* opens, a darkly clad clown witch is promptly ignored by the evil stepsisters. A title card reads "Egotism and Cruelty." Then the witch encounters Cinderella (Mary Pickford) and, unlike her sisters, she offers the witch assistance. The title card reads "Love of one's neighbor and friendliness." The old clown witch then transforms into a fairy godmother.

Cinderella's clown witch plays a similar narrative role as the western's elderly folk witch; she serves to define the heroine's goodness. She is a moral compass. The evil stepsisters ignore the old woman and therefore are defined as bad. Cinderella does not and is marked as good. Using the nonthreatening clown aesthetic makes the situation believable rather than dangerous. If the witch had a frightening appearance, the audience may have experienced more sympathy toward the stepsisters and their refusal to help. The style also makes it easier to digest her later transformation into a fairy godmother.

The Fantasy Crone, Ethics, and Exchange

The classic fantasy crone is the dominant fantasy witch construction of the period, which is not surprising considering the repetition of classic fairy tales and literature, such as *The Woman Who Did Not Care* (1913), *Feathertop* (1913), *Snow White* (1916), *Cinderella* (1914), *The Babes in the Woods* (1917) and *The Seven Swans* (1917). These crones are typically depicted wearing dark cloaks and having some object related to fantasy witchcraft such as a cauldron, broom, or crow. For example, in *Cinderella*, a fantasy crone, completely unrelated to the film's clown witch, appears a third of the way into the story. Her stooped, dark form stands over a bubbling cauldron as she holds a wand and broom. Her visual construction is a stark contrast to the whimsical and patchwork styling of Old Mombi or Cinderella's fairy godmother in disguise.

It is important to note that the silent fantasy witch, clown and crone, is rarely the primary antagonist. She is typically doing the bidding of an evil figure, or even in some cases, the hero. As such, these witches tend to be morally ambiguous figures who barter in magic. In this way, the clown witch and the fantasy crone are no different. It is simply their visual construction that creates the delineation between the two characters. Outside of that visual difference, they maintain similar narrative purposes, which are often a supporting role as magic-for-money businesswomen.

In *Snow White*, Witch Hex aids the Wicked Queen in her multiple attempts to kill Snow White. In *The Seven Swans*, the Wicked Queen calls on the witch to turn the brothers into birds. In *The Babes in the Woods*, the evil stepmother and Bad Prince employ a witch to capture and kill the young children in order to inherit their wealth. Even in the Oz film *His Majesty, the Scarecrow of Oz*, Old Mombi the clown witch is not acting alone. At the bidding of King Krewl, she freezes the heart of Princess Gloria.

While the motivation for providing aid to the villain is not always made clear, there always appears to be an exchange. The witch sells magical services for a price, and it is either money or another favor that drives her actions rather than ideological evil. In *The Babes in the Woods*, the Bad Prince promises the witch riches for her help. In *Cinderella*, a title card reads "Ignorance and Superstition. The sisters go to a fortuneteller." After being handed coins, the fantasy crone reads their palms and says, "A member of your family will be chosen to be the Prince's wife." Old Mombi is, according to title cards, always ready to make a "dishonest dollar." The motive is personal profit, and magic is the business.

This moral ambiguity is inherited from classic fairy tales, in which the magical woman is entirely separated from the story's antagonist. In fact, in many of the original stories, both villains and heroes will barter with a witch. How she is positioned in the narrative changes depending on who is asking for help. In both *Cinderella* and *The Story of the Blood Red Rose*, it is the young heroine who engages in the transaction. Although there is reciprocity between the characters, the relationship between the heroine and the witch is not contractual; it is based purely on happenstance. The heroine helps the witch, and in return, the witch helps the heroine. In these instances, the witch plays the role of a moral compass, helping to define the heroine as good. As noted earlier, Cinderella is defined as being kind because she helps the elderly clown witch; her evil stepsisters do not.

When the witch barters with the villain, she ceases to be a moral compass and, instead, is a tool used against the young maiden by an evil despot. As such, the witch becomes the mystical obstacle aimed at preventing a young girl's evolution into a socially acceptable woman. King Krewl, the Wicked Queen, and the Bad Prince all hire the witch to kill the heroine. In the historical dramas, the mystical obstacle was an unacceptable social decision leading to an accusation. In the western, the obstacle was a lack of social grace or knowing too much. In both cases, the young heroine's own actions under her own power cause the tension and, therefore, she herself ultimately houses the symbolic "supernatural" danger that interferes in her ability to take her proper role in society. However, in the fantasy film, the heroine is never the witch herself, rather the mystical obstacle is embodied in an entirely separate female character, typically a fantasy crone.

Even when the crone acts as aide or moral compass, she is always the physical incarnation of the forbidden mystical element that seduces the young girl due to her liminal state of beingness. The suggested tension in this age-related character dynamic is partly derived from the original fairy tales. However, the uneasy relationship between the crone and heroine is only an undercurrent in early silent films because most of the witches are minor characters and operate from a point of moral ambiguity. They do not contain the intensity that is seen in later adaptations such as Disney's *Snow White and the Seven Dwarfs* (1937). Rather than diving deep into character motivation and narrative complexities, these silent fantasy films are focused on faithful adaptation, the implied voyeuristic entertainment of the "child-woman" and, more simply, providing light children's fare for a growing viewer demographic.

A Closer Look: *The Annette Kellerman Spectacles*

Two unique fantasy films offer a look at the ways silent fantasy crones were narratively constructed. *Neptune's Daughter* and *A Daughter of the Gods* were big-budget fantasy spectacles with original scripts starring Australian film actress Annette Kellerman. Both films are lost. No visuals remain of their witch characters and there is only a little narrative detail left to provide insight into their roles and motivations. While there is some remaining footage of *Neptune's Daughter*, the scenes do not contain images of the Sea Witch; the only surviving stills are of Kellerman. This is not surprising since both films were designed purely as star vehicles. In fact, *A Daughter of the Gods* is considered the first million-dollar movie, as well as the first to have a nude scene with a major star. Most of the surviving stills are of those nude scenes.

Australian actress Annette Kellerman stars in A Daughter of the Gods *(1916), one of the first extravagant fantasy spectacles and the first film to contain a nude scene. [Source: Bain News Service, Publisher. Library of Congress, Library of Congress, Prints & Photographs. Copyright: Public Domain]*

In *A Daughter of the Gods*, the witch appears to be the primary villain and a businesswoman, who makes her magical deal with a sultan. If he helps her capture and kill the young goddess, she will resurrect his son. Just as with other silents, the film places the fantasy crone in direct conflict with the young heroine. Her allegorical goal is to curb or stop the process of maturation into a socially acceptable adult woman, as with *Snow White* or *The Babes in the Woods*. Unfortunately, not much more is known. There are no visuals that show how the witch was dressed or narratively framed.

In *Neptune's Daughter*, the mermaid heroine makes the deal with the film's witch. In this case, the magical woman is a sea witch who enables the heroine to become human. While this plot detail suggests inspiration from Hans Christian Andersen's "The Little Mermaid," the film is not considered an adaptation of the story, but it likely was inspired by the work. From the few surviving details, it appears as if the sea witch plays the role of the amoral fantasy witch who assists the heroine for a price. She represents the mystical that seduces the adolescent female during her dangerous stage of growth and thereby gives her a chance at unfettered feminine power and an escape from social obligations. In that role, the fantasy crone is both a moral compass defining the heroine and an obstacle to her assimilation into society.

Fantasy Witchcraft and Its Literary Origins

There are five legendary authors who have had the most influence in creating the American cinematic witch, particularly the fantasy crone. They are L. Frank Baum, Nathaniel Hawthorne, the Grimm Brothers, and William Shakespeare. Baum's influence, as already discussed in detail, was limited at this point in time to his young fans and their families. His many creative endeavors eventually bankrupted him and, while his books were popular with children, the films never succeeded. In fact, *The Wonderful Wizard of Oz* was largely considered cinematic poison for decades. Eventually, however, that changes, and the power of his influence through his story and his witch characters is unmistakable.

Unlike Baum, novelist Nathanial Hawthorne's influence on witch films is significant right out of the starting gate. During the early silent period, there were two adaptations of his "moralized legend" *Feathertop* and one adaptation of *The House of the Seven Gables*. In this period, there were two 1913 adaptations of his short story, including Kinemacolor's *Feathertop* and Éclair American's *The Woman Who Did Not Care*. Both of these shorts may have been cinematic recordings or adaptations of Percy MacKaye's successful 1908 theatrical adaptation of Hawthorne's *Feathertop* called *The Scarecrow*.

Historians, such as Gretchen Adams, consider Hawthorne along with his publisher, Samuel Goodrich, to be two of the biggest influencers who perpetuated Salem's witchcraft legacy into the twentieth century.[78] It was a cyclical cultural engine; the fascination with Hawthorne's stories of New England witchcraft and moral panic, particularly *Feathertop*, inspired filmmakers to keep making cinematic adaptations, which in turn kept the public's interest in the history alive.

While, like Hawthorne's works, classic fairy tales were told and retold many times, it is *Hansel and Gretel* that was adapted the most. And like Hawthorne's works, the fairy tale's influence emerged in the film industry's infancy with the 1909 Edison short *Hansel and Gretel*, followed by *The Babes in the Woods* (1917). German authors Jacob and Wilhelm Grimm first published the story in 1812, giving readers a look at the classic eastern European legend of the fearsome old witch of the woods. While other Grimm stories such as "Sneewittchen" (or "Snow White") were also adapted many times, it is "Hansel and Gretel," with its iconic fantasy crone, that was adapted most frequently and most consistently over time and in almost every decade.

The Brothers Grimm did not create their fairy tales, nor did they invent the witch; they published well-known European-based oral tales that had been shared for generations. The witch depicted as an old crone was not new to them, which leads to the last of the influencers: William Shakespeare. The year 1916 sees the first feature-length US cinematic adaptation of one of his most famous tragedies: *Macbeth*. While there were three recorded short adaptations prior to this film, two did not contain the witches and the third, recorded in 1898, has left little information behind other than its existence. All three are lost. Unfortunately, the 1916 version, directed by D. W. Griffith, is also lost and most of the reviews make no mention of the famous weird sisters. What is known is that all three of the *Macbeth* witches were portrayed by men, suggesting that they were covered up with dark cloaks to hide their gender. The use of men in these roles mirrors imagery from other theatrical performances as well as many still renderings of the famous Shakespeare trio (e.g., Henry Fuseli "The Weird Sisters," 1782; Henri Fuseli "Macbeth, Banquo and the Witches," 1793–1794).

Macbeth's influence on cinematic witches cannot be understated, but its influence is not from the repetition of adaptations; in fact, *Macbeth* isn't adapted very frequently at all. What makes the play so influential is the popularity of the three weird sisters, whose likeness has been copied and adapted across cultures, time, and narrative forms of expression. Written in the 1600s, Shakespeare's tragedy was birthed during the Jacobean era and the notorious European witch hunts. The witch-related language and symbols employed by the playwright were undoubtedly familiar to his

---

78. Adams, *The Specter of Salem*, 38–39.

audiences. Historian Diane Purkiss suggests that the weird sisters were originally "a low-budget, frankly exploitative collage of randomly chosen bits of witch-lore, selected not for thematic significance but for its sensation value."[79] In other words, the concept of three old women dealing in magic and divination was not invented by Shakespeare. In fact, the sisters are reminiscent of the Greek Fates and other similar mythological figures.

Whether Shakespeare's original intent was pure sensationalism or not, the characters' cultural influence has far exceeded comic relief due to a cultural fascination, for better or worse, with witchcraft. Their influence has touched everything from classic art (e.g., Daniel Gardner, "The Three Witches from Macbeth" 1775) to the extratextual repetition of their most famous lines in popular cinema, including "Double, double toil and trouble" (e.g., *Double, Double, Toil and Trouble*, 1993) or "Something wicked this way comes" (e.g., *Something Wicked This Way Comes*, 1983). With periodic adaptations and the play being required school-age reading, the weird sisters stand out as powerfully influential witches in American cinema, after making their debut in the silent era.

Myra, Spiritualism, and the Occult

As noted in chapter 1, the witch was not associated to the occult or religion during the early days of filmmaking. Witches were accused women, wild women, or fantasy creatures. Magic and the practice of witchcraft were products of superstition, ignorance, and backward cultures. While theological language describing witches still lingered in film reviews, the rhetoric was never meant to suggest a belief that the witch was truly a product of occult or satanic practice. For example, in a review of *His Majesty, the Scarecrow*, William Ressman Andrews writes, "The grinning hag, accoutered with all the traditional regalia of her office, peaked hat and bizarre garments, goes to her task with a diabolical zest."[80] Nowhere in the actual film is there a devil construct as Andrews suggests. The language is just descriptive. This is true of all other film reviews using such language, except the reviews of one production: *The Mysteries of Myra*.

As far as it is known, the serial *The Mysteries of Myra* was the only witch-related production during this time to openly embrace the occult as a subject and maintain a strong bond between theology and magic. The serial's narrative and repeating plot rely on a mix of Spiritualist philosophy, psychology, ceremonial magick, and Eastern spirituality. As film archivist Eric Stedman writes, "Myra was the first film to bring all of the then-modern spiritualism and parapsychology together to the front in a

79. Purkiss, *A Witch in History*, 207.
80. William Ressman Andrews, "The Scarecrow of Oz," *Motion Picture News* (October 24, 1914): 61.

'serious,' at least pseudo-scientific and contemporary setting." [81] While the serial still frames these disciplines as evil in Christian terms, *The Mysteries of Myra* makes no attempts to filter or hide such activity or occult ritual work. In fact, it was this very detail that made the series both unusual and successful.

Produced and directed by Theodore and Leopold Wharton, *The Mysteries of Myra* was a 1916 serial with fifteen episodes and two more unreleased. Many of the reels are lost. However, fragments have survived along with stills, synopses, and other production information. In one episode after another, the Black Order, a secret society of devil worshippers, use various forms of occult practice to capture and kill the young Myra in order to gain her inheritance. The serial's plot synopses describe the inclusion of occult practices like ritual magic, possession, clairvoyance, astral bodies, levitation, and elementals.

Occult Influences

Unlike the purely speculative Spiritualist underpinnings of Baum's written works, *The Mysteries of Myra* flaunts its religious and occult influence in full view, and those representations were crafted with the help of experts. Stedman notes that "elements related to devil-worship might have been derived from old books of magic, such as *Dogme et Rituel de la Haute Magie* (1861) by Éliphas Lévi, which contains a representation of the Black Order's magic circle." [82] The source of such information was author, Spiritualist, and famed psychic and paranormal investigator Hereward Carrington. who consulted on the production and offered storylines to scriptwriter Charles Goddard. In fact, the serial's main male protagonist, Dr. Payson Alden, is based on Carrington himself. [83]

Additionally, infamous British occultist Aleister Crowley, who was once dubbed "the most wicked man in the world," was the model for the Grand Master played by Michael Rale. Crowley's organization, the Order of the Golden Dawn, formed the basis of the serial's Black Order. The association is unmistakable. Surviving images of the Grand Master are direct copies of Crowley's own famous publicity photographs, most notably the image of him wearing his iconic triangle hat and resting his hands on his fists with thumbs up. Due to these obvious replications, there has been speculation on whether Crowley consulted on the serial's production. Photos have even surfaced that show a man who resembles Crowley on the *Myra* set. However, it is unlikely.

---

81. Eric Stedman, *The Mysteries of Myra: A Serial Squadron Lost Serial Photonovel* (California: Eric Stedman, 2010), 7.

82. Stedman, *The Mysteries of Myra*, 10.

83. Stedman, *The Mysteries of Myra*, 396.

Spiritualist Hereward Carrington designed the character of
the Grand Master after legendary occultist Aleister Crowley.
[Source: Ithaca Made Movies. Copyright: Public Domain]

Crowley was in fact living in New York at the time of *Myra*'s production in Ithaca and could have been on location. However, Crowley makes no mention of the film serial in his detailed diaries. Furthermore, Carrington wrote in a published personal account that he did not meet the famed occultist until after the start of World War I in 1917.[84] It is most likely the case that Carrington, in his paranormal investigative work, knew of Crowley and the Order of the Golden Dawn, and he used both as inspiration for the film's villain and evil occult order.

The Mysteries of Myra went on to inspire similar film works on paranormal and adjacent subjects, if not specifically witchcraft, through the end of the decade. While the Grand Master was never labeled a witch or warlock in the serial, his role is iconic and he is the earliest depiction of the male occultist, which is later repeated regularly either

---

84. Hereward Carrington, "The Strangest Man I Have Ever Known: Aleister Crowley," edited by Michael Kolson (Seattle: Night of Pan Books, 2011) on *Gorish* (blog), Blogger, March 8, 2015, http://gorish .blogspot.com/2015/03/the-strangest-man-i-have-ever-known.html.

on its own or in relationship to satanic witchcraft (e.g., *House of the Black Death*, 1965). Both Crowley and eventually Church of Satan founder Anton LaVey served as two of the most influential figures on the characterization of male occultists in American cinema.

Adolescent Femininity and the Mystical

Along with its overt display of occult practice, the serial is yet another example of the contemporary interest in adolescent femininity. Myra is an ordinary teen girl who is repeatedly threatened by practitioners of magic. The serial's title, *The Mysteries of Myra*, is meant quite literally because her own father was once of the Order. But the title also points to the theoretical parallel between female adolescence and magic. In this case, the theme manifests as an occult world seeking to capitalize on the pliant nature of a sweet young woman in an effort to disrupt proper social norms by stealing her rightful inheritance and, ultimately, her proper future.

This is similar to the narrative in *The Babes in the Woods* and coincides with any fantasy in which a magical figure attempts to kill a young heroine. Anselmo-Sequeira notes that Myra is the antithesis to most other serial heroines of the time in that she is younger and depicted as "delicate" with "no special physical ability."[85] This construction makes her more susceptible to magical influence and better supports the gender-based themes that dominated witch-related films of the period.

Fantasy Witchcraft

Despite the serial's focus on the occult and ceremonial magic, it is important to note that *The Mysteries of Myra* also includes a fantasy witch. The character only appears in episode thirteen, aptly named "Witchcraft." She is a typical fantasy crone with elongated facial features and dark clothing. However, this witch is in no way affiliated with the Black Order, rather she acts in predictable fashion by serving as a moral compass for the heroine. Myra saves the witch from a lynching and, in return, the witch saves her from the Black Order. The fantasy crone always deals in quid pro quos and, in this case, the exchange benefits Myra, defining her as good.

---

85. Anselmo-Sequeira, "Apparitional Girlhood," 31.

Myra earns the help of a woodland witch in her fight against the
Black Order in episode 13 of the 1916 serial The Mysteries of Myra,
starring Jean Sothern as Myra and an unknown actress as the witch.
[Source: Ithaca Made Movies. Copyright: Public Domain]

Stedman describes the "Witchcraft" episode as "outright fantasy," which distinguishes it from the proto-horror elements found in the rest of the series.[86] Stedman notes that midway through the serial, the tone clearly shifts from a linear narrative focused on occult or Spiritualist concepts to fantastical "monster of the week" stories. It is believed that Hereward Carrington, the main source of occult material, left the project, leaving serial writers to invent their own narratives.

The inclusion of an iconic fantasy crone is part of this narrative shift. She is distinct from the magical Black Order, demonstrating once again that witchcraft and the occult were not connected in the minds of American filmmakers and viewers. While the series was billed as horror, episode thirteen and others like it are classified as fan-

---

86. Stedman, *The Mysteries of Myra*, 10.

tasy. Occult practice and witchcraft were separate elements, at least in American cinematic language. One was a dangerous, satanic-based or a mystical reality; the other was a product of superstition, backward cultures, and pure fantasy.

Conclusion

In 1913, the American film industry had expanded beyond its nickelodeon roots and was moving to the West Coast. Seven years later, the move was complete, and the industry was organizing into what would become modern Hollywood and the famed studio system. During this period, innovations in technology and experimentation with the medium were changing the way filmmakers told their stories. Films increased in length and were no longer the characteristically short demonstrative films or theatrical recordings.

Despite the evolution, as noted by film historian Jennifer Bean, the filmmaker's underlying goal still had not yet developed beyond the "look what we can do" stage. Bean writes, "The focus of interest remains insistently on the turn of the century, where the hype over attractions has accentuated a film form potentially dominated by exhibitionism rather than voyeurism, by surprise rather than suspense, and by spectacle rather than story.[87] Depth and intensity of character development had yet to reach its full form. The witch, for example, was simply a whimsical novelty, an indicator of genre, a secondary villain, and a narrative device. Like American cinema, she hadn't come into her own yet.

With that said, silent cinema is no less indicative of cultural trends regarding gender and female agency than any other period in Hollywood's history. The majority of these films highlight the lingering Victorian cultural obsession with teenage girls or what Studlar termed "child-women." Embedded within that popular trend was a connection, for better or worse, between female adolescence and the mystical. Although the conclusion is always the same, the films do offer room for subversive readings. For example, *Joan the Woman* contains narrative elements that allow for the enjoyment of active feminine power even within an otherwise oppressive narrative. As Blaetz posits, *Joan the Woman* "reveal[s] much about popular notions of female heroism during the First World War."[88] This could be compared to the "Rosie the Riveter" campaigns of the 1940s.

---

87. Jennifer M. Bean, "Introduction: Toward a Feminist Historiography of Early Cinema," in *A Feminist Reader in Early Cinema*, ed. Jennifer M. Bean and Diane Negra (Durham: Duke University Press, 2002), 6.

88. Blaetz, *Visions of the Maid*, 64.

It is here in this early stage of American cinema that we witness the beginnings of the dual nature of the witch archetype as both a display of oppression based on conventional gender roles and one that also inspires and empowers female agency. However, this is only just the beginning. Moving into the 1920s beyond the silent era, the witch does begin to evolve, becoming more central to the narrative, and finding herself in new cinematic formats as genres lose and gain popularity.

Chapter 2: Filmography

A Puritan Episode	1913	unknown
The Witch of Salem	1913	Raymond B. West
In the Days of Witchcraft	1913	Fred Huntley
Ivanhoe	1913	Herbert Brenon
The Mountain Witch	1913	George Melford
The Woman Who Did Not Care	1913	unknown
Feathertop	1913	unknown
The Witch	1913	O. A. C. Lund
The Witch Girl	1914	Walter Edwin
Cinderella	1914	James Kirkwood
His Majesty, the Scarecrow	1914	L. Frank Baum
The Story of the Blood Red Rose	1914	Colin Campbell
Neptune's Daughter	1914	Herbert Brenon
When Broadway Was a Trail	1914	O. A. C. Lund
A Witch of Salem Town	1915	Lucius Henderson
Fanchon the Cricket	1915	James Kirkwood
The Mountain Girl	1915	Paul Powell
Witchcraft	1916	Frank Reicher
Snow White	1916	J. Searle Dawley
Macbeth	1916	John Emerson
The Mysteries of Myra	1916	Theo & Leopold Wharton
A Daughter of the Gods	1916	Herbert Brenon

The Witch	1916	Frank Powell
Joan the Woman	1916	Cecil B. DeMille
The Babes in the Woods	1917	Chester & Sidney Franklin
The Seven Swans	1917	J. Searle Dawley
The Witch Woman	1918	Travers Vale
The Star Prince	1918	Madeline Brandeis
The Sins of Roseanne	1920	Tom Forman

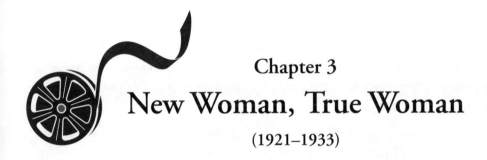

Chapter 3
New Woman, True Woman
(1921–1933)

The late teens and early twenties are largely considered a period of stabilization for the American film industry during which industry executives began forming what would become the studio system. By 1920, Hollywood had fully embraced the extravagance for which it was famous from spectacles to lavish lifestyles. In *A History of Narrative Film*, Dr. David Cook writes, "New money, new power, and the 'new morality' of the postwar Jazz Age all combined to make Hollywood in the 1920s the modern Babylon of popular lore." [89]

Much of the work to establish the studio system and its unique cinematic language was done in the late teens. As explained by historian William Everson, "The films of the late teens were, in film-making parlance, rather like 'establishing shots' used functionally to get movies under way. They established the art and industry that took off in the twenties." [90] Everson's observation applies directly to the period's witch films. The early twenties saw a repetition of narratives that were popular in the late teens such as fairy tale adaptations (e.g., *Hansel and Gretel*, 1923), fantasy spectacles (e.g., *Folly of Vanity*, 1924) and literary adaptations (e.g., *Puritan Passions*, 1923). Iconic witch characters appeared in their expected roles, including the disfigured elderly woman in dark cloaks and a pointy hat, the accused woman, the wild young adolescent, and the archetypical woodsy folk witch.

---

89. David A. Cook, *A History of Narrative Film* (New York: W. W. Norton & Company, 1996), 196.

90. Everson, *American Silent Film*, 124.

However, in 1924, the trajectory of Hollywood's witch construction veers drastically from that course. The female witch, in nearly all forms, disappears from the silver screen entirely. Her only consistent incarnation can be found within animated shorts (e.g., *Felix Switches Witches*, 1927) and a few low-budget live-actions. There are no Salem-based films, no western adventures or dramas with witches, no more live-action fairy tales or literary adaptations. This sudden shift begs the question: why did live-action female witches disappear and then why, at the end of this period in 1933, did they return? To understand this change, it is important to look at both the changes in the industry itself and at the changes in broader culture that point to the "new morality" of the Jazz Age.

Shifting Gender Roles and the Cinematic Witch

The disappearance and reappearance of the live-action female witch follows a similar pattern to the cultural negotiation of gender politics within 1920s Hollywood cinema as a whole. In other words, the general trends in the representation of non-magical heroines runs congruently with the appearance or disappearance of witches. When independent female characters dominate the silver screen, the witch virtually disappears. When the cultural and cinematic interest in the modern Jazz-era heroine wanes, the witch returns. It is an observable inverse relationship.

The New Woman and the True Woman

In her essay "Cinema and the Modern Woman," Veronica Pravadelli describes how pre-1919 silent cinema was notably influenced by what has been labeled the "cult of true womanhood."[91] Recalling historian Dr. Barbara Welter's scholarship on the topic, Pravadelli notes that this character construction is marked largely by "a strict moral code based on four traits: domesticity, religiosity, sexual purity, and subordination to the male."[92] In witch films, this is evidenced by the codification of the witch as wild femininity or as a woman acting outside of accepted norms. As shown in earlier chapters, younger witches are typically reincorporated into society either by a hero's rescue (e.g., *Witchcraft*, 1916) or by a traditional heterosexual marriage (e.g., *In the Days of Witchcraft*, 1913). The young woman who chooses otherwise is killed (e.g., *Joan the Woman,* 1916). As for the old witch or the indigenous witch, she is simply cast aside. Despite any possible subversive film readings of female agency, the witch

---

91. Barbara Welter, "The Cult of True Womanhood: 1820–1860," *American Quarterly* 18, no. 2, part 1 (Summer 1966): 151–174, https://doi.org/10.2307/2711179.

92. Pravadelli, "Cinema and the Modern Woman," 4.

exists as the antithesis of the "true woman." In other words, she is an example of what not to be.

However, the 1920s saw a marked change in a woman's role in mainstream society, as well as the way she defined herself. This gender shift is partly what defines the "new morality." Influences were, in part, the suffrage movement, the growth of consumer culture, and technological advancements that allowed for greater middle-class leisure. By 1920, household items like the refrigerator, vacuum cleaner, the electric iron, and even the automobile were revolutionizing home life, consequently freeing women to explore hobbies outside the home. In her essay "The New Woman and Consumer Culture," historian Sumiko Higashi defines this social change as a time of self-making.[93] It was not a complete reissuing of gender roles, rather it was a release and an exploration of the possibilities.

In a cultural environment open to such exploratory discourse, there is no need to strictly define gender boundaries and related norms. There can be no antithesis to a "true woman" when there is no standard of truth to work against and when society itself supports experimental self-making. During the 1920s Jazz era, the term "true woman" was in flux, giving way to what is often termed the "new woman," as in Higashi's essay. While not all boundaries surrounding gender roles shifted, many did, and others were challenged. With that in mind, progressive female viewers may not have been as interested in traditional cinematic reincorporation narratives or examples of "what not to be." Therefore, there was less cultural need for the witch figure as an allegorical representation of the woman who knows too much, or subversively a woman empowered by her own oppression. In that environment, there could be no such thing.

This socio-culture reality may also explain, at least in part, why live-action witches then returned in the 1930s. Pravadelli notes, "Sometime around 1933–1934 the dominant mode of female representation veers toward the convergence of normative forms of desire."[94] The ambiguity and the exploration within narrative films had come to an end, just after the US suffered a catastrophic stock market crash leading to the Great Depression. As Pravadelli suggests, Hollywood returned to "a rational mode of storytelling which, in turn, supported traditional forms of identity and lifestyle especially for women"[95] In that framework, the concept of the "new woman" is supplanted by the silent era's "true woman." This so-called cinematic age of order, which replaced the Jazz

---

93. Sumiko Higashi, "The New Woman and Consumer Culture: Cecil B. DeMille's Sex Comedies," in *A Feminist Reader in Early Cinema*, ed. Jennifer M. Bean and Diane Negra (Durham: Duke University Press, 2002), 298.

94. Pravadelli, "Cinema and the Modern Woman," 14.

95. Pravadelli, "Cinema and the Modern Woman," 14.

Age, resurrected hardened support for traditional gender roles and, perhaps unsurprisingly, resurrected the live-action witch.

Other Factors

There were, of course, many other cultural, economic, and technological factors influencing change within the fledgling Hollywood industry, some of which may have also contributed to the disappearance and reappearance of witches in live-action movies. As noted earlier, the studio system was by this point in full operation with strong financial backing from Wall Street; feature films were now common, and a system of movie theaters spanned across the country. By the end of this period both color and sound had revolutionized the viewing experience and expanded the possibilities in creative storytelling, contributing to the birth of new genres and original content.

Coinciding with shifting gender roles and viewer tastes, filmmakers were less interested in the story of the "child-woman," which was a throwback to Victorian sensibilities and interests. The narrative of young girls caught in between womanhood and girlhood by mystical forces and magic was no longer drawing audiences as society moved beyond its Victorian legacy into the new century. While the theme of merging female adolescence with magic doesn't entirely disappear, it just goes into a hiatus, eliminating yet another typical reason for a live-action film to host a witch.

Lastly, the period's industry changes also brought shifts in genre popularity, which also contributed to the witch's disappearance. As noted, genre was the main determining factor on whether a witch appeared or not in the silent era; the character did not yet hold her own power at the box office. Therefore, the disappearance of witches around 1924 was also partly due to genre shifts. With industry expansion, filmmakers depended less and less on adapting literature and fairy tales or showcasing history. The new popular genres, such as the gangster film and the musical, didn't necessarily provide an obvious fit for the witch. While the western was still popular, its narratives shifted focus from tales about life on the frontier to the more well-known cowboy narrative focusing predominantly on negotiations of masculinity.

Similarly, this is the time when the American horror film first became popular, but the witch had yet to be established as part of that cinematic world. While witches were already populating foreign horror films (e.g., Benjamin Christensen's *Häxan*, 1922), early American horror focused on mad scientists and monsters. Like the cowboy western, classic horror films were typically male-dominated universes that championed rational law and science above all. In both the western and the horror film, there was little room for the narrative-based gender negotiations or fantasy escapism that was implied when introducing an iconic witch character. Consequently, witches were left to the fledgling animation industry, where fairy tales still reigned supreme and the fantastic was written directly into its highly artistic mode of storytelling.

The Films

From 1921–1933, there were only four live-action films containing a female witch. They were all made by smaller studios and they are all lost. Those films included two adaptations: *Hansel and Gretel* (1923) and *Puritan Passions* (1923); an adventure film, *Devil Within* (1921); and a melodramatic fantasy spectacle, *Folly of Vanity* (1924). Additionally, there were some live-action adventure films that contained a character labeled a witch doctor. These include lost films like *Kivalina of the Ice Lands* (1925), *Tropic Madness* (1928), and *Nagana* (1933) and one surviving film *White Zombie* (1932). The extent to which these adventure films apply to this study will be discussed later.

The rest of the period's films are cartoon shorts made by the emerging animation industry (e.g., *Felix Switches Witches*, 1927; *Betty Boop's Snow-White*, 1933). The shorts were screened before the feature film and were enjoyed by both children and adults. Animation itself was not new, but it was during this era that this unique art form was solidifying its place within the larger film industry. Most importantly, it was within a handful of these cartoon shorts that a new type of cinematic witch was born: the Halloween witch. This character eventually went on to become one of the most prolific constructions in American entertainment.

Live-Action Fantasy: Adaptation and Spectacle

As noted, the beginning of the period saw more of the same cinematic witch-related fare that had been offered in previous decades, including adaptations and large fantasy spectacles. Even Baum's *The Wonderful Wizard of Oz* (1925), which was still considered box office poison, received another cinematic adaptation. Produced by actor Larry Semon, this version did not contain the witch and was another box office flop. The one witch-related fairy tale that was successfully adapted, unsurprisingly, was *Hansel and Gretel* (1923) starring popular child actress Baby Peggy. The other live-action fantasy film, *The Folly of Vanity* (1924), is not an adaptation but rather an over-the-top spectacle similar to those found in the latter teens (e.g., *A Daughter of the Gods*, 1916). *The Folly of Vanity* is a melodrama; however, it contains a fantasy sequence with a witch.

Famed child star Baby Peggy appeared with Buddy Williams in
Hansel and Gretel (1923). Starring (from left to right) Johnny Fox,
Buddy Williams as Hansel, and Baby Peggy as Gretel.
[Source: Universal Studios/PhotoFest. Copyright: © Universal Pictures]

Both fantasy films, *Hansel and Gretel* and *The Folly of Vanity*, incorporate the typical silent era crone. Even in character construction, the narratives carry forward the trends of the earlier period. In each film, the fantasy crone uses her magic to interject tension into a relatively smooth linear narrative progression. In one, she is morally ambiguous, serving as an ethical measure for the heroine, and in the other, she is a villain. However, in both cases, she is not the primary focus of the film.

In the 1923 version of *Hansel and Gretel*, the witch is the villain; however, she is one of many obstacles that are set before the child protagonists as they proceed on their journey. The children must contend with miniature figures and goblins before even arriving at the witch's house.[96] This version of the tale models Madeline Brandeis's film *The Star Prince* (1918), in which two children also take a journey that presents many difficult challenges. Like the Brandeis film, *Hansel and Gretel* was made specifically to entertain young audiences. Therefore, there was no need to focus on an overbearing evil witch and the intensity such a conflict would bring. The adaptation was meant to be amusing, light, and not at all frightening.

---

96. "*Hansel and Gretel,*" *The Film Daily* 26, no. 64 (December 16, 1923): 12.

The Folly of Vanity's crone is part of an underwater fantasy segment. When heroine Alice jumps into the ocean to escape the film's villain, she is transported to Neptune's kingdom. Once there, Alice is introduced to a group of voluptuous mermaids, King Neptune, and his "underling, a witch." [97] The entire scene was reportedly colorized in order to enhance its spectacle quality and to suggest a dream sequence. Most critics panned the film for its ostentatious display of sexuality and the extreme lunacy specifically found in that fantasy segment. In a 1925 *Exhibitor's Trade Review*, a staff reporter wrote, "[*Folly of Vanity*] is merely an excuse for making a frank exhibition of undraped feminine physical charms." [98]

As with the earlier Annette Kellerman fantasy spectacles, the witch plays a minor role within an exaggerated, over-the-top production. She is a character-driven plot device that helps move the narrative forward. During the dream sequence, the witch informs Neptune that Alice, a guest at his court, has the mark of vanity. In response, Neptune expels the heroine from his world, resulting in her finally learning about the pitfalls and evils of greed. Once back on land, Alice returns to the arms of her husband and all ends well. The witch provides the narrative catalyst that allows the heroine to return to what the movie deems is her proper ethical base—humility, marriage, and a rejection of greed. In this film, as with other earlier fantasy films, the witch is a minor character who acts as a moral compass.

Puritan Passions, Wild Women, and the Satanic Witch

The third live-action witch film released during the early 1920s is the drama *Puritan Passions*, which is yet another adaptation of Nathaniel Hawthorne's popular short story *Feathertop*. Unlike the older silent shorts, *Puritan Passions* deviates considerably from its origins. As such, the film introduces a new concept into witch films: satanic witchcraft. Although the theme was not new to Western culture, it is an element of witch construction that had yet to be fully integrated into Hollywood's language. As noted earlier, theologically based definitions of witchcraft had largely been abandoned or suppressed from public discourse. The success of *Puritan Passions* did not alter this trend. It would be decades before satanic witchcraft was overtly expressed again in mainstream American cinema (e.g., *The Undead*, 1957).

---

97. Mordaunt Hall, "Der Letzle Mann—The Screen," *New York Times*, January 28, 1925, https://www.nytimes.com/1925/01/28/archives/the-screen.html.

98. "*Folly of Vanity*: A Study in Nudity," *Exhibitor's Trade Review*, February 14, 1925, 85.

Immediately after *Puritan Passions*'s release, reviewers took note of the atypical and somewhat darker premise of this literary adaptation. An *Oakland Tribune* reviewer called it "one of the most novel and unique film plays ever produced."[99] *Exhibitor's Trade Review* remarked, "The music has a weird haunting strain in keeping with the spirit of the picture."[100] That same magazine also counseled film exhibitors to "shoot carefully on this and you won't go wrong."[101]

The primary reason for the noted reviewer reactions lies in the narrative itself. *Puritan Passions* is an adaptation of Percy MacKaye's theatrical rendering of Hawthorne's story. First performed in 1908, MacKaye's play *Scarecrow* pays tribute to Hawthorne's work but is not a faithful dramatization. In the preface to the printed script, MacKaye wrote, "it is fitting, I think, to distinguish clearly between the aim and the scope of 'Feathertop' and that of the play in hand, as much in deference to the work of Hawthorne as in comprehension of the spirit of my own."[102]

Construction of the Witch

It is within this difference that the witch shifts construction from an iconic silent cinema fantasy crone, as seen in the earlier adaptations of Hawthorne's work, into a wild woman or elderly folk witch. In the silent era *Feathertop* adaptations, the crone's magic is never sourced as is the case in Hawthorne's original story. She just has magical ability and, as such, she is a fantasy witch. In MacKaye's play, the witch's magic is a gift from Satan. It is this narrative detail, which was carried over into *Puritan Passions*, that elicited the reactions calling the film "dark," "haunting," and "novel," and at the same time, it changed the categorization of the story's witch.

Not only is Goody Rickby, the witch, not a fantasy crone, she is also atypical for the period's elderly folk witches. Rickby is defined as a victim of social abuse, which then becomes the justification for her turning to witchcraft and Satan. With that backstory, MacKaye created a sympathetic satanic witch who is more similar to witch characters found in the late 1990s and 2000s horror films (e.g., *The Craft*, 1996; *Salem*, 2014–2017) than in those in this period.

Taking that a step further, Rickby is a blend of two types of witches: the accused woman and the elderly folk witch. Her backstory tells the classic tale of a young, accused woman. As the story goes, Rickby was once the mistress of Gillead Wingate,

---

99. Review of *Puritan Passions*, *Oakland Tribune*, September 23, 1923, 17.

100. Review of *Puritan Passions*, *Exhibitor's Trade Review*, October 20, 1923, 991.

101. Review of *Puritan Passions*, *Exhibitor's Trade Review*, 724.

102. Percy MacKaye, *The Scarecrow: Or, The Glass of Truth; A Tragedy of the Ludicrous* (New York: MacMillan Co. 1908), xiv.

a prominent and pious man living in Salem. Eventually he grows weary of her and leaves her poor and alone with their young son. When the child becomes sick, Wingate refuses to help and the child dies. Rickby is scorned and labeled a witch. With that narrative backstory, Rickby begins her adult life as an accused woman. She is Hawthorne's Hester Prynne from his 1850 novel, *The Scarlet Letter*.

Osgood Perkins stars as Dr. Nicholas and Maude Hill as the witch Goody Rickby in Puritan Passions *(1923).*
[Source: Photofest. Copyright: Public Domain]

However, the film's plot begins many years later, and Rickby has transformed into a folk witch. She is now an elderly woman who has since made a pact with the Devil that grants her the power of witchcraft. Despite her satanic dealings, the film still portrays Rickby as a victim of circumstance. She couldn't marry the man or save the child, so she was pushed into partnering with the Devil and, as such, gains a child— the Scarecrow. Rickby is therefore constructed as a tragic and reluctant villain, not a self-possessed, evil woman like most satanic witches (e.g., *Witchcraft*, 1988). In fact, her visual appearance is haggard, as would be expected of a silent-era western folk witch, but it is also softened through costuming. In one of the few remaining film stills, Rickby stands next to the Devil wearing a large dark period skirt and white blouse. She does not visually resemble the dark, harsh forms of classic satanic-themed elderly folk witches (e.g., *Twilight Zone*, "Jess-Belle," 1963). She looks more like the elderly folk witches and healers of the early silent era (e.g., *Rose O' Salem-Town*, 1910).

Despite Rickby's story being the center point of the narrative, Goody Rickby is not the primary villain, which mirrors the construction of other witches of the era. She is a reluctant antagonist who does not own her own power. In fact, Rickby is actually a narrative addendum who simply paves the way for the power struggle between the main male characters and for related themes of morality. Rickby's abuse and retribution are what push the plot into being, after which she takes a back seat. The witch, once again, is a narrative device, serving as a measure of another character's morality. In fact, in most of the contemporary reviews of *Puritan Passions*, writers focus on the performances of Osgood Perkins as the Devil and Glenn Hunter as the Scarecrow. There is no mention made of Maude Hill's performance as Goody Rickby.

Theology and Witchcraft Representation

Regardless of Rickby's limited narrative role, the film's inclusion of the Devil is still vital to the study of Hollywood witches. Not only is this the first American mainstream film to show a witch purposefully cavorting with Satan, but it is also the first to clearly define the origins of a witch's power in theological terms. Here, Rickby is a witch because the Devil gave her powers, not because of her relationship to society or an accepted fact of her fantasy construction. In other words, *Puritan Passions* is the first film to put the witch back into a traditional Christian framework—one that had been mostly lost with the coming of an Enlightenment-based culture.

In fact, the film adaptation advances its theological theme even more profoundly than MacKaye's play. In the theatrical version, the final scene takes place in a parlor. At the end, both Rickby and the Devil leave without consequence, and the Scarecrow, while a hero of sorts, dies. In the film, the final scene takes place in a church. Within that distinctly religious space, the villain is revealed, and the Devil and witch are vanquished. The real hero, the Scarecrow, earns his soul and becomes human in a "Pinocchio" finale. As described by actor Osgood Perkins in 1923, the scene ends as sunlight falls upon a passage from a prayer book that reads "'How shall they which are dirt gain a soul and be saved from Satan and the Eternal fires of damnation? And the Prophet answered, 'By Love, Alone.'" [103] These are not words from the original

---

103. Osgood Perkins, synopsis, *Motion Picture Classic*, July 1923, quoted in John T. Soister et al., *American Silent Horror, Science Fiction and Fantasy Feature Films, 1913–1929.* (Jefferson, North Carolina: McFarland, 2012), 472.

script. MacKaye's play is more faithful to its origin text with a tragic hero in the Scarecrow, while the film has a classic moral hero with, what one might call, a Hollywood ending.

The Magical Other and Island Magic

Outside of the films already discussed, the only other live-action witches to appear at this time are the practitioners of foreign magical systems or religions. These are represented typically by minor characters such as the indigenous folk witch, as seen in the last period, or the witch doctor. In the previous era, the magical other was most typically constructed as a Native American or, using the film's label, "Indian." During this period, the witch as a magical other includes indigenous characters from other lands, typically Africa, the islands of the South Seas, or Haiti.

These characters work within the narrative in the same way as past indigenous witches, and their constructions, visual and narrative, play off a deeply embedded cultural bias that stems from a colonialist attitude toward non-Western societies. For example, in a scene from the film *White Zombie* (1932), a white Christian missionary tells the hero "There are superstitions in Haiti that the natives brought here from Africa." Then, after learning that his wife may have been taken by a "witch doctor," the hero exclaims, "In the hands of natives? Better dead than that."

The Indigenous Folk Witch

In the lost film *The Devil Within* (1921), the magical character is an indigenous folk witch from a South Seas island. She is the only folk witch to appear during this period and as is typical, she is a minor character who only briefly interacts with the narrative to disrupt the story and challenge the protagonist. According to a 1922 review in the *Wakefield News*, *The Devil Within* tells the story of "a bestial captain," who confiscates an idol while visiting a South Seas Island. After a dispute with "natives," a witch "calls down the curse of Vishnu upon the head of the Captain."[104] The witch's magic then follows the hero through the rest of the film. Her actions redirect the narrative, forcing the captain to face his own cruelty. The indigenous folk witch acts as an ethical measure for the main character. The film title's reference to the Devil is only meant as a reflection of the hero's inner struggle.

As a wild woman construction, the indigenous folk witch's magic must be sourced. In this film, the witch appears in her native South Seas island. There she is accepted, magic and all, as an integral part of the social experience. The witch holds important

---

104. "Review of *The Devil Within*," *Wakefield News*, July 15, 1922, 6.

jobs, such as being a consult to the king, the priest, or the medical doctor. She and her use of magic are normalized within that cultural framework; yet she still stands out as abhorrent within the overall narrative and in relationship to the viewer. In other words, she is not "us." She is othered along with her entire culture, and it is always this otherness, whether defined by ethnicity, race, nationality, or something else, that justifies the use of magic. Films with similar content include the earlier lost silent film *The Sins of Roseanne* (1920), which contains an indigenous folk witch from South Africa. Additionally, the witch in *The Folly of Vanity* (1924), although a construction of pure fantasy, relies on a similar model. She is a minor character from a non-American society who uses magic to affect change and to challenge moral judgment.

The Witch Doctor

Female indigenous folk witches, like all others, disappear from the screen in 1924. After this point, the only live action witches left were a few so-called witch doctors. Found in adventure films, these minor characters are typically morally ambiguous magic-for-money figures who, like the indigenous folk witch, perpetuate a cultural stereotype of the magical man in non-Western societies. The witch doctor is often consulted when something, mystical or otherwise, has gone wrong. Examples of these characters appear in *Tropic Madness* (1928), *Nagana* (1933), *White Zombie* (1932), and *Kivalina of the Ice Lands* (1925). All but one of the above films is lost and, consequently, it is difficult to know the true nature of these characters' roles, what they look like, how long they are even on-screen, and, most importantly, whether they are truly considered "witches" within the film's universe.

The term "witch doctor" itself has colonialist origins and is largely considered pejorative by contemporary anthropologists. It was brought to non-European nations in the eighteenth century by English-speaking explorers who categorized indigenous religions and magical folk practices as purely superstition. The term carried over into the twentieth century, affecting American culture as a whole, not only Hollywood. Therefore, subjective extratextual presumptions are often applied to a character or narrative that do not have any basis in the actual film. In other words, film reviewers and archivists may have used the term "witch doctor" or "witchcraft" without the filmmaker using it. This was not uncommon. Since most of these characters are minor and many of the films are lost, it is often impossible to know the true nature of each character's construction and whether they fit the scope of the study. One exception is Halperin Productions' horror film *White Zombie*.

A Closer Look: *White Zombie*

The independent film *White Zombie*, starring Bela Lugosi, is considered the first American zombie horror film. While far more a classic monster picture than a witch film, *White Zombie* demonstrates several key components that link it to the canon of witch films. The film contains three magical men who do, in fact, practice or have knowledge of island magic. In reviews, Lugosi's character is often called a Voodoo priest; however, the film makes no mention of Voodoo. This is a primary example of extratextual assumptions made by a reviewer. The film itself labels all three characters "witch doctors."

Generally speaking, the cinematic witch doctor is the male equivalent of the indigenous folk witch. In this film, two of the witch doctors are so called "natives" and the third is the film's villain, played by Bela Lugosi. The two indigenous witch doctors are old, wear robes, and have large necklaces of shells and bones around their necks. Their magical expertise is accepted by their own culture and they are minor players acting as set dressing, cultural indicators, and sideshow elements. Additionally, one of these indigenous witch doctors serves as a source of information, which is typical for magical men. Where a woman folk witch is more commonly a source for spell craft, the male witch is a source of occult knowledge. In this film, the hero, Neil, visits the witch doctor to learn what might have happened to his wife.

Because *White Zombie* takes place in Haiti, "native" culture is defined by a population of Black locals as established right from the opening shots of a funeral ritual. Despite this racial alignment, two of the witch doctors are white and the other, it appears, is in blackface. This is another indicator of Hollywood's treatment of race in its early days. Black actors were confined to minor and supporting roles. Lugosi's character is visually characterized far more like his famous Dracula character than a Haitian witch doctor. His Hungarian accent, dark clothing, high collared cape, and trademark widow's peak suggest an eastern European mad scientist rather than a mystical priest. Given that he makes no mention of religion, Christianity or otherwise, his witch doctor descriptor is even less believable.

While *White Zombie* has elements of the period's witch films, it is still a mad-scientist themed horror film. In fact, as is revealed in the end, the Dracula-like witch doctor isn't even performing magic; he's just using drugs and mind control. Regardless, the film sits on the edge of the witch film canon and demonstrates the representation of one type of magical man—the witch doctor. Moreover, it is important to note that, while the female live-action witch disappeared from 1924–1933, the magical man as "witch doctor" remained to a degree, reinforcing the theory that the disappearance was linked to shifting gender roles.

The Animated Shorts

In 1924, after the live-action female witch all but disappears, the animated witch takes center stage. Over the following nine years, Hollywood's classic fantasy crone is iconized through the reduction of narrative, thematic, and visual elements within the confines of the comedic animated short. Hollywood animators fully embraced and then perpetuated the well-established archetype in a highly concentrated form and, in doing so, developed an identifiable fantasy-based Halloween witch that has survived virtually untouched ever since.

In the early days of animation, shorts were meant to be secondary amusement or purely whimsical children's fare and nothing more. In his book *Animating Culture*, historian Eric Smoodin writes, "Exhibition practices relegated cartoons to less important positions on the film bill than those held by the feature film or the newsreel." [105] The animated short was a minor comedic novelty that drew from culturally recognizable elements to attract an audience and a quick laugh. Depth of character construction was unimportant. These films functioned in the same way as the early live-action movies that were released at the turn of the century. Like those films, the shorts were simply meant to showcase the new technology and demonstrate what could be done. Narrative depth and structure were not a priority.

Despite this minor position within overall entertainment, silent animated shorts played an important role in the study of Hollywood witches for two main reasons. They solidified the permanence of an iconic figure, the Halloween witch, and they served as virtually the only home to witch characters from 1924–1933. Working in this cottage industry at the time were Max Fleischer, Pat Sullivan, Walt Disney, Ub Iwerks, and Otto Messmer. These artists along with others had to rely on preconstructed cultural cues to create their works due to the condensed and conceptual nature of the drawn visual product. The fantasy crone was one of those well-known figures. However, her appearance and nature prior to this era were not uniform across productions. Through these early animated shorts, that changes. She becomes a singular identifiable entity.

All of the period's shorts use straightforward, basic visual cues made up of elements that were already known to audiences and that were often associated with Halloween. Without fail, the animated witch is depicted as the disfigured fantasy crone in a dark ragged dress and pointed hat. Surrounding her are the trappings of witchcraft, such as a broom, a black cat, crows, spiders, cauldrons, bats, pumpkins, owls, and the full moon. These are the chief markers of the animated Halloween witch in

---

105. Eric Smoodin, *Animating Culture: Hollywood Cartoons from the Sound Era* (New Brunswick, NJ: Rutgers University Press, 1993), 1.

her simplest form, and there was little variation after this point. The archetype is re-peated over and over again, regardless of studio or artist. There was still one impor-tant iconic element missing from these early characterizations: *green skin*. That visual detail only appears after 1939.

One of the earliest surviving shorts containing a witch is *Felix Switches Witches* (1927), starring Pat Sullivan and Otto Messmer's famous cartoon cat. The short dem-onstrates the basic characteristics that define the early animated fantasy crone. In this monochromatic cartoon, the witch wears a ragged black dress and pointed hat, and she carries a broom. Her face is exaggerated, marked with an elongated nose and a wart, and she has an extended chin. The magic that comes from her hands is con-veyed by thin black lightening-style bolts. In colorized shorts, such as Disney's *Babes in the Woods* (1932), the same visual characterizations are evident, adding only mi-nor color adjustments. The witches are either dressed in solid black or in black and gray, and their hair is either white or gray.

There are ten animated shorts containing this figure. Four of the films were made in the 1920s including *Felix Brings Home the Bacon* (1924), *Felix the Cat at the Rain-bow's End* (1925), and *Felix Switches Witches* (1927) plus Kinex Studio's stop-motion animated short *Snap the Gingerbread Man in "The Witch's Cat"* (1929). During the 1930s as animation gained in popularity, production increased, and more artists en-tered the industry. In 1931, Charles Mintz Productions offered *Halloween* starring Toby the Pup. Max Fleischer produced three Betty Boop witch shorts, including *Betty Boop's Snow White* (1933), *Mother Goose Land* (1933) and *Betty Boop's Hallow-een Party* (1933). Walt Disney and Frank Moser of Terrytoons both released adapta-tions of the classic fairy tale *Hansel and Gretel*. Disney's was titled *Babes in the Woods* (1932) and Moser's, *Hansel and Gretel* (1933).

Adaptations

Disney and Moser's shorts, as well as Fleischer's adaptation of *Snow White*, are all attempts to render classic stories for pure entertainment. However, unlike the silent live-action fairy tale adaptations, the animated fantasy crone is in fact the primary villain. The plot of an animated short must be simple, and the narrative must be high-ly concentrated due to its short run span. There is no room to engage in varied con-flicts and multiple obstacles as was done in the 1918 live-action film *The Star Prince* or the 1923 adaptation of *Hansel and Gretel*. Each narrative conflict, as a result, must be a simple good versus evil scenario with the witch as singular, comedic evil force.

For example, in Disney's adaptation, the animated siblings march happily into the woods, momentarily surprised by several natural objects, such as a gnarly tree and flock of birds. However, this is short lived, and the children quickly arrive at a village populated by happy gnomes. It is at this point the witch appears as a shadow on the ground created by her flight above. She then becomes the children's only obstacle. However, unlike the original and many of the adaptations, this animated witch doesn't eat children. She just turns them into stone or animals. Disney's *Babes in the Woods* does not have the depth of character construction or level of horror that the studio's later full-length fairy tale adaptations would have. She is evil but comedic, borrowing from the silent Victorian clown witch.

Fantasy Originals

Several shorts use well-known fairy tale iconography to construct a new and original story. These recognizable images are nods to the child viewer's imagination and to an adult's sense of nostalgia. In other words, the films rely not on well-known narratives but on a basic understanding of cultural cues. The period's shorts that depend on a knowledge of popular tales include *At Rainbow's End*, *Mother Goose Land*, *Snap the Gingerbread Man in "The Witch's Cat,"* and *Felix Brings Home the Bacon*. In these cases, the witch is not the main character, but rather an icon within a larger fantasy universe.

For example, in *Felix Brings Home the Bacon*, Felix the Cat discovers Old Mother Hubbard has no food for her poor dog. He then goes in search of food, encountering Little Red Riding Hood and eventually a broom-flying witch. Audiences recognized the literary cues and, therefore, were able to follow the simple narrative to conclusion. This includes understanding that the witch is a villain.

A 1924 advertising poster for the cartoon short Felix Brings Home the Bacon.
[Source: Soulis Auctions Copyright: Public Domain]

In this Felix short, both Old Mother Hubbard and the witch wear similar pointed hats. However, the character construction difference lies in the rest of their appearances. Old Mother Hubbard has a white shawl and shoes, white hair, and a normal size nose and chin. The elderly witch dresses in black and has elongated facial features. The use of the hat for Old Mother Hubbard is derived from Victorian drawings of Mother Goose, who often resembles a witch. This styling is also found in Fleischer Studios' Betty Boop short *Mother Goose Land*. In this case, Mother Goose has lost her whimsical clown costuming entirely and looks exactly like a Halloween witch. According to Jeffrey Barton, a researcher at Cotsen Children's Library at Princeton University, the shift to a more witchy, folk appearance and away from Victorian whimsy was the trend in children's publications at the time.[106] While this may attest to malleability and popularity of the witch character, it may simply have been a contemporary attempt to use throwback illustrations for classic children's stories.

Halloween Celebrations

The three remaining animated shorts focus specifically on holiday-inspired stories drawing upon the popularity of Halloween. These films include *Toby the Pup's Halloween*, *Felix Switches Witches*, and *Betty Boop's Halloween Party*. The shorts rely on not only the iconic symbols and elements of the holiday and the witch but also include actual Halloween activities, including bobbing for apples, costuming, hauntings, trick-or-treating, and howling black cats. They are specifically holiday specials released during the October season.

For example, in *Toby the Pup's Halloween*, Toby is hosting a holiday party and all is going well until he declares that it's "the witching hour." At that point, a classic Halloween witch appears riding a broom against the full moon. A similar image appears at the start of *Betty Boop's Halloween Party*. A silhouette of a witch riding a broom flies across the night sky. The figure is marked by the points of her hat, her nose, her elongated chin, the broom, and a flowing cape. This is the Halloween witch in silhouette, and it is the same recognizable silhouette that Disney relied upon in *Babes in the Woods*.

All of these shorts, holiday-based or not, rely on the same iconography. The differences are mainly in their narratives. Holiday specials focused on Halloween celebrations, whereas the adaptations and children's stories relied on popular literature. In cultural terms, the witch had long been associated with both fairy tales and October festivals. However, through these early animated shorts, the witch character was

---

106. Jeff Barton, "Mother Goose Gets a Makeover…" Princeton University Library Blogs, October 30, 2015, https://blogs.princeton.edu/cotsen/2015/10/mother-goose-gets-a-makeover/.

condensed, visually and narratively, and its influence on cultural meaning intensified through regular repetition of its visuals and lore. Halloween iconography merged with that from literature to create a singular distinct type of fantasy crone called the Halloween witch.

Conclusion

At the start of the 1920s, the American film industry was well on its way to forming its famed studio system. Through the next decade, sound and color were both introduced and films continued to evolve narratively with new genres and new depths in character and story development. At the same time, society shifted. Most notably, there were significant changes in the negotiation of what it meant to be a woman in America. The flapper, the washing machine, and the hard-won voter registration card were liberators, allowing for the birth of what film theorists have labeled the "new woman." With those social changes, the depiction of female witches, accused, wild, or otherwise, disappeared from live-action narrative films. As markers of what not to be, witches were no longer of interest in a world where women could engage in their own self-making.

Although the period begins in 1921 with typical silent-era witch characters (e.g., *Hansel and Gretel*, 1923; *Folly of Vanity*, 1924), live actions female witches eventually disappear. From 1924–1933, the female witch only lived through cartoons while a few male witch doctors remained in live-action films. This newly born animated witch was comedic in nature, but she was not visually designed as a clown; rather, she resembled a darker fantasy crone. This change in visual portrayal not only remained unaltered for decades to come, it also threw the door wide open for the Halloween witch as primary antagonist to evolve into a truly frightening villain. This would come a decade later in 1939, after live-action witches returned to the silver screen.

Chapter 3: Filmography

The Devil Within	1921	Bernard J. Durning
Puritan Passions	1923	Frank Tuttle
Hansel and Gretel	1923	Alfred J. Goulding
Felix Brings Home the Bacon	1924	Otto Messmer
The Folly of Vanity	1924	Maurice Elvey
Felix the Cat at the Rainbow's End	1925	Otto Messmer
The Wonderful Wizard of Oz	1925	Larry Semon
Kivalina of the Ice Lands	1925	Earl Rossman
Felix Switches Witches	1927	Pat Sullivan
Tropic Madness	1928	Robert Vignola
Snap the Gingerbread Man in "The Witch's Cat"	1929	Unknown
Toby the Pup's Halloween	1931	Arthur Davis, Dick Huemer, and Sid Marcus
Babes in the Woods	1932	Burt Gillett
White Zombie	1932	Victor Halperin
The Wizard of Oz	1933	Ted Eshbaugh
Betty Boop's Snow White	1933	Dave Fleischer
Nagana	1933	Ernst L. Frank
Mother Goose Land	1933	Dave Fleischer
Hansel and Gretel	1933	Frank Moser
Betty Boop's Halloween Party	1933	Dave Fleischer

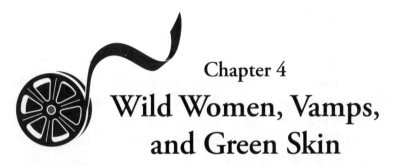

Chapter 4
Wild Women, Vamps, and Green Skin
(1934–1940)

The early 1930s saw a major change in the way Hollywood conducted its business. After decades of complaints that the studios were perpetuating cultural depravity and a real threat of reduced ticket sales, industry leaders finally decided to put teeth into their self-censorship system. As a result, the ambiguity and exploration found in Jazz-era narrative films comes to an end just as American society is forced to face the ramifications of a catastrophic stock market crash and financial crisis. As historian Veronica Pravadelli observes, Hollywood returned to "a rational mode of storytelling which, in turn, supported traditional forms of identity, lifestyle, especially for women." [107] Within that framework, the concept of the "new woman," made popular in the 1920s, is supplanted by the silent era's "true woman."

The period opens in 1934, the year that the industry began enforcing its censorship code. Pravadelli writes that it was "sometime around 1933–1934 [that] the dominant mode of female representation veers toward the convergence of normative forms of desire." [108] The change is observable. Betty Boop is a primary example. She was redrawn that same year going from a Jazz era flapper to a girl next door. It should then come as no surprise that this so-called cinematic age of order, which resurrected

107. Pravadelli, "Cinema and the Modern Woman," 14.
108. Pravadelli, "Cinema and the Modern Woman," 14.

hardened support for traditional gender roles, also resurrected the live-action witch. The period ends in 1939 with the release of MGM's *The Wizard of Oz* and the birth of Hollywood's most famous cinematic witch: The Wicked Witch of the West.

The MPPDA and a Codified Morality

While the reason behind the reappearance of witches in film is largely speculative, the formation of a new censorship organization, as noted, corresponds directly to that change. The year 1934, which saw both the return of the witch and the return of the "true woman," was the same year that Joseph Breen took over the Motion Picture Producers and Distributors of America's (MPPDA) Production Code Administration (PCA) and began strictly enforcing censorship policies on all Hollywood films.

Several years earlier, the MPPDA created the PCA in response to public pressure, lost revenue, and looming federal censorship. With the help of a Jesuit Priest, the MPPDA created a regulatory code for all films released within its system. However, it wasn't until 1934 that the censorship code, known more commonly as the Hays Code after MPPDA director William Hays, or simply the Production Code, was actually enforced. Joseph Breen, a publicity man and Catholic journalist, became its enforcer. In his book *Hollywood's Censor*, film historian Thomas Doherty writes, "Breen's imprint on the Hollywood films he censored—or regulated—went deeper ... he was an activist editor ... Bringing a missionary zeal to his custodial trust, he felt a sacred duty to protect the spiritual well-being of the innocent souls who fluttered too close to the unholy attractions of the motion picture screen." [109]

It is no coincidence that Pravadelli and other researchers cite 1934 as the notable time of change in the representation of female agency within American cinema. Breen's influence on a film's moral construction significantly impacted the depiction of sexuality and gender roles. The code reads, for example, "The sanctity of the institution of marriage and the home shall be upheld. Pictures shall not infer that low forms of sex relationship are the accepted or common thing." [110] Essentially the PCA used the code to put a damper on anything that was deemed improper.

Written by Jesuit Priest Father Daniel Lord and editor Martin Quigley, the Production Code was based on a specific theological morality. It was sold as a way to rein in Hollywood's perceived excess and displays of depravity, and it mirrored American society's overall search for grounding after suffering economic collapse. The code's preamble reads, "During the rapid transition from silent to talking pictures [produc-

---

109. Thomas Doherty, *Hollywood's Censor: Joseph I. Breen & The Production Code Administration* (New York: Columbia University Press, 2007), 9.

110. Doherty, *Hollywood's Censor*, 352.

ers] realized the necessity and the opportunity of subscribing to a Code to govern the production of talking pictures and of acknowledging this responsibility." [111] That social responsibility to which the code refers is dedicated to "spiritual and moral progress ... higher types of social life ... correct thinking." [112]

Regulations and Restrictions

Despite its Catholic base, the Production Code itself had no text regulating the portrayal of witchcraft. The age-old connections made within Catholic theology between witches and Satan had long been forgotten or suppressed by mainstream US culture, as already observed. While the PCA did regulate many details of production from song lyrics, costuming, dancing, and what it labeled "scenes of passion," witchcraft was not a concern.

The code had other focuses, such as how a woman should dress or how she should or shouldn't act, and the proper displays of patriotism and religiosity. For example, during the production of the 1933 Paramount film *Spitfire*, the PCA sent a letter to RKO executive Merian C. Cooper to tell him that "the expression 'Lord God' does not seem to be used reverently and we believe it should be modified under the Code." [113] Also banned were words labeled as "profanity" or "vulgarity" as well as the suggestion of "sexual perversions." In the same letter, the PCA requested the removal of the words "hussy" and "damn" from the *Spitfire* script. The word "witch" was never mentioned.

In order to be screened in US theaters, all films had to receive a PCA stamp of approval. In a letter to the PCA in 1936, concerned Walt Disney Studios executive William E. Garity wrote, "As you know, we have started the production of the feature cartoon [...] The question arises as to the advisability of the going ahead on this feature without the approval of your organization of our script." [114] Garity goes on to welcome the PCA to review the *Snow White* script and to speak with "Walt [to discuss] the picture from the censorship angle." [115]

---

111. Doherty, *Hollywood's Censor*, 351.

112. Doherty, *Hollywood's Censor*, 351.

113. James Wingate to Merian C. Cooper, October 10, 1933; source: *Spitfire* Production Files, MPAA PCA records, Margaret Herrick Library, Academy of Motion Picture Arts and Sciences, Beverly Hills, California.

114. William E. Garity to Douglas McKinnon, March 2, 1936; source: *Snow White and the Seven Dwarfs* Production Files, MPAA PCA records, Margaret Herrick Library, Academy of Motion Picture Arts and Sciences, Beverly Hills, California

115. William E. Garity to Douglas McKinnon, March 2, 1936.

Witchcraft and the Production Code

The fact that witches were left out of a code created under Catholic supervision and based on a Christian morality, once again, demonstrates the lack of any real connection made between theology and witchcraft. A 1936 pre-production studio report on the film *Maid of Salem*'s script clearly demonstrates this point. When discussing one character's "charge of sexual intercourse with the Devil, resulting in pregnancy," Paramount producer Howard Estabrook wrote that "modern audiences might be puzzled by an idea so far removed from current experience" and, in the same document, references the characters' "witchcraft delusions."[116] Estabrook also remarks that the Code would require a tempering of that theme, but he expressed more concern that viewers would interpret the charges of witchcraft as strange or even silly, causing a failure in the story's effectiveness.[117] The script, he said, would be revised.

While the code didn't explicitly ban witchcraft narratives, there was enough censorship to prevent the witch archetype from expanding into the horror genre and taking on one of its most well-known forms—the satanic witch. As noted earlier, there were limitations placed not only on the depiction of sexuality, but also religiosity. During the production of *Maid of Salem*, for example, Breen sent a letter to John Hammell of Paramount Pictures, requesting that the studio remove anything that "could be interpreted as reflecting adversely upon the clergy as a whole."[118] Considering this regulation along with the one that limited expressions of evil as alluring or sexy, the satanic witch could not be comfortably rendered in a Code-era production. It isn't until the 1950s, after Breen retires, that filmmakers begin to push back against the Code's restrictions and the witch enters into horror—reconnecting, for better or worse, with her theological roots.

The Films

This period does not contain many witch films, but those that were produced had a significant impact on the depiction of Hollywood witches. After a ten-year hiatus, live-action female witches first reappear in Paramount's *Spitfire* (1934), *Maid of Salem* (1937), and the independent film *The Devil's Daughter* (1939). All three provide variations on previously used themes, but none add anything revolutionary to the

116. Howard Estabrook, "Maid of Salem: Notes on the first draft of treatment," June 13, 1936; source: Howard Estabrook papers, Margaret Herrick Library, Academy of Motion Picture Arts and Sciences, Beverly Hills, California.

117. Howard Estabrook, "Maid of Salem: Notes on the first draft of treatment," June 13, 1936.

118. Joseph Breen to John Hammell, August 27, 1936; source: *Maid of Salem* Production Files, MPAA PCA records, Margaret Herrick Library, Academy of Motion Picture Arts and Sciences, Beverly Hills, California.

construction of the cinematic witch paradigm. *Maid of Salem*, starring Claudette Colbert, is a historical drama set in Salem Village. The main character is the prototypical accused woman. The film also contains Tituba (Madame Sul-Te-Wan), an indigenous folk witch. In *Spitfire*, Trigger Hicks (Katharine Hepburn) is a poor and reclusive young wild woman with a healing gift. Finally, *The Devil's Daughter* provides a unique depiction of the magical other.

Although the construction of the characters fits neatly into previously seen models, the films are notable on several other counts. They bring back witch-related themes that had disappeared for ten years, such as rural mountain life and the Salem witch trials. They are the first live-action mainstream productions containing witches to be scrutinized under the new censorship code. Finally, the depth of character development found in the female leads is something that was not seen in the silent era and, as such, it allows for a broader subtextual expression of female agency within a traditional sociocultural framework.

The remaining four productions are fantasy-based, both animation and live-action. Two are animated shorts and the other two are features. Similar to the Paramount films, they capitalize on a cinematic element that had previously worked, in this case its literary adaptation. All four heavily rely on the American viewer's adoration and familiarity with children's tales. However, two of the films render the adaption outside the realm of light children's fair: Disney's *Snow White and the Seven Dwarfs* (1937) and *The Wizard of Oz* (1939). Together, the two films introduce three of the most iconic and influential fantasy witches: The Wicked Queen, the Wicked Witch of the West, and Glinda.

These three fantasy witches embody several classic witch constructions: the fantasy crone, the Halloween witch, and the fairy good witch. Additionally, there is also a new construction found within these three iconic characters: the fantasy vamp as portrayed by the Wicked Queen in Disney's *Snow White and the Seven Dwarfs*. Derived from the word vampire, "vamp" was a term coined in the silent era for female characters who were shockingly beautiful temptresses. Betty Boop, for example, is considered an animated vamp. The term caught on and was used for both fictional characters and actresses who embodied those qualities. Disney's Wicked Queen fits the description. She is an incarnation of the middle-aged fantasy witch, who is often associated with an obsessive desire to maintain youth and beauty.

As a result, *Snow White and the Seven Dwarfs* is not only the first mainstream American animated feature film and the first in Disney's long run of full-length fairy tale adaptations, it is also the first Hollywood full-length production to marry witchcraft directly with mature female sexuality, beauty, and body image. *Snow White and the Seven Dwarfs* together with MGM's 1939 film *The Wizard of Oz* introduced new iconography and narrative threads to the witch canon, thereby shifting the representation of American cinematic witches permanently.

The Wild Woman: *Spitfire*

The first live-action witch film to be released after the hiatus was Paramount's *Spitfire* (1934), which is an adaptation of Lula Vollmer's play *Trigger*. Vollmer was raised in North Carolina and most of her work focused on country living or the lives of everyday people. These slice-of-life stories were popular during the Great Depression when Americans often relied on the movies to temporarily escape from their daily struggles. *Spitfire* tells the story of a barely literate, reclusive mountain girl who has faith healing powers. As a result, she is shunned by the townspeople and called a witch, and her practice is labeled "deviling." Prior to the film's release, a 1934 *Picture Play* article titled "The Witch," displayed promotional photos of Hepburn on the film's rural set.[119]

From New Woman to True Woman

Spitfire works more or less through a classic reincorporation narrative in which the heroine, Trigger Hicks, evolves from an aggressive renegade or witch into a proper woman. In the opening scenes, Trigger is a bully. She throws rocks at the townspeople, is rude to her friend, and admits to stealing. The early talk of witchcraft is visually reinforced when Trigger picks up a wandering black cat. However, the film slowly reveals Trigger's character complexity. By the end of the movie, she has transformed from a young wild woman to "true woman." When she is unable to save the Sawyer family's sick baby through her magic, Trigger is shown in soft-focus and close-up crying over its dead body. The scene depicts her as a compassionate, vulnerable mother figure, which is a stark contrast to the opening scenes of her throwing rocks and flirting with male strangers.

This character arc is supported by other filmic elements. Trigger's vocal quality and costume lines soften over time, as does the camera's embrace of her face. In early scenes, her close-ups are only filmed in hard-focus and her dress has straight simple lines. Additionally, in those opening scenes, her top shirt buttons are open exposing her upper chest. Trigger is sharp tongued, wild, and aggressive, which, along with her costuming, suggests a traditional masculine quality to her character.

---

119. "The Witch," review of *Spitfire*, *Picture Play* 39, no. 6 (February 1934), 47.

Katharine Hepburn as Trigger Hicks, a young Appalachian girl with healing powers, talks to God and dreams of a better life in Paramount's film Spitfire *(1934). [Source: RKO Radio Pictures/Photofest. Copyright: © RKO Radio Pictures]*

However, as the film progresses, she is increasingly framed in soft-focus, culminating in a very classic studio close-up as she cries over the baby. Her face is washed in cloud-like blur, making her look almost angelic. Additionally, mid-way through the film, Trigger changes into a dress that has a high collar and is decorated with fringe, puffy-sleeves, and a small bow at the center. This new look offers a far more traditionally feminine appearance than her earlier costume. Near the film's conclusion, Trigger tells George Fleetwood, her romantic interest, "I want to be like you so I don't have to throw stones and holler."

Trigger is redeemed both narratively and visually, drawing in viewer sympathy. As such, she is vindicated from her transgressive status as a witch, and she is reframed as a naive young woman. She begins as the young aggressive wild woman and ends the film as a sensitive mother figure who cares about the well-being of the townsfolk, loves a man, and believes in God. In that respect, she is reincorporated back into society, moving from father to husband and from wild woman to "true woman," both thematically and visually.

Feminist Undercurrents in *Spitfire*

It is important to note that Trigger does not end the film married, as one might expect. She does give up her magic and abandon her cabin home, but Triggers also leaves the town as well as the hero. She tells her new lover, George, that she wants "to be somebody." This narrative twist does not fit the typical reincorporation narrative. While Trigger is redeemed from her witch status and is narratively reframed within societal standards of goodness, the plot doesn't completely follow suit. Her full redemption is only based on a promise to return, which the viewer and George only trust because of her overall shift in character. At the very end of the film, Trigger is dressed in dark, conservative clothing as she literally and figuratively walks away from the wild, defined by her rural town and her past, into the symbolic real world.

The film's ending provides a subversive undercurrent of meaning aimed at the female viewer. This narrative element may be the result of the original play being written by a woman, as was *Fanchon the Cricket* (1915). In both cases, there is an anomaly built into the story. The 1915 movie contains a positive mother-daughter "witch" bond; the 1934 film has the witch put off marriage to travel the world. Before leaving, Trigger promises to return to her fiancée in twelve months, but first, as she says, there is something she must find out for herself. The unusual show of independence is an anomaly for the wild woman construction, particularly for this period. However, as noted, her promise to her future husband, supported visually by a change in costume, indicates to the viewer that her rejection of magic and wild behavior was, in fact, honest and that she will return to fulfill her proper role as wife and mother.

Expressions of Religion in *Spitfire*

It is important to note that *Spitfire* contains a strong religious component, which is essential to the construction of Trigger as a witch. Trigger talks to God, to her father, and to herself throughout the entire film. Her praying defines the source of her healing power, which is a critical aspect of the wild woman construction. Magic that is proven to be strictly faith-based is defined as reasonably safe in traditional Hollywood language under the Code. More specifically, Christian religious prayer and conviction are typically markers of good character, even when used in magical terms.

Therefore, it is the theological origin of her healing powers that afforded her leniency in her desire to travel and also allowed her to be easily redeemed as she changes her behavior. Aside from *Joan the Woman* (1916), *Spitfire* is the first witch film to depict religion-based magic or faith healing as witchcraft. While never overwhelmingly popular, the theme does dot the witch film landscape over the years with the majority of such films being produced after 1980 during the Satanic Panic and the rise of the evangelical Christian movement (e.g., *Resurrection*, 1980; *The Gift*, 2000).

It was *Spitfire*'s religious theme, not the suggestion of witchcraft, that concerned PCA director Joseph Breen. As noted earlier, several expletives written into the original script were cut, such as "damn" and "hussy." Concerns were also raised over the appropriate use of the words "lord" and "good lord." In 1933, PCA administrators notified RKO producers that state and international film boards might censor the film or parts of it due to its use of religious language and displays of sexuality.[120] That, in fact, was proven to be the case. Quebec's film board removed the kissing scenes and the British film board deleted the dialogue that contained heavily religious language. Regardless of international reactions, the PCA itself had few problems with *Spitfire* after it was edited, and the film received its certification.[121]

The Accused Woman: *Maid of Salem*

The second mainstream witch film released after 1934 was Paramount's *Maid of Salem* (1937). It is a historically inspired witch trial film set in the famous Massachusetts town. It is based on a short story titled "Between Two Worlds" originally written by screenwriter Bradley King. As noted earlier, the film opens with a direct claim at historical accuracy, saying "Our story, based on authentic records of the year 1692, opens in the colony of Massachusetts Bay, at the Port of Salem, a gateway to the vast territories of the new world." This language frames the narrative in the viewer's known reality, historically speaking. Before even one line of dialogue is spoken, the viewer has a definitive idea of what to expect of the movie.

As with past witch trial films, *Maid of Salem* defines a belief in witchcraft as purely a product of ignorant minds and suspicious behavior, and the film's narrative is grounded deep in that premise. Even Tituba, the film's indigenous folk witch, eventually denies her own magical ability, saying the potion was just a sleeping brew and her tales of witchcraft were just stories to entertain. Similarly, one of the film's title cards states that "a night of terror ... followed by rumors ... brought panic to the superstitious minds of the villagers."

---

120. James Wingate to Merian C. Cooper, December 9, 1933; source: *Spitfire* Production Files, MPAA PCA records, Margaret Herrick Library, Academy of Motion Picture Arts and Sciences, Beverly Hills, California.

121. Joseph Breen, British Film Board censorship report, February 20, 1935; source: *Spitfire* Production Files, MPAA PCA records, Margaret Herrick Library, Academy of Motion Picture Arts and Sciences, Beverly Hills, California.

Claudette Colbert stars as Barbara, a Salem woman who is accused of practicing witch-craft and tried before the town in the historically inspired film Maid of Salem *(1937).*
[Source: Paramount Pictures/Photofest. Copyright: © Paramount Pictures]

Claudette Colbert plays Barbara, an average Puritan woman who is well-liked in the village. However, Barbara expresses more freedom and inner strength than other village women, which is visually cued by her lighter clothing. As the film opens, she demonstrates her individuality by ignoring her guardian's mandate to not give candles to a recluse, and later, she wears a fancy bonnet to a church service. Additionally, Barbara is an unmarried adult woman who has fallen in love with a renegade American freedom fighter.

Right from the opening credits, the film sets Barbara up as a natural victim of the coming trials. She is independent, young, and beautiful and, therefore, an easy target. Based on the jealousy of other women, angry children, the judgment of a town drunk, and religious extremism, Barbara is arrested and accused of witchcraft. When she takes her place in court, she is dressed in rags with her unkempt hair flowing freely. Visually speaking, the town's mania has turned her into what one might label a witch.

While *Maid of Salem*'s plot negotiates through its traditional reincorporation narrative, it never posits Barbara as guilty. The film's symbolic purpose, like other Salem stories, is to illustrate the dangers of a moral panic. Because the narrative follows Barbara for much of its screen time, the viewer is able to witness the truth in her actions, including her care for children, her attention to community, her honest romantic feelings, and even her innocence when interacting with married men. She is always framed in soft-focus, properly dressed, and shown performing acts of service for others. While she does fall in love with the escaped freedom fighter Roger Coverman, he is the film's rational hero and the counterpoint to the mania. Roger is largely defined by his heroic deeds in service to American nationalism and freedom. This is an important thematic element in a film released in 1937, during the Depression and on the eve of World War II.

Throughout the film Barbara is attempting to be the "true woman," but the cast of superstitious characters want to frame her as a wild woman. That is the crux of the accused. Unlike the wild woman witch, the accused woman does fit into society but innocently missteps or unintentionally veers off the expected path. It is the townspeople that cause Barbara's change in appearance after her arrest, not her. Paralleling her costume change, the film's lighting shifts. As panic grips the village, the scenes literally darken, and the individual shots become more congested. An hour into the film a title card reads, "Fear reigns in Salem [...] Old grudges are paid by the fatal charge of 'witchcraft.'"

Religion and Witchcraft in *Maid of Salem*

While the film's story revolves around the notion of paranoia, it does not posit religion as the source of the problem or the religious figures as the antagonists. It is not a call for secularism. The Production Code Administration would not have allowed that conclusion. In 1936, Joseph Breen told Paramount's John Hammel to remove anything that "could be interpreted as reflecting adversely upon the clergy as a whole." [122] While Breen accepted the point that one of the historical religious figures was caught up in the chaos, he insisted that the writers introduce another minister who would "represent the liberal viewpoint [...] and will protest against the witchcraft hysteria of the time." [123]

---

122. Joseph Breen to John Hammell, 27 August 1936.
123. Joseph Breen to John Hammell, 27 August 1936.

As with *Spitfire*, witchcraft itself was not a PCA concern. There were only two mentions of the subject in the files. One was the concern over whether modern audiences would be able to understand the superstition at all. The second was the request to change the script's witch burnings to hangings, which echoed viewer complaints about earlier Salem films. In 1936, Breen wrote, "It is our impression that there were no burnings—rather was the alleged punishment confined to hangings." [124] Unlike in past Salem films, the change was made.

Near the end of the film, the speech given by Barbara reflects the nuanced relationship that the narrative has with religion and witchcraft. Reduced to rags, she stands against a room of aggressive Puritans, saying, "I deny there is such a thing as witchcraft." After being pressed further and in tears she says, "I will not confess a lie, or deny God to save my life." Her face is continually framed in soft-focus to reflect her angelic-like innocence and subsequent victimization. In this moment, she is a woman standing against the world, demonstrating a powerful moment of pure agency and personal choice. There again lies the subversive reading that exists in many of these classic Hollywood witch films.

However, in the end, Barbara as the accused woman and victim must endure a white knight rescue as narrative redemption for her misstep. While Barbara stands weakly on the gallows awaiting her hanging, Roger Coverman rides up on a horse through the crowd to reveal the truth. She had been protecting him and was not cavorting with any devil. Not only is the heroine rescued by her lover, she also finds a savior in the film's liberally minded religious cleric. Dressed in official uniform, he turns to the village leaders and says, "Have you not had enough? Will you be satisfied only with this girl's death?" Barbara is redeemed in the end and free from her witchcraft accusations, and in her acceptance of the rescue, she apologizes for her transgressions. She is the true woman after all.

The Indigenous Other

Barbara was not the only witch in *The Maid of Salem*. The film also contains the famed character Tituba, who was written into the plot through the historical remnants of Salem's legacy. From adaptation to adaptation, the construction of Tituba is not always the same. However, what is identical across retellings is her use of what is defined as witchcraft and her teaching of it to the village children. Regardless of historical fact, she is typically blamed as the source of the town's moral panic.

Maid of Salem's Tituba, played by Madame Sul-Te-Wan, is constructed as indigenous folk witch who is othered not by a reclusive lifestyle in the wild woods or her

---

124. Joseph Breen to John Hammell, 14 May 1936.

South Seas island surroundings but purely by her ethnicity and race. When she is first introduced, Tituba is telling a group of young girls and women a story of the "spirits and bad ones" dancing with Satan in the jungles of Africa. Later she is seen alone, stirring a cauldron over her fireplace. When Goody Goode enters, she says the pot contains a potion that takes the spirit "to the witches' feast." It is just like the elixirs that she once made "in her own country."

Based on definitions outlined by film historian Donald Bogle, Tituba is constructed as a type of mammy figure, which he labels "the aunt jemima." [125] It is one of the few film roles open to Black actors in mainstream productions during this period in Hollywood's history. Dressed in dark clothing, Tituba wears a scarf around her head, a costume piece iconic to the mammy. As Bogle explains, the aunt jemima is typically a woman who "wedge[s] themselves into the dominant white culture" and is often depicted as a buffoon.[126] In *Maid of Salem*, Tituba plays the role of village entertainer and jester. She is depicted as more a curiosity than a woman or even a human, a fact that is supported when one of the male villagers calls her "creature."

Like most other indigenous folk witches of the period, Tituba is a minor character, but her actions become a catalyst for the mass hysteria and the famous trials. When she discovers that Anne has stolen a witchcraft book, she turns both the book and the child over to Master Goode. This makes Anne furious, causing her to begin pointing fingers. When Tituba is later captured and accused, she reveals that her storytelling and potion making were just a game and she "meant no harm." She admits to having no magic. However, to save her life, she confesses and names others. In this scene, Tituba's crouched, dark form is centered within an angry mob of standing white men. She shakes and screeches like a scared animal, which visually correlates to the suggestion that she is a creature. That is the last moment that she appears on-screen.

Tituba ignites both the fury and the imagination of the villagers. The film sources her magic as either being an outright lie or a product of her primitive upbringing. The villagers use her to start the hunt for other witches and then simply discard her. In the end, Tituba isn't punished or killed as white witches might be, because she's ultimately not considered a threat or even human. She is just forgotten.

The earlier silent Salem films do not contain a Tituba character because they were not attempting to retell actual events, nor were their narratives character driven. In addition, most silent era indigenous folk witches were depicted as "Indian women" living just outside the village. In these films, the magical other was defined as a Native American and not a Black woman, which is an indicator of silent filmmakers' interest

125. Donald Bogle, *Toms, Coons, Mulattoes, Mammies, and Bucks: An Interpretive History of Blacks in American Films* (New York: Continuum, 1996), 9.

126. Bogle, *Toms, Coons, Mulattoes, Mammies, and Bucks*, 9.

in exploring Americana. Although "Indian" healers were othered, they were still defined as part of American lore, whereas Black women healers were not. They are from somewhere else.

Tituba, played by Madame Sul-Te-Wan, tells Goody Goode, played by Beulah Bondi, stories of magic and dancing from her homeland.
[Source: Paramount Pictures/Photofest.com. Copyright: © Paramount Pictures]

Unlike the silent era "Indian" folk witches, Tituba lives within the village and is accepted as part of the village. Her liminality as a folk witch is not defined by a physical space, but solely defined by race and nationality. Her skin and her heritage symbolically act as the wild wood does for the white elderly folk witch. It is Tituba's very beingness that isolates and others her. She does not need an "Indian" village or a forest cabin. Tituba is something that is "not us," as defined by the contemporary viewer. Consequently, she is primitive, suspect, and ultimately disposable.

A Different Perspective on Witchcraft and Race

In 1939, *The Devil's Daughter* was released with an all-Black cast. The film was specifically produced for Black audiences and only released to theaters that permitted

Black spectators. It was what was called a "race film." *The Devil's Daughter* tells the story of Sylvia Walton, a successful New York career woman who returns to Haiti to claim her inheritance after her father dies. Her sister Isabelle, who was left out of the will, is there waiting. Wanting to scare them away and claim the inheritance for herself, Isabelle pretends to be a witch and Vodou priestess.

Unlike Tituba, Isabelle, the Haitian witch, is the main antagonist. The hero and heroine by contrast are depicted as American and Christian. As such, Isabelle's adherence to Haitian magic is not linked to nationality and race; it is linked to nationality and religion. Isabelle is othered not by her skin color but by her religious beliefs and culture. The film's demonization of Vodou and Haitian society is notable, but also typical for the era. While a full analysis of Vodou depictions in American film deserves a closer look, it is beyond the scope of this particular study. However, with that said, *The Devil's Daughter* is an important marker alongside the period's limited and unflattering constructions of Black magical characters in mainstream films. It is a historical counterpoint to *Maid of Salem* and demonstrates the variance in cultural lines being used to define witchcraft, magic, religion, and race.

Animation: Cartoon Shorts

Although the animation industry continued to grow, the period did not see an increase in the number of witch-related shorts. The 1930s is considered the beginning of animation's golden era and many of the most famous and enduring characters, including Porky Pig and Donald Duck, made their debuts at this time. Like the live-action film industry, animators moved away from strict literary adaptations as the medium established itself as credible and valuable. Cartoon shorts were increasingly character driven as audiences looked forward to watching the antics of their beloved favorite. There was no witch character, however, that fit that model.

During this period, there were only two notable animated shorts. Betty Boop's *Baby Be Good* (1935) and *Greedy Humpty Dumpty* (1937). *Greedy Humpty Dumpty* is a throwback to the 1920s cartoon offerings. It depicts a fairy tale land similar to *Mother Goose Land* (1933). Its unnamed witch is just one of the many fairy tale characters who are forced into labor by the embryonic despot. Joining her are Little Boy Blue, Old Mother Hubbard, Mother Goose, and many other recognizable story time figures. As with past animated witches, she is dressed in ragged dark clothing and a classic conical hat with a big round brim. She has white hair and an elongated nose and chin. Like her 1920s counterparts, the witch's broom head spins like a propeller as she takes off. This is a cultural reference to the emergence of airplane travel, which began commercially in 1914.

The period's second short, Betty Boop's *Baby Be Good*, was produced in 1935, after Joseph Breen took hold of the PCA and is a solid counterpoint to earlier Betty Boop shorts and a good example of just how the PCA helped to redefine the construction of female characters on film. Betty arrived on the scene in 1930 as a parody of several famous 1920s jazz singers. She was the embodiment of flapper culture. Betty was her own woman, having no male counterpart and no family. In her shorts, she goes on adventures, parties with demons, wears short skirts, and fends off aggressive, muscle-bound male characters. In many ways, Betty was the epitome of the new woman.

Like most animated characters of the era, Betty Boop was solely created by male artists. Film historian Karl F. Cohen notes that animators in the Fleischer studios were all young, single men who drank "bootleg whiskey from Friday evening until Monday morning." Most did not have high school degrees and they enjoyed spending their weekends with prostitutes.[127] As such, Betty Boop was quite literally a product of the male gaze in a way that only cartoons can be. She became manifest only through the imaginations of men. However, Betty was not created to be a weak woman, and it was through her power and her open displays of sex appeal that female viewers connected to her as widely as men.

Then, in 1934 Betty Boop changed. Most remarkable is the length of her skirt, which goes from a micro mini to an A-line falling to her knees. Her low back bustier is replaced by a short sleeve button up with a white collar, bow, and trim, as seen in *Baby Be Good*. Cohen writes, "She started out as a popular star with innocent sex appeal and ended up looking like a schoolmarm."[128] After witches return to the screen, Betty Boop evolves into the "true woman," losing her freewheeling behavior and open displays of female sexuality.

In *Baby Be Good*, Betty appears mid-short as a good fairy, flying on a broom with a star-topped wand and a long flowing gown. She is the epitome of the good witch or fairy godmother. Her power comes from her wand as with most good magical characters like Glinda in any *Oz* adaptation. What is even more notable in Betty's transformation is her central motivation. Betty Boop is no longer depicted throwing parties (*Betty Boop's Halloween Party*, 1933) or dancing with devils (*Red Hot Mamma*, 1934). In this short, Betty is depicted as a mother or caregiver, reading stories and punishing naughty children. Boop, in her own right, typifies the transition of female character construction from the "new woman" back to the "true woman."

---

127. Karl F. Cohen, *Forbidden Animation: Censored Cartoons and Blacklisted Animators in America* (Jefferson, NC: McFarland & Company Inc, 2004), 17.

128. Cohen, *Forbidden Animation*, 22.

Animation: The Vamp, the Crone, and Disney

While most animators may have given up on their witch characters, it was Walt Disney's animation studio alone that instead pushed the envelope on what was possible and defined new ways to imagine the iconic character with the release of the first full-length American animated film: *Snow White and the Seven Dwarfs*. In that film alone, Disney birthed two of the most iconic American witch constructions in one single villainous character: The Wicked Queen. For most of the film, she is a vamp witch, beautiful and treacherous. Toward the end, she transforms into the fantasy crone, dark and evil.

In a 1938 article for *The New York World-Telegram*, Disney said that he chose the Grimm Brothers story for personal reasons. He wrote, "You see, it has been one of my favorite stories ever since I was a kid." [129] Another reason he cited was the film's salability in the foreign market. He explained, "'Snow White' is a tale loved in practically every country in the world." He goes on to say that the fairy tale also gave the animators "an opportunity to use small birds and animals which have always been popular with [their] fans." [130]

Just as producers did in the early days of live-action filmmaking, Disney chose to test his innovative project using a well-known story and recognizable visual elements that had proven to be successful. [131] He hoped that these elements would help to ease viewers into accepting the new full-length cartoon format. The strategy worked. Production began in 1934 and after four years of work the film was released to rave reviews, earning special Oscar recognition in 1938.

One Woman: Two Witches

In terms of the witch, *Snow White and the Seven Dwarfs* contains one character, the Wicked Queen, who takes on two forms: the vamp witch and the fantasy crone. This dual construction mirrors, to some extent, the character construction of the original tale. Near the end of the story, the Grimm Brothers wrote, "Then with the art of witchcraft, which [the queen] understood, she made a poisoned comb." [132] However, that is the only time that the word "witch" is found in the entire text, and the word

---

129. Walt Disney, "Temperamental Dwarfs Held Up 'Snow White,' Walt Disney Reveals," *The New York World-Telegram*, January 8, 1938, 48.

130. Disney, "Temperamental Dwarfs," 40.

131. Disney, "Temperamental Dwarfs," 40.

132. Jacob Grimm and Wilhelm Grimm, "Little Snow-White," First published in *Children's and Household Tales*, vol. 1–2 (Germany: Dieterich, 1857), trans. D. L. Ashliman,. http://www.pitt.edu/~dash/grimm053.html.

"magic" is only used once in reference to the mirror. In fact, Grimms' queen does not even use witchcraft to disguise herself as, what the Grimm Brothers called, "an old peddler woman." To do so, she "[colors] her face."[133] In the original story, the queen is never labeled a witch, and the use of that narrative detail defines just one of her many evil acts, which include several attempted murders.

In most cinematic adaptations of the classic tale, the Queen is not a magical practitioner at all; she does not personally "understand" witchcraft. For example, in the 1916 film *Snow White*, the Queen must elicit help from a fantasy crone in order to enact her magical intent, and that character breakdown follows suit in later adaptations as well, such as *Snow White and the Three Stooges* (1961). In condensing the narrative to fit into animation's mode of storytelling, Walt Disney incorporated the original tale's character construction, but he exaggerated the magical aspect. In doing that, Disney created the first Hollywood fantasy vamp witch, forging a direct link between magic, mature female desire, and the body.

The Vamp

The Wicked Queen in her vamp form is considered beautiful, as described in the Grimm Brothers' original tale, and this character detail was replicated in the film's production elements. She is an animated version of classic 1930s femme fatales, modeled on actresses such as Joan Crawford, Marlene Dietrich, and Greta Garbo. In her essay "Somatexts at the Disney Shop," film theorist Elizabeth Bell writes, "Disney transforms the vain, active, and wicked woman of folktales into the *femme fatale*, the 'deadly woman' of silent film and of Hollywood classic film."[134]

This visual detail is not simply based on spectator reaction. It was intentional. In his book *The Art of Walt Disney*, Christopher Finch notes that Disney production files describe the Queen's beauty as "sinister, mature, [with] plenty of curves."[135] In a 1938 *Photoplay* article detailing the inside story behind the making of the animated film, writer Kirtley Baskette notes that "experiments on [the Queen's] lovely cruel mouth and eyes alone represent drawings enough to paper a house."[136] As a result,

---

133. Grimm and Grimm, "Little Snow-White," http://www.pitt.edu/~dash/grimm053.html.

134. Elizabeth Bell, "Somatexts at the Disney Shop," in *From Mouse to Mermaid: The Politics of Film, Gender, and Culture*, ed. Elizabeth Bell , Lynda Haas, and Laura Sells (Bloomington: Indiana University Press, 1995), 115.

135. Christopher Finch, *The Art of Walt Disney: From Mickey Mouse to the Magic Kingdoms* (New York: Abrams Books, 1975), 66.

136. Kirtley Baskette, "The Amazing Inside Story of How They Made 'Snow White,'" *Photoplay* 52, no. 4 (April 4, 1938): 68.

the Queen embodies what feminist film theorists, such as Barbara Creed or Mary Ann Doane, might call the treacherous or monstrous-feminine.

Taking that concept further, the Queen as vamp exists in a more concentrated form than her live-action femme fatale counterparts. She exists wholly in the symbolic realm because she was crafted by the imagination and, more specifically, by the minds of men. The original written fairy tale did not describe the Queen's physicality; the Grimm Brothers simply called her "a beautiful woman."[137] Any physical details are left to the reader's imagination. Therefore, Disney animators had full interpretive rein of what "beautiful" meant. In that context, the Queen is not a vamp or femme fatale herself; rather she represents one, as interpreted, and presented by male animators of the late 1930s. She is a symbol, a fantasy, and an exaggeration, like Betty Boop.

As the main villain, the Queen's presence is visually consuming. She is often drawn in close-up and, in some cases, her face fills the entire screen, leaving the viewer with no visual escape. Her long dress is predominantly black and purple, and her head is framed completely with a black hood, which is set off against a high white collar. These details, together with her pale skin and exaggerated makeup give the Queen a vampiric image, which is suggested by her bat-like shadow. The Queen not only is the bad mother, but she also represents a monster.

The Bad Mother and Mystical Adolescence

There has been much written about the mother-daughter character dynamic commonly found in traditional European fairy tales and their corresponding modern retellings. In these classic stories, the female antagonist is defined as the bad mother who interferes in an adolescent girl's life. That theme coincides with the representation of witchcraft and witches, particularly going forward. As discussed in chapter two, historian Diana Anselmo-Sequeira posits that early silent films depicted the young girl as existing in a dangerous liminal space, where she could be easily influenced by the mystical unknown, and that only through marriage could she be rescued from a dangerous fate.[138] In those cases, the occult or witchcraft was depicted as a symbolic enticement from which the confused teen needed to be rescued.

Applying Anselmo-Sequeira's theory to the mother-daughter fairy tale thematic, the bad mother as witch monster exists as the personification of that dangerous mystical element that seeks to influence or to harm the impressionable adolescent girl, who then must be saved by a hero, heterosexual marriage, and traditional domesticity. Disney's feature is a perfect example. Snow White falls victim to magic and can

---

137. Grimm and Grimm, "Little Snow-White," http://www.pitt.edu/~dash/grimm053.html.
138. Anselmo-Sequeira, "Apparitional Girlhood," 33.

only be saved by true love's kiss. The poisoned apple, made by her stepmother, is the symbolic mystical enticement and an extension of the witch.

In her book *A Skin for Dancing In*, Tanya Krzywinska posits that the fairy tale mother-daughter dynamic is Oedipal in nature. Using Disney's *Snow White* film as an example, she suggests that the tale is "structured around a teenage girl's fantasy of the mother as sexual competition" or her "unconscious desire to commit matricide." [139] Krzywinska is speaking specifically of bad mothers as witches, who hold a distinct role in the relationship due to their access to magic as symbolic of internal female power. She is a threat to the princess both literally and existentially.

The witch, as such, becomes intrinsically wrapped in the ideology of the monstrous woman, which is depicted through the visual characterization of the Disney Queen as an actual vampire. The magical bad mother has an independence, knowledge beyond the knowable, and a power that exceeds the realms of the established community, just like any other witch. In addition, as remarked by Elizabeth Bell, these magical bad mothers typically are "living and thinking only for themselves as sexual subjects, not sexual objects." [140] The Queen, absent a husband or love interest, still seeks to retain her beauty. Her sexuality is her own, as is her power.

As noted earlier, Disney's *Snow White and the Seven Dwarfs* is the first mainstream American film to fully tap into this ideology and make it horrific. The power of the mature feminine becomes defined by the use or misuse of internal forces as symbolized by magic. The vamp witch not only knows too much but she uses what she knows of herself and society to take action for her own needs. The Queen relishes her power and wields it unchecked. She is a character of action, unlike the heroine who is largely reactive, except when choosing to clean the dwarves' home and make them dinner, modeling traditional domesticity.

The polarity between the characters demonstrates the idea posited earlier of the "true woman" versus the "new woman." Snow White is an example of the "true woman," where the Queen might be considered the "new woman." This extreme polarization of the two female characters is echoed visually through their colorization. Snow White is dressed in bright colors of the daytime, such as blue, yellow, white, and with touches of red. The Queen's clothes are made up of colors of the night, such as blacks and purples with shocks of white.

However, it is in this very polarization where a female viewer might locate a subversive reading of the Disney film. Krzywinska makes this point, suggesting that female viewers might, if only quietly, align with the frustrations found within the Queen's character. She writes, "We might celebrate, with a suitable cackle, the fact

---

139. Krzywinska, *A Skin for Dancing In*, 137.
140. Bell, "Somatexts at the Disney Shop," 116.

that she poisons the saccharine heterosexual romance and the cute idyll of woodland life, both grounded in a patriarchal valorisation of passive, innocent and youth femininity." [141] Krzywinska's characterization of the witch may partly explain why she has endured in popularity. The Queen gives off a strength that was unknown in a female viewer's real life. The witch serves as an escape from the limitations imposed by traditional gender structures and modes of behavior.

The Fantasy Crone

Along with intensifying the presentation of the vamp witch, Disney animators also included some very identifiable, classic witchcraft iconography as well. However, much of that doesn't appear until the Wicked Queen descends into her chamber to physically transform. In a darkly lit stone room, she stands over a bubbling cauldron, where there are bones, skulls, and her pet crow. When the Queen does change, she takes on a classic fantasy crone appearance, one that is known to nearly all viewers. In this elderly stooped form, the Queen wears a black hooded cloak and has elongated facial features and fingers. She is easily identifiable as a witch, the weird sister, the Baba Yaga.

Comparing the Queen in this form to Disney's older fantasy crone found in the short *Babes in the Woods* (1932), it is easy to see how animators intensified the characterization just as they did with her vamp form. In the earlier work, the witch is gangly and ragged. Her clothing is made up of an assortment of darker colors, rather than solid black. Her face, which was drawn in the stylized simplicity of Disney's *Silly Symphonies*, is framed only by white hair and a gray hat. In addition, the 1932 crone never gets close to the camera. In essence, the witch in *Babes in the Woods* is a simple caricature of what the Wicked Queen becomes. She is the Halloween witch or comedic buffoon commonly found in cartoon shorts. By contrast, the 1937 Disney crone is an evil villain of the highest order.

Interestingly, the Queen as crone does perform one narrative function that is in fact common to elderly witch characters, fantasy or otherwise. Her presence helps to define the heroine as morally good, as was done in the opening scene of the silent film *Cinderella* (1914). The naive Snow White, like Cinderella, kindly engages with an old beggar woman. Snow White invites the crone in and takes the apple. This moment demonstrates that Snow White is compassionate and gentle. She sees no danger in the stark crone figure. However, the audience knows better, which is what creates tension in that scene. Despite using the same trick as Cinderella's fairy godmother, the Queen's goal lies beyond a simple exchange.

---

141. Krzywinska, *A Skin for Dancing In*, 137.

Religion, Alluring Evil, and the PCA

The original Grimm tale contains religious undertones not found in the Disney film. For example, the Grimm brothers describe the wicked woman, who understood witchcraft, as ungodly. This type of faith-based description is completely absent from Disney's *Snow White and the Seven Dwarfs*. In cinematic terms, the Wicked Queen is a product of fantasy and does not need her magic sourced. It just exists. What "wicked" actually means is left up to the viewer's own ideological worldview. Disney's witch was clearly designed as evil and beautiful, and that was enough to elicit fear.

Despite the clear connection between evil and alluring beauty, the film's script did not raise concerns at the Production Code Administration. As noted earlier, Garity, a Walt Disney producer, reached out to the PCA prior to the start of production to ensure that the project would not violate the code. In fact, the chairman of the MPPDA and overseer of the PCA, William Hays, considered Disney "the best representative of the industry's moral standards."[142] The medium of animation provided a buffer that allowed Disney to connect evil and sexuality without being censored. *Snow White and the Seven Dwarfs* received its PCA approval and premiered on December 21, 1937.

Nearly a century later, the Wicked Queen in both of her forms reigns as one of Disney's most beautiful characters and one of the most frightening. Not only is she the first vamp witch, but she is also the first witch to truly inspire horror and to take on a focused role as a powerful and threatening antagonist. But the Queen would not stand in that space alone for long. Less than two years after the release of *Snow White and the Seven Dwarfs*, the film's level of intensity in witch construction was matched and even exceeded by her live-action predecessor: The Wicked Witch of the West.

The Halloween Witch and the Good Fairy: *The Wizard of Oz*

In August 1939, MGM released *The Wizard of Oz*, the next adaptation of Baum's classic story. Although not the first, it is undoubtedly the one that stands out as a cultural icon existing beyond the limited scope of the 1930s silver screen. Within the MGM film, the Wicked Witch of the West was designed with an entirely different look than anything found in the past. Her appearance alone solidified standards for the Halloween witch, creating a legacy that lasted well into the next millennium (e.g., *Oz the Great and Powerful*, 2013). At the same time, the film produced Glinda the Witch of the North, a new model for the good witch.

Up until this point, the Oz property was still considered box office poison. The silent films of the 1910s, the live-action adaption in 1925, and Ted Eshbaugh's 1933

142. Marc Eliot, *Walt Disney: Hollywood's Dark Prince: A Biography* (New York: Carol Publishing Group, 1993), 97.

animated short, which did not contain a witch, all failed to produce the fiscal returns or even enough viewer excitement to warrant more production. However, MGM decided to take the chance.

In the months surrounding the release of Disney's *Snow White and the Seven Dwarfs*, film critics wondered if anyone could compete. A *New York Times* article reported, "With the industry convinced that 'Snow White' will be a box-office success, there is a wild search by producers for comparable fantasies." [143] MGM's search produced *The Wizard of Oz*. After the film debuted in August 1939, reporters speculated whether the new fantasy film could topple Disney's reign. *Cincinnati Enquirer* critic E. B. Radcliffe wondered if "Disney's power to bewitch film fans [would] decline because of *The Wizard of Oz*" and if "Walt's wizardry [was] topped by Mervyn's magic." [144]

The Wicked Witch of the West

It is not surprising that the two fantasy films are often compared, being released less than two years apart. But more poignantly the two wicked witches are also discussed side by side. While there are certainly similarities, the two characters are vastly different in their construction. The Wicked Queen focuses on her own beauty, the Wicked Witch seeks only power; beauty is far from a concern. Therefore, the Wicked Witch is not a vamp, nor is she a fantasy crone. However, she is closer in visual structure to the latter. The Wicked Witch is the epitome of the Halloween witch—a figure that had been coalescing over the last decade within the animated short (e.g., *Felix Switches Witches*, 1927).

Like those cartoon drawings, the Wicked Witch is a condensed form of the fantasy crone who is commonly associated with Halloween. She is highly symbolic, being built almost entirely on recognizable cultural cues. Even the use of orange smoke surrounding her arrivals and departures reflects the color of the fall season. As for her clothing, the Wicked Witch is dressed in solid black, draped with a cape and topped with the classic pointed hat. She flies on a broomstick, stirs a cauldron, gazes into a crystal ball, and has magic powers. In addition, the Wicked Witch cackles loudly and has an elongated nose, chin, and fingernails. She is the live-action version of what was found in animated shorts.

143. "Screen News Here and In Hollywood," *The New York Times*, February 19, 1938, 19.

144. E. B. Radcliffe, "Is Walt's Wizardry Topped by Mervyn's Magic?" *The Cincinnati Enquirer*, August 27, 1939, 47.

The Wicked Witch of the West drops in on Glinda and Dorothy in Munchkinland
in the MGM adaptation of Baum's classic story The Wizard of Oz *(1939);*
seen from left to right: Margaret Hamilton, Judy Garland, Billie Burke.
[Source: MGM/Photofest. Copyright: © MGM]

In a 1977 essay, actress Margaret Hamilton recalled the amount of time that the studio spent creating her iconic look, including the best fit and shape of the chin and nose, and whether the dress sleeves would "have a medieval look." She wrote, "details were considered, and accepted or turned down on the basis of the whole effect."[145] Perhaps the most striking feature of the MGM Wicked Witch and the most recognizable is her green skin. This visual detail was not used for any witch prior to 1939. Whether in paintings, stories, or films, there is no evidence to suggest that green skin was ever even considered a mark of witchcraft practice. While Baum's own Wicked Witch was described as having one eye, he made no mention of a green skin tone.

---

145. Margaret Hamilton, introduction to *The Making of the Wizard of Oz*, by Aljean Harmetz (New York: Hyperion, 1998), xxxvi.

The unique color choice was applied to the character by *The Wizard of Oz* film crew. According to Hamilton, the green makeup was used to solve a technical problem discovered during wardrobe testing. She wrote:

> Black [clothing] next to your skin seemed to give rise to a thin line of white on the edge of the black, which did not look like edging but rather like a separation. But with *Oz* the problem was solved—perhaps that was why they chose green makeup for my face, neck, and hands. The problem of the thin white line was only apparent when black was the basic color.[146]

Hamilton notes that she wasn't aware at first why they had decided to use the green makeup, but later learned of the problem caused by the Technicolor process. By covering her in green makeup, she could wear the black dress without her head and hands looking disembodied. As a result of that choice, Halloween witches forevermore became associated with green skin.

While there is no definitive explanation for why filmmakers chose green, it could be speculated that the color is commonly associated with monsters, greed, and the sick. On the body, green symbolically exists in the realm of the unnatural, the inhuman, or the abject. In addition, during this period of time, classic monsters were popular subjects in horror films. Therefore, the use of green skin could have been a visual cue aligning the Wicked Witch with the horrific. Just as Disney created the first truly frightening animated witch character, MGM did the same in live action. While neither film can be classified as horror, both have witches that are codified as monsters using symbolic language. If Disney's Wicked Queen is Dracula, the Wicked Witch is Frankenstein.

The concept of both characters existing as female versions of classic monsters is also supported by their surroundings. Neither one, for example, lives in a cabin in the woods—a setting more typical to the fantasy crone witch (e.g., *Brave*, 2012). In the case of the Wicked Witch, she lives in a dark gothic stone castle, surrounded by a thick leafless forest. Her space is more reminiscent of Dracula's home or a mad scientist's lab than the typical fairy tale witch's cottage. *Snow White*'s Wicked Queen lives in a similar setting. As such, the two female antagonists are concrete examples of the monstrous-feminine working within the fantasy genre just outside the realm of horror.

As noted earlier, both *Snow White* and *The Wizard of Oz* mark a dynamic shift in the intensity of the fantasy witch. They are no longer relegated to plot devices, secondary villains, or comedic foils. Both wicked witches are overwhelmingly evil and

---

146. Hamilton, introduction to *The Making of the Wizard of Oz*, by Aljean Harmetz, xxxv.

are the only adversaries on the heroine's journey. In her book *The Making of The Wizard of Oz*, Aljean Harmetz remarked on this point, characterizing it in terms of a cinematic loss of innocence. She wrote, "The primacy of the [Wicked] Witch was dramatically unavoidable, but it coarsened the movie." Harmetz then describes the film as a "familiar nightmare set in Technicolor to a lovely musical score." [147]

The Witch Woman as Villain

Although many similarities can be found between the two wicked characters, there are just as many differences. The Wicked Witch, as noted, is not interested in beauty, and this is a decisive point. Her only focus is to obtain her dead sister's shoes in order to grow her magical power. There is no other goal or purpose stated. The Wicked Witch's primary objective is to exist as an ever-lurking source of terror, and this idea is supported by the film's structure.

The witch only appears in twelve minutes of the entire movie; however, she commands full attention when on the screen. Typically standing center or above the central action, her black form creates a monolithic dark presence that draws the eye. There are close-ups of her green face, and her classic cackle pierces through the soundtrack and stops all other noise. The Wicked Witch exists as an ever-presence along Dorothy's quest. It isn't until the end scenes, when her clothing blends with the dark scenery of the castle, that she weakens in narrative terms.

In her book *The Monstrous-Feminine*, theorist Barbara Creed notes, "[The witch] is thought to be dangerous and wily, capable of drawing on her evil powers to wreak destruction on the community." [148] This statement captures the primary concept behind the characterization of the Wicked Witch. She is the monstrous-feminine not because of an extenuated display of sexuality or attention to beauty, but rather because of an internal power and the willingness to use it to disrupt the conventional. Once again, this is where a female viewer might find a subversive reading in the MGM film text. The witch is active, independent, and self-empowered. She is not subservient to any man and finds her success outside of social convention.

In 1995, that subversive reading manifested into Gregory Maguire's novel *Wicked: The Life and Times of the Wicked Witch of the West*, and later, into the Tony-award winning musical adaptation, *Wicked: The Untold Story of the Witches of Oz*. In those later texts, the Wicked Witch's "powers to wreak destruction on the community" are simply reframed as reactions to a corrupt government and unfair social order. Ma-

---

147. Aljean Harmetz, *The Making of the Wizard of Oz* (New York: Hyperion, 1998), 39.

148. Barbara Creed, *The Monstrous-Feminine: Film, Feminism, Psychoanalysis* (London: Routledge, 1993), 76.

guire's story not only inspired fans, but also has been used to promote anti-bullying campaigns across the United States and United Kingdom.

Mothers and Daughters

Like the Disney film, *The Wizard of Oz* evokes the mother-daughter narrative dynamic. The Wicked Witch represents the bad mother who hunts the younger heroine and, visually speaking, the two female characters are diametrically opposed. Dorothy is dressed in whites and light blues—the colors of daytime. The Wicked Witch is in black—the color of the night. However, the tension between the Disney characters is slightly different than in *Oz* because the animated film introduces a love interest and focuses on female beauty and sexual maturity. These elements are absent from the MGM film.

The Wizard of Oz's Dorothy was originally written to be far younger than Snow White, despite the appearance of actress Judy Garland. Dorothy is not a teenager on the verge of maturity, and therefore thematic tensions concerning maturity and sexuality do not play a role in MGM's fantasy. Instead, the polarization occurs through motivation and ethics. Dorothy wants to empower other people and to go home to continue her role as a proper little girl. The Wicked Witch wants to empower herself and terrorize the community.

The ruby slippers become the central point of contention. If those sparkling shoes are read as a symbolic point of femininity, then the fight over them becomes a symbolic battle over female agency. Once again, it is the "true woman" as represented by Dorothy fighting against the "new woman" represented by the Wicked Witch. Within this classic fantasy film, even absent all sexual excess, there lies a very base dynamic commonly found within American cinematic witch ideology; it is the battle of what it means to be a woman—subservient to the patriarchal order or free.

Glinda the Good

Unlike her evil counterpart, Glinda is visually constructed as an angel, a fairy, or something of heaven. She wears pink and white and lightly glitters. Her hair falls down around her shoulders in golden waves and her face is always framed in soft focus. Where the Wicked Witch arrives from the ground with orange smoke reminiscent of hellfire and dies melting downward, the good witch descends from the heavens to help and, when done, ascends back into the clouds. Later in the film, she even appears simply as a soft god-like image in the sky.

Despite the use of the term "witch," Glinda is visually constructed within a definitive Christian theological framework. While mostly subtle in nature, the religious cues are more overtly realized during the black and white scenes. Auntie Em says to her cruel neighbor, Almira Gulch, "For twenty-three years, I've been dying to tell you what I thought of you. And now, well, being a Christian woman, I can't say it." This statement defines Auntie Em as morally just and good through her connection to Christianity. She is a good Christian woman who loves children and animals. These are classic Hollywood cues. By contrast, Almira Gulch, who eventually turns into the Wicked Witch, is the antithesis.

In Baum's original story, there are two good witches and two bad witches. MGM followed the structure for the bad witches but did not for the good witches. Baum's good witch of the north is a "little old woman," and his Witch Glinda of the south is "beautiful and young." [149] That latter description does fit the MGM character and, at the same time, it matches the trends in construction of good magical women as fairy godmothers. In the 1910 film *The Wonderful Wizard of Oz* Glinda the Good is also fairy-like in appearance, descending from the sky.

Aside from visuals and any theological suggestions, Glinda's nonthreatening nature is also defined in the way she uses magic. Her power only comes from her starry wand, suggesting that Glinda's magic was bestowed upon her, rather than being internal to her. It can be taken away. The Wicked Witch, on the other hand, uses internal power. Her magic comes from her body and is something that cannot be taken away. Allegorically speaking, the woman as a bad witch is a self-empowered woman with her own agency; the woman as a good witch does not own her power and she is limited.

Despite these distinctions, MGM did not remove Glinda's full title as Selig Polyscope did in the early silent film. Glinda is still called a witch, which is an anomaly. Typically, good magical women are godmothers and nannies or other women who care for children. After Dorothy arrives in Munchkinland, Glinda and Dorothy have a brief exchange explaining this point.

> Dorothy says, "Witches are old and ugly."
>
> After the Munchkins giggle, Glinda says, "They're laughing because I am a witch. I'm Glinda, the Witch of the North."
>
> Dorothy retorts, "You *are*? Oh, I beg your pardon! But I've never heard of a beautiful witch before."
>
> Glinda responds, "Only *bad* witches are ugly."

The exchange adds another layer to the definition of what it means to be good: you must be beautiful. Good witches are then identified by graceful movements, love of children, socially given power, a heaven-based Christian aesthetic, and ideal beauty.

---

149. Baum, *Oz: The Complete Collection*, vol. 1, 11, 175.

Evil witches are defined by ugliness, a disregard for dogs, a hell-based Christian aesthetic, Halloween iconography, and full self-empowerment. Where the Wicked Witch is the bad mother, Glinda is the good mother.

Box Office Flop ... Again

Despite the hype around the film's release, *The Wizard of Oz* was not universally loved. There were critics who believed it was too frightening for a fantasy film aimed at children or simply thought it was uninteresting. In fact, the British film board censored the movie outright as an adults-only film, reporting that the "Witch and grotesque moving trees and various hideous figures would undoubtedly frighten children." [150] At the same time, the film was nominated for several academy awards, including best picture. While it lost that honor to Victor Fleming's other directorial venture *Gone with the Wind*, *The Wizard of Oz* did take home awards for best original song, "Somewhere Over the Rainbow," and best score.

Initially the film lost money and did not earn universal praise. However, reactions shifted slowly over time. As noted by Harmetz, critics largely changed their tune when the film was re-released in 1949. She attributes this change of heart partially to nostalgia, as many of the new critics had seen the film as a child.[151] Then, when television became ubiquitous, the movie began playing annually every Halloween and, as a result, it became a holiday classic.

As Harmetz notes, the 1939 critics made little to no mention of either witch character. Despite that fact, the Wicked Witch would eventually go on to become the most commonly evoked aspect of the movie, even outside of the context of the original film.[152] By 1950, animated witches were uniformly drawn with green skin. Margaret Hamilton began making appearances that directly referenced her iconic character (e.g., *Comin' Round the Mountain*, 1951). And by the turn of the millennium, *The Wizard of Oz* had become a Hollywood icon that, nearly eighty years after its initial release and poor showing, had produced a cultural legacy surpassing even its original story within the global pop culture mindset.

---

150. Breen, British Film Board censorship report. December 8, 1939; source: *The Wizard of Oz*, Production Files, MPAA PCA records, Margaret Herrick Library, Academy of Motion Picture Arts and Sciences, Beverly Hills, California.

151. Harmetz, *The Making of the Wizard of Oz*, 300.

152. Harmetz, *The Making of the Wizard of Oz*, 297.

Conclusion

In 1934, the American film industry took a sharp right turn, so to speak, after the hiring of Joseph Breen as director of the Production Code Administration. The enforcement of its censorship code shifted the way Hollywood told stories. In a 1938 report, director William Hays discusses the success of the new program, saying, "The motion picture public is no longer the millions more or less conditioned to the suggestive and sensational. It is a universal public attracted to the movie theater by a vast variety of clean and artistic entertainment." [153] The code was a success and led what Hays called a new "economic foundation."

As the country battled through the Depression, the live-action witch returned to the screen in the form of the accused woman, the indigenous other, and the wild woman. Despite similarities to their predecessors, there were marked changes in the exploration of the lead female characters, which allowed for a display of strength not previously seen in witch figures.

As the period comes to a close, several of the most iconic and most frightening American witches are born in what was generally considered fantasy children's fare. Disney produced the first fantasy vamp, thereby linking magic to female power and the body for the first time in Hollywood's history (i.e., *Snow White and the Seven Dwarfs*). Then MGM produced the first horrific Halloween witch and an atypical example of a goodly fairy witch (i.e., *The Wizard of Oz*).

By the end of the period, the witch was no longer the silent film's secondary character, unworthy of mention or consideration in reviews, nor was she simply a comic buffoon. By 1939, the witch had become the center of the film's narrative, whether good or evil, with extreme close-ups and depth of character construction. She had monologues calling for morality and private scenes praying to God. Within the protective framework of fantasy, the witch took center stage as a single, powerful, and terrifying monster—one that has continued to frighten children decades after her original creation.

---

153. William H. Hays, "Self-Regulation in the Motion Picture Industry," *Annual Report to the Motion Picture Producers and Distributors of American, Inc.*, March 28, 1938, page 8; source: Core Collection Pamphlets, Margaret Herrick Library, Academy of Motion Picture Arts and Sciences, Beverly Hills, California.

Chapter 4: Filmography

Spitfire	1934	John Cromwell
Betty Boop's Baby Be Good	1935	Dave Fleischer
Maid of Salem	1937	Frank Lloyd
Greedy Humpty Dumpty	1936	Dave Fleischer
Snow White and the Seven Dwarfs	1937	David Hand et al.
The Devil's Daughter	1939	Arthur H. Leonard
The Wizard of Oz	1939	Victor Fleming et al.

Chapter 5
War and Weird Women
(1941–1950)

Despite the remarkable changes made within witch films by the late 1930s, the follow-ing decade did not capitalize on that period's dynamic and creative momentum. The intense fantasy witches found in *Snow White and the Seven Dwarfs* (1937) and *The Wizard of Oz* (1939), for example, did not significantly inspire other filmmakers to move in that direction. This was most likely due to the coming of catastrophic world events that affected the film industry as a whole and the productions it released. In 1941, the US entered World War II and Hollywood followed suit in backing the na-tional war effort. As noted by historians Kristin Thompson and David Bordwell, "Af-ter Pearl Harbor ... the film industry supported the war cause wholeheartedly." [154]

The period itself ranges from 1941–1950. It begins after the start of war in Eu-rope, and it ends with the dawn of television's Golden Age. As influencers, both of these two sociocultural events had significant impact on Hollywood output and, as a by-product, the production of witch films. Although the United States did not en-ter World War II until December 1941, the rising conflicts of the European theater affected the industry almost immediately as foreign markets were either completely gone or severely limited. Hollywood lost much of its international revenue stream and had to focus on national distribution. By 1942, Hollywood shifted its attention even further to participate in supporting the cause, which included marked changes in genre interests and popularity. When the war ended and American society began

---

154. Thompson and Bordwell, *Film History*, 235.

to settle down, Hollywood found itself facing a new problem and perhaps its biggest challenge to date: television.

Witches and Wartime Hollywood

At this point in time, witches remained genre-dependent constructions, and shifts in genre popularity necessarily affected the appearance and use of witches in cinematic entertainment. For example, fantasy stories, fairy tales, and literary adaptations only appear before and after the war. Even Walt Disney, who did continue to explore children's stories, did not capitalize on the success of *Snow White and the Seven Dwarfs* by creating another animated full-length traditional princess film with an evil witch. The studio's new shorts and films, allegorically speaking, explored male heroism and the lessons of boyhood (e.g., *Pinocchio*, 1940; *Dumbo*, 1941; *Bambi*, 1942). While other works, such as *Fantasia* (1940), showcased technology and artistry, and still others focused on Americana and the war itself (e.g., *Song of the South*, 1946 and *Victory Through Air Power*, 1943).

Despite the genre shifts, there were several witch films released between 1942 and 1945. Like the industry's general output, these wartime witch films reflect the country's growing nationalism, an "us against them" ethos, and the ideology behind cultural preservation. Film historian Eric Smoodin describes this shift as "[creating] ... a sense of ideological wholeness ... to smooth over the potential disturbance of difference." [155] Unlike in the pre-war years or after, the live-action witch character and her magic are depicted as an outsider and, allegorically, an invader of American society (e.g., *Weird Woman*, 1944).

Due to this new construction within the witch narrative, the role of Salem changed as well. The city's historical baggage takes on a cued meaning within cinematic language. Up until this point in time, most Salem witch films or those set in a small New England town depict the famous trials in some form. They are historical dramas or try to be (e.g., *Maid of Salem*, 1937). However, during this period, Salem becomes a backdrop, a mythological universe so to speak—one that cues the audience that the upcoming story will involve witchcraft.

While the thematic tension behind these witch trial films is built primarily on the polarity between reason and superstition, films that used Salem as a setting for an invasion story rely on a totally different motif: the balance between normalcy and chaos (e.g., *I Married a Witch*, 1942). Once again, this coincides with the wartime efforts to, as Smoodin said, "smooth over the potential disturbance of difference." The use of Salem

---

155. Smoodin, *Animating Culture*, 71.

in this decorative way evolves into a standard for witch films and can be found regularly going forward, particularly in horror and comedy (e.g., *The Witches of Eastwick*, 1987).

The Films

For this period, there were nine relevant films and shorts included in the study. The era begins with two shorts that tell their stories using new innovative cinematic techniques: George Sidney's proto-horror short *Third Dimensional Murder* (1941) and George Pal's fantasy short *The Sky Princess* (1942). In both cases, the witches take on typical fantasy forms: the Halloween witch and fantasy crone, respectively. After the war, the industry released two films that retold two famous stories: Orson Welles's adaptation of *Macbeth*, and Victor Fleming's prestige film *Joan of Arc* (1948). In addition, witches appeared in a few character-driven animated shorts as comedic antagonists to their popular heroes (e.g., Mighty Mouse in *The Witch's Cat*, 1948).

While the fanciful, epic, and innovative appeared in the years surrounding the war, the period from 1942–1945 saw none of this. During those years, there are three key live-action witch features, including *I Married a Witch* (1942), *The Woman Who Came Back* (1945), and *Weird Woman* (1944). These films focus on real-world living, a woman's role in society, and community safety. Each of these films contains a different witch construction. The first is a fantasy vamp, the second an accused woman, and the third a young wild woman. It is not surprising to find films devoted to women's issues dominant during a period when women were on the home front expected to bolster nationalism and maintain traditional American society. Allegorically speaking, these films explore the disruption that a woman with too much power can cause to an otherwise peaceful town. The stories warn of the dangers of unchecked femininity as an alien invader and, once again, as the disrupter of normalcy.

Animation and the Halloween Witch

Similar to the last period, animation did not offer an uptick in witch characters. Animators continued to move further and further away from retelling classic stories and toward building their own original works. They relied on recognizable and branded casts of characters, focusing less on familiar narratives. In other words, producers were more interested in feeding viewers with regular doses of Woody Woodpecker or Droopy Dog than with retellings of Grimms' fairy tales. During this period, Paramount's *Superman* made his debut, Warner Brothers enjoyed success with its new *Bugs Bunny* shorts, and MGM featured *Tom and Jerry* among others.

Additionally, many of the released animated shorts focused on pro-American themes and wartime propaganda (e.g., *Out of the Frying Pan into the Firing Line*,

1942). As Smoodin notes, "the film bill constructed a space where much might be displayed, but only one thing, finally, was on view: a national consensus accepting hardship and responsibility in order to achieve an American-made peace." [156] These trends did not provide the typical settings, narratives, or scenarios for the generic buffoonery of the classic animated Halloween witch.

With that said, there were three notable witch-related shorts made during the era, including *The Sky Princess* (1942), *The Witch's Cat* (1948), and *Which is Witch* (1949). The first one is a George Pal stop-motion animated short produced and released before the onset of war, and it mimics, in its own unique way, the witches of the 1930s. The second is a Terry Toon's *Mighty Mouse* short that was released in 1948 after the war. It also includes a classic animated Halloween witch. Finally, the third short, *Which is Witch?* stars Looney Toons' famous rabbit Bugs Bunny as he encounters an African witch doctor.

A Closer Look: *The Sky Princess*

George Pal's *The Sky Princess*, released in 1942, contains an iconic witch figure who was styled very clearly after MGM's Wicked Witch of the West from its 1939 classic film. Since it was produced only a few short years after *The Wizard of Oz*, young viewers would have recognized the visual similarities. Like the Wicked Witch, Pal's character wears long dark clothing, flies on a broom, and cackles loudly. More strikingly, the Puppetoon witch has green-blue skin, which makes her the second witch character to have this distinguishing feature. However, unlike MGM's witch, Pal designed his Puppetoon to have straggly white hair similar to other 1930s animated figures and piercing red eyes.

Although *The Sky Princess* is a fairy tale and loosely based on Charles Perroult's classic fairy tale *Sleeping Beauty*, an element that is amplified by the use of the waltz from Tchaikovsky's ballet of the same name, the short is far more than pure children's entertainment. It was an exercise in a unique cinematic technology: stop-motion animation. It was part of Pal's Puppetoon series, which was distributed by Paramount between 1940 and 1947. Pal, who created dozens of these shorts using his hand-crafted puppets, is largely considered one of the pioneers of this type of animation. The Puppetoon series only ended after the costs to make a single film became prohibitive.

While *The Sky Princess* remains a minor film in the overall trajectory of Hollywood witch construction and was not even one of Pal's more well-known shorts, the characterization of his witch demonstrates how film language progressively builds on itself to produce cultural meaning. In this case, the witch has green skin and is the

---

156. Smoodin, *Animating Culture*, 75.

film's primary villain and a source of evil. Pal incorporated the use of these character details, which had developed and solidified in the 1930s and, in doing so, he helped maintain the construction of this type of witch in the minds of the viewers and propel the language into the next decade.

A Closer Look: *The Witch's Cat* and *Which is Witch?*

The two other character-driven shorts were released well after the end of World War II. *The Witch's Cat* stars Terry Toons' Mighty Mouse and was released in 1948. *Which is Witch?* stars Looney Toons' Bugs Bunny and was released in 1949. The two witches are different but indicative of the era's representation of what was considered fantasy magic and superstitious witchcraft.

Like any superhero story, Mighty Mouse cartoons relied on a clear good versus evil polarity. In this case, the hero's story is framed by the cartoon's comedic and fantasy setting. *The Witch's Cat* opens with jack-o'-lanterns singing a festive Halloween song on their way to a masquerade ball. The witch appears shortly after riding her broomstick against the backdrop of a full moon. As she flies through the air, she looks at the camera and says, "I am a wicked old witch, wicked old witch." She is the antagonist that the rodent superhero must vanquish.

The cartoon is Halloween-centric, and the witch's design follows suit. She is wearing dark clothing and a pointed hat. She has exaggerated facial features, stirs a cauldron, and owns a black cat. Unlike Pal's puppet, however, this animated character does not have green skin. She is simply a 1940s rendering of the characters found commonly in the 1920s and 1930s. As the antagonist, this witch is the classic animated comic buffoon.

In contrast, the 1949 *Looney Tunes* short *Which is Witch?* contains a character who was not found in past cartoons and is reminiscent of characters found in live-action adventure films. During this short, Bugs Bunny foils the plans of an African "witch doctor." The male figure is drawn with overexaggerated facial features and colorized with a clown-like design. Unlike other franchises, Warner Brothers' *Looney Tunes* based much of its content on lived experience rather than pure escapist fantasy. Many of its shorts are steeped in satire, commentary, and cultural mocking, for better or worse.

Which is Witch? relies heavily on visual stereotyping and an imperialist sensibility common to animation in the early part of the century. Even as some studios began to curb their racial stereotyping by the 1930s, "sensitivity took a back seat to the war effort," as noted by historian Karl F. Cohen.[157] The concepts used to construct the animated caricature of the African man are similar to those used to create the caricature of the white crone witch, as seen in *The Witch's Cat*. In both cases, unnatural and

---

157. Cohen, *Forbidden Animation*, 50.

exaggerated physical humanity creates a proscenium that allows for comedic pleasure through an othering process. Comedy disarms the character of any perceived ethical harm and excuses the viewer's voyeuristic enjoyment of witchcraft and other acts deemed immoral or otherwise problematic. This method of visually disarming something or someone through comedy is similar to what was done in the silent era with the clown witch costume. However, it is important to note that, in the case of the witch doctor, there are heavy racist implications in the design.

Wartime and the Witch Invader

The dominant witch films during the war era were live-action stories that focused on a woman's psyche and her function within society. Each of the three films produced during this time were set in small close-knit communities with hardened social structures and traditional gender roles. Women act as wives, mothers, and bridge players and are often jealous and emotional. Men are doctors, professors, politicians, and rational thinkers. Two of the films use small-town New England as their setting, including *I Married a Witch* (1942) and *The Woman Who Came Back* (1945). Similarly, the third film *Weird Woman* (1944) uses a small college town as the signifier defining acceptable and rational American society.

Together, the three films typify how a basic character narrative can move fluidly from one genre to another, including changes in witch construction. In all three, the witch is depicted as a stranger in town who invades a peaceful setting, disrupting would-be romance, the male protagonist's career, and other societal expectations. In addition, all three stories end with the standard assimilation narrative in order to put an end to the chaos caused by a woman's perceived irrationality and mischievous behavior. With that said, the three films are not the same genre-wise. *I Married a Witch* is a fantasy-based screwball comedy containing a fantasy vamp witch and the first full-fledged comedic male witch. *The Woman Who Came Back* is often classified as horror but operates more like a mystery. In this film, the witch is an accused woman. Finally, *Weird Woman*, also considered horror, works more like a whodunit, and the witch is constructed as a young wild woman due to her "pagan" religious beliefs.

Fantasy Meets Reality: *I Married a Witch*

René Clair's screwball comedy *I Married a Witch* is based on Thorne Smith's novel *The Passionate Witch* and stars Veronica Lake as Jennifer the witch and Frederic March as Wallace Wooly. The novel was written predominantly in the early 1930s. However, Smith died in 1934 before finishing the story; it was later completed by author Norman Matson and published in 1941. Paramount picked up the project immediately, releasing the film a year later in the summer of 1942. While the book and movie have similar elements, they are not related in terms of witch construction or overall theme. *The Passionate Witch* is a pulp-style novel written from Wooly's perspective. It contains lurid details, sensationalized ideas about witchcraft, and an open use of Christian rhetoric.

Jennifer, a young and mischievous witch, creates a love potion to toy with a man's heart in I Married a Witch *(1942), starring Veronica Lake.*
[Source: United Artists /Photofest. Copyright: © United Artists]

The film, on the other hand, is told from Jennifer's perspective. It was produced under the Production Code and therefore contains only masked expressions of sexuality and religiosity. *I Married a Witch* is a prototypical screwball comedy with quick dialogue, physical gags, and a romantic tug-of-war. In the book, Jennifer is the antagonist. In the film, she is the heroine. These differences affect the characterization of the witch and her movement within the story.

Sexuality and Religion in *The Passionate Witch*

The Passionate Witch contained many details that were outside the limits of what Hollywood censors would have allowed. As noted earlier, the novel's depiction of Jennifer is far more lurid than what was found in the movie. For example, Smith describes Jennifer as "lustrous," "a wench," "evil," and "monstrous." She leads the hero to drink and to break his vow to never marry or love another woman after his first wife's death. Smith's witch is unethical and has no remorse. She is the aggressive, evil seductress—a detail emphasized by artist Hebert Roese's accompanying book illustrations.

In addition to the novel's over-sexualized presentation of the witch, Smith also included strong religious language and suggestions of occult practice, both of which serve to draw moral lines between the hero and the magical temptress. For example, Wooly calls Jennifer as "pagan as ever the golden calf had been." [158] The comment not only demonstrates Wooly's own devout religious belief, but also presents the witch as an antithesis to that moral system.

Within this specific religious framework, Jennifer is the false idol. Halfway through the novel, Wooly catches her performing an animal sacrifice. Smith writes,

> Jennifer sliced the rooster's throat expertly, with a tight-lipped smile, and the blood pumped out, splashed her hands, her clothing. She was clumsily filling a cup with blood. Now she dropped the rooster. She was talking in a language he had never heard. [159]

Later, Jennifer is heard speaking backward, and she is unable to say the Lord's Prayer. These direct references to theology and belief serve to differentiate the good characters from the bad through a Christian lens. The hero as a man of faith is good; the witch as a follower of Satan is bad.

Sexuality and Religion in *I Married a Witch*

Little of the book's overt sexuality or religious composition is present in the film adaptation. While 1937 saw the first truly evil cinematic witch (i.e., Disney's the Wicked Queen), Hollywood had not yet fully realized the highly sexualized, satanic-based character as found in Smith's novel, and it would not be until Roger Corman's film *The Undead* (1957) that such a witch would be rendered in mainstream American movies. In *I Married a Witch*, Jennifer is not defined as an evil seductress who dabbles in the Devil's work; rather she is the precocious unwed young woman playing

---

158. Thorne Smith, *The Passionate Witch* (New York: Sun Dial Press, 1942), 46.
159. Smith, *The Passionate Witch*, 86.

around with things she doesn't completely understand. In the opening scene, Jennifer is described as "young, and beautifully fair. Fairer than all women that ever were." As such, she begins the film defined similarly to the fairy tale heroine awaiting her prince. This construction is vastly different from the novel, but it worked for both the film censors and the screwball genre that sought to merge fantasy with reality to advance its comedy.

With that said, the film harbors an irony in its construction, making it the perfect example of how the Production Code Administration's censorship affected witch-themed movies in general. The Code's religious bias, which strictly forbids the presentation of "evil as alluring," is one of the factors that forced Paramount filmmakers to de-sensationalize and limit sexual expression and its associations with evil in the adaptation.[160] As a result, the need for heavy religious dialogue to counter that point or to distinguish good from evil became superfluous. That is not to say that the film is completely without religious expression and, in fact, that is actually where the irony lays. The film's existing religious piety can be found in the production's tempering and avoidance of sexual expression and other acts deemed sinful. In other words, religious expression is what curbed religious expression.

In January 1942, the PCA sent a message to Paramount executive Luigi Luraschi telling him that the film's script was "flatly in violation" of the code. The offending elements included, "suggestions of nudity," "sex suggestiveness in Jennifer's attitude in forcing herself upon Wally," and an "overemphasis on liquor and drinking."[161] In February, the PCA sent another letter informing Luraschi that improvements had been made. However, the PCA continued on to insist that the Paramount writers remove any "play upon nudity," references to gambling, and "undue exposure" of the female body.[162] Due to these conflicts, the start of shooting was delayed. The production crew finally received the green light April 17.

It is important to note that, just as with past films, witchcraft itself was not an issue for the PCA. This point is well-illustrated in an interoffice memo sent by Paramount executive Alfred Levitt. He described the *I Married a Witch* script as "imaginative," "playing upon the wife's lack of mortal experience for comedy." He called Jennifer "ingenious" and "aggressive," rather than "evil" and "lustrous," as in the novel. Levitt

---

160. Doherty, *Hollywood's Censor*, 352.

161. Joseph Breen to Luigi Luraschi, January 14, 1942; source: *I Married a Witch* Production Files, MPAA PCA records, Margaret Herrick Library, Academy of Motion Picture Arts and Sciences, Beverly Hills, California.

162. Joseph Breen to Luigi Luraschi, February 11, 1942; source: *I Married a Witch* Production Files, MPAA PCA records, Margaret Herrick Library, Academy of Motion Picture Arts and Sciences, Beverly Hills, California.

likened the film to Shakespeare's comedy *A Midsummer Night's Dream* "for its back-firing love philtre."[163] Unlike in the original novel but common to Hollywood films, witchcraft is viewed as superstition and fantasy. As such, the theme only serves as a catalyst, in this case, for the zany humor secured within the screwball comedy, which is a genre known for highlighting eccentric behaviors and, as Thompson and Bordwell write, "[ignoring] contemporary social problems."[164]

Despite any adjustments made to the film in the wake of PCA objections, sexual expression and its connection to witchcraft were not entirely lost. This is evident in the film's not-so-subtle promotional material. In one of the studio's photos, actress Veronica Lake, who was by this point a 1940s sex symbol, is wearing black lingerie and a pointy black witch hat. In some of the photographs, Lake is shadowed by a silhouette that looks eerily like the Wicked Witch of the West—a visual cue that was not lost on 1942 audiences.

The same image is replicated in drawings on the film's theater posters, which include the phrase "No man can resist her." Through these clever marketing choices, filmmakers formed a definitive visual connection between the witch as an iconic antagonist and the witch as seductress. However, it is important to note that Jennifer, although mischievous at times, is never overtly evil in the film itself.

Fantasy Vamp to Wild Woman

Through the studio's promotional work alone, Jennifer can be defined as the first live-action fantasy vamp witch and the next step in development after Disney's Wicked Queen. They both derive power from their physical being and play with the innocent for their own gain. At the beginning of the film, Jennifer says to her father, "'Twould be nice to have lips; lips to whisper lies; lips to kiss a man and make him suffer." Jennifer understands that sexuality is power, and she uses her body to that end. Despite the filmmakers' attempt to downplay this point for censorship and genre reasons, the depth of her true character, in terms of sexuality at the very least, remain hidden just below the surface and sometimes even not.

As with past witch films, *I Married A Witch* offers the female viewer an opportunity for a subversive reading through the witch's brief show of freedom. Jennifer spends a fair amount of screen time flitting about, displaying ownership of her body and her choices. Through that play, the viewer can find a space to identify with her

---

163. Alfred Levitt, Interoffice Communication, January 19, 1942, page 19; source: *I Married a Witch* Memoranda, Paramount Pictures Scripts, Margaret Herrick Library, Academy of Motion Picture Arts and Sciences, Beverly Hills, California.

164. Thompson and Bordwell, *Film History,* 231.

and bask in her freedom. However, Jennifer only enjoys her agency when the narrative indulges in the fantastic. By the final scene, Jennifer's antics are fully contained; fantasy gives way to reality, and the free woman is assimilated into traditional society. Jennifer moves from father to husband, gives up her magic, and by doing so, gains social respectability. When the credits run, she is no longer a witch.

Due to this assimilation narrative, Jennifer is not the powerful, antagonistic fantasy vamp figure seen in *Snow White and the Seven Dwarfs* (1937), the original novel, or in post-Code comedies or horror films (e.g., *Love at Stake*, 1987; *Witchcraft II: The Temptress*, 1989). The live-action screwball narrative forced the fantasy vamp witch character into the position of the untamed young wild woman often found within that genre (e.g., *Bringing Up Baby*, 1938 or *The Philadelphia Story*, 1940). By the end of the movie, Wooly has been charmed by Jennifer's crazy behavior, resulting in the couple falling in love and getting married. In the final shot, Jennifer is happily sitting in a wingback chair knitting; her hair is tied up in a neat bun. The shot is evenly lit and framed predominantly in comfortable medium shots. This visual is a stark contrast from her earlier appearances when her hair is flowing free and her clothes are unkempt and purposefully inappropriate for the setting. It is even more of a contrast to the opening flashback scenes that are dark, dense, and crowded.

The mixing of fantasy and reality is the primary drive for *I Married a Witch* and its comedy. It wonders: "What if witches really did exist?" and takes off from that point. We know, as viewers, that witches don't exist and that the entire film is just a big joke. This tension is similar thematically to that found in witch trial films: *superstition versus reason*. The conclusion is always the same: the witch must be assimilated. Therefore, it is through the juxtaposition of fantasy and reality that Jennifer walks a line between vamp witch and wild woman. She begins as a full-fledged fantasy vamp, who is then forced through a typical wild woman narrative and made to choose between fantasy or reality. Allegorically speaking, that choice is magic over marriage, agency over subservience, individualism over conformity. Jennifer chooses reality and is assimilated into traditional social models. This narrative structure and witch construction are seen again in later productions such as *Bell, Book and Candle* (1958) and *Bewitched* (1964–1972).

Salem and the Witch Invader

I Married a Witch is not a historical drama or trial film; however, it consciously uses the New England small town setting and Salem's cultural mythos to prime the audience for a movie containing a witch. In this way, Salem and New England become signifiers, rather than concrete locations. Not only is New England a cue for a story involving witches, but it is also used as an allegorical symbol of Americana, the nation's roots, and American society—an important detail for films produced during the wartime years.

Prior to 1942, films based loosely on the historic American witch trials all begin with the narrative chaos setting at zero, meaning the story introduces us to the film's universe in its normative state. The skies are bright, and the characters move about the space with typical, daily concerns. These films then proceed to tell the history, whether accurately or not, of a moral panic involving witchcraft. In those retellings, some action, idea, or inanimate object within the town becomes a catalyst for the tensions that ultimately lead to the trials (e.g., children's games, a book on witchcraft, African stories, flirtations, herbal knowledge, a rejection of sexual advances, frilly bonnet). In *I Married a Witch*, the disruption to the town's normative state is not caused by an inanimate object or internal problem, but rather by a person who comes from somewhere else. In this case, the witch is an alien invader.

The Proper Setup for a Witch Film

I Married a Witch begins with the presentation of a pseudo-history based on the Salem story. "Long ago, when people still believed in witches…" Then the film cuts to a bonfire on a hill. A Puritan leader explains that we are witnessing a witch burning and an exorcism of evil, one of the only religious references in the entire film. He then announces an intermission before the burning of the second witch. The camera tracks back through a large crowd of onlookers who treat the burning like a theater performance complete with a food vendor selling "pop maize." The shots are dark and congested. This is chaos at its peak, but as a comedy, the scenes are couched in humor and skepticism. There is no foreboding or fear as there might be in a horror film.

After that opening, the New England setting and Salem mythos become functionally irrelevant to the story itself. In fact, the entire historical premise found in the movie plays no part in Smith's original novel. Therefore, the filmmaker's inclusion of Salem as a signifier was a conscious artistic choice. However, it is also clear that the studio's interest in representing any historical accuracy was limited. During production, Paramount executive Luigi Luraschi sent a letter to director René Clair and producer Preston Sturges telling them to ensure that the film establishes hangings, not burnings, as the "method of punishing witches in New England." He notes that

"New England is sensitive about this point" and that it had come up during the 1937 production of *Maid of Salem*.[165] However, Luraschi then adds:

> This point was handled satisfactorily in the script of February 7th where you stated the fate of witches was—"First you hang them— Then you burn them—Then you plant an oak tree over their ashes." This phony formula technically will placate the New Englanders since we mention the hanging.[166]

Luraschi's interest in historical accuracy only went as far as "placating" his New England viewers. However, the script was never revised, and the film opens on a scene depicting a burning with no mention of hangings.

The Foreign Invader

After the film establishes the witchcraft theme through Salem's mythos, the New England setting becomes a stand-in for small-town America. As such, it is the perfect location for a social disruption caused by a foreign or invading element. It is important to note that, while *Maid of Salem*'s Tituba is framed by her otherness, she is still a working member of Puritan society. Although she is one of the catalysts for the trials, she is not an invader. Moreover, it is her stories that act as the precipitous of chaos, not her.

Jennifer and her father, however, are both invaders to the film's normative universe. Not only are they unknown to the townspeople, but they are also nonhuman. Part of the film's comedy stems from their unfamiliarity with mortal life, as well as their lack of concern for social mores, including proper dress and alcohol consumption. Jennifer, specifically, is posited as more of a threat than her father, because she upends traditional gender roles. She seeks to disrupt normalcy and the established order as defined by the hero's political career and his romantic intentions. The fantasy vamp witch and her drunk father, in this case, are the foreign invaders, representing wild womanhood, unfettered feminine sexual expression, male impotence, and lawlessness. The New England town is the antithesis, representing the patriarchy, defined order, and tradition. In the end, the town goes back to its normal state as the witch

---

165. Luigi Luraschi to Preston Sturges and René Clair, May 4, 1942; source: *I Married a Witch* Production 1941–1942, Paramount Pictures Production Records, Margaret Herrick Library, Academy of Motion Picture Arts and Sciences, Beverly Hills, California.

166. Luraschi to Sturges and Clair, May 4, 1942.

intruder is schooled in the ways of proper behavior and, as a result, actively chooses to reject her alien existence, as represented by fantasy, immortality, and witchcraft.

More Witch Invasions

During the war years, *I Married a Witch* was not the only film to capitalize on a narrative in which a small peaceful town is invaded by a witch. In 1944, Universal Pictures released *Weird Woman*, one of its low-budget *Inner Sanctum* mysteries starring Lon Chaney, Jr. and based loosely on Fritz Lieber Jr.'s 1943 novel *Conjure Wife*. *Weird Woman* is the first in a string of cinematic adaptations of Leiber's novel, which include the British film *Burn, Witch, Burn* (1962) and the American comedy *Witches' Brew* (1980).

Anne Gwynne stars as Paula, a young wife struggling with
fitting in to American society after growing up in the South Seas.
[Source: Universal Pictures /Photofest. Copyright: © Universal Pictures]

Weird Woman tells the story of sociology professor Norman Reed who marries Paula, an American girl he met while studying in the South Seas. While both Leiber's original novel and the film pit superstition against the rational, the book posits witchcraft as an American reality, delving deeply into the world of evil magic. However, as would be expected, the theme shifts completely in the cinematic adaption. The film's writers removed the reality of American-based witchcraft by constructing it as an element of an indigenous spiritual practice found in the South Seas. Paula, who grew up on those islands, is a follower of the native religion, which includes magical work, healings, a high priestess, and as noted in the film, "weird pagan" rituals. However, once back in the United States, her nontraditional beliefs are at odds with proper academic society, and she is labeled a witch. Paula is a classic wild woman who must eventually choose between her upbringing and American society.

A year later, in 1945, Republic Pictures released the low-budget film *The Woman Who Came Back* directed by Walter Colmes. It tells the story of Lorna Webster's return to her childhood home in a small New England town where eighteen women were once burned for witchcraft. Lorna eventually reveals that she had been avoiding the town due to her own ancestors' involvement in those burnings three hundred years ago. During the film, her mental anguish builds, consuming her, and convincing her that she is indeed a witch herself. By the end, the town is also convinced. Lorna becomes the classic accused woman, even in her own mind. As such, she must ultimately be saved and proven innocent by a rational hero.

In these two films, the narratives open with a clear presentation that witchcraft is considered superstition, replicating Hollywood's well-established ideology regarding the practice. *The Woman Who Came Back* begins with a newsreel-style voice-over explaining in detail how the town once experienced the "Black Terror," or "the branding of innocent people as witches with the penalty of death by burning at the stake." *Weird Woman* begins with an *Inner Sanctum* opening, and moves to a shot of the hero, Norman Reed, writing at his desk. In voice-over, he thinks: "Man's struggle upward from his dark past is the struggle of reason against superstition." Norman continues this line of commentary throughout the film.

Like Jennifer in *I Married a Witch*, both Lorna and Paula enter a quiet town in a distinctly disruptive manner. Jennifer is nearly naked. Lorna is emotionally troubled and anxiety-ridden, being brought into the community after nearly drowning in a bus crash. *Weird Woman*'s Paula clings to her new husband, intimidated by the new world. She clutches her prized magical medallion and performs rituals in graveyards at night. Allegorically speaking, these three witches represent the irrational feminine. Not only must a rational man save the small town from her as the witch invader, but he must also save the witch from herself. Wooley marries Jennifer after she gives up her fantasy magic and immortality, and she becomes real. Similarly, Lorna is saved by both the preacher, who is one masculine voice of reason, and the doctor, who loves her and works to prove that she is not a witch.

In *Weird Woman*, Paula is rescued from the "pagan rituals of the islands" and converted to an American ideology by her new husband. Early in the film Norman states that Paula had "lived too long with the high priestess" and that she was "enslaved by superstition." At the end of the film, Norman says, "You know, all of the magic that you or anyone else needs, is a generous heart and a steady mind. Paula, will you try and believe that?" Paula answers yes; they kiss and the credits role. The invasion is over, the witch is vanquished, and America is saved.

The Irrational Feminine

In all three films, the witch as heroine is defined by confusion, superstition, ineptitude, odd behavior, and love, which is contrasted to the man-hero, who is defined as rational, authoritative, and knowledgeable. The heroine's irrationality not only destabilizes her surrogate community but also forces the hero to question his own direction, career, and beliefs. He must maintain his own rational balance, which he is ultimately able to do. The comparison between the hero and the heroine creates a definite gender-based valuation that posits male rationality as good and female irrationality as bad, or at least problematic. This is not new. The juxtaposition is just another iteration of the reason versus superstition debate. The dichotomy derives, as in the past, from a gender-based, contrived mythology that posits women as emotional and wild and men as rational and structured. With that setup, the hero can then save the town from the heroine-witch and the woman from herself.

Just as the irrational woman theme is atypical for the fantasy vamp witch, as noted earlier, it is also new for the accused woman construction. In the older trial film *Maid of Salem*, for example, the accused woman, Barbara, is never irrational, keeping her calm even well into her courtroom speech. The chaos is found only in the townspeople. Barbara is neither an invader nor an example of psychological instability. She is a victim. However, in *The Woman Who Came Back*, Lorna is presented as unstable from the opening sequence, during which she enters the town both visually and mentally a mess after a bus crash and a frightening encounter with an old lady.

Furthermore, the witch is not the only irrational woman in the films. Due to the hero's attraction to her, the witch develops enemies in other prominent female characters. These townswomen are either former lovers (e.g., *Weird Woman*), nosey society ladies (e.g., *Weird Woman*), family members (e.g., *The Woman Who Came Back*), or crushes (e.g., *Weird Woman*, *I Married a Witch*). While they operate as minor antagonists, these secondary female characters exhibit, like the heroine, emotionally driven and erratic behaviors. This allows for a polarizing tension that places the rational hero at the center. He intervenes to alleviate that tension, ending a virtual whirlwind of feminine psychological instability.

It is important to note that all three of these films were made during a time when women were being called into action to serve the war effort by maintaining the American way on the home front. Irrationality, fantasy, and superstition were not affordable luxuries at the time; society needed women to buckle down, so to speak, and focus on preserving the safety of the nation by doing what was needed to support the troops. As with many films produced during this time, these three witch films work primarily to create "a sense of ideological wholeness … to smooth over the potential disturbance of difference," as Smoodin said about animation.[167]

The witches, who came from elsewhere, must be assimilated into society by means of accepting local standards and traditions. Their irrationality and the irrationality they provoke in other women must be calmed and contained. *Weird Woman*'s hero, Norman, says, "Paula, will you try and believe that?" She responds, "Yes, Norman." All three witches give up their craft, their beliefs, their fears, their irrationality, and their alleged superstitious ways to become functional members of America's small-town society, and the disturbances are thereby smoothed over.

A Note on Othering

The three live-action witches found between 1942–1945 were all invaders and, due to the perceived difference, were treated as "others" for the purpose of fulfilling the narrative. The witches are different from the townspeople due to their mental condition, their beliefs, or in the case of *I Married a Witch*, their nonhuman form. However, none of these witches are "othered" as defined generally by this study; they are not characterized by an intrinsic otherness. They are othered by narrative alone. This is an important point. All three of these women are racially white and defined as American. While they are strangers to the film's established small-town universe, they are not strangers to the overarching cultural understanding of "us," as put forth by classic Hollywood ideology. Therefore, they can and must be assimilated.

This type of "othering" is distinctly different from the "othering" found in, for example, *Maid of Salem*'s Tituba. Plot-wise, Tituba is fully accepted in the film's universe, and she is known to its people. However, she is not white and not defined as being American; this racial and ethnic difference is intrinsic to her beingness. Therefore, Tituba is othered on a character level, not a narrative level and, consequently, she can never be assimilated. Her otherness is permanent, as discussed more fully in chapter four. This type of "othering," which is based on race, ethnicity, or nationality,

---

167. Smoodin, *Animating Culture*, 71.

was common during Hollywood's golden era. Another example can be found in the 1949 Bugs Bunny cartoon mentioned earlier. The African witch doctor is drawn with an unnatural and exaggerated physicality that derives from an imperial understanding of African culture. In that case, the othering plays for comedy.

A similar character-based othering is found at the heart of *Weird Woman*. Paula is raised within a South Seas island culture, which is visually depicted in flashback at the beginning of the film. While hiking in the jungle, hero Normal Reed comes upon a group of islanders engaged in religious ritual. Men are drumming and women are dancing. During this scene, the women are scantily clad with short shirts and bare midriffs. This is unusual costuming for the era. While the PCA would not permit this level of nudity for most female characters, the code did permit such dress when a film depicted "native life." [168] In 1939, the PCA made a resolution emphasizing this point. If the costuming was exclusive to the native scenes and not otherwise "objectionable," then the rules on nudity or "undue exposure" could be relaxed. [169]

Although not officially written into the censorship code, the same idea applies to the film's presentation of witchcraft. Paula is a wild woman and, as such, her magic must be sourced. In this case, the source is her island-based upbringing and religious beliefs. Just as the code deemed "native" costumes only appropriate when depicting cultures outside of traditional American society, witchcraft was also only considered plausible in that same context. The rules of acceptability change outside of the boundaries of what is defined as American. The island dance costumes and the practice of witchcraft are allowable within the representation of another culture, one that is typically posited as being backwards.

Weird Woman repeatedly makes that point. In a confrontation scene, Norman tells Paula that she is "turning the clock back to the Dark Ages." She responds, "some things don't belong to any special age." He later tells her that she lived in "the jungle" way too long. Just as with all wild women, the movie ends with her accepting his ideology and embracing American life. While the island scene is short, the othering of that land and its people is what essentially sources Paula's magic and propels the film forward, ending with the rejection of foreign culture as inferior to the American way. The narrative-based othering of Paula is relational and contingent on assimilation, while the othering of the South Seas indigenous people and their culture is intrinsic to their beingness and is permanent.

---

168. Doherty, *Hollywood's Censor*, 356.
169. Doherty, *Hollywood's Censor*, 356.

The Male Clown Witch and Family Relations

Along with all its other unique depictions of witchcraft, *I Married a Witch* also contains the first strong male witch character. As noted in the introduction, magical men exist in many forms throughout Hollywood's history. However, not all magical male figures are considered witches. Those included in this study must be defined in some way as a witch through the film's own structure. Jennifer's father, Daniel, who is introduced in the opening witch trial sequence, is burned for the practice of witchcraft. While he is also called a sorcerer, he is a witch by the film's own narrative standards.

Daniel takes on the construction of comedic male clown witch in his actions but not in his appearance. He dresses in nondescript era-appropriate clothing. The comedy is resident in his slapstick behavior as well as the fact that he is male. Witchcraft itself was still considered silly and unreal. To have a man be a witch would be considered even more ludicrous. Therefore, the male witch, even without any elaborate attire, is a natural comedic character. Daniel is a buffoon who can't control his daughter and is more interested in alcohol consumption. He is a symbol of male impotence in that sense and pure comic relief to the film's romantic tension between the two main characters.

At the same time, Daniel also plays an important role in defining the heroine and helping her through her character arc. In the original novel, there was no father figure. The temptress was free and completely on her own. Daniel's presence as the father de-sensationalizes the witch's wild femininity by creating a traditional family structure that posits the witch as a spoiled brat needing a husband rather than as a mature, sexualized woman serving a demonic monster. Jennifer's move from witch to woman is paralleled by a move from an impotent father who could not control her to a strong husband who can. While Daniel as a male witch also feeds the fantasy aspect of the film, he ultimately is woven into the structure of traditional reality, supporting Jennifer's movement out of fantasy into reality.

Toward a Horror Film Witch

At this point, it is important to stop and recognize that by 1940 an evolution was in process for the Hollywood witch. She was slowly becoming a monster unto herself and moving closer to becoming a regular feature of the horror film. *The Wizard of Oz* was the first film to suggest a biologically based inhumanity for the witch with the use of green skin, which likened her to the classic horror monster Frankenstein. Similarly, Disney's Wicked Queen, although depicted as a human woman, is visually likened to another popular horror monster, the vampire. While neither film would ever be classified as horror, they contain the first two witch characters that inspired true fear in the same way such a monster might.

Small Evolutionary Shifts

In 1942, Paramount's *I Married a Witch* takes the concept a step further in that Jennifer is depicted as being inhuman and immortal; she exists as another species that can reproduce and have families. However, she is not defined through a frightening physicality like the Wicked Witch. On the contrary, it is her extreme allure that is considered transgressive. As the marketing poster claimed, "No man can resist her." Jennifer's sexuality is what is considered dangerous, and that construct will eventually find its way into the monster-witch form. However, not at this time.

In 1944 and 1945, *Weird Woman* and *The Woman Who Came Back* become the first two witchcraft-based feature films classified as horror, although neither one is true horror and neither of these two characters are monsters. Like Jennifer, it is their transgressive behavior that becomes the narrative's problem, not a fear-invoking monstrosity. While none of the films mentioned contain a true horror witch, they all contain small shifts in construction that slowly lead to the birth of something far more frightening.

Included in that evolutionary process was an experimental MGM horror short called *Third Dimensional Murder* (1941), also known as *Murder in 3-D*. Beginning with a crime drama voice-over, the short introduces an investigator who is researching a murder at the Old Smith Mansion. Once in the haunted home, he is attacked by several classic horror characters, including Frankenstein, skeletons, a "headhunter," a suit of armor, and a Halloween-style witch. The purpose of the film is simply to use a familiar movie setting and characters to showcase the new 3D technology. The viewer is placed in the position of the investigator as monsters chase or claw for him, and various items are thrown about the interior space. The story is irrelevant, and the only purpose in making the film at all was to show off technology.

However, this minor MGM film is important in this study because it is the first Hollywood film to place a fantasy Halloween witch fully within a horror monster narrative. In 1916, the proto-horror series *The Mysteries of Myra* did contain a witch in its thirteenth episode. However, the narrative was largely defined by fantasy, and the witch operated as a fantasy crone not a horror monster.[170] Although *Third Dimensional Murder's* witch only appears briefly, she is visually styled after the Wicked Witch of the West. This detail is not surprising considering the short was an MGM production.

Filmmakers lifted the frightening fantasy witch out of the earlier movie and placed her in a space typically inhabited by classic horror monsters. A 1941 viewer,

---

170. Stedman, *The Mysteries of Myra*, 10.

who had previously been terrified by the Wicked Witch's hands clutching for Dorothy, might be equally as unnerved by the suggestion of her presence in the Old Smith Mansion. *Third Dimensional Murder* may not be a landmark film in its own right, but it demonstrates another step pushing the fantasy witch character into the realm of the monstrous-feminine.[171]

Monstrous-Feminine and the Abject

When considering the horrific elements found in witch construction, it is important to note the difference between the witch as a model of transgressive or nontraditional womanhood and the monstrous-feminine, as defined by this study. The transgressive witch, as already seen in many films, is defined by her aberrant behavior; she knows too much, lives in solitude, practices herbalism, flirts with men, or does not follow society's rules in some way. Transgressive femininity is common to witch constructions across genres. The monstrous-feminine, by contrast, is a concrete and symbolic demonstration of this concept, and it finds its home predominantly in the horror film or similar. In other words, a witch constructed as the monstrous-feminine breaks boundaries far beyond just behavioral expectations, and this is often reflected in her visual appearance. This extreme representation forces her to enter the realm of what theorist Julia Kristeva calls *the abject*.

In her seminal work, *Powers of Horror*, Kristeva defines the term as that which "disturbs identity, system, order. What does not respect borders, positions, rules. The in-between, the ambiguous, the composite."[172] While that definition does apply to transgressive behavior, the abject has permanence that extends beyond action. The Wicked Witch, for example, looks human, but she has green skin, which is unsettling. She is not different enough from us to become an object clearly separate from who we are. She is still human, but she has green skin. As such, this visual detail causes a disintegration of human identity and an ambiguity in the character's construction. Is she a monster or is she human? This is the place of the uncomfortable unknown and the place of horror. Unlike behavioral transgressions, it cannot be undone.

It is interesting to note that, while American feature horror films had yet to incorporate a monstrous witch, they had already included characters that depicted the monstrous-feminine in other ways. Films like *Jungle Woman* (1944), *The Cat Creeps* (1946), *Captive Wild Woman* (1943), *Cat People* (1942), and *The Black Cat* (1941) all negotiate a woman's sexuality and power as allegorically defined through her appearance as an animal, particularly a cat. The women are not witches; however, they

---

171. Creed, *The Monstrous-Feminine,* 3

172. Julia Kristeva, *Powers of Horror: An Essay on Abjection*, tr. Leon S. Roudiez (New York: Columbia University Press, 1982), 13.

are close cousins. By breaking down the structure of the body and what it means to be human, these characters enter the realm of the abject and, thereby, create a monstrous form of femininity—one that not only ignores the established rules of behavior, but also the natural or biological systemic order. Is she a cat or is she human?

The horror film allows for the blurring of these lines in the extreme and also seeks to break down the cinematic proscenium that provides a comfortable distance between the viewer and the film text. As Kristeva observes, horror "does not respect borders, positions, rules."[173] The genre attempts to shift that paradigm, disrupting the systemic order of genre safety, and merge the film's universe, even if only for an emotional moment, with the viewer's reality. This is what causes the visceral reaction of fear, the jump moment, and the scream.

The Wicked Witch, of course, was created within a fantasy narrative, and therefore, she is not truly a horror witch. No borders were broken, and the viewer knows that the film is not real. The fantasy framework maintains Kristeva's systemic order. This is also true of comedy as seen in *I Married A Witch*. The boundaries created by genre and censorship are partly what kept the witch out of the horror realm and out of abjection for so long. Her construction remained defined only by transgressive behavior and not a monstrous femininity. However, that begins to shift slowly through the 1940s and into the next decade.

Macbeth and the Old Religion

After the war was over, the interest in films with invading witches ended and American society was working to reestablish itself in a new peacetime. It was during this post-war calm that Herbert Yates of Republic Pictures gave famed actor Orson Welles the opportunity to bring his unique vision of Shakespeare's *Macbeth*, and consequently its witches, to the silver screen.

After decades of staging the tragedy in the theatrical world, Welles was eager to produce the play as a film. His cinematic adaptation was finally released in 1948 and was as untraditional in production as any of his previous theatrical versions, such as his Voodoo *Macbeth* staged in 1936. In *The Magic World of Orson Welles*, biographer James Naremore wrote, "Every time Welles adapted *Macbeth*, his basic strategy was much the same: he gave it a primitive, exotic setting and tried to eradicate its Renaissance manners."[174] The 1948 film is no exception. It is based largely on Welles's Utah

---

173. Kristeva, *Power of Horrors*, 13.

174. James Naremore, *The Magic World of Orson Welles*, 2nd ed. (Dallas, TX: Southern Methodist University Press, 1989), 137.

theatrical staging and, as Naremore described it, the production was a "courageous experiment." [175]

Welles Edits Shakespeare

As noted in chapter one, Shakespeare's original play contains arguably three of the most famous literary crone witches in Western history. The play was written during the Jacobean era and the notorious European witch hunts. While historians believe that the witches were largely intended as sensational reflections of their contemporary society, their symbolic legacy has been imprinted on Western culture in such a way to make them the three most influential witch characters in modern history.

Despite the weird sisters' prominence, the changes that Welles made to his experimental cinematic adaptation significantly affected the presentation of Shakespeare's infamous magical trio. The first notable deviation directly involves their famous lines. In the original play, act 1, scene 1, begins with a witch saying, "When shall we three meet again / In thunder, lightning, or in rain?" [176] In Welles' version, the first line in the opening scene begins with the delivery of the famous phrase: "Double, double, toil and trouble / Fire burn and cauldron bubble," which was lifted from act 4, scene 1. The trio then stands over their cauldron while uttering portions of other various speeches originating from both act 1 and act 4. The scene finally ends with the famous declaration: "Something wicked this way comes."

Using these familiar lines at the beginning had two primary effects. First, Welles eliminated the appearance of the witches in act 4. By moving the text, he salvaged the well-known lines. This leads to the second effect. Using those phrases right at the beginning of the film grabbed the attention of the 1940s viewer through a general and collective understanding of the play and the famous sisters as witches. By doing this, the film could potentially draw in a larger audience base, making Shakespeare more palpable.

However, the script changes were not the only deviations Welles made in the depiction of the trio; he imagined them as symbols of mystic femininity and as priestesses of an old nature-based religion. Using both creative visual cues and well-established witch iconography, he attempted to juxtapose the rational world of men with the mystical world of women through the presence of the witches. Within the first few minutes, the film tosses out several well-established cultural symbols associated with witchcraft, such as boiling cauldrons, frogs, newts, bats, snakes, and the word "wicked." These iconic images are rooted in Shakespeare's original work and in Western culture.

---

175. Naremore, *The Magic World of Orson Welles*, 137.

176. Shakespeare, *Macbeth* (New York: Penguin Books, 1984), 25.

Visually speaking, the trio does not deviate from expectations. The witches recall not only past film and theatrical productions (e.g., *Macbeth*, 1916) but also many of the classic paintings that were inspired by the original play. For example, in Henry Fuseli's *Macbeth, Banquo and the Witches* (1793–1794), the weird sisters are dressed in hooded cloaks from which only crone-like facial features and long fingers can be seen. Crouched on a dark rock before Macbeth and Banquo, Fuseli's three witches appear, as museum curator Deanna Petherbridge described, "misty" and "ghostly." [177]

In the opening scene of Welles's film, the trio is similarly perched on a dark rock against the misty night sky. They wear dark cloaks that obscure their facial features and only expose their gangly hands and hair. Like the painting, the film's lighting gives the witches a ghostly or mystical look. Near the end of this scene, as the witches run away from Macbeth, they stop for a moment and turn toward the camera. A single light casts a glow down on their bodies causing, just for that one single long shot, their hair to be almost luminescent. Then the trio disappears into the fog.

Religion in Welles's *Macbeth*

After that first scene, the witches no longer appear in physical form. They become a disembodied presence, which suggests that they exist solely as part of Macbeth's psyche, as mystical fates, or as spiritual guides. This nuance in his construction lends itself to Welles's own claim that his witches were designed to be Druidic priestesses. In an interview with Peter Bogdanovich in 1969, Welles says that the film's main point was "the struggle between the old and new religions." He explains, "That's the whole device of the picture … [It] is based on this struggle between, not between good and evil, but between two religious systems. One underground and one overground." [178] The witches' mystical presence defines them as part of "the underground [world of] Druidical people," which is then juxtaposed to that of the new Christian order.

Despite Welles's testimony, the reading of the witches as Druids or as priestesses of an ancient Scottish paganism was not clearly depicted, either thematically or visually. In the 1969 interview, he laments that reviewers had missed this point. Although the nuance may have been lost in production, what is clear is that the witches are the antithesis to the male-based, Christian social structure. This dynamic is presented in the first few minutes of the film when the witches confront Macbeth. The camera cuts to a Celtic cross on a long, thin pole. Then, it pans down to Angus, who is hold-

---

177. Deanna Petherbridge, *Witches & Wicked Bodies* (Edinburgh: National Galleries of Scotland in association with the British Museum, 2013), 83.

178. Peter Bogdanovich, *Interviews with Orson Welles*, Internet Archive, 1969–1972, 27:12, https://archive.org/details/InterviewsWithOrsonWelles.

ing the religious staff. Next, the camera cuts to a long shot of the witches standing on the rocky cliff. When Angus arrives, they turn and scurry away with their black cloaks flowing behind them. Macbeth tries to follow, but he can't. Through this series of shots, it appears that Christianity has forced what Welles called the "old religions" to retreat into the mists. The scene contains an almost Arthurian ambiance.

Christianity is associated with the male world defined by well-lit daytime scenes and a focus on prayer. These scenes mostly take place within the walls of a man-made castle that is populated by mostly men. The antithesis to that are the dark scenes, which are dominated by rocks, clouds, trees, and the presence of women. This is also the space where the violence of mutiny occurs. The wild, untamed, natural world, which Welles associates with the old religion, is gendered as female. The lit, structured, law-abiding, pious world is gendered male.

Because the "old ways" were not as clearly defined as Welles might have thought, the weird sisters are more functionally symbolic of the wild and the untamed, as is typical of any crone witch. Much of that construction comes directly out of the original play. Shakespearean scholar Janet Adelman writes in "Born of Woman: Fantasies of Maternal Power in *Macbeth*":

> Largely through Macbeth's relationship to [the witches], the play be-
> comes … a representation of primitive fears about male identity and
> autonomy itself, about those looming female presences who threaten
> to control one's actions and one's mind, to constitute one's very self,
> even at a distance.[179]

The envisioning of the witch as the manifestation of transgressive femininity and the interloper of the proper or accepted patriarchal society is nothing unique. Welles's visual construction of the witches as mystical, even without the Druidic detail, only strengthens this theme. Despite his sincere and creative attempts to alter the narrative to introduce unique themes, the weird sisters are, both thematically and visually, classic renderings of the *Macbeth* witches and the modern Hollywood fantasy crone.

Return of the Classic Accused Woman: *Joan of Arc*

Not only did 1948 see the release of a new cinematic adaptation of *Macbeth* containing three of the most famous crone witches, but it also saw a new cinematic version

---

179. Janet Adelman, "'Born of Woman': Fantasies of Maternal Power in *Macbeth*," in *Shakespearean Tragedy and Gender*, ed. Madelon Sprengnether and Shirley Nelson Garner (Bloomington: Indiana University Press, 1996), 105–106.

of the classic accused woman story: Joan of Arc. Just as Welles's *Macbeth* was the first major studio adaptation of Shakespeare's play since 1916, Sierra Pictures' *Joan of Arc* (1948) was the first major American retelling of that story since Cecil B. DeMille's film *Joan the Woman*, which was also released in 1916. The earlier two films were produced during World War I and the latter two were released just after World War II. While these correlations are interesting, they are most likely happenstance and only indicators of the ebb and flow of genre popularity.

The 1948 *Joan of Arc* film was directed by Victor Fleming, who died shortly after it was released, and starred the illustrious Ingrid Bergman as Joan. The production was one of several Joan of Arc projects being explored in the 1930s and 1940s. However, it was the only one that was produced. During that period, the PCA expressed repeated concerns over the presentation of Joan's story due to the reported backlash against DeMille's silent film. In a 1934 letter to RKO producer N. P. Whitman, PCA director Joseph Breen explained how the French and English governments had protested the depiction of the clergy in the 1916 film. And how Roman Catholics had objected to the narrative's suggestion of a romance. Due to that history, Breen told producers that he had spoken to various religious authorities and that they could not assure that there [wouldn't] be protests.[180]

The prospect of retelling the well-known legend within the contemporary Hollywood system proved too risky for some studios. RKO opted not to pursue the project, as did producer David Selznick after he made several inquiries. However, in 1947, Sierra Pictures was created by Bergman, Fleming, producer Walter Wanger, and several others to specifically create a Joan of Arc film. It was to be based on Bergman's theatrical success as Joan of Lorraine in a play of the same name. Filming began that year with great anticipation from both the creators and Breen himself.

As a legendary historical figure, Joan is the epitome of the witch as an accused woman and has come to represent such in Western cultural mythology. Like the town of Salem, she encapsulates society's struggles with reason, superstition, faith, and political control. In addition, the Joan story often hits right at the center of the struggle of the empowered woman within a hardened patriarchy, and as such, she is the clear embodiment of the witch's reality.

---

180. Joseph Breen to N. P. Whitman, January 19, 1934; source: *Joan of Arc* Production Files, MPAA PCA records, Margaret Herrick Library, Academy of Motion Picture Arts and Sciences, Beverly Hills, California

Ingrid Bergman stars in the prestige film Joan of Arc *(1948).*
[Source: RKO/Photofest. Copyright: © RKO]

However, each retelling of her story reflects the time in which it was created, and as a result, Joan's characterization changes as well. DeMille's *Joan the Woman* was produced, for example, during World War I and, as historian Robin Blaetz argues, the film was allegorically concerned with readying the country for war and with "popular notions of female heroism."[181] *Joan the Woman* served as propaganda, inspiring women to work beyond their typical homemaker roles. Unlike DeMille's silent, the 1948 film was produced after a world war just as women were returning to the home front to resume their traditional roles as housewives. In her study, Blaetz considers why a story about female heroism in war would be produced after a period of time in which women were being called into action, after the Rosie the Riveter period. This

---

181. Blaetz, *Visions of the Maid*, 51.

question becomes even more interesting considering the cultural implications found within DeMille's earlier version.

The difference lies in the focus of the narrative. *Joan the Woman* emphasizes Joan's personal story, including a love interest. This early film was less concerned with the implications of politics, war, and her divine visions. By contrast, the 1948 *Joan of Arc* film is predominantly concerned with political maneuvering, religious structures, and battle scenes. This latter film lives in what is defined as a masculine universe with Joan appearing as a pawn. Within that construction, she is a forlorn child who leaves her proper place only to become lost in a world in which she does not belong. The film does not focus on her legendary heroism as its own valor—a point that is underscored by the many high angle close-ups of Bergman's face. In these shots, the camera looks down on her, almost with pity, as she muses poetically about her plight and her love of God and nation.

In many ways, *Joan of Arc* is similar to the live-action witch films produced during the war. From the beginning, Joan is marked as different, wearing a bright red skirt that contrasts the drab grays and browns around her. She is also portrayed as psychologically distraught, having already heard the divine voices for years. Once she leaves home against her father's will, Joan enters the realm of men and becomes the witch-invader. She disrupts what has become a settled society in France, challenging the status quo. Like Jennifer, Paula, and Lorna, Joan is the transgressive woman defined by an irrationality that defies the systemic order.

In her study, Blaetz notes that after the war, magazine articles began to appear that lamented the "loss of femininity in American women, who were described as increasingly unstable and dangerous."[182] This observation not only supports the gender struggle present within the film, but it also supports the overarching theme defining female irrationality as transgressive behavior. Throughout *Joan of Arc*, there is a running commentary that Joan is out of place. Her hair is cut short; she wears men's clothing. She doesn't understand the warrior culture. Near the end of the film as the trial breaks her down, Joan begs to be surrounded by women in a church prison. "Give me women about me," she cries. She has had enough.

The difficulty for filmmakers was in adapting the legend and historical data with a contemporary allegorical message that posits the heroic woman as transgressive, out of line, and irrational. Blaetz notes, "In its attempt to fit Joan into traditionally feminine roles while maintaining that these subservient roles are heroic, the film categorizes Joan in contradictory ways."[183] This is demonstrated, for example, by those

---

182. Blaetz, *Visions of the Maid*, 119.
183. Blaetz, *Visions of the Maid*, 137.

high-angle camera positions used during many of her speeches, as noted earlier. The power of her words and her purpose are undercut by visuals that suggest weakness or subservience. As the story ends, the film cuts between a sympathetic priest and a close-up of Joan on the stake as smoke billows about her. These close-ups are now presented from straight or low angles, both of which are visuals that lift her up and herald her memory, in a sense. The priest's speech focuses not on Joan's transgressions or her punishment, but on her effort to fight for national freedom. With those words and the imagery, Joan is redeemed. She transforms through sacrifice, not rescue, into a version of Lady Liberty. In the final heavenly shot of the sky and sun, the film thanks Joan, the American, for her sacrifice.

Joan of Arc was approved by the PCA, but it ultimately was a box office flop. Critics had mixed reviews, and many viewers believed that the 145-minute prestige film was too long and slow moving. Its struggle to win fans was not aided by the revelation of a scandalous affair between Italian director Roberto Rossellini and lead actress Ingrid Bergman. After the short run, Sierra Pictures folded, never to produce another film. Then, in 1950, RKO re-released a shorter version of *Joan of Arc*; however, the second release fared no better. Regardless of its failings, *Joan of Arc* fits in with the canon of witch films of the time due to its focus on the irrational woman as a disrupter of established society.

Conclusion

Despite a world war and its influence on film production, the period offered a number of critical steps forward in the evolution of the Hollywood witch. It is a period of subtle shifting and the perpetuation of larger changes made in the earlier decade. The witch begins to test the waters of the horror genre in various disjointed ways, and green skin survives its source, moving into new texts.

The witch becomes a symbol of female irrationality and aggressive sexuality, both of which are framed as disrupters of peaceful society and a man's world. She is slowly becoming a monster in her own right. Lastly, while this point was ignored by critics, this period saw for the first time witchcraft linked to the practice of an ancient religion. This detail would not be included again until the 1970s. The various changes made during this era are steps forward on the witch's journey as she moves into the 1950s and the time of television.

Chapter 5: Filmography

Third Dimensional Murder	1941	George Sidney
Sky Princess	1942	George Pal
I Married a Witch	1942	René Clair
Weird Woman	1944	Reginald LeBorg
The Woman Who Came Back	1945	Walter Combs
Mighty Mouse, "The Witch's Cat"	1948	Mannie David
Macbeth	1948	Orson Welles
Joan of Arc	1948	Victor Fleming
Looney Tunes, "Which is Witch?"	1949	Friz Freleng

Chapter 6
Bell, Book, and Satan
(1951–1960)

As the 1940s ended, a new dawn had arrived for American mass-market visual entertainment. Hollywood had faced, or was about to face, several pivotal challenges that
would ultimately disrupt the industry's status quo eventually leading to the dissolution of the classic studio system. In 1948, the US Supreme Court held that the eight
majors were guilty of monopolistic practices and forced them to release their theater
chains. From 1947 to 1954, the infamous McCarthy era "witch hunts" left many tal-
ented filmmakers blacklisted as communists and no longer able to work. At the same
time, the coming of television presented the film industry with its biggest competitor
for the American viewing audience.

With all these industry changes, the PCA began to lose its grip on film content. In
1952, the US Supreme Court made a landmark decision that heralded a fundamental
ideological shift in the understanding of the film industry's role in American society.
The court "ruled that motion pictures [were] a significant medium for the communication of ideas." [184] That decision overturned the court's 1915 ruling labeling the
movie industry as simply "a business" unprotected by any First Amendment rights.
After 1952, Hollywood filmmakers were protected by the US Constitution's right to
free speech, giving them more power to ignore the PCA. Then in 1954, Joseph Breen,
the PCA's administrative director and notorious film censor, retired, leaving the aging
self-censorship organization without its pivotal leadership.

---

184. Doherty, *Hollywood's Censor*, 302.

For the construction of narrative witches, these industry changes were only background noise. They did not overtly affect the presentation of the witch, at least not yet. Those shifts were, however, precursors for things to come, laying the foundations that would allow for significant changes in the representation of witchcraft onscreen as well as an explosion of new characters. While significant character changes wouldn't be realized for at least another decade, there is evidence of subtle shifts in representation by the end of the 1950s as women as witches begin to question rather than wholly reject their inner power allegorically presented as witchcraft, magic, and the mystical.

The Coming of Television

Before 1947, the number of televisions in American homes was in the thousands. By 1960, that number was well into the millions. The steep increase presented a major technological shift in the consumption and production of visual entertainment.[185] American viewers no longer had to leave their living rooms to watch newsreels, cartoons, or to see their beloved stars perform. While this new technology had been around since the 1930s, the war had significantly curtailed production and distribution. With post-war prosperity came new cultural growth that allowed for a quick buildup of a lucrative television market, complete with its own censorship code and standards. Within a few years, Hollywood was able to adjust to the competition, discovering that television provided a new avenue for its film products, both new and old, and the industry successfully transitioned to accommodate new viewing trends.

To this point, the study has focused solely on film content, both features and shorts. Due to the coming of television, the study must also include episodes and shows. Not doing so would be irresponsible as the two industries were, and still are, closely connected, particularly in the making and remaking of cultural meaning. For example, in 1952 the National Association of Broadcasters established a censorship code to guide content in the new market, and that new code contained similar language to the one established for film. The broadcasting code regulated everything from fiction to news to advertising. Shows that complied were marked with a "Seal of Good Practice," which was shown before or after airing.

Moreover, as time goes on, many of the most well-known American witches, such as Samantha, Morticia, and Sabrina, make their debuts on television rather than film. The animation industry eventually moves its distribution from the big screen to the small screen. Finally, it is television that turns MGM's *Wizard of Oz* from its status

---

185. Mitchell Stephens, "History of Television," Mitchell Stephens Class Pages, last modified 2000, https://stephens.hosting.nyu.edu/History%20of%20Television%20page.html.

as box office poison to a beloved classic and powerful cultural influencer unlike any other.

The Films and Shows

This period is chiefly defined by the dawn of television's Golden Age and ends in 1960 just after the birth of the legendary television show *Twilight Zone*, a signal of the cultural change and a new growing interest in the paranormal and occult. Over this nine-year period, witch-related entertainment is predominantly reflective of the contemporary conservative climate, sharing much in common with past decades. With only a few exceptions, the period provides a little bit of everything already offered in years past, from western folk witches (e.g., *Wanted: Dead or Alive*, "The Healing Woman") to witch doctors (e.g., *Captive Girl*, 1950) to animated Halloween witches (e.g., *Bewitched Bunny*, 1954).

There was a full re-emergence of genre-based witch characters that hadn't been used in bulk since the silent period. Adaptations continued to be popular. Shakespeare's *Macbeth* was produced in 1954 and 1960; Nathanial Hawthorne's *Feathertop* (1955) returned to the screen for the first time since the silent era. *Hansel and Gretel* was adapted at least three times. More distribution opportunities meant more productions and therefore more opportunities for the witch to appear. Buried within this amalgam of normalcy, so to speak, are oddities and fresh concepts of witchcraft. In fact, it is at the end of this period that the industry birthed the first true satanic witch (*The Undead*, 1957) and two more vamps who pushed against the limits of the aging censorship code (e.g., *Damn Yankees*, 1958; *Bell, Book and Candle*, 1958)

Fairy Tales and the Fantasy Witch

Paralleling film and animation pioneers, early television producers were equally attracted to fairy tales because the stories stood the test of time and always drew an audience despite the newness of the technology. As a result, the fantasy witch re-emerged both in animated and live-action forms after a hiatus in the 1940s. From 1951–1960, there were five different fairy tale productions containing a witch. Of those, three were adaptations of the Brothers Grimm's story *Hansel and Gretel*. The fourth fairy tale was an adaptation of *Rapunzel*, also a Grimm tale. Finally, Walt Disney returned to his roots with *Sleeping Beauty* (1959).

Hansel and Gretel, Again and Again

As noted, adaptations of *Hansel and Gretel* appear more frequently in this study than any other fairy tale due to the story's prominent witch character. During this period, the famous story was not only adapted wholesale, but it also finds itself the inspiration for narratives outside of its classic rendering, such as in the 1954 *Looney Tunes'* vignette *Bewitched Bunny*. It is not surprising, therefore, that *Hansel and Gretel* would lead the 1950s resurgence of witch-containing fairy tale productions.

While the three television adaptations of *Hansel and Gretel* use the same basic narrative, the presentations are not alike; nor are the witches. The 1951 stop-motion animated television short, titled *The Story of 'Hansel and Gretel,'* was created by Ray Harryhausen and released by Bailey Films Inc. In this adaptation, the witch character is a stereotypical fantasy crone with elongated facial features and a black cloak. She was also crafted with green skin, making it the third production to characterize the fantasy witch in that way and the first *Hansel and Gretel* production to do so. Visually speaking, Harryhausen's witch is a combination of the crone from Disney's *Snow White and the Seven Dwarfs* (1937) and MGM's infamous Wicked Witch of the West from *The Wizard of Oz* (1939).

During that same year, Harryhausen and Bailey Films also produced *The Story of 'Rapunzel'* using the same stop-motion animated technology. In this case, the witch is Rapunzel's adoptive mother, and she looks nearly identical to the *Hansel and Gretel* witch. However, in *The Story of 'Rapunzel,'* the witch does not have the iconic green skin. This distinction changes the symbolic significance of the character from witch as monster to witch as bad mother. As such, Harryhausen's witches together demonstrate two of the most common visual codifications of evil femininity within the presentation of classic fairy tales.

In 1954, RKO Radio Pictures produced their own adaptation of *Hansel and Gretel*. Using Engelbert Humperdinck's 1893 opera, the television special is a stop-motion animated musical retelling of the story titled *Hansel and Gretel: An Opera Fantasy*. Directed by John Paul, this version contains a witch named Rosina Rubylips voiced by Anna Russell. The character is atypical of the era in that her clothing and hair are reminiscent of the fanciful, less frightening clown witches of the Victorian period. She wears a high collar, a white frilly apron with her hair tied up in a bow. At the same time, however, Rosina's elongated facial features, black dress, and lanky hands provide the needed visual cues to mark her as the story's witch. Unlike the Harryhausen shorts, RKO's operatic adaptation eventually became a holiday television classic, airing regularly in December for over thirty years.

Rosina Rubylips the witch, voiced by Anna Russell, happily discovers the wandering siblings in the 1954 film Hansel and Gretel: An Opera Fantasy. *[Source: RKO Radio Pictures/Photofest. Copyright: © RKO Radio Pictures]*

Moving even further from the traditional depiction of a fairy tale witch, NBC television produced a live-action *Hansel and Gretel* special in 1958. It is a comedic musical adaption starring Barbara Cook, Red Buttons, and Hans Conried as the witch. Casting a male actor as a female witch added an extra dose of comedy to the already farcical environment. Despite this gender play, the viewer knows immediately that Conried is the witch due to several visual cues. He is wearing, for example, a long curly wig, black robes, and a big pointy hat. Conried was also fitted with an elongated nose and exaggerated chin. Together with the other three television fantasy witches mentioned above, this NBC special demonstrates that even the most minimal use of deeply embedded visual cues are easily interpreted by the American viewer regardless of any twists in the narrative or presentation. Each of the four witches, although different in appearance and voice, are readily identifiable as just that—the witch.

A Closer Look: Disney's *Sleeping Beauty*

One of the most dramatic examples of a change in fantasy witch construction appears in Disney's retelling of Charles Perrault's classic story "Sleeping Beauty." After a string of moderately successful non-princess films in the 1940s, Disney decided to return to its *Snow White* formula and it did so successfully in 1951 with the production of Cinderella, the studio then began immediate production on *Sleeping Beauty*. However, after Disney invested ten years and $6 million on the project, the new princess film was met with a poor reception, becoming its biggest setback to that point. *Sleeping Beauty* was considered too frightening and too artistically stylized by both reviewers and the public. Disney himself called it "an expensive failure." [186]

While there is a definite marked change in *Sleeping Beauty's* artistry from earlier works, the film's witch, Maleficent, takes her cues directly from her magical predecessor, The Wicked Queen. As with *Snow White and the Seven Dwarfs*, Disney did not use the animated Halloween witch commonly found in its animated shorts (e.g., *Trick or Treat*, 1952). *Sleeping Beauty* dances with horror images and toys, once again, with the notion of dangerous female sexuality.

Like the Wicked Queen, Maleficent was crafted with a striking, almost mesmerizing physical beauty. She stands tall and thin, with high cheekbones and dark lashes. She is draped in colors of the night: black and purple robes with a horned hat, all of which enhance her dramatic features. During the christening scene, Maleficent raises her arms to cast the spell and, doing so, her robes with scalloped edges spread out like bat wings. Just as the Wicked Queen is visually likened to a vampire, Maleficent is likened to a bat and a devil. She is a fantasy vamp witch: beautiful, powerful, and dangerous.

Rather than using a classic fantasy crone to replicate Perrault's magical character, Disney animators chose the vamp witch model and evil mother, creating a derivative of its successfully frightening Wicked Queen. Both characters are dominated by colors of the night, punctuated with touches of white and red. They wear heavy makeup against pale faces and are followed around by a crow, which is an iconic element of witchcraft. With that said, Maleficent takes on a monstrous form that is not found in either Disney's characterization of the Wicked Queen or in Perrault's original 1697 story. In Perrault's tale, the magical character did not have a name, nor was she called a "witch." Perrault labeled his antagonist an "old fairy" with no other description. At the beginning of the story, she casts a sleeping spell on the kingdom in response to not being invited to the christening. After that point, she is never mentioned again. The old fairy is simply a catalyst for the rest of the story. As such, Disney's adaptation is only loosely based on Perrault's work.

As was done with the Wicked Queen and the Wicked Witch of the West, Disney animators distilled the essence of Perrault's old fairy into a singular form of feminine

---

186. Heather Urtheil, "Producing the Princess Collection: An Historical Look at the Animation of a Disney Heroine," Emory University Film Studies Department (Atlanta, Georgia: 1998), 30.

evil and then re-expanded her out into a powerful enemy who haunts the entire narrative. This construction creates an extreme but highly simplified narrative tension between the polarities of good and evil, as defined by a traditional Christian moral lens. In a 1953 memo, Disney producer William B. Dover called Maleficent an "evil fairy" and "mistress of the black arts."[187] She is defined visually and narratively as a devil figure and witch who disrupts a Christian ritual and threatens the life of the baby and then later haunts the virginal young girl. The social valuations are clearly written into the film.

The Witch as a Monster

While Maleficent was modeled on the earlier Disney witch, there is one big difference. Maleficent is a literal monster. Because Perrault's original character is described as a fairy and nonhuman, Disney animators had creative leeway to push the boundaries of her physicality. They could break rules in her construction that could not be done with a human character. In other words, her fairy status explains her ability to transform into a dragon, along with her bat-like appearance and her horns. She is a nonhuman monster from the start. Although the Wicked Queen was also visually likened to Dracula and is clearly evil, this detail is confined to her humanity. In other words, she does not become a literal monster, but remains only a human one. She is the bad mother.

Maleficent, on the other hand, lives in a place of ambiguity, similar to the Wicked Witch of the West. She is only nearly human, which is suggested by her blue-green skin and fairy existence. As discussed in chapter 5, the distortion of what is natural to the body creates what theorist Julia Kristeva labels an abjection, or something that breaks a boundary of systemic order. In this case, the order is the physical body. Maleficent is horrifying because she is both treacherously beautiful in her humanity but also deeply repulsive in her inhumanity. This is what evokes the horror.

The difference in characterization between the two Disney witches informs the way they die. The Wicked Queen runs off a cliff while being chased. Nobody kills her. The evil human woman as bad mother dies by her own mistake. Maleficent, on the other hand, is killed by impalement when Prince Philip, the hero, stabs her in dragon form with his sword. This is defined as a beast slaying, not a woman killing, and that detail is important in the shifting configuration of the Hollywood witch. Maleficent is a fantasy vamp due to her extreme beauty, but she is also defined by her monstrosity.

---

187. William B. Dover to Production Code Administration, July 20, 1953; source: *Sleeping Beauty* Production Files, MPAA PCA records, Margaret Herrick Library, Academy of Motion Picture Arts and Sciences, Beverly Hills, California.

She is not simply a danger to one princess; she threatens an entire kingdom. In that role, the witch monster must be killed by the male rational hero, allegorically speaking, with the phallus as symbolized by the sword. Adolescent femininity must once again be rescued from outside mystical influences by a heroic male, and transgressive womanhood, in whatever form, must be contained, assimilated, or killed. The themes are not new.

After *Sleeping Beauty*'s failure, Disney did not attempt the princess fairy tale formula again. The studio went back to exploring male coming of age stories (e.g., *The Jungle Book*, 1967) and simple renditions of its buffoonish fantasy witch (e.g., Mad Madam Mim in *Sword in the Stone*, 1963). It would be another thirty years before Disney Animation Studios would attempt another fairy tale adaptation in which they re-create their fearsome witch (i.e., *The Little Mermaid*, 1989).

The Animated Halloween Witch

The animated Halloween witch enters this period as the same iconic and very commercialized version of the fairy tale witch that had been distilled and solidified in the cartoon shorts of the 1920s and 1930s. Examples include Disney's *Trick or Treat* (1952) and *Tom and Jerry*'s "The Flying Sorceress." With the coming of television, the industry got a boost, providing a new venue and captive audience for animated shorts. Unlike the past in which most animated witches were designed as generic characters who never appear more than once, this period saw the birth of iconic animated witches who become a regular and recognizable part of their animated universe. Such characters include the Sea Hag, Witch Hazel, and Wendy the Good Little Witch. While these characters generally maintain the look born in the silent era, they do contain expressions of their time and, more notably, they all demonstrate the growing cultural influence of MGM's *The Wizard of Oz* (1939).

The Sea Hag

In her debut animated appearance, the Sea Hag, Popeye's nemesis, plays a classic narrative role for the witch. She is the comedic foil. Visually speaking, the Sea Hag cuts a tall, skinny, awkward profile with exaggerated facial features. Her appearance is taken directly from Elzie Crisler Segar's 1929 *Thimble Theatre* comic strip, from which she originally came. In Segar's original drawings, the Sea Hag was depicted with a light human skin tone and she wore a dark dress with a head cover. When she first appeared in Paramount Cartoon Studios' animated series *Popeye the Sailor Man*, the Sea Hag sported similar clothing but her skin was green. In the adaption of the well-known comic strip character, animators took advantage of a new cultural cue for the bad witch.

The Sea Hag appears periodically throughout the popular series, debuting September 17, 1960 in an episode titled "The Last Resort." In addition to giving her green skin, Paramount animators also chose to define her magic with the term "Voodoo." In episode eighteen, titled "Voo-Doo to You Too," the Sea Hag employs a "Voodoo doll" and turns Olive Oyl into a zombie. While this character detail was unusual for the animated witch, the connection made between witchcraft and Voodoo was, in fact, taken from Segar's original stories, mirroring a broader cultural understanding of magic. Not only does the Sea Hag practice "Voodoo," she also stars as the evil witch in an adaptation of the fairy tale *Snow White* titled "Olive Drab and the Seven Swea-Peas." Voodoo, witchcraft, and evil magic were often conflated and indistinguishable.

Witch Hazel

Unlike the Sea Hag, *Looney Tunes*' Witch Hazel fits more in line with traditional cartoon witch constructions. Animator Chuck Jones based his famous character on the 1952 Disney short *Trick or Treat*, who was also named Witch Hazel. Jones is said to have created his animated Witch Hazel right after seeing the Disney short. In a 1989 interview, voice actress June Foray said that Jones was so enamored by Disney's witch that he approached Foray, who had voiced the character and asked her to be the *Looney Tunes*' witch.[188] With the exception of Witch Hazel's first appearance in *Bewitched Bunny* (1954), Foray became the recognizable voice of the character for decades.

It is important to note that the name Hazel, in both cases, is a play on words taken from a common trademarked product of that era. The name was not only used for the Disney and *Looney Tunes*' witches but also for the witches in *Tom and Jerry*'s "The Flying Sorceress" and Casper's *Which is Witch*. Additionally, Hazel is the name of Ethel Barrymore's elderly folk witch character in the live-action feature film *The Story of Three Loves* (1953). Like green skin, the name Hazel became a cultural cue for a cinematic witch, and other names would follow including Sarah, Mags, Margaret, Thelma, Zelma, and Velma.

Looney Tunes' Witch Hazel may have been modeled on Disney's witch, but the two characters are not identical. The earlier character lacked green skin and behaved as a morally ambiguous trickster and a foil to the emotionally unbalanced Donald Duck. She is not the short's true antagonist. Contrary to that, Jones's Hazel is far more exaggerated in appearance and in behavior. She is the story's villain, who whimsically

188. Michael Mallory, "Which Witch is Which?" *Animation Magazine*, October 23, 2014, http://www .animationmagazine.net/top-stories/which-witch-is-which.

moves about the *Looney Tunes* world, playing off culturally identifiable pieces of Halloween's animated witch iconography, including broomsticks, cauldrons, and magic mirrors. As is typical for *Looney Tunes* characters, Hazel manifests satire aimed at both the animation world and Hollywood in general. In some respects, Jones's Witch Hazel is a comedic mirror to MGM's Wicked Witch and she even sports the green skin to prove it.

While animation is largely considered secondary entertainment, the final scene of Jones's *Bewitched Bunny* offers a telling look at the period's cultural understanding of the witch in terms of gender politics. After Bugs Bunny accidently turns Hazel into a flirty female bunny, he walks off saying, "Oh sure. I know. But aren't they all witches inside?" While the comment is meant as a joke aimed at the male viewer, it highlights the misogynistic bias present in that medium. All women are witches inside, and witches eat children, are ugly, have green skin, and are capable of magic. Taking that further, if Bugs is a stand-in for the typical American male, then witches, according to the short's narrative, seek to literally devour masculinity. The only way to stop the witch is to assimilate, or in this case transform, the monstrous woman into the perfect woman as defined by conventional heteronormative structures, which in this cartoon's case are marked by youth, beauty, red lips, swinging hips, and sex appeal.

The Animated Child Witch

While *Looney Tunes'* Witch Hazel and other similar Halloween witches continue to make regular appearances, this period offered a new addition to the animated witch canon: the child witch. She is readily identifiable as Casper the Friendly Ghost's good friend Wendy, who was introduced in a 1954 comic book but made her first animated appearance in the 1958 Paramount Studios short "Which is Witch?" Like Casper, Wendy is depicted as a friendly version of a more typically fearsome character. The innocence of childhood, as emphasized by height, small noses, and large eyes, eliminates the horrific nature of the Halloween icon. Instead of wearing black, Wendy is dressed in red and has well-kept blonde hair and blue eyes. She is the Shirley Temple of the witch world and is visually juxtaposed to her three aunties, Thelma, Zelma, and Velma, who are all drawn as traditional Halloween witches with dark robes, pointy hats, and green skin. While they are characterized as monsters, she is an angelic human. The comparison is not unlike that made between Glinda and The Wicked Witch of the West.

In the various *Casper* series that aired from 1958 onward, several other young witches make cameo appearances. In the 1958 episode "Which is Witch?" a brown-haired girl wearing traditional black clothing is depicted as Wendy's roommate. Her name is Hazel, and she is no less a doll-like figure than Wendy. In another episode also named "Which is Witch?" Wendy and Caspar confront an unruly little witch girl named Wild Cat, who resembles the other two young witches. However, unlike Wendy or Hazel, Wild Cat is mischievous and must be redirected and convinced to "become good." A child witch, like a young wild woman, cannot end the narrative as a mischievous character; she must be assimilated. This is a child-directed version of the standard assimilation theme. It is meant as a direct teaching lesson for the young viewer. The cartoon's message is "be a good friend and citizen."

Literary Adaptations

Along with a renewed interest in fairy tales and the continuation of the animated Halloween witch, the 1950s also saw the adaptation of witch-related literature, specifically Shakespeare's *Macbeth* and Nathanial Hawthorne's short story *Feathertop*. As noted earlier, this revival, so to speak, coincides with the entertainment industry's trend in presenting familiar material when launching a new mode of storytelling. All of these adaptations were produced for television. *Macbeth* aired in 1954 as a live telecast, which was released as a made-for-television film in 1960. The *Feathertop* adaptation aired in 1955 as part of CBS' General Electric Theater broadcast and the story was later adapted again in 1961.

George Schaefer's *Macbeth*

The 1954 version of *Macbeth* was produced by George Schaefer and starred British actor Maurice Evans and Australian actress Judith Anderson. The film was created for the *Hallmark Hall of Fame* television series and was the first live telecast in color of a Shakespeare play. Schaefer's adaptation was then later recorded and released in 1960. Filmed on location in Scotland, the 1960 version earned five Emmy Awards, including best actor, best actress, and program of the year. Because the original was not recorded, all assumptions about the adaptation's presentation are based on the 1960 filmed version.

Unlike Orson Welles, Schaefer stuck close to Shakespeare's original text. However, like Welles, he did make some changes that significantly affected the play's famous witches and the gender balance of the entire production. Schaefer opened with the classic scene of the three weird sisters chanting around a cauldron. Their faces appear in a triad looking down on the camera, which is placed in the cauldron. They are designed in the manner of the classic fantasy crone with unkempt white hair and bent hands. Their scratchy voices shake as they speak their lines. Several minutes later, when the trio is shown in long shot, all three are cloaked, hunched over, and limping. The entire sequence is punctuated by smoke, darkness, and shadow.

After that scene, the witches never appear again. They are not even mentioned. Their narrative role remains only introductory, as a premonition for the coming story. While Welles also removed the later physical presence of the witches, the trio did remain as a mystical force and a narrative voice. In Schaefer's adaptation, the witches are simply gone. This significantly undermines the gender dynamics of the original play, setting the notion of evil femininity squarely on the shoulders of Lady Macbeth as nearly the only female figure in the entire rendering.

Schaefer's version is dominated by the politics of men and, as such, Lady Macbeth becomes the instigator of all sordid affairs. While she is defined as an evil seductress, she is never called a witch. As for the play's famous witches, they are relegated to throwaway roles, perhaps only present at all because they are iconic to the play. As a result, the trio introduced a patriarchal-driven story that blames a single woman as the instigator of all men's evils, paralleling the biblical notion of original sin and mirroring the more conservative cultural climate.

Feathertop Reinvented

Similar to *Macbeth*, Nathanial Hawthorne's classic moral tale *Feathertop* was also adapted for television viewers. The last cinematic rendering of the popular story was *Puritan Passions* released in 1923, and that production proved to be even darker and more contemplative than the original tale. However, the 1955 adaptation moved in the exact opposite direction. It was decidedly apolitical in nature with softened edges that would attract a wide audience during prime time viewing hours. It aired as an episode of the General Electric Theater broadcast hosted by actor Ronald Reagan. The show starred Natalie Wood as a young woman who falls in love with a scarecrow disguised as a nobleman.

While the 1955 *Feathertop* adaptation, along with the musical version that aired in 1961, appear on the surface to be far too whimsical to contain the political undertones found in Hawthorne's original tale, there are historians who suggest that producers simplified and repackaged Hawthorne's story in such a way as to support a sense of community belonging within a growing middle-class American suburban family culture and support a wave of growing American nationalism and conservatism found in the 1950s. Rather than being critiques of the superficiality found in conventional American society, the two adaptations promoted the benefits of such convention through the notion of marriage, love, and happy endings.[189]

---

189. Laurence Raw, *Adapting Nathaniel Hawthorne to the Screen: Forging New Worlds* (London: Scarecrow Press, Inc., 2008), 45.

With that reading in mind, it is not surprising that the witch shifts roles from a fantasy crone or elderly folk witch to something less threatening. Neither the 1955 adaptation nor the 1961 version grapple with the moral significance embedded in the traditional role of crone character, as found in both Hawthorne's original story and MacKaye's 1908 theatrical derivative. These contemporary *Feathertop* witches are reduced to minor antagonistic roles as a singular villain. The elimination of the witch's moral role coincides directly with the elimination of societal critique and the reimagining of a complex story into a simplified tale of good versus evil with a romantic ending. As noted, the producer's main interest was simply to create family fun entertainment that confirmed American life rather than critique it.

Westerns, Americana, and the Elderly Folk Witch

The revived popularity of the western in both television and film was also propelled by a growing American nationalism. With the genre's re-emergence came the reappearance of the silent era's classic wild woman witch. While the silent era western focused on landscapes and lifestyles, the 1950s cowboy western grapples with social structures and the negotiations of masculinity. What is a man's role in his world? What are his goals, and where are his ethical boundaries? This is defined by taking decisive action, by the dichotomy of good versus evil, by a man's loyalty to the homestead and family, and by the ethical choices he makes within the social confines of his masculinity. The classic cowboy western is a man's world, and the witch as a wild woman is typically constructed as a threat to those masculine structures. Therefore, she exists comfortably as an antagonist in these popular narratives.

Within the cowboy western's universe, the wild woman is a disruption to order, as she does not follow conventional gender roles or abide by expected social structures. Just as in the silent era, the young wild woman must be assimilated, typically through marriage. In doing so, she turns from witch to wife and mother. The old wild woman, or elderly folk witch, is permitted to exist, remaining the crazy, non-sexualized, amoral hag living at the edge of existence. While these two descriptions are gross generalizations, they loosely apply across productions. However, at the same time, there is a distinct difference in the witches presented in the early 1950s to those released at the end of the period, which is indicative of the growing tensions with regard to gender roles within American society.

The Elderly Folk Witch

During the first half of this period, westerns contained only the iconic old wild women, similar to what was found in the silent era (e.g., *Blackened Hills*, 1912). This elderly folk witch, for example, appeared in shows such as *The Gene Autry Show*, "The Trail of the Witch" (1952), *The Adventures of Kit Carson*, "The Haunted Hacienda" (1953), and *Wanted: Dead or Alive*, "The Healing Woman" (1959).

In two of the three shows, the elderly folk witch is given the common witch name "Mags" or "Maggie." The reason for the repetition of this name is not entirely clear. One of the Salem witch trial's victims was an elderly woman named Margaret Scott and the United Kingdom boasts the legend of Maggie Wall. Additionally, the actress who played the famous MGM Wicked Witch was, in fact, named Margaret. However, it is more likely that the western's elderly folk witch became associated with the name Margret due to naming trends. Around 1915, the name Margaret reached a peak in popularity and then steeply declined after 1920. As such, those women who had been named Margaret in the early part of the century would have been middle aged or older by 1960. As a result, the name could have become culturally associated with older women, including aunts and grandmothers.[190]

A Closer Look: "The Healing Woman"

Similar to the silent era, one of the main conflicts within the western narrative is order versus chaos. Masculinity, embodied in the cowboy, symbolizes order while femininity represents the wild. On a thematic level, this conflict appears in witch films across genres, but in the western it is literalized. During this period, the 1959 *Wanted: Dead or Alive* episode "The Healing Woman" provides a good example of this contemporary version of the conflict.

The story's central tension is created through the juxtaposition of modern medicine and folk healing with the noted gender implications. The town has both a medicine woman named Maggie Blake and a modern male doctor. Early on the doctor tells hero Josh Randall (Steve McQueen) that "[Maggie] couldn't take a bullet out of a cake of soap." However, she is good at midwifery and "putting kids to bed when they are sick," or other actions largely considered women's work. Randall later says, "A doctor's a man; not a magician." This language establishes clear boundaries between the folk witch, who exists outside the male establishment, and the doctor, who thrives within that world.

---

190. "Margaret: Popularity in the United States," Behind the Name, accessed February 24, 2021, https://www.behindthename.com/name/margaret/top.

Pleading with Amanda Summers, Josh Randall explains the dire
medical condition that her son faces in Wanted: Dead or Alive, *"The Healing*
Woman" (1959). Starring (left to right) Virginia Gregg, Steve McQueen.
[Source: CBS/Photofest. Copyright: © CBS]

The episode's conversation naturally evolves into a science versus belief argument with superstition relegated to the antagonists. It is not entirely dissimilar to the witch trial films that pit reason against religion (e.g., *Maid of Salem*, 1937). In this situation, science becomes the so-called Excalibur of the hero, who wields it unrelentingly until proven right. Randall says to the ailing boy's mother, "If you think that that witch is going to cure a stomach full of poison with a couple of dead frogs…" In the end, it is the mother who chooses the doctor over the healing woman. Science and the male hero with his gun and sense of reason bring the mother to her senses and save the boy's life. To borrow language from earlier decades, it could also be said that the "true woman" as the mother wins over the "new woman" as the healer.

The Elderly Folk Witch Outside the Classic Western

Another notable example of the traditional western folk witch is found in the feature film *Comin' Round the Mountain* (1951), during which the comedy duo of Abbott and Costello negotiate the cultural "backwoods" of Appalachia. The film is not a traditional western but plays off its themes for comedy. It is light on depth but heavy on chatter and physical gags. It is a true modern comedy of errors in the Shakespearean sense. That comedic structure, however, allows the iconic western elderly folk witch to cross over into a somewhat magical realm, rather than just being an herbalist as in the *Wanted: Dead or Alive* episode.

When the comedy opens, Wilbert Smith (Lou Costello) has been locked into an arranged marriage with one of his cousins. Frustrated by this turn of events, he decides to ask a local woodland witch for help. Dragging his friend Al (Bud Abbott) along, Wilbert approaches the witch's cabin in a scene that is reminiscent of Dorothy and her three companions approaching the Wicked Witch's castle in *The Wizard of Oz*. The camera pulls back on a shot of the dilapidated cabin shadowed by gnarled trees while sinister music and a hooting owl can be heard in the background. As they approach, Wilbur tries to run, saying, "I'm scared." But Al grabs him and insists on moving forward. This filmic nod to MGM's classic film does not go unsatisfied. Aunt Huddy the witch is played by none other than Margaret Hamilton. Although she does not have green skin and is costumed more like "a gypsy" or woodland folk witch, Hamilton is unmistakably the same character in voice, posture, and movement. This is one of Hollywood's very poised, self-reflexive moments. Casting Hamilton was purposeful, and audiences recognized the joke.

While Aunt Huddy is a classic folk witch, the comedic environment allows for the presence of what might be considered real magic. Aunt Huddy, like Popeye's Sea Hag, practices what the film terms Voodoo. By the end of the scene, the character interactions devolve into a battle of poppets, pins, and pain as Wilbert and the witch poke each other repeatedly. *Comin' Round the Mountain* exists purely as a parody of the western homestead story, and the witch here mocks the Mags and Maggies of the television shows while referencing Hamilton's classic role. She is a comedic marker of the "backward" beliefs of mountain people, as well as a Hollywood hat tip.

Female Agency and the Young Wild Woman

By the end of the period, the witch of the westerns shifted from the elderly folk witch to the young wild woman. With this change, the question of the woman's power, allegorically depicted as magic, takes center stage. Is the young wild woman's magical power real and, if so, from where is it sourced and how is it tamed? In the silent westerns, the containing of a woman's power was never a point of contention and her magic or belief in magic was simply accepted as a symptom of her condition or poor upbringing. In these westerns, even when the conclusion results in traditional social reincorporation, the acknowledgement of a true, rational, independent feminine power is suggested.

For example, in *Bonanza*'s "Dark Star" (1960), *Maverick*'s "The Witch of Hound Dog" (1960), and even in the earlier non-western action-adventure film *Saadia* (1953), the alleged witch is a beautiful, young, unwed woman who believes that she has supernatural power. In *Dark Star*, she is gypsy-born and claims to have been "bewitched by the devil," and threatens to turn the hero into a toad. In *Maverick*, the young girl says, "I can't help being a witch" and when the hero says he doesn't believe in witches, she responds, "You don't believe in me?" In *Saadia*, the heroine is convinced she is bewitched by a local sorceress. These two shows and film dance around the idea that the young wild woman may simply be crazy while not completely abandoning the possibility that she does have power. The conclusion is not definitive. The source of her power is never fully explained. The wild woman embraces the term "witch" or "evil," but is also unsure and even scared by the possibilities. This is strikingly different from the film *Spitfire* (1934) in which Trigger never calls herself a witch, but rather insists that her faith-based power is from God. It is also unlike the silent wild woman, who doesn't have a power at all and easily accepts redemption.

If magic is defined allegorically as an enticement for the adolescent female mind or the young, unattached woman, then the woman who contemplates the reality of magical liminality is also contemplating her personal power. In most narratives, the mystical experience happens to the young wild woman without her consent, whether by a local sorceress, a witch, or an unexpected divine gift. However, she is always given the opportunity to relinquish her power. In the past, when she doesn't, she is killed. By contrast, the contemporary young wild woman, such as in "Dark Star" and "The Witch of Hound Dog," accepts her magical fate and allegorically her unique intrinsic power. "You don't believe in me?" the witch says. These characters turn down redemption and hold to their true selves and, unlike in the past, they just disappear from the story without consequence. The new narrative solution to the disruption of the social order is allowing the witch to simply go away.

A Closer Look: "Make Me Not a Witch"

The questioning of a young woman's personal agency is a theme that not only appears in television westerns. It also plays out in the growing number of paranormal suspense shows that gained popularity at the end of this period. For example, in 1959, *Alcoa Presents: One Step Beyond* aired an episode called "Make Me Not a Witch" that told the story of twelve-year-old Amy Horvath who develops a psychic ability. This is the first television show to depict the witch as a wild girl and psychic adolescent. This theme eventually takes center stage in Brian De Palma's horror film *Carrie* (1976) and then is repeated many times over.

At the beginning of "Make Me Not a Witch," Amy's parents confront the reality of her psychic gift. Amy's father says to her mother, "You gave me a female with the devil inside." As suggested by that statement, the *Alcoa* episode incorporated a Christian-based understanding of witchcraft, which had been largely abandoned to this point. This theme is another marker of changing content within mainstream entertainment. Films and television productions were beginning to acknowledge the broader spectrum of historical meaning behind the concept of witchcraft. In this case, the young wild woman herself is terrified that she has become a witch and turns to a priest for help. Like the characters in the westerns, Amy recognizes her power and addresses it. Amy is not the naive wild girl of the silent era.

However, "Make Me Not a Witch" is not a 1950s western in which a young wild woman never finds the source of her magic and redemption is rejected. Amy is too young to just disappear without explanation. Furthermore, Amy cannot be easily assimilated through other typical means: marriage or death. Therefore, her power must be handled, and religion is the answer to the question of her magic's source. God gave Amy the gift, which defines her as good. In that sense, she is Casper's Wendy. In the end, Amy proves her goodness by using her power to save two other children, after which she loses her power.

The show's conclusion is vastly different from that presented in *Spitfire*. Trigger's faith-based power was never confirmed by the film, fully examined, or explained by a priest or otherwise. Amy's is fully acknowledged and explained. However, in both productions, the faith-based healers lose their powers, which is the most common ending for wild women witches. She must give up her power, God-given or not, in order to exist in proper society. Amy is no different.

"Make Me Not a Witch" contains a more traditional narrative due to the witch being a child, rather than a teenager approaching womanhood or a young attractive woman. However, like her western show counterparts, there is a moment of acceptance. The narrative acknowledges her power and treats it as real, not the product of insanity or wild behavior. This detail mirrors the period's overall relationship with witchcraft and female agency. The witch, girl or woman, begins seeing her power and questioning its source. "What is this power I have?" "Am I a witch?" This is a gendered power shift in the allegorical use of witchcraft in narrative storytelling. By the close of the period, the young wild woman believes in her own power and narratives begin to dance with the reality of witchcraft.

The Witch Doctor

As with past periods, there were very few male witches depicted in television or film and most that appeared were either meant for comedy or background noise (e.g., *Bell, Book and Candle*, 1958). However, with the continued popularity of action-adventure films, variations on the witch doctor became the dominant depiction of the male witch at this time. Most of these films are set in Africa, the South Seas, or Mexico. Such films include *Captive Girl* (1950), *Bride of the Gorilla* (1951), *Jungle Gents* (1954), *White Goddess* (1953), *White Witch Doctor* (1953), and *Voodoo Woman* (1957). As in the past, these films continue to rely on the colonialist or imperial aesthetic that posited that all things non-Western were uncivilized, superstitious, and un-American. The use of the term "witch" in these cases is a direct reference to this model.

Witch doctors are typically minor characters, sometimes less than even that. They are ornamental props, serving as indicators of the backward civilization. Due to this fact, most of these films are not necessarily witch films and therefore are not central to this study. However, one film deserves a brief look due to the centrality of the concept of the witch doctor character construction and its negotiation of gender roles. The 20th Century Fox film *White Witch Doctor* (1953) starring Susan Hayward and Robert Mitchum, demonstrates how the action-adventure film uses the witch doctor in a similar way to other witch constructions and how the concept of magic weaves its way through racist narrative structures and character constructions to negotiate the thematic tension between wild nature and civilization. The film also offers a unique look at a woman defined as witch doctor.

A Closer Look: *White Witch Doctor*

White Witch Doctor tells the story of an American nurse, Ellen (Susan Hayward), who finds herself in the Congo caring for indigenous populations. Sent by a Christian missionary organization, Ellen is guided by Lonni Douglas (Robert Mitchem), an animal trapper and explorer. Through her use of modern medicine to save local villagers, she becomes known as Little Momma as well as the "white witch doctor." During several scenes, the village witch doctors, all men, stare curiously on as she performs what they call "white" magic. The shots go back and forth between soft close-ups of her face and then medium crowded shots of the witch doctors wearing what is defined as traditional clothing, face paint, and elaborate headdresses.

The dichotomy presented here is one that supports the colonial aesthetic, as discussed earlier. The single white savior brings Western "magic" to save the African population from disease and itself. It is a variation on the wild versus civilized theme.

The indigenous witch doctors use rocks, incense, and rattles to cure the sick. Their work is labeled witchcraft and focused on ridding the body of demons and not viruses. Ellen's magic, by contrast, is based on modern Western medicine, which is recognizable to the contemporary viewer. Therefore, Ellen is characterized as civilized and the villagers are not.

While this theme is found in many witch films, there is one notable difference in *White Witch Doctor*. In this case, the medical doctor and the symbolic voice of reason is a woman, and the irrational and uncivilized characters are men. In that way, the film retains a strong feminist current. Perhaps unsurprisingly the novel on which the film was based was written by a woman, Louise A. Stinetorf.

Despite this distinction, the narrative still boasts a traditional social hierarchy. The white witch doctor as woman symbolizes the rational in juxtaposition to the village's traditional healers, but she is wild in comparison to the white rational male hero, Lonni, and within her own cultural social structure. Ellen is not a doctor; she is a nurse. She points this out throughout the film. In addition, Ellen must be saved from a local tribe as well as from herself. As such, Ellen is defined as a wild woman in terms of witch construction. Her abandonment of civilization, her lack of a husband, and her intense desire to help the indigenous people is what define her as wild, and in the end, she must accept redemption through rescue.

Unlike Ellen, the male witch doctors are allowed to exist in their own symbolic irrationality because they are Black African men who live in the Congo. This defines them as backwards and ignorant; the narrative permits them to remain as such. While the film has a moderate feminist undercurrent that is atypical to similar contemporary witch films, that theme is subservient to a larger overarching gender bias as well as the common ethnic and racially based hierarchy that defines the witch doctor.

Dawn of the Horror Witch

While the power dynamic with regard to female agency did subtly shift as the period progressed, there still were few, if any, witches in American horror films. As already noted, prior to 1950, the genre remained focused on monsters, mad scientists, giant creatures, and the like. While gender politics did play out within those narrative structures, the monstrous women were not witches; rather they were spin-off monsters, such as in *The Bride of Frankenstein* (1935) or animal-like creatures, such as in *Cat People* (1942). Outside of that, women were depicted as young, beautiful, naive victims who must be saved from the monstrous male villain (e.g., *White Zombie*, 1932).

However, as a witch's relationship to magic changed over time, the American film industry began to incorporate the witch into the horror genre as more than a victim of her own mind (e.g., *Weird Woman*, 1944) or her transgressive social behavior (e.g., *The Woman Who Came Back*, 1945). As the Production Code Administration slowly lost its grip and female characters began to question their roles within society, the horror witch slowly emerged. In doing so, she brought with her the deeply embedded and theological baggage that had followed her for centuries and was infamously written in the Inquisition's witch-hunting guide the *Malleus Maleficarum*, first published in 1486

The *Malleus Maleficarum*, translated as *The Witches' Hammer*, was the standard text on witchcraft for centuries, helping to foster the belief that witches were aggressive, secretive, promiscuous, and seductive beings and, as written in the influential medieval document, they "copulate with those Devils known as Incubi." [191] Due to censorship, early American filmmakers had limited ability to capture this medieval construction. As noted, the code strictly controlled the presentation of sexuality, religiosity, and even that which was deemed "gruesome." As the codes reads, for example, "[evil] must not be allowed to appear so attractive that the audience's emotions are drawn to desire or approve so strongly that later the condemnation is forgotten and only the apparent joy of the sin remembered." [192] As such, it is not surprising that witches were absent from horror until the PCA could no longer strictly control content.

Censorship and Roger Corman's *The Undead*

The first notable film containing a true horror witch is Roger Corman's *The Undead* (1957). While the film is not frightening by most standards, *The Undead* weaves its story using Catholic-based ethics, pop psychology, and an array of Hollywood witch tropes. It opens in modern-day America as a mad scientist, Quintus, hires a prostitute as the subject for his mind experiments. Quintus believes that through hypnosis he can induce time travel and he is successful. The film then rewinds to a fantasy-like medieval Europe, complete with witches, devils, imps, knights, and a hero with an Arthurian-derived name: Pendragon. The bulk of the film is a cross between fantasy and horror.

Originally called *The Hypnosis of Diana Love*, Corman's film was approved by the PCA in 1956, but not after significant changes were made to the script and the production design. In July of that year, PCA director Geoffrey Shurlock presented Corman with twenty-two violations found in the original script. None of the complaints

---

191. Heinrich Kramer and James Sprenger, *The Malleus Maleficarum*, tr. Reverend Montague Summers (1486; trans., 1927; New York: Dover Publications, 2012), ii.

192. Doherty, *Hollywood's Censor*, 360.

referred to witchcraft. As was typical, the letter focused on the presentation of sexuality, "gruesomeness," and religiosity. For example, the film contains a dance sequence that was deemed problematic. Shurlock writes:

> The stage directions for this dance with "figures slithering over and around one another" depicting "evil incarnate" and "wantoness" gives us serious concern. In no event, should this "slithering" be in any way suggestive nor should any part of the dance portray sex suggestive or indecent body movements.[193]

As exemplified in Shurlock's note, the PCA was concerned not only with suggestive sexual displays in both costuming and movement, but it was also concerned with the representation of evil, defined by satanic witchcraft, presented as something alluring. With that said, the PCA made no mention of the construction of the witches themselves outside of that scene.

The Undead's Witches

The Undead contains three witches: an accused woman, an elderly folk witch, and a vamp witch. However, they are not a magical sisterhood; rather they epitomize the tensions between female characters often found in classic fairy tales, such as in Perrault's "Cinderella." They represent the archetypical maiden, mother, crone unit with the maiden caught between a magical grandmother and an evil mother.

Helene (Pamela Duncan) is the film's heroine who becomes the prototypical accused woman. She is sentenced to death for the practice of witchcraft, which is perpetuated solely by the jealousy of another witch. There is nothing transgressive or non-normative about Helene's character. However, it is important to note that Helene embodies the past life of Diana Love, a prostitute who is put under hypnosis. As such, the fantasy flashback serves as a redemption story for Diana, as the experience forces her to confront her transgressive ways. This narrative technique was used in the silent film *Folly of Vanity* (1924) with the heroine descending into a fantasy undersea world to face herself.

The second witch is Meg Maud (Dorothy Neumann) who is a typical elderly folk witch living a liminal existence between what is socially acceptable and what is not. Her face is deformed, her hair is stringy, and she shuffles about, cackling. Meg Maud

---

193. Geoffrey Shurlock to Roger Corman, July 10, 1956; source: *The Undead* Production Files, MPAA PCA records, Margaret Herrick Library, Academy of Motion Picture Arts and Sciences, Beverly Hills, California.

is similar to other elderly witches, even in name. The source of Meg's magic is revealed to be Satan. However, as Meg explains, her mother learned Satan's tricks and then disavowed him—an act that caused Meg to lose her beauty. Through this explanation, the elderly folk witch's magic is sourced and her existence is justified. Meg is defined as good by the renunciation of satanic evil.

The third witch is Livia (Allison Hayes). She is the moral and visual antithesis to Meg Maud. Livia is a beautiful vamp witch, who is depicted as powerful, jealous, and manipulative. She can transform into a cat or lizard, like other non-witch female horror characters, and she is accompanied by an imp-like creature who does her bidding. Unlike Meg's mother, Livia's did not renounce Satan, making her an agent of the Devil. During a confrontation scene, Meg tells Livia, "I am thy match, witch. But I am not thy kind." It is Livia's jealousy and her attraction to the film's hero that incite her to accuse Helene of witchcraft. She is the classic horror vamp.

As with past transgressive witch characters, Livia provides the opportunity for the female viewer to engage in a subversive pleasure that is counter to what is experienced in daily life. In the book *A Skin for Dancing In*, Tanya Krzywinska explains:

> [Livia's] association with bestiality and perversion is written into the film at both surface and subtextual levels, making her ripe for a subversive reading. We know that she is in the pay of the Devil and walks the earth free of the constraints of motherhood or family, an obvious, if forbidden, attraction for many women.[194]

Livia presents a moment for the female viewer to touch her own desire and power outside the bounds of social norms. However, Livia ultimately must die. By contrast, the elderly folk witch is left to her devices, and Helene confesses. In doing so, she offers her future prostitute self redemption for her transgressive, sinful existence. The female characters are, in the end, all handled as expected.

While *The Undead* is classified and promoted as horror, it indulges far too much in the fantastic to truly be a horrifying film. Much of the proposed horror imagery was removed from the script due to PCA objections, including blood dripping down Livia's face, close-ups of a hanged man, and the chopping off of heads.[195] Corman's film operates more like a low-budget modern fairy tale dipped carelessly into one of television's paranormal suspense thrillers. However, the film is notable as the first full

---

194. Krzywinska, *A Skin for Dancing In*, 122.
195. Shurlock to Corman, July 10, 1956.

attempt at presenting a true horror witch. It was released in 1957 as part of a double feature with the low-budget horror film *Voodoo Woman*.

Religion, Beauty, and the Vamp

A year after *The Undead* was released, the successful Broadway show *Damn Yankees* was adapted for the big screen, starring the original show's cast and actor Tab Hunter in the starring role. Similar to Corman's film, *Damn Yankees* contains a witch who displays unrestrained female sexuality. Lola (Gwen Verdon) is a 172-year-old witch who sold her soul to the Devil (Ray Walston) to become a beautiful seductress. Halfway through the film, she sings her signature song "Whatever Lola Wants." Lola is dangerous, not because she mixes poisons in a cauldron, but because she is a temptress who seeks to destroy men's lives. She is another Hollywood vamp witch and the figurative embodiment of the transgressive feminine wielding an irresistible sexuality that is the undoing of any mortal man. She is the symbol of the empowered woman that thrives within a culture in which female sexuality is feared.

Damn Yankees takes the concept of the vamp witch a step further than similar past constructions such as Jennifer in *I Married a Witch* (1942) or even the Wicked Queen in *Snow White and the Seven Dwarfs* (1937). Jennifer embodies female sexuality with only a light tone of mischief. She is a biological witch with no further sourcing. The Wicked Queen's construction merged a narcissistic obsession with female beauty and the notion of pure evil. She is designed as a transgressive human woman who knows the art of portions. Lola, like Livia, projects the same level of narcissism as the Queen but their obsession is combined with a sexuality as explicitly defined in religious ideology. These two witches were once human women who made a conscious choice to sell their soul to the Christian Devil for eternal life and beauty.

The production notes for *Damn Yankees* are unavailable but, according to the notes for *The Undead*, it was the overt expression of religiosity, absent the witch, that evoked the most ire from the PCA. In fact, the religious rhetoric was even more problematic for censors than the film's sexual content or gruesome displays. In 1956, PCA director Shurlock told Roger Corman that, in *The Undead*, "the use of 'holy water' on the grinding wheel would be offensive and should not be mentioned." [196] Shurlock also required that Corman remove the nun from the list of Helen's "future selves" and requested that the line, "For the sake of God" be added at one point in order to "eliminate any question of irreverence." [197] These were typical concerns raised by the PCA based on code specifications. Once again, the witch is not mentioned.

---

196. Shurlock to Corman, July 10, 1956.
197. Shurlock to Corman, July 10, 1956.

The restrictions placed on religious expression coupled with the American ideological concept that witchcraft was only superstition kept satanic-based witchcraft mostly out of film narratives. A 1953 internal memo regarding a proposed film, *The Witch of Guadalupe*, demonstrates this point. The PCA told producers at United States Pictures that there was "no Code prohibitions against telling stories about superstition and witchcraft." [198] Continuing on, the note explains that the proposed story was acceptable as long as writers did not "haphazardly jumble together superstition and religion in such a way as to reflect unfavorably on religion." [199] That statement demonstrates the guiding point for the PCA's control of films through the 1960s. Witchcraft was still fantasy and superstition; religion, by contrast, was sacred and something to protect.

Despite the use of religious themes within other genres, it is not until the release of *The Undead* that this theme is overtly expressed in connection to witchcraft. Corman's film uses language such as the witch's sabbat, "sell your soul," and "altar of the profane." Meg Maud crosses herself with holy water. Livia admits to being an agent of the Devil, who makes an appearance himself at the end of the film. A year later, *Damn Yankees* does the same within a comedic musical. Lola confesses to having sold her soul to the Devil. When she resists him, he "threatens to give her back her broom," suggesting that he will turn her back into the hag she once was. Near the end of the film, he does just that and Lola transforms from *The Undead*'s Livia to Meg Maud.

Conflicting Messages and the Female Body

In merging religiosity with both female sexuality and witchcraft, *The Undead* and *Damn Yankees* offer a conflicting message about socially acceptable displays of femininity. They simultaneously suggest that female beauty is alluring to men and something a woman should seek out. But yet, the quest for beauty is ultimately evil and immoral in Christian terms. At the same time, the films posit that ugliness and advanced age, while morally good, are repulsive and often a retribution for social nonconformity. The only answer, therefore, is once again for the woman to relinquish her self-making and her magic, or symbolically her power, and align herself with notions of physical modesty and conventional marriage and motherhood as defined by 1950s standards. This echoes strongly through the character arc of *The Undead*'s heroine Helene and the presence of Meg Boyd, the suburban housewife in *Damn Yankees*.

---

198. J.A.V., Interoffice Memo for the Files, June 3, 1956; source: *The Witch of Guadalupe* Production Films, MPAA PCA records, Margaret Herrick Library, Academy of Motion Picture Arts and Sciences, Beverly Hills, California.

199. J.A.V., Interoffice Memo for the Files. June 3, 1956.

While the vamp witch construction was not new, its merger with religiosity and conflicting messages on female beauty brought the American cinematic witch one step closer to the realization of a full witchcraft-based horror film. However, that is where the period's changes stopped. *The Undead* is too steeped in fantasy to embody the gripping danger or extreme sexuality found in later horror films (e.g., *Blood Sabbath*, 1972). Similarly, *Damn Yankees* embeds its vamp witch within a fantasy-based musical comedy. Lola and the Devil are caricatures who dance and sing their way around Washington, DC. While this vamp witch does not denounce her satanic pact, she does demonstrate deep remorse, allowing the viewer to empathize with her impossible position. In the end, she stays with Satan, retains her beauty, and disappears. The film is pure musical comedy. Genre and related narrative devices prevented these two highly sexualized vamp witches from being truly frightening and from being censored out of the scripts. Despite any limitations, both characters do demonstrate the loosening of PCA's restrictions on feature films.

The Witch Next Door: *Bell, Book and Candle*

It was at the end of this period that one of the most famous American vamp witches arrived on the scene: Gillian of *Bell, Book and Candle* (1958). Often mistaken for a remake of *I Married a Witch*, *Bell, Book and Candle* was based on a play written by John Van Druten, which ran on Broadway from November 1950 to June 1951. In 1953, David Selznick purchased the film rights, but he never moved forward with production and sold the property to Columbia Pictures in 1956.

Although Columbia Pictures was prepared to produce *Bell, Book and Candle* that very year, the first screenplay attempt was rejected by the PCA. As in the past, it was not witchcraft that was the problem, but rather the sexually suggestive elements found in costuming and language. In a letter to producer Harry Cohn, director Shurlock said that *Bell, Book and Candle* was unacceptable due to "clear cut indications of an illicit sex relationship between the two leads, which is not treated either with any voice for morality or any compensating moral values."[200] After adjustments were made, *Bell, Book and Candle*'s script was finally approved in November 1956.

Anecdotally, screenwriter Daniel Taradash said that actress Kim Novak jumped into her witchy role immediately, spending the first couple of weeks of production

---

200. Geoffrey Shurlock to Harry Cohn, October 22, 1956; source: *Bell, Book and Candle* Production Files, MPAA PCA records, Margaret Herrick Library, Academy of Motion Picture Arts and Sciences, Beverly Hills, California.

walking around as if she was a witch.[201] The film was released in January 1959 and has since become one of most recognizable witch films in Hollywood's history, even outranking *I Married a Witch* in the collective American cultural memory.

While *Bell, Book and Candle* and *I Married a Witch* are not related in terms of source material, the two vamp witches and their respective stories are similar. Not unlike her predecessor Jennifer, Gillian embodies the idea of a witch next door found in a narrative text that pits fantasy against reality. One way both films make that connection is by anchoring their narratives in the Salem mythos. While the 1942 film offers a flashback to witch hangings, *Bell, Book and Candle* only makes a few references to New England lore. When love interest Shep Henderson (Jimmy Stewart) asks if Gillian's been up to un-American activities, she responds, "No. I'd say very American. Early American." This comment also capitalizes on the contemporary sociopolitical climate. The original play was written and produced during the height of investigations by the House Un-American Activities Committee as well as the McCarthy trials. It was a time when government officials as well as the public had become intimately involved in defining what exactly it meant to be an "American." With that in mind, Gillian's line is a nod to that premise and defines witches as being "very American."

The Vamp: Fantasy versus Reality

Both Gillian and Jennifer spend their screen time seeking out the hero's attention using magic, which results in them falling in love and eventually having to relinquish their magical power. Like Jennifer, Gillian is defined as a fantasy vamp witch through visual cues and mannerisms. She wears black clothing, owns a cat, speaks slowly, and moves seductively through her scenes. Her magic is not sourced; it just exists. At one point, Gillian's appearance recalls the exaggerated features of Disney's animated Wicked Queen. In the famous close-up of Gillian holding her cat Pyewacket, her dark eyebrows are set off harshly against her light skin, mimicking the cat's ears. This image recalls a similar close-up of the animated Queen holding the heart box. Like Gillian, the Queen's dark, arched eyebrows stand out dramatically against her pale skin.

From the film's start, Gillian is portrayed as a fantasy-based temptress. When Shep first meets her, she tells him, "I love it when a man is above me." While Gillian is talking about his apartment being one floor above hers, the sexual overtones are clear. Later, in two-shot, the couple sits on a couch with Gillian dressed in a long, tight black evening gown, which has a low open back. She is draped across the couch, facing away

201. Patrick McGilligan, ed., *Backstory 2: Interviews with Screenwriters of the 1940s and 1950s* (Los Angeles: University of California Press, 1997), 324.

from the camera toward Shep. Through this scene, she emits an aggressive sexuality and that eventually results in her successfully casting a love spell on him.

Despite Gillian's and Jennifer's shared vamp construction, Gillian walks a different line between fantasy and reality. Unlike her predecessor, Gillian wants to be what she calls "humdrum." She forbids the practice of witchcraft in her home and tells Aunt Queenie that she just wants to "spend Christmas […] at a church somewhere listening to carols." This line is a signifier of what she, and Hollywood language, considers normal. Gillian, unlike Jennifer, does not want to be a witch, and this difference provides a basis for the film's tone. Where Jennifer's character arc is simplistic and permits female viewers the space to engage in silly escapism, Gillian's arc is more complex, demonstrating a struggle with personal identity. Through that character depth, the film retains a melodramatic feel alongside its comedy and, at the same time, captures the period's witch-based theme that allows for the questioning of a woman's innate power and the ownership of her desire.

Aunt Queenie (Elsa Lanchester), Nicky Holroyd (Jack Lemmon),
and Gillian Holroyd (Kim Novak) discuss the use of magic
in Bell, Book and Candle *(1958).*
[Source: Columbia Pictures/Photofest. Copyright: © Columbia Pictures]

As the film continues, Gillian's reluctance to engage in witch culture becomes increasingly evident. Her independence and control of her sexuality fade into the background giving way to a classic assimilation narrative. Just as in *I Married Witch*, the witch as heroine must move out of the fantasy space across forms into reality. Like Jennifer, Gillian begins as a fantasy vamp, moving over into the role of wild woman as projected on her by the male hero. Once there, she can then be tamed. While Jennifer does not plan for that to happen, Gillian is looking for it; she wants to be in love, which is a classic subtheme of the 1950s melodrama.

Gillian's transition from fantasy vamp to wild woman is visually indicated by costuming and shot framing. She moves from black clothing with seductive lines to brighter colors and higher collars. As time progresses, there are fewer extreme close-ups, as the camera holds its distance from her body. Where the film's comedic witches remain in their fantasy structure, Gillian transitions out. The magic is gone. This character evolution is complete when she admits to being in love with Shep and finds herself able to blush and cry. As the film posits, witches can do neither.

The significance of power loss being defined as the ability to blush and cry cannot be understated, as they both are symbolic of demure feminine emotional expression. Women cry and blush. Like Jennifer, Gillian exchanges her freedom of expression and innate power for the conventional emotions and behaviors associated with modest femininity. As such, the film ends with the couple in each other's arms; the wild woman has been assimilated and is, once again, in a position to be married and live a long "humdrum" life.

The Witch Family and the Codification of Queerness

Outside of Gillian's own search for identity as represented by her relationship to magic, the film has a subtextual layer of meaning primarily supported through the presence of other witches. As with Jennifer, Gillian has a family made up of nonhumans living in human society. While keeping their magic secret, these witches peacefully maintain homes, businesses, and social lives. However, they also maintain a separate subculture. The film's primary symbol of this culture is the Zodiac Club.

These urban witches are defined by eccentric behavior and, in the case of the women, colorful clothing. Aunt Queenie (Elsa Lanchester) and Bianca De Pass (Hermione Gingold) are two primary examples of the witches populating that world. Both are contemporary clown witches in style and behavior. They have short curly red hair. They laugh loudly and engage in mischievous activities through spellwork. They are contemporary versions of the whimsical female clown witch, which was made popular in the silent era through a Victorian aesthetic. In this film, the character is reimagined with a 1950s urban bohemian flare.

The other prominent member of Gillian's family and witch society is her brother Nicky Holroyd (Jack Lemmon). Like Jennifer's father in *I Married a Witch* (1942), Nicky provides a point of comic relief, playing off the film's straight man and love interest, Shep Henderson. Nicky's free-spirited antics dance in the background, destabilizing the dramatic environment in order to create tension for the love story. He is the prototypical male clown witch, laughing in the streets and getting himself and others into trouble.

Together with Aunt Queenie, Bianca, and the other witches, Nicky serves to define the witch society in normative terms and provides a stable reality for the nonhuman witches, making them more relatable to the viewer. At the same time, the film's witchcraft culture has another layer of meaning that was written into the original play. It serves as an allegory for gay life in 1950s New York City, a level of meaning that was largely lost on mainstream audiences.

Playwright John Van Druten spent much of his life hiding his queer identity, expressing his experiences only in writing. Theater historian Dr. Maya Cantu called *Bell, Book and Candle* a "subtle affirmation of Van Druten's homosexual identity in the midst of the McCarthy-era witch hunts."[202] That point underscores the subtext of the entire film, from Gillian's own personal conflict living between the worlds to the Zodiac Club and beyond. Often the film's dialogue between witches offers the most revealing evidence of the script's codification of queerness. For example, Aunt Queenie says, "I sit in the subway sometimes, on buses, or the movies, and I look at the people next to me and I think: 'What would you say if I told you I was a witch?'" While comical to the average viewer, the statement's underlying meaning would not have been lost to a member of the gay community living in the conservative US culture of the 1950s.

Witchcraft Worlds

Although this subtext derives from the original play, it was not abandoned when producing the film; nor could it be, as the premise of a hidden subculture is essential to even the most superficial retelling of the basic story. As such, this level of meaning offers a new dimension to Gillian's own identity crisis and her final decision to give up her magic for heterosexual love. But, more importantly, it offers a new perspective on the representation of witchcraft. *I Married a Witch* did not have a witch world. Jennifer and her father were the only magical characters in the film. They were invaders. By contrast, *Bell, Book and Candle* has an entire world of witches. Gillian and her family are part of that hidden witchcraft universe thriving in the shadows of society.

---

202. Maya Cantu, "John Van Druten Biographical Program Note, London Wall, Mint Theater Company," *Academia* (February 2014): 5–7. https://www.academia.edu/5279265/John_Van_Druten _Biographical_Program_Note_London_Wall_Mint_Theater_Company.

When an entire witch-based culture exists within a film that is set in the viewer's reality, as with *Bell, Book and Candle*, that magical world and its relationship to what is defined as normalcy become equally as important as any single character construction. The magical subculture exists as an alternative to the viewer's reality, a counterpoint to defined acceptability as in this film, or an escape from reality (e.g., *The Owl House*, 2020) or even a native magical land that connects the character to their heritage and identity (e.g., *Twitches*, 2005). How a cinematic witch world operates within the narrative depends on American society's overall relationship to magic at the time the film was produced. For example, is witchcraft considered wholly transgressive or an acceptable personal identity and path to empowerment? In the case of *Bell, Book and Candle* and those productions found in the decade immediately following (e.g., *Bewitched*, 1964–1972), witchcraft is mostly transgressive. The period's fantasy witches and their subcultures, therefore, are depicted as strange and silly but not real. Yet, at the same time, they contain weighted, even if codified, sociocultural meanings reflective of their time and creators.

Conclusion

The period from 1951 to 1960 saw a burst of witch constructions that predominantly mirrored the past. This was partly due to the introduction of television. As with film and animation, the new visual technology relied on well-known stories to attract its audiences, such as *Macbeth*, *Hansel and Gretel*, and *Feathertop*. In addition, with television there was increase in productions, providing ample opportunities for the witch to appear in a greater variety of genres and stories. The conservative social era brought with it the popularity of Americana, such as the western and with that the elderly folk witch. Disney returned to its princess formula and introduced another fearsome vamp witch. Fairy tales and adaptations punctuated the decade.

However, by the late 1950s changes in the industry began to affect the construction of witches and the representation of magic. The western shifted from old folk witches to young wild women who acknowledge their power. Could witchcraft be real? Could women have innate power? What or who is the source of the power? Religion, specifically the age-old concepts of satanic devotion, began to seep into stories, even if only through comedy and fantasy. The industry also birthed another one of its most famous vamp witches, Gillian, in a film that offered a new powerful, although hidden, social undercurrent in the representation of a magical world. While the period feels traditional in many ways, it was also the very beginning of the end of the Hollywood studio system and its antiquated censorship system.

Chapter 6: Filmography

Comin' Round the Mountain	1951	Charles Lamont
The Story of 'Hansel and Gretel'	1951	Ray Harryhausen
Story of 'Rapunzel'	1951	Ray Harryhausen
Trick or Treat	1952	Jack Hannah
The Gene Autry Show, "The Trail of the Witch"	1952	George Archainbaud
The Adventures of Kit Carson, "The Haunted Hacienda"	1953	John English
Story of Three Loves	1953	Vincente Minnelli
White Witch Doctor	1953	Henry Hathaway
Saadia	1953	Albert Lewin
Hansel and Gretel: An Opera Fantasy	1954	John Paul
Looney Tunes, "Bewitched Bunny"	1954	Chuck Jones
Macbeth	1954	George Schaefer
Feathertop	1955	Don Medford
Tom and Jerry, "The Flying Sorceress"	1956	Joseph Barbera, William Hanna
The Undead	1957	Roger Corman
Bell, Book and Candle	1958	Richard Quine
Omnibus, "The Lady's Not for Burning"	1958	Christopher Fry (writer)
Casper the Friendly Ghost, "Which is Witch?"	1958	Seymour Kneitel

Hansel and Gretel	1958	Paul Bogart
Damn Yankees	1958	Georgia Abbott, Stanley Donen
Alcoa Presents: One Step Beyond, "Make Me Not a Witch"	1959	John Newland
Sleeping Beauty	1959	Clyde Geronimi
Wanted: Dead or Alive, "The Healing Woman"	1959	Donald McDougall
Bonanza, "Dark Star"	1960	Lewis Allen
Macbeth	1960	George Schaefer
Maverick, "The Witch of Hound Dog"	1960	Leslie Goodwins
Popeye the Sailor	1960–1962	(Multiple)

Chapter 7

Toward a New Hollywood

(1961–1968)

The 1960s was a difficult decade for America's film industry. Television was stealing away audiences, studios were losing money, and fewer and fewer films were produced. According to historians Thompson and Bordwell, "Hollywood was unsure about what the public wanted." [203] One of the primary reasons for the industry's problems was a shifting cultural climate. During this period, a number of national events destabilized society, including the continuation of a Cold War, the assassination of President John F. Kennedy, and the public emergence of an organized civil rights movement led by Martin Luther King Jr. In 1963, Betty Friedan's *The Feminine Mystique* was published, signaling the beginning of second wave feminism. Then, in 1964, the Vietnam War escalated, and an increasing number of military personnel were sent to fight. By 1965, a new generation of young people, who felt they had nothing to lose, began to push against the boundaries that defined America's cultural hierarchies and challenge the perceived utopia of the 1950s.

With such a seismic cultural shift, old Hollywood narratives and the traditional ways of telling stories were no longer attracting crowds. Even by the late 1950s, emerging filmmakers had started pushing the limits of allowable content, flouting the PCA's authority, and publicly demanding adjustments to what appeared to be an antiquated censorship system. This continued into the 1960s when many independent filmmakers began distributing their films without the PCA stamp of approval. In fact,

---

203. Thompson and Bordwell, *Film History*, 513.

as Thompson and Bordwell note, the censorship administration often unintentionally created "lucrative publicity" for the films it rejected.[204]

As the PCA slowly lost control, the door opened to increased violence, sexual content, and challenging subject matter. Films began to reflect the evolving American sociopolitical landscape, which included, as noted, the amplification of race and gender politics, environmentalism, feminism, and New Thought religions. Similarly, television producers, through their own medium, aired shows that also challenged these boundaries, although the effort was somewhat masked due to broadcast rules and the presence of the television set in the home.

Emergence of the Modern Witchcraft Movement

Before looking closely at the films and shows, it is important to examine how the shifting sociopolitical climate directly influenced witchcraft representation through a growing interest in occult practice. While modern Witchcraft and other similar spiritual traditions were not overtly depicted in American films or television until the 1970s, it is during this era that the modern Witchcraft movement began to spread, enabling it to eventually influence scripts and character construction.

It was in 1954 that English Witch Gerald Gardner emerged on the world's occult scene with the release of his most recognizable and influential book, *Witchcraft Today*. By the 1960s, the Craft, as it came to be known, spread to the US through several practitioners and associates of Gardner, including author and Witch Raymond Buckland. At the same time, American figures like Carl Llewellyn, Frederick Adams, Laurie Cabot, and others were growing and expanding uniquely American New Age, Witchcraft, and occult industries. Additionally, but not necessarily central to the Witchcraft movement, Anton LaVey launched his famous Church of Satan in 1966.

Modern Witches did not typically practice openly during this era, as the movement was just beginning. Fear of community backlash was ever present. However, at the same time, the work being done during this era became the backbone of the later and very public modern Pagan movement, which did directly influence Hollywood films beginning in the 1970s (e.g., *Mark of the Witch*, 1970; *The Craft*, 1996). In fact, prior to this decade, the last time that a modern occult practitioner had influenced, even indirectly, any witch production was 1916 when Aleister Crowley served as the model for *The Mysteries of Myra*.

While modern Witchcraft may not have directly influenced films during this period, the changes in cinematic witch construction from 1961–1968 do parallel the movement's growth. Furthermore, it was the same seismic-level societal shifts that

---

204. Thompson and Bordwell, *Film History*, 515.

both allowed for the expansion of the modern Witchcraft movement as a viable spiritual path and forced the breakdown of traditional modes of operation within the film industry, including the dissolution of the PCA. That breakdown eventually opened the door for a true revolution in witchcraft representation on-screen, including depictions of actual occult practice.

The Films and Shows

The loosening of the PCA's control over film content offered filmmakers an increased opportunity to dive into the age-old mythos of the witch as a sexualized and evil being. While this character detail appeared in the late 1950s, representations of satanic witchcraft became more prevalent. The period's witchcraft narratives also continued the contemplation on the origins of female agency and identity, allegorically defined as magic, and those discussions eventually became central to her story. Old genres such as fantasy disappeared, and suspense and horror became dominant. As a result, the witch became a more complex character, less genre bound, and a signifier in her own right.

Although television content tended to be more conservative and consistent in expression than film, the small screen took the lead in many of these changes. Its paranormal suspense shows explored mystical and occult topics, both of which helped to propel the witch further into the horror genre. More importantly, it was television that introduced two of the most famous American entertainment witches: Samantha (*Bewitched*, 1964-1972) and Morticia (*The Addams Family*, 1964–1966). Both shows offered entertainment and laughs while engaging with current sociocultural issues.

However, it was the big screen that introduced the most shocking representation of witchcraft to date. In 1968, just before the PCA was dissolved, Paramount Pictures released Roman Polanski's film *Rosemary's Baby* (1968). The landmark film marks the end of Hollywood's golden era, giving way to the construction of a true horror witch as she had never been seen before in American cinema.

Fantasy, Fairy Tales, and Adaptations

As seen in the past, witch-related fantasy films were typically popular during periods in which new technology was introduced or during periods of relative social conservativism. Conversely, the genre's popularity tends to decrease during times of social instability and upheaval. Therefore, it is no surprise that the interest in fairy tales and fantasy adaptations waned during the 1960s. Nearly all of the witch fantasy films reviewed were released before 1965. Most are comedies or over-produced dramas that mix fantasy and lore and rely on well-established fantasy tropes.

While traditional in their source material, the films all contain twists within their presentations. For example, the 1961 adaptation of Hawthorne's *Feathertop* was a feel-good musical comedy, as discussed in chapter 6. In 1963, Walt Disney Studios released an animated version of the King Arthur legend titled *The Sword in the Stone*, featuring a witch named Mad Madam Mim. She is a fanciful fantasy crone acting as both comedic foil and antagonist. She is traditional in construction, which fits the Disney character brand. While both films are considered adaptations, they do not closely follow their origin texts and stories. Despite the twists, neither film is particularly progressive or reflective of the period.

Similarly, the Three Stooges offered their own unique rendition of The Grimm Brothers' tale *Snow White*. This live-action comedy, titled *Snow White and the Three Stooges* (1961), did not include a traditional witch. Instead, the film relies on a narrative structure similar to that of the 1916 adaptation, in which a non-magical evil queen employs a magical character to accomplish her scheme. However, unlike the 1916 version, the Stooges' witch is a fantasy magician and not a classic fantasy crone. This character choice coincides with the increase in magical male figures during this period and will be discussed later. In fact, this film is not unique in that regard. The 1962 United Artists film *Jack the Giant Killer* is a fairy-tale inspired fantasy film that reimagined the medieval world with a male witch at the helm of an evil empire of monstrous witches.

Other period fantasy films with witches include *The Magic Sword* (1962), *Atlantis, The Lost Continent* (1961), *The Magic Christmas Tree* (1964) and *Blackbeard's Ghost* (1968). Most of these films were not particularly successful and, as noted, the genre largely fell out of favor by 1965 as Hollywood struggled to appeal to an audience made up of younger viewers who, for the first time, had grown up entirely with access to daily visual narrative entertainment.

The Wizard of Oz as Influencer

Despite a growing disinterest in fantasy narratives, the one origin text that does not escape filmmakers' periphery is Baum's *The Wonderful Wizard of Oz* and, more specifically, MGM's 1939 adaptation. As was seen in the colorization of Maleficent and other 1950s animated witches, *The Wizard of Oz* continued to exert a subtle but growing influence on the cultural understanding of what it meant to be a witch. This influence was not due to happenstance or a nostalgia-based cult following. It can primarily be blamed on television. In 1956, CBS aired the film for the first time during prime time and then again in 1959, marking the beginning of the film's annual television run that lasted thirty-two years. This yearly tradition helped to transform *The Wizard of Oz* from just another golden era classic movie into a cultural behemoth.

As in Disney's *Sleeping Beauty* (1959), the MGM film's influence is found most readily in the use of the green face. What was once just a solution to a technological problem took on a new life in Hollywood language, creating meaning where there was none and expanding far beyond the scope of its original creative source. The use of green skin becomes increasingly common, particularly in defining the animated Halloween witch, as seen with *Looney Tunes*' Witch Hazel, *Popeye*'s Sea Hag, *Casper*'s three aunties and, in this period, *Honey Halfwitch*'s Cousin Maggie.

But green skin was not the only influencer. By this period, MGM's film had become so popular that it was increasingly referenced in both television and film productions. For example, in 1964, Orrin Enterprises produced a low-budget, live-action television special called *The Magic Christmas Tree*. It contains a typical fantasy crone figure who transforms into a classic Halloween witch without the green skin. However, the campy film steals the structure of *The Wizard of Oz* by opening in black and white and moving to color during the dream sequence. Additionally, the popular television show *The Addams Family* cast Margaret Hamilton as Morticia's witch mother. Although Hamilton's character bears no resemblance to the Wicked Witch, the casting reference was not lost on audiences at the time.

Not only did this period see productions reproducing elements from the MGM film, it also saw the first attempt to adapt Baum's original work since 1939. Producers Arthur Rankin and Jules Bass created the animated television movie *Return to Oz* (1964). In this reimagined tale, the Wicked Witch is presented as an all-green figure and Glinda is designed in fairy-like pink. The film was a spin-off from the Rankin-Bass television series called *The Tales of the Wizard of Oz*. Each short in that series lasted only five minutes and shared the antics of the Lion, the Scarecrow, the Tin Man, and other Oz characters. The witches play no part in the series. While Rankin and Bass took their inspiration from the original books, they also capitalized on the very recognizable imagery from MGM's film, as evidenced by the coloring of their witch characters in *Return to Oz*.

By the mid-1960s, MGM's *The Wizard of Oz* had almost entirely usurped the cultural power of the original stories, becoming a baseline for future adaptations. By 1968, the film had reached a popularity level and influence that could only be matched, in terms of witch films, by Shakespeare's *Macbeth*, the legendary tales of *Joan of Arc*, and the history of Salem. This cultural power would only continue to expand, eventually finding expression beyond film and television.

Animation and the Halloween Witch

To this point, the animated cartoon witch was largely reliable and consistent in construction. However, she, like all witch characters, did not completely escape unchanged from the period's larger industry and cultural shifts. First, by 1968, animation studios had fully redirected their attention from the big screen to the small screen, finding success with younger audiences who were captivated by this form of storytelling. Mainstream cartoons that may have once been produced for general audiences were moving completely toward becoming purely children's entertainment.

Secondly, with a decline in fantasy, the witch was no longer featured. Those that did appear were characters already popular in well-established series such as *Loony Tunes'* Witch Hazel, *Popeye's* the Sea Hag, and *Casper's* three aunties. With that said, there were a few newcomers such as *Honey Halfwitch* (1965–1967) and a few single Halloween-based shorts such as *Underdog*, "The Witch of Pickyoon" (1965). However, like live-action fantasy, most of these were produced before 1965.

A Closer Look: *Honey Halfwitch*

The Paramount series *Honey Halfwitch* ran from 1965–1967 and its evolution exemplifies changing viewer interests as well as the awareness of Hollywood's successful witch tropes. Making her debut in Paramount's *Modern Madcaps'* "Poor Little Witch Girl," Honey was originally called simply Halfwitch. She is "half wizard" and "half girl" with red shoulder-length hair. She wears a large black pointed hat and simple black dress. She lives with her elderly cousin, Maggie, and a vampire bat named Fraidy, who sports a top hat and has an iconic Transylvanian accent. In every way, the original episode visually celebrates Halloween's cultural legacy from jack-o'-lanterns and spiderwebs to brooms and jars of potions. In cinematic terms, this short offers a classic animated setting for the witch.

After the April 1965 release of "Poor Little Witch Girl," Paramount Cartoon Studios launched a series called *Honey Halfwitch*, featuring the little witch, now called Honey, and her cousin Maggie. In the following eight episodes of the series, Honey and her cousin appear the same as in the original short. They live in a cottage within a fantasy forest, encountering robed wizards, dragons, and other magical creatures. Like *Casper the Friendly Ghost*, the series relied on the fantasy adventures of a young witch and her crone companion. Honey is designed like Wendy, and Maggie is a classic fantasy crone with black clothing and exaggerated facial features. However, it is important to note that, unlike Wendy's aunts, Maggie does not have green skin.

Honey was produced with the hopes of reviving Paramount's animation division, which had been financially struggling for several years. Created by newly hired executive producer and veteran animator Howard Post, Honey was, in some ways, a child's version of the popular show *Bewitched*. However, not long after the initial episode, Post resigned and animator Shamus Culhane took his place. According to author

Leonard Maltin, Culhane was "determined to revamp and reorganize the studio." [205] While Culhane was developing new projects, he was committed to releasing Post's *Honey* series. However, in 1967, he gave the series a notable facelift, making it more current and, hopefully, more popular.

The difference is remarkable right from the opening sequence of episode ten. While Post's original sequence is largely fantasy-based and resembles that of *Bewitched*, Culhane's sequence has a contemporary urban aesthetic, abandoning the sparkles and dark blue background. Paralleling this design change, Culhane moved Honey and Maggie's forest cottage out of the woods to the top of a high-rise apartment in 1960s America. He completely abandoned the fantasy setting.

Additionally, the characters themselves were redrawn to reflect popular animation trends. The new Honey resembles the characters in Charles Schultz's *Peanuts* specials, which were first made popular at this time. And Cousin Maggie, who previously could be likened to *Looney Tunes'* Granny or a classic animated Halloween witch, was redesigned with a taller more exaggerated physique, long white hair, and green skin, recalling *Looney Tunes'* Witch Hazel or even Wendy's aunties. For the final two episodes, animators changed her hair again to wiry black hair, reinforcing this point.

In reimaging *Honey Halfwitch*, Culhane pulled from animated witch tropes that were successful and recognizable at that time. Honey became more relatable and more real. Rather than a fantasy child witch with a comical accent, she became a witch-version of a Peanuts character, designed to be a typical American kid. In the episode "Alter Egotist" (1967), Honey's primary goal is to find a friend, a quest not unfamiliar to the average young viewer.

Despite the changes, *Honey Halfwitch* was not successful, and Paramount shut down its cartoon studios in 1967. Along with it went the *Honey* series. However, the show's narrative and visual shift demonstrates the efforts being made by animators to meet the expectations of a changing audience in an evolving social climate. Culhane employed new, contemporary witch signifiers to help boost the likability of the characters and reimagined the narrative so that it distanced itself from traditional fantasy and aligned with reality. In his attempts to find viewers for the unique series, Culhane demonstrated the industry's movement in general.

---

205. Leonard Maltin, *Of Mice and Magic: A History of American Animated Cartoons*, rev. and updated ed., with Jerry Beck (New York: Plume Group, 1987), 321.

The Wild Women of Paranormal Television

While fantasy programming was waning, paranormal suspense thrillers were not. The genre first arrived on the scene in the late 1950s but hit its stride in the 1960s with popular shows such as *The Outer Limits* and *The Twilight Zone*. Prior to this period, there was only one series with a notable witch episode: *Alcoa Presents: One Step Beyond*: "Make Me Not a Witch." As noted in chapter six, the show offers a version of the classic reincorporation narrative that characterizes the mystical as a disruptive power in the woman's maturation process. At the same time, the heroine, Amy, confronts her power asking, "Am I a witch?" This direct address and acknowledgment of her unique beingness was new to the witch narrative at that time and was a sign of what would come in this era.

Similar to the Alcoa episode, the paranormal suspense thrillers of the 1960s ground their narratives in the exploration of the unexplained, including mysticism, within the viewer's reality. The center of these stories, including the earlier one, is the power itself, whether that is witchcraft or not. However, unlike the Alcoa episode, the 1960s paranormal shows do not focus on the witch as a nonconformist or confused wild child, but rather they present the witch as truly mystical. She is the unexplained, and her magical existence is a reality. With that said, it is not hard to see how these shows crossed a line into horror.

The majority of witch-related paranormal shows appear in the series titled *Thriller*, which was a horror-inspired show narrated by Boris Karloff. In both "A Wig for Miss Devore" (1962) and "God Grante That She Lye Stille" (1961) the witch is an undead woman who either seeks to remain alive and beautiful through magic or who haunts the establishment where she was killed. In another episode titled "La Strega" (1962), an elderly folk witch casts a spell on a defiant couple. All three shows capitalize on traditional witch narratives, such as a beauty-seeking woman or the vengeful villain. These themes, although limited in this period, re-emerge in 1970s horror. Television's paranormal suspense shows were the gateway.

A Closer Look: *Twilight Zone*, "Jess-Belle"

A 1963 *Twilight Zone* episode offered its own take on witchcraft through a western-inspired setting. The show "Jess-Belle" contains two wild women: one old and one young. Granny Hart is an elderly folk witch who lives in the woods and, like *Comin' Round the Mountain*'s Aunt Huddy, is a real magical practitioner. Jess-Belle is a young wild woman who was scorned by her lover and only wants acceptance in conventional society, similar to Trigger Hicks in *Spitfire* (1934). As is typical to *The Twilight Zone* series, writers infuse a recognizable genre, in this case the western, with elements of horror to invoke fear. Those elements include theology, devil worship, psychosis, sexuality, and murder. The series was bred to challenge viewer expectations and push the limits of convention and understanding. The "Jess-Belle" episode does just that with its presentation of witchcraft.

When the episode opens, Granny Hart stands center screen in a medium shot muttering and chanting "bubble, bubble" and stirring a boiling pot. This is strikingly reminiscent of the opening scenes of almost any *Macbeth* production. The camera is placed inside the hearth, so the flames are ominously dancing in the foreground as she chants, suggesting satanic practice. Throughout the rest of the show, Granny moves between being a traditional amoral folk witch who exchanges cash for magic and a horror folk witch whose power is sourced from the Devil. When Granny is alone in her cabin, the shots are dark, and her face is obscured by hair, a cloak, or a broken mirror. When someone enters the home, the shots are well lit; Granny's cloaks are gone, and her hair is typically pulled back. In one frame, she is the dark, satanic folk witch, and in the other she is the small town's crone in the woods.

Counter to Granny is Jess-Belle, a poor young wild woman who is lost in love. Her heartache sends her to Granny for a love spell. At first, Granny responds, "Womankind has her own kinda witchcraft for that." But Jess is not convinced and accepts a magical bargain that comes "with a price," which she later learns is her soul. As Granny explains, the soul "is always in the bargain when you barter with witches." Prior to the bargain, Jess-Belle was already an outcast due to her poverty and her pursuit of a man above her station. She longs for the wild woman assimilation narrative; she wants to be married and transition into a conventional life. However, Jess bartered herself out of that narrative option by becoming a witch. When Jess begs for a reversal, Granny Hart tells her to accept her new role as an antagonist: "Be a witch. Take a witch's pleasure. Take the man you bargained for."

Jess rejects the advice and tries to fix what she has done. She confesses to her mother, "My prayers aren't answered in heaven no more," when advised to "kneel down" and ask "God for help." However, it is too late, and in the end, Jess-Belle is killed, making her the tragic hero. Despite efforts to redeem herself, Jess-Belle is not afforded a white knight rescue. She does not earn her spot as wife and mother. In this construction, once a satanic witch, forever a satanic witch. Thematically speaking, the narrative drives this point home through Jess-Belle's nightly transformations into a panther. She is a horror witch, although reluctantly, whose behavior and construction move far beyond simple social transgressions into the world of the monstrous. From that place, there is no redemptive return. While the elderly horror witch survives unscathed, the young horror witch experiences only tragedy.

Rise of the Male Witch

Paranormal suspense producers not only stepped outside of traditional constructions with their female witches, but they also took the lead in bringing the male witch to a new prominence. Rather than making minor appearances in the background as comic relief or as indigenous witch doctors, the magical man steps to the forefront as the primary antagonist and, perhaps more notably, as the leader of witches. This is an important point as it parallels the growing focus on the paranormal and a re-emerging interest in the occult, more specifically ceremonial magic. During the period, the male witch takes on three main forms: the fantasy magician, the occultist, and the witch doctor.

Before going forward, it is important to acknowledge the general difference between these newly constructed magical men and their female counterparts. Where the female witch derives her power from earth-bound elements, nature, love, desire, and sexuality, the magical man typically finds his source of power in celestial bodies, cerebral knowledge, science, occult mysteries, and other iconic elements of the "paranormal." The male witch controls his world and understands it; the female witch embodies power and wields it. She typically wears black, greens, and sometimes purple; he typically wears black, gold, and red. Where she functions from the outskirts of society, he functions from within community. She wants romantic love, eternal beauty, and solitude; he wants to rule. In addition, these new magical men are often depicted as leaders of a coven or a cult. While in the past most evil female witches are transgressive loners with the exception of the sisterly triad, this period sees the construction of the witch in society, cult, or coven with the male witch as the leader.

The Fantasy Magician

The fantasy magician, whose female counterpart is the fantasy crone, makes regular appearances in both television and film and is predominantly found in fairy-tale inspired or high fantasy productions, and sometimes science fiction. In *Jack the Giant Killer* (1962), for example, the fantasy magician is named Pendragon and bears the title the Black Prince of all Witches. While his name recalls the Arthurian legend, Pendragon's title reflects the Christian-based concept of Satan as the king of witches. Pendragon wears a dark shirt with gold stripes, and his cape bears a high red collar. As is typical for the fantasy magician, Pendragon has dark hair, a dramatic widow's peak, arched eyebrows, and a goatee shaved into points. This gives him a decidedly sinister look recalling the archetypical male evildoer such as Bela Lugosi's Dracula or Ming the Merciless in the *Flash Gordon* comic book series.

Pendragon's universe is constructed with a smattering of occult imagery, including symbols from astrology and ancient religions, as well as stolen narrative pieces from the Arthurian legend and a Renaissance-like production design. He is surrounded by strange monster-like beings called witches. These characters are anomalies, and it isn't until the 2010s that witches take on a physically monstrous appearance beyond recognition of any humanity (e.g., *Hansel & Gretel: Witch Hunters*, 2013).

Despite its campy style, *Jack the Giant Killer* provides a good example of the fantasy magician character. Similar magicians can be found in *Snow White and the Three Stooges* (1961), *Atlantis: The Lost Continent* (1961), and *The Magic Sword* (1962). In television, a fantasy magician appears in a 1967 *Star Trek* episode called the "Catspaw." Additionally, and as a sidenote, a related fantasy figure who does not always fit the study is the elderly wizard, such as the Merlin character in Disney's film *The Sword in the Stone* (1963) or the wizards found in Paramount's *Honey Halfwitch*.

The Male Occultist

A second type of the male witch found in the period is the occultist, who is typically associated with Satanism or other ritualistic cult practice. He exists predominantly in the horror film and the paranormal suspense thriller, and his female counterpart is the satanic witch. The male occultist undoubtedly finds his visual inspiration in famous historical figures such as Aleister Crowley, as well as in the horror film's popular mad scientist and assorted representations of occult practitioners as seen in foreign films and other media.

In the 1965 horror film *House of the Black Death*, two brothers, Belial (Lon Chaney Jr.) and Andre Desard (John Carradine), lead a community of satanic cultists. The film, also titled *Blood of the Man Devil*, was billed as involving "male witchcraft in evil terror," and the two brothers are sometimes labeled as warlocks. Belial and Andre are prototypical male occultists. In contrast to Pendragon, the brothers are severe in appearance with little to no facial hair; they wear dark clothing and hooded cloaks. They speak slowly in a deep, deliberate voices and rarely smile. As with most fictional occultists, the brothers practice a religion that is defined by satanic rhetoric, iconography, and ritualistic behaviors. Visually speaking, Belial has horns and a cloven foot caused by his worship, likening him to the Devil.

House of the Black Death is the first film to present a coven-based witchcraft narrative and a magical practice with both men and women combined. Therefore, it offers a clear juxtaposition between the male occultist and the female horror witch. The women cult members wear hooded dark robes during ritual just like the men, and they are equally as severe in manner and speech. However, at several points during the film, Belial asks a young witch (Sabrina) to dance for him. She disrobes, revealing a burlesque costume and commences a seductive dance before the entire coven. At no point do the male witches disrobe or display sexuality for any purpose.

This narrative detail reflects the difference in characterization of the female and male witch. The male witch, whether occultist or fantasy magician, never expresses raw sexuality. His world is about "power over" and not "pleasure for." Or better yet, his pleasure is the power over, and therefore his sexuality is reactionary and only serves his own needs. On the other hand, the female witch wields her sexuality or, in cases like *House of the Black Death*, bleeds it. This characterization becomes more evident after the Production Code gives way to the rating system and satanic horror films become popular.

Other examples of the period's male occultist can be found in the *Twilight Zone* episode "Still Valley," the *Thriller* episode "The Weird Tailor," and William J. Hole's low-budget film *The Devil's Hand*, all released in 1961. In these productions, the use of magic is directly associated with an evil ritual practice, gaining control over death or enemies, and growing personal power. While "Still Valley" is a contemplation on morality with the protagonist eventually giving up his magic, "The Weird Taylor" and *The Devil's Hand* are more typical occult horror stories.

The Witch Doctor

While the other two male witch constructions are relatively new, the period's witch doctors remained unchanged from past decades. They are mostly secondary characters or character props found in action-adventure films set in South America, Africa, or the South Seas. Their presence helps to define the film's cultural setting as exotic, dangerous, and primitive. As such, the witch doctor is most typically characterized as racially non-white and non-American. He dresses in elaborate costumes that might include face paint, headdresses, large jewelry, and often a bare upper torso. During this period, witch doctor films and shows include *The Spiral Road* (1962), *How to Stuff a Wild Bikini* (1965), *Mister Moses* (1965), *Gilligan's Island*, "Voodoo" (1966), *The Death Curse of Tartu* (1966), and *Valley of Mystery* (1967).

One might assume that progressive 1960s audiences were no longer interested in the colonialist values being portrayed by the witch doctor within the action-adventure genre. While that may be true, any rejection of the stereotype had yet to be incorporated into narrative entertainment. Moreover, even when the witch doctor in this iconic form does begin to disappear, witch films and shows continue to use black and brown bodies as signifiers of foreign or evil mysticism and witchcraft. (e.g., *Blood Orgy of the She Devils*, 1973; *Something Wicked This Way Comes*, 1983). The use of such cues external to the action-adventure genre or absent a true witch doctor are found in both *The Devil's Hand* (1961) and *How to Stuff a Wild Bikini* (1965).

The opening credit sequence of *The Devil's Hand* has an island ambiance, which sets the tone for a narrative that ultimately takes place in California. The film's occultist, Francis Lamont, is a white man who is portrayed as an average American. He owns a doll shop in the city center and wears nondescript suits. At one point, Francis explains that his unique religious practice originated abroad and that he worships Gamba, the Devil God. During his ceremonies, a young Black man wearing no shirt beats two drums. In several scenes, the camera rests solely on this figure before backing up to show the entire ritual. In addition, the cult leader's main magic is defined by poppets that read as "Voodoo" dolls in traditional Hollywood language. While the film may not contain a witch doctor or be set in a foreign land, it relies on established cinematic cues around foreign mysticism that have included the iconic witch doctor character traditionally found in the action-adventure film.

Similarly, the Annette Funicello beach musical *How to Stuff a Wild Bikini* uses an unrestrained mix of witchcraft tropes to build a farcical portrayal of the witch doctor and his role within a story set in Tahiti. In this case, Bwana, the witch doctor, is played by Buster Keaton in one of his final film roles. Not only do Bwana's scenes comedically mimic the portrayal of the Hollywood-based witch doctor, but they also offer unrelenting mockery of the entire concept of witchcraft and island culture, throwing everything at the viewer for a laugh. In this way, Keaton's character is a mix of witch doctor and male clown witch.

Both films are largely unremarkable, but *How to Stuff a Wild Bikini* does have one notable moment. At the end of the film, Keaton calls for his daughter to help with a spell. When she appears on camera, the viewer is delighted to see none other than *Bewitched*'s star Elizabeth Montgomery, who was married to the film's director, William Asher. In her cameo, she offers a knowing grin, a wink, and a classic *Bewitched* wrinkle of the nose. The viewer is rewarded.

After 1968, the witch doctor's appearance does decline. However, this change was not due to a cultural distaste for the embedded racism found within the character construction, as noted earlier. The decline was predominantly caused by a growing disinterest in the genre itself or, more specifically, in its classic style of execution. Genre popularity shifts are often the primary reason for the appearance and reappearance of characters and that applies to magical men as well as women. The action-adventure as a genre was evolving and the witch doctor's decline was part of that evolution.

Paranormal Suspense to Horror

While paranormal suspense shows were mostly popular in the early part of the period, they helped usher in and even introduce many elements that had largely been missing from Hollywood's witchcraft representations, such as rituals, occult paraphernalia, covens, and satanic worship. These elements began to bleed into the period's limited number of horror films. These films were mostly low-budget or independent films that flouted censorship rules and ignored PCA regulations.

One of the earliest horror films of the period was the Roger Corman film titled *The Terror* (1963) starring Boris Karloff and a young Jack Nicholson. Like Corman's earlier film *The Undead*, *The Terror* bridges the gap between the mad scientist narrative and the horror witch film. It tells the story of a young man who stumbles upon a secret, which includes a woman's ghost, a satanic pact, and a forbidden love affair. The film contains a single elderly folk witch who is played by Dorothy Neumann, the same actress who played *The Undead*'s Meg Maud.

Lt. Andre Duvalier (Jack Nicholson) confronts Katrina (Dorothy Neumann),
a local witch, about her son Eric in Roger Corman's 1963 film The Terror.
[Source: American International Pictures/Photofest.
Copyright: © American International Pictures (AIP)]

While *The Terror* is a horror witch film, it doesn't capture the shifting trends with regard to witchcraft and displays of sexuality that were found in his 1957 film *The Undead* or Harold Daniels's *House of the Black Death*, released in 1965. In comparing Corman's earlier work to Daniels's film, it is easier to see the coming changes in construction. Near the end of Corman's 1957 film, a group of actresses, dressed as darkly clad ghouls, dance around the graveyard. Their bodies are mostly covered, and their dance is defined as a celebration of the witches' sabbath. The sequence is symbolic of the film's emotional tension as all the characters come together for the final conflict. The ritual dance is a working part of the narrative.

By contrast, Daniels's 1965 film contains two dance sequences, and both are performed by a scantily clad young coven member and witch (Sabrina). When requested by the High Priest, she disrobes and dances for him and his guests. Her dances do not advance the plot and they play no other role than to define the cult practice as salacious and inappropriate. The sequences act primarily as visual pleasure points for the characters and viewers alike.

A Closer Look: *The Naked Witch* and Low Budget Schlock

Despite the changing climate, the juxtaposition of overt sexual pleasure and witchcraft, as found in *House of the Black Death*, was largely avoided or significantly masked in mainstream productions, with a few exceptions. However, the period's growing indie market bore no allegiance to the crippled PCA and it began to capitalize on the characterization of the vamp witch within the horror genre. Highly sexualized witches not only appeared in low-budget horror films, like Daniels's *House of the Black Death*, but also in a growing sexploitation or "nudie" industry. Such films include the previously mentioned *The Devil's Hand* (1961) as well as *The Devil's Mistress* (1965) and *The Satanist* (1968).

Included in that list was Larry Buchanan's *The Naked Witch*. Filmed in Texas in 1961 but not released until 1964, this low-budget horror film tells the story of a resurrected, vengeful, and naked witch. While Buchanan's film is a cheap thrill in terms of overall production, it is one of the first notable films to cross horror and paranormal suspense through a dead witch narrative, although the theme also appears in the *Thriller* episode "God Grante That She Lye Stylle" released in 1961. Within its campy construction, *The Naked Witch* contains many of the basic iconic elements in the paranormal horror film: old legends, stakes through the heart, foreign culture, the living dead, scorned love, and a naked woman. Buchannan captured it all.

To make the low-budget film, Buchanan was given a meager eight thousand dollars by Claude Alexander, who he described as being "an independent road-side distributor of exploitation product." [206] Alexander granted Buchanan full creative authority as long as he stayed on budget and kept the film to eighty minutes. As Buchanan remembers, Alexander said, "make a drive-in picture with lots of nudity and

---

206. Larry Buchanan, *"It Came From Hunger!" Tales of a Cinema Schlockmeister* (Columbia, SC: Larry Buchanan, 1996), 48.

very little dialogue."[207] The story itself was inspired by Buchanan's own personal trip to Luchenbach, Texas, where he said the old German folkways still thrived. In the city's history, he found the tale of "a witch who returns from the grave after 100 years to kill and maim the descendants of those who had put her to the stake."[208] In the end, Buchanan's film did well enough for a low-budget drive-in film, but it is largely considered, as his memoirs might call it, "schlock."

It is important to note that Buchanan's *The Naked Witch* is not the same film as *The Naked Witch* (1967). The two are often confused in databases and articles. Buchanan's 1961 film is considered a low-budget horror film that tells the story of a woman who was once accused and burned as a witch. The 1967 film, which is sometimes titled *The Naked Temptress*, is a lost sexploitation film directed by Andy Milligan and set in New Jersey. Milligan's film tells the story of two women accused of witchcraft due to love affairs and an interest in orgies. Aside from the title and budget point, the only other commonality between the two films is that they are both named "Naked Witch" and are built on the concept of women being accused of witchcraft due to transgressive behavior.

Emerging Themes in Horror Witch Narratives

Through these independent horror witch films and the paranormal suspense thrillers, themes begin to emerge that will continue to dominate horror witch films into the future. Most of the recurrent themes involve a woman's quest for love, beauty, or revenge. *The Naked Witch* seeks revenge, Miss Devore seeks everlasting youth and beauty, Jess-Belle seeks love. None of these themes are new to narrative film. Disney's Wicked Queen wants to retain her youth and beauty and Mother Rigby seeks revenge. However, the true horror narrative works in extremes. It is not enough to simply associate a woman's independent actions, her power, or her appearance to witchcraft and magic. The narrative must also define that power through a hyper-sexualized beauty, obsessive female narcissism, or a literal monstrosity.

These extremes in character construction were not limited to the period's horror films. For example, in the fantasy spectacle *Jack the Giant Killer*, Pendragon turns his captive princess into a witch. When that happens, she changes from wearing soft pastels and renaissance garb into a bright red gown and dramatic headdress. Her eyes become snake-like and her makeup dramatic. The princess turns from an innocent girl next door to a sexualized vamp who loves looking at her reflection in the mirror. This transformation is indicative of demonization of a woman's femininity as represented by witchcraft, linking it to a narcissistic pleasure. It also reinforces a concept seen in many past films that good women take care of others while evil women do for themselves.

---

207. Buchanan, *"It Came From Hunger!,"* 48.
208. Buchanan, *"It Came From Hunger!,"* 49.

While these themes appear in other genres as shown, it is in the horror film that they are fully realized in order to evoke both extremes of pleasure and repulsion at the same time. The witch exists as both an object of desire and as an abomination. Miss Devore is attractive with her wig, but she is grotesque with it gone. The Naked Witch is beautiful and naked, but simultaneously she is both a killer and, quite literally, dead. The beautiful Jess-Belle is a shape-shifter with no soul. That is how horror works. The quest for beauty, love, or everlasting life is not simply a human desire for these witch characters. It becomes a ravenous need guiding a transgressive woman into a monstrous state in which she seeks her goal at any cost. The witch is literally becoming a monster.

Old Time Religion

Along with expressions of female sexuality and power, filmmakers were also increasingly exploring themes related to satanic worship and religion. As the Code broke down, Hollywood's aversion to expressing traditional themes found in Catholicism began to wane. The late 1950s saw this shift happening (e.g., *The Undead*, 1957), and that trend continued into the 1960s in both television and film. For example, Roger Corman's *The Terror* is filled with traditional Catholic ideology. The film's witch, Katrina, is killed by burning after trying to enter the "house of God." She is called a heretic with the "power of darkness."

Through paranormal suspense and the limited number of horror films, filmmakers were reconnecting the witch with her historical and theological roots as an agent of Satan. In past decades, witchcraft was an allegory for a woman's innate power, sexuality, and internal spirit, all of which had to be controlled. During this period, film narratives reimagined witchcraft as not an innate power or beingness, but as one given to the woman by a mystical man, Satan. It is the wild woman's narcissistic desires that lead her to seek out this power. In other words, magic is no longer a woman's power, but a gift bestowed to a desperate woman by a man (i.e., *Damn Yankees*, 1958). Her transgression is not one of personal expression but solely the result of extreme self-absorption. This is an ironic truth given the coming of second wave feminism where gender roles were being questioned.

Witch Next Door: *Bewitched* and *The Addams Family*

As the interest in paranormal television and fantasy waned, there was a notable decrease in the overall number of narrative witches in American entertainment. However, those productions that remained offered new and emerging constructions and treatments of witchcraft. The witch and her magic were moving from a state of virtual irrelevancy to something worth examining in and of itself, whether they be evil or not. These emerging expressions of witchcraft paralleled shifting gender dynamics in American society as well as a woman's social currency, which was similarly moving from virtual irrelevancy to something more.

In the second half of the period, television produced two of its most famous fantasy witches: Samantha and Morticia. Both are versions of the witch next door. Samantha is a comedic fantasy witch and Morticia, a fantasy vamp. Due to these classifications, their power is not sourced. The fantasy genre is enough to justify their use of magic and they are accepted as such into their universe. Unlike past witches next door, Samantha and Morticia remain full fantasy witches to the bitter end, self-empowered, and adored within the text and without. They do not cross over into the world of the wild woman as did Jennifer or Gillian. They do not give up their magic, or in the case of Morticia, a goth appearance, for love and marriage. These two suburban fantasy witches exist with no excuses and no compromise.

A Closer Look: *Bewitched*

Six years after the release of the film *Bell, Book and Candle* (1958), the television show *Bewitched* once again blended witchcraft fantasy with contemporary reality. Beginning its run in 1964, the series was an immediate success. The show was first imagined by television executives Bill Dozier and Harry Ackerman. Shortly after, they hired screenwriter Sol Saks, who has repeatedly admitted in interviews that his inspiration was the two older films *Bell, Book and Candle* and *I Married a Witch*. In 1965, Ackerman said, "[*Bewitched*] is a simple, honest extension of an elemental comedy idea that had gone about as far as it could go. We hit on a simple thing that sang and led us to marvelous story ideas: a witch trying to kick her witchdom." [209]

The series begins with the witch, Samantha (Elizabeth Montgomery), already married to her husband, Darrin (Dick York). It goes on to tell the story of a 1960s suburban housewife grappling with the mundane experiences of motherhood and marriage, as well as the added difficulty of maintaining the walls between her magical family and her human existence. Visually, Samantha is the typical 1960s television housewife. She has blonde hair and blue eyes with a neat contemporary hairstyle and conservative yet fashionable clothing. Samantha looks appropriate. She is, in appearance, the "true woman" trying to maintain that socially acceptable lifestyle.

---

209. Joseph N. Bell, "TV's Witch to Watch," *Pageant*, April 1965, http://www.harpiesbizarre.com/vintage-witch2watch.htm.

Elizabeth Montgomery as Samantha Stephens and Agnes Moorehead as
Endora befuddle Darrin (Dick York) with magic in Bewitched *(1964–1972)*
[Source: ABC/Photofest. Copyright: © ABC]

However, like the two older films on which the show was reportedly based, *Bewitched* springboards off the collision between witchcraft fantasy and a conventional modern reality; this dance is what creates the comedic tension. In some ways, *Bewitched* is act 2 for the older films with Samantha in the role of the married Gillian or Jennifer. Whereas the two older characters both lived in fantasy while trying to retire to reality, Samantha lives in reality while fighting off fantasy.

Unlike her predecessors, Samantha is not forced to abandon her magic in order to experience what Gillian labeled the "humdrum." However, as Ackerman suggested, Samantha is working to "kick her witchdom" habit. She repeatedly promises Darrin that she would not use magic. Despite all her efforts, she can't fully escape being a witch. Therefore, Samantha is not a wild woman waiting to be assimilated; she is a fantasy witch. And it is the tension created by the show's lurking witchcraft within the framework of contemporary reality that creates the comedic situations. For example, in the pilot, Samantha's mother, Endora, repeatedly moves Darrin, who is wearing only pajamas, into the crowded hotel lobby in order to keep him from entering the honeymoon suite.

Witchcraft in *Bewitched*

In defining witchcraft, *Bewitched* capitalized on well-known fantasy iconography. In the first episode, when Samantha reveals the truth to Darrin, she says, "I am a witch. A real house-haunting, broom-riding, cauldron-stirring witch." In the same episode, Endora explains that humans believe that witches wear those "big ugly hats and fly around on broomsticks." Ironically, this was the exact imagery used in the animated opening credit sequence. The cartoon Samantha flies into the frame on a broomstick across the moon, wearing the iconic hat and dress. Then, in a different frame, she transforms into a cat. In several episodes, Endora and Samantha make trips to Salem to attend council meetings and a witch conference. Despite the use of this iconography, the show only toys with—rarely ever fully emerging into—the Halloween realm. The symbols are predominantly used as kitsch in a show that, beneath the surface, explores suburban life, gender roles, and social difference.

Bewitched's magical world is also defined through its secondary magical characters and their eccentric appearance and behavior, including Endora and Uncle Arthur. The latter is a male clown witch, similar in construction to Gillian's brother Nicky. Uncle Arthur (Paul Lynde) only appeared in ten episodes. Endora, as noted, is Samantha's mother. Visually she has curly red hair, wears dramatic eye makeup, and dresses in vibrant colors that offset the pastels and drab palette of suburban life. Like Aunt Queenie and Bianca, Endora (Agnes Moorehead) is a contemporary clown witch. Hers and Uncle Arthur's eccentricities are what distinguish the witch world from the human world—something for which they have little care or love. In the pilot, Endora expresses this disdain for humanity, explaining that humans are prejudiced against witches.

Endora plays the important role of magical caretaker, a character who is most typically portrayed as an auntie or a cousin (e.g., *Honey Halfwitch*, 1965–1967; *Bell, Book and Candle*, 1958). However, Endora is Samantha's mother, which is a rare character relationship. The mother-daughter bond is typically one of antagonistic conflict, not loving support (e.g., *Snow White and the Seven Dwarfs*, 1937). Samantha and Endora's relationship, although not perfect, adds another level of comedic tension through the parody of a contemporary mother-daughter relationship. Endora is constructed as the prototypical mother-in-law who is unhappy with her daughter's choices in marriage, parenting, and homemaking. At the same time, Endora's presence normalizes Samantha's existence as well as witch culture in general. Even witches have meddling mothers.

Bewitched in a Changing Culture

Bewitched was popular right from the start and had a long run that ended in 1972. Since its airing, the show has received a variety of conflicting readings from women and feminist writers. One common criticism is that Samantha, like the typical sitcom housewife, is suppressing her agency, symbolically presented as witchcraft, in order to live within her husband's world. Samantha is trying to kick her witchcraft habit. She wears conventional clothing and exhibits no aggressive sexuality or playful seduction. Her personal mission is to maintain a well-appointed human existence and serve as a proper wife in a proper setting, bearing the resemblance to June Cleaver of *Leave it to Beaver* (1957–1963). Her eagerness to fill this conventional role is a source of contention for critics. In her essay "Retelling Salem Stories," Marion Gibson notes that "Scriptwriter Lila Garrett saw Endora as offering an alternative to liberal women viewers who 'were a little annoyed at times to see a woman like Samantha, who was that capable, insisting on staying at home all the time.'"[210]

In other readings, *Bewitched* was read as a reflection on the 1960s social climate. As such, the show subverts the 1950s family media model in which the father always "knew best" (e.g., *Leave it to Beaver*; *Father Knows Best*, 1954–1960). While Samantha attempted to sincerely play at that classic family game, she was consistently thwarted by other magical characters and mundane situations. Darrin was often the victim of circumstance and Samantha would come to the rescue. In the pilot, after she tells him that she's a witch, Darrin says, "We'll talk about it tomorrow." She replies, "Now." Samantha is not a pushover; she sits at the center of the show's universe on the edge between fantasy and reality. Through this reading, Samantha is reimagined as a progressive example of the feminine spirit. And it is witchcraft, as part of her existence, that pushes against of the limits of convention. Samantha is a witch, and she cannot stop being a witch. It is not a choice, like the witches of horror. She is who she is, and her power is part of it.

A third reading takes this social perspective a step further, positing that the show is reflective of the civil rights movement. This thesis was suggested in 1965 by the show's own producers. Danny Arnold said, "I saw a great opportunity to accomplish something. Fantasy can always be a jumping-off place for more sophisticated work […] What we do in this series doesn't happen to witches; it happens to people. But the

---

210. Marion Gibson, "Retelling Salem Stories: Gender Politics and Witches in American Culture," *European Journal of American Culture* 25, no. 2 (August 2006): 97, https://doi.org/10.1386/ejac.25.2.85/1; Herbie Pilato, *Bewitched Forever: The Immortal Companion to Televisions Most Magical Supernatural Situation Comedy* (Irving TX: Tapestry Press, 2004), quoted in Gibson.

messages are funnier when they happen to a witch—and therefore less offensive." [211] Arnold goes on to explain how the show "pointed the finger at bigotry." He says:

> Samantha's husband was prejudiced about witches—who are definitely a minority group. He thought they were all ugly old crones, and his wife had to break down this prejudice. It is a direct parallel to some of our social problems of today. But through fantasy, we can get a more vivid portrayal. Humor can then come out of touchy subjects." [212]

With that reading in mind, humans are, allegorically speaking, the white Christian majority, and witches are the other. Samantha and Darren's life together models the struggles of couples within interracial, interfaith, or intercultural marriages.

In addition, the character of Uncle Arthur is often read, even at the time, as a positive gay role model. With that in mind, the witchcraft world, like that of *Bell, Book and Candle*, could be a stand-in for a hidden but lateral gay subculture or that of any marginalized American community. These progressive readings are not a stretch knowing that television content was more conservative and conventional than Hollywood, mainly because television shows were easily accessible to children within the home space. Regardless of any backlash, *Bewitched* has since been recognized as a progressive expression of a changing American society hidden within a conventional setting, making the show a well-played narrative irony masked in comedy and, quite possibly, a true reflection of American society as it was.

The Addams Family

The third sociopolitical reading of *Bewitched* also applies to the popular sitcom *The Addams Family*, which aired at the same time. The show was based on a series of single-frame print comics originally created by Charles Addams, debuting in 1938. *The Addams Family*, in comics or on television, follows the daily life of an eccentric family of horror-inspired characters as they exist in modern suburban America. Like *Bewitched*, the show merges fantasy, in this case horror, and reality to create its satirical comedic tension. In this macabre family, Morticia Addams (Carolyn Jones) is the witch.

Visually speaking, Morticia is everything that Samantha is not. She fully embodies the seductive vamp witch with an iconic tight black dress, pale skin, dark arched eyebrows, red lips, and long dark hair. Where Samantha could be Gillian turned housewife, Morticia could be Livia (e.g., *The Undead*) without the satanic elements.

---

211. Bell, "TV's Witch to Watch."
212. Bell, "TV's Witch to Watch."

Like Livia, Morticia is constructed to be shockingly beautiful and vibrantly sexy, and unapologetically so. The show relishes in this aspect of her character, as seen partly through her husband Gomez's lustful behavior and suggestive remarks. But Morticia is more than that; she is also a mother and a wife. The show offers the possibility that a beautiful and sexualized woman could actually care for others as well as herself, subverting both horror and fantasy standards.

Thematically speaking, the show works like *Bewitched* in terms of its allegorical social context. Where *Bewitched* creates a mixed marriage, *The Addams Family* places an entire group of people, defined as nonnormative, within a conventional suburban environment. The show asks and answers the question: "what happens when a family, who is not like us, moves into the neighborhood?" The show then answers this question through its satirical comedy, but as noted by *Bewitched* producer Danny Arnold, "[f]antasy can always be a jumping-off place for more sophisticated work." [213]

As an aside, the possibility of reading witch productions as allegory for racial tensions can be taken further if one includes the use of green skin as a marker of difference. Over time, green skin became a signifier of the woman who is transgressive, monstrous, nonhuman, amoral, or evil. While that visual element originally was a technical solution meant to define the witch as a monster, it evolved in meaning with repeated use. However, at the same time, green skin is predominantly taken for granted as simply fantastical. It is not until much later that this visual element is drawn into witch narratives as openly symbolic of social difference, race, or otherwise (e.g., Broadway's *Wicked*, 2003).

Long before that happens, *Bewitched* and *The Addams Family* exist as two notable shows that invest in contemporary social conversations and, at the same time, demonstrate the evolution of the witch into something more than just a transgressive woman who needs saving. While the earlier witch next door characters were forced to conform, Samantha and Morticia are not. The former tries, but she is unable. Samantha can't deny who she is. The latter owns her identity and makes no apologies. Morticia is her own woman and thrives in her magical existence. Both series challenge the assumption of cultural uniformity as well as the limitations on the powers allowed to women within contemporary America.

The End of an Era: *Rosemary's Baby*

Due to Hollywood's financial difficulties and its struggle to draw audiences away from the television, the PCA was no longer regularly issuing approval certificates as early as 1966. However, the administration continued its work. If the film did not

---

213. Bell, "TV's Witch to Watch."

meet code standards, the film was stamped with the label "Suggested for Mature Audiences." [214] Then, in November of 1968, the Production Code Administration and its infamous moral code were completely abandoned in favor of the MPAA (Motion Picture Association of America) rating system. However, before that happened, one last witch film was released, and it was a harbinger of what was to come for the Hollywood witch.

In 1968 just before the removal of Hollywood's production code, Paramount Pictures released Roman Polanski's first American film titled *Rosemary's Baby* (1968). Based on Ira Levin's book of the same name, the film is considered to be a classic and tells the story of a young couple who encounter a satanic coven living next door to their new apartment. After some time, the young wife, Rosemary Woodhouse (Mia Farrow), is drugged and raped by the Devil. As a result, she becomes pregnant and eventually produces a demon child. *Rosemary's Baby* was so well received that it had already become a cultural icon by 1973, when it was mentioned in George Romero's film *Hungry Wives*. In that scene, two friends are driving to a tarot reading, and one advises, "If the mousse tastes chalky don't eat it. You know. It's the *Rosemary's Baby* bit."

Polanski and the Production Code Administration

Polanski's film was produced before the Production Code Administration was completely dismantled, and the conversations that ensued between the producers and the censorship office demonstrate the prevailing attitude of filmmakers at the time. In a 1967 memo, PCA administrator Morris Murphy notes that Paramount producer William Castle claimed that he "did not wish to submit [their] lengthy letters to Mr. Roman Polanski." According to Castle, Polanski "wanted no interference of any kind in making the picture and that in order to keep him on the project as it were, they had decided to leave him alone." [215] Similarly, Paramount studios refused to yield to most PCA requests. In another memo dated Feb. 29, 1968, Murphy notes that the administration would grant the film its certificate despite the studio not eliminating the phrase "Oh shit!" [216] The film was approved in March and released to theaters in June of 1968.

---

214. Thompson and Bordwell, *Film History*, 515.

215. Morris Murphy, Interoffice Memo for the files, August 14, 1967; source: *Rosemary's Baby* Production Films, MPAA PCA records, Margaret Herrick Library, Academy of Motion Picture Arts and Sciences, Beverly Hills, California.

216. Morris Murphy, Interoffice Memo for the files, February 29, 1968; source: *Rosemary's Baby* Production Films, MPAA PCA records, Margaret Herrick Library, Academy of Motion Picture Arts and Sciences, Beverly Hills, California.

Polanski and the producers had no interest in being censored and they directly flouted the system, which exemplifies what was happening in the industry overall. Arthur Penn's film *Bonnie and Clyde* had all but shocked the American public in 1967, and a growing influx of foreign and young filmmakers were actively resisting the antiquated studio system, which was still stuck in its moral supremacy founded in the 1930s. After MPAA director Jack Valenti dismantled the PCA and removed the code, *Rosemary's Baby* was given an R rating, suggesting that no one under sixteen should be permitted to see the film without a parent or guardian.

Satanic Witch Horror

While Polanski was not the only filmmaker to push against the ailing PCA, his film is a landmark in this study due to the timing of its release. *Rosemary's Baby* heralds a flood of satanic witch horror films and typifies the witch films of the early 1970s. Polanski presents a proto-typical coven-next-door narrative, in which a young un-suspecting couple move happily into a new home. Over time, they discover that their friendly neighbors are a bit odd, which eventually leads to the wife suspecting some-thing more sinister. In this film, Rosemary Woodhouse discovers that her elderly neighbors practice witchcraft, and the narrative's tension increases from there as she attempts to escape the grips of the coven.

After Rosemary and her actor husband Guy (John Cassavetes) move into their lush New York City apartment, the warning signs appear immediately with oddly placed furniture, weird noises, strange herbal remedies, and the overly friendly neighbors. Throughout the film Rosemary is consistently trying to brighten up her surroundings with yellows and whites, but the shots visually never change. She can-not alter the atmosphere or her fate. Through the subdued backgrounds, Polanski was able to maintain a calm tone that pulsates slowly throughout the film, allowing for suspense and the creep factor to fester. He also accomplished this through sug-gestive action and visual cues rather than shocking imagery. These techniques mimic Rosemary's own fears and the thematic concept that evil lurks under the surface of what appears to be a mundane life.

The film's horror witches, Minnie and Roman Castavet, enforce this idea because they are characterized as a typical New York City elderly couple. They are not defined as witches by pointy hats or hooded cloaks, but rather simply by their beliefs and practice. The only witch character trope offered is Minnie's interest in herbs and her rejection of modern medicine. Unlike in *House of the Black Death* (1965), the Casta-vets's coven does not live on a compound away from society. Its leaders live in the urban apartment; one member is a doctor and, eventually, another is Rosemary's own husband. They are male and female, young and old. In that way, the Castavets and their coven members are contemporary witch next door figures, but with a horrific twist.

Neighbor Minnie Castavet (Ruth Gordon) and her friend Laura-Louise (Patsy Kelly) visit Rosemary (Mia Farrow) and gift her a locket filled with tannis root in the 1968 horror film Rosemary's Baby. *[Source: Paramount Pictures/Photofest. © Paramount Pictures]*

The film's most shocking and disruptive scene is the ritual invoking Satan to Rosemary's bedroom, which results in the pregnancy. This rape scene is the centerpiece of the entire film, propelling the plot and defining the witches in practice. During that sequence, Rosemary is the only person that is clearly shown for any length of time, and the shots are mostly of her face in close-up or extreme close-up. The Devil is represented only through his body parts—hands, arms, eyes, and shadow. The witches stand as a crowd around the bed; they are naked but only shown from the shoulders up. The sequence is dark, wild, and confusing in both sound and imagery. That cinematic atmosphere parallels Rosemary's own confusion.

Equally as jarring is the final scene in which Rosemary comes to terms with the reality of the rape scene. Her baby is a demon, and her husband is a Satanist. She tries to run, but as she does, the baby cries. Rosemary is drawn back in, and the film ends with evil thriving in New York City. In this film, Polanski created an allegory for the contemporary social upheaval and the surging backlash against the establishment.

The New Old Witchcraft

According to a 2017 *Vanity Fair* article, author Ira Levin had "'mixed feelings about *Rosemary's Baby*,' including religious guilt" due to the fact that it played a part in popularizing occult, Satanist, and witchcraft practice.[217] As noted earlier, by the late 1960s the modern occult movement was expanding alongside a countercultural movement of free thought and progressive politics. Levin, a Jewish atheist, said, "I really feel a certain degree of guilt about having fostered that kind of irrationality."[218]

Polanski, an agnostic, expressed similar sentiment as recorded by film critic James Greenberg. Polanski said, "[The Satanist] aspect of the book disturbed me. I could not make a film that is seriously supernatural. I can treat it as a tale, but a woman raped by the devil in today's New York? No, I can't do that. So I did it with ambiguity."[219] Polanski purposefully never shows the baby, and the rest of the scenes, even the rape scene, are ambiguous, as noted. While many people believed the story was about Devil worship, Polanski maintained it was not. Greenberg writes:

> I don't think anyone—except for a few crazies—truly believed Rosemary had been violated by the devil. But the important thing is that for two hours Polanski made it feel like it *could* happen. And in his great films, of which this is surely one, there is always that shadow of a doubt.[220]

Despite Greenberg's assumption and Polanski's skilled camera work, in a changing climate with an increasing interest in the occult, Levin was closer to the truth. The film did spark the imagination of younger audiences, who were increasingly interested in progressive topics. The National Catholic Office for Motion Pictures also believed it was real enough to give the film a rating of "C" for condemned.[221] Additionally, many fans began to believe the film was cursed due to a number of deaths

---

217. Rosemary Counter, "The Most Cursed Hit Movie Ever Made," *Vanity Fair*, June 1, 2017, https://www.vanityfair.com/hollywood/2017/06/the-most-cursed-hit-movie-ever-made-rosemarys-baby.

218. Counter, "The Most Cursed Hit Movie Ever Made."

219. James Greenberg, *Roman Polanski: A Retrospective* (New York: Harry N. Abrams, 2013), 97.

220. Greenberg, *Roman Polanski: A Retrospective*, 97.

221. "Recent Classifications and Guide to Current Films," The National Catholic Office for Motion Pictures 33, no. 20 (June 27, 1968).

and career failures associated with its cast and crew. The most public one was the brutal murder of Polanski's wife, Sharon Tate, by cult leader Charles Manson.[222]

Despite Polanski's or Levin's reservations, the film's narrative goes more completely where no other mainstream witch production had. *Rosemary's Baby* fully embraces witchcraft as a satanic practice with witches who show no remorse for their beliefs. The film offers no narrative nuance in their characterization, nor does it inflict a plot-based judgment with regard to their ethical choices, as in *House of the Black Death*. While witchcraft is designated as evil, the film just presents it as reality without killing or punishing the characters. The Castevets are what they are, as is Samantha, Granny Hart, or the Naked Witch. Furthermore, there are many witches like them, all living in contemporary society. That point, once again, is the essence of the film's horror. Evil, whether by Devil or human corruption, lurks just below the surface of American normalcy.

Although *Rosemary's Baby* was not the first horror film to include a satanic theme, it was the first mainstream film to do so with a post-Code sensibility. Furthermore, it was the first to do so successfully with an artistic flare and depth of meaning. The film's influence cannot be understated. Once Hollywood was released from the shackles of censorship in 1968, more filmmakers followed Polanski's lead. The gates were open, and beginning in 1970, all hell broke loose, so to speak. A flood of horror witch films hit the market, although not one ever came near in execution to the beauty and horror of *Rosemary's Baby*.

Conclusion

The 1960s was a difficult era for Hollywood as the sociocultural changes left the industry unsure of its audience. Emerging independent directors and producers flouted the censorship administration, and an increasing number of films were released without the seal of approval. Moreover, television, which continued to flourish, stole audiences away from the big screen, offering an ever-growing range of popular content.

With all this flux and instability, the representation of witchcraft began to change. Traditional genres, such as fantasy and fairy tale adaptations, disappeared. Paranormal suspense shows and the occasional low-budget horror film presented witch characters that had rarely, if ever, been seen in Hollywood, such as the satanic witch or the ghost witch. And, moreover, male witches as leaders of covens made their first appearances. Television brought two of its most famous witches: Samantha and Morticia. These two shows not only reflected a change in the representation of the witch and her relationship to her power, but they shared an interest in the sociopolitical

---

222. Counter "The Most Cursed Hit Movie Ever Made."

climate. Their families reflect the 1960s suburban reckoning with regard to race, religion, and ethnicity.

Finally, as the period closed, Hollywood had its own reckoning. In the face of a dying industry, the MPAA dismantled its decades-old Production Code in favor of a rating system. It was the end of Hollywood's golden era. As that happened, Paramount released one of the most iconic American witch films: *Rosemary's Baby*. Unbeknownst to its producers, the film would go on to become a signifier of what's to come in terms of the presentation of witchcraft, the occult, and the horror genre overall. It also marks the beginning of the first true wave of American witch films and shows.

Chapter 7: Filmography

Feathertop	1961	Dean Whitmore
Snow White and the Three Stooges	1961	Walter Lang
The Twilight Zone, "Still Valley"	1961	James Sheldon
Thriller, "The Weird Tailor"	1961	Herschel Daugherty
Thriller, "God Grante That She Lye Stille"	1961	Herschel Daugherty
The Devil's Hand	1961	William J. Hole Jr.
Atlantis, The Lost Continent	1961	George Pal
The Tales of the Wizard of Oz	1961	Harry Kerwin
Thriller, "A Wig for Miss Devore"	1962	John Brahm
The Spiral Road	1962	Robert Mulligan
Jack the Giant Killer	1962	Nathan Juran
The Magic Sword	1962	Bert I. Gordon
Thriller, "La Strega"	1962	Ida Lupino
The Twilight Zone, "Jess-Belle"	1963	Buzz Kulik
The Terror	1963	Roger Corman
The Sword in the Stone	1963	Wolfgang Reitherman
The New Casper Cartoon Show	1963–1969	Seymour Kneitel
Bewitched	1964–1972	Sol Saks (creator)

The Magic Christmas Tree	1964	Richard C. Parish
The Naked Witch	1964	Larry Buchanan
Return to Oz	1964	F. R. Crawley et al.
The Addams Family	1964–1966	David Levy (creator)
Underdog, "The Witch of Pickyoon"	1964	Gary Mooney
House of the Black Death	1965	Harold Daniels
Mister Moses	1965	Ronald Neame
How to Stuff a Wild Bikini	1965	William Asher
The Lucy Show, "Lucy and the Monsters"	1965	Jack Donohue
The Devil's Mistress	1965	Orville Wanzer
Honey Halfwitch	1965–1967	Howard Post (creator)
Gilligan's Island, "Voodoo"	1966	George Cahan
The Death Curse of Tartu	1966	William Grefé
Valley of Mystery	1967	Joseph Lejtes
The Naked Witch	1967	Andy Milligan
Star Trek, "Catspaw"	1967	Joseph Pevney
The Satanist	1968	Zoltan G. Spencer
Blackbeard's Ghost	1968	Robert Stevenson
Rosemary's Baby	1968	Roman Polanski

Chapter 8
Horror and Exploitation
(1969–1978)

By 1969, the cultural revolution was in full swing, the country was at war, and Hollywood was experiencing epic changes to its industry structure. The classic studio system was dead, and the censorship code had been abandoned after nearly a decade of deteriorating influence. Rather than undergoing PCA scrutiny to receive a seal of approval, mainstream films now received an audience rating of either G (General Audiences), PG (Parental Guidance), or R (Restricted). These changes resulted in what is sometimes referred to as the "New Hollywood," which included increased opportunities for independent filmmakers, foreign directors, and new up-and-coming young directors.[223]

The changes also provided space for evocative screen content, including graphic violence (e.g., *The Wild Bunch*, 1969; *The Godfather*, 1972) and nudity (e.g., *Vixen!*, 1968; *Blood Sabbath*, 1972), both of which found a natural home in the rebirth of the horror genre. Similarly, this was the decade that birthed the teen slasher film and gave way to the modern pornography film industry. Legendary director John Ford blamed this on economics, saying "Hollywood now is run by Wall St. and Madison Ave., who demand 'Sex and Violence.'"[224] To an extent that was true. These themes and narratives, which were previously kept off the screen, did help increase ticket sales. However, the reason for their presence was more than simply a function of economics. It was also a product of a society that included a pervasive counterculture movement,

---

223. Thompson and Bordwell, *Film History*, 516.
224. Thompson and Bordwell, *Film History*, 515.

racial tensions, war protests, a sexual revolution, and a growing teen culture. In addition, there was newly revived interest in the occult and what eventually became known as "New Age" spirituality.

Modern Witchcraft Meets Hollywood Witchcraft

Once again, it is important to acknowledge the intersections between the burgeoning modern Witchcraft movement and related occult movements with the American entertainment industry. As noted in chapter seven, it was not until the late 1960s that modern American Witches and other occultists began to significantly organize in contemporary terms. By 1968, there were a host of formal institutions and traditions, including the Church of Aphrodite, the Church of All Worlds, Seax Wicca, FeraFeria, and the New Reformed Orthodox Order of the Golden Dawn. In 1968, the Council of Themis formed as the first umbrella Pagan organization.[225]

After 1968, the list of Pagan and occult organizations grew significantly, and with that came widely available publications, including books, journals, and magazines. In 1969, Anton LaVey published *The Satanic Bible*, followed by *The Satanic Witch*, and Sybil Leek published *Diary of a Witch*. That same year, Raymond Buckland released *A Pocket Guide to the Supernatural*, followed by *Witchcraft from the Inside*. And, Isaac Bonewits, a leader in the modern Druidry movement, published *Real Magic*. Additionally, British screenwriter Paul Huson published his own book *Mastering Witchcraft*. In 1971, *The Witches' Almanac* began publishing its popular annual, and the Church of All Worlds launched the very first publicly available Pagan magazine called *Green Egg*. This was just the tip of the iceberg.

By the mid-1970s, modern Witches were increasingly stepping out of what they called "the broom closet" and becoming more visible to the general population. In 1970, Salem Witch Laurie Cabot opened her first store, and then in 1977, she was named the Official Witch of Salem by Massachusetts Governor Michael Dukakis. This, along with the continued popularity of the television show *Bewitched*, ushered in a new era for the city of Salem, whose residents had yet to fully embrace their long-held label as *America's Witch City*. According to historian Dr. Emerson Baker, "Witchcraft cast a long shadow over Salem." However, he noted that along with *Bewitched*, the arrival of modern Witches and Wiccans and the public nature of Cabot's work in the 1970s helped the city embrace what had largely been considered a dark point in the area's history.[226]

---

225. Chas Clifton, *Her Hidden Children: The Rise of Wicca and Paganism in America* (Lanham, MD: AltaMira Press, 2006), 7–9.

226. Emerson W. Baker, email message to author, January 14, 2016.

As the Pagan movement emerged further out of the shadows, its proponents forced a discourse that attempted to reframe the practice in the public's eye. Newly formed national Witchcraft and Druid organizations, such as the Church of All Worlds, Covenant of the Goddess, Circle Sanctuary, and eventually Ár nDraíocht Féin: A Druid Fellowship, made their services and practices more available to an American public flirting with a revived interest in the occult. As a result, the Witchcraft movement evolved from presenting as purely an occult ritualistic secret society to a true, bona fide religion. Witchcraft, Wicca, and Druidry were no longer simply counterculture entertainment dabbling in socially forbidden acts, but rather they were serious religions with deities, clergies, and rites. Then as the 1970s came to a close, two landmark American Pagan books were published: *Drawing Down the Moon* by celebrated NPR journalist Margot Adler and *The Spiral Dance* by Reclaiming founder and activist Starhawk.

Modern Witchcraft in Hollywood Film

The emergence of these organizations, the presence of LaVey in Hollywood, and the printing of major Witchcraft publications provided easy access for Hollywood writers and producers to exploit occult material in order to provide their counterculture-hungry audiences with a continued stream of tantalizing realistic material. The elements taken from modern Witchcraft practice or LaVey's Satanism began to appear within mainstream films and television shows as early as 1970. Witch and author Raymond Buckland was hired as technical adviser for the film *Necromancy* (1972) starring Orson Welles and was in contact with Hollywood producers, although received no other credits.

In the 1970 horror film *Mark of the Witch*, for example, the main character, Jill, uses the phrase "Blessed be," which has Masonic origins and is commonly used in modern Witchcraft communities as an ending to conversation or prayer. Jill also refers to the *Witch's Rune*, which is a chant written by Doreen Valiente, who was Gerald Gardner's High Priestess and largely considered "the mother of modern Witchcraft."

Despite using elements from genuine practice, *Mark of the Witch* does not present a realistic picture of contemporary Witches. The film drops those details into a narrative containing a sensationalized mix of culturally understood iconography associated with cult ritual, paranormal activity, Salem mythology, and medieval-based Catholic witchcraft. For example, in the film's first ritual sequence, Jill calls the directional quarters and recites the names of ancient deities, such as Diana and Artemis. The invocations recited are often performed in modern Witchcraft rituals. Then, after a dead witch takes possession of her body, Jill attempts to seduce the professor and claims, "I'm a High Priestess of the old religion, or the Craft, whatever you choose to call it" and speaks of her "coven." Jill transforms into a vindictive three-hundred-year-old resurrected witch, similar to those found in paranormal suspense, "nudies," or other period witch horror narratives. Modern witchcraft elements and rhetoric were used predominantly as decoration to lend the script an air of authenticity.

Mark of the Witch is not the only period film that contains references to authentic Witchcraft practice. *Blood Orgy of the She Devils* (1973) and *Hungry Wives* (1973) both use language taken directly out of printed modern Witchcraft material. The former two films contain the rhyme "Water and Earth where you are cast, no spell nor adverse purpose last, not in complete accord with me, and as I will, So Mote It Be." The ending phrase, "so mote it be," was originally Masonic but was incorporated into Gardner's practice and is commonly used by modern Witches. The rest of the rhyme was originally published in Paul Huson's book *Mastering Witchcraft*.[227]

In fact, Huson's book provides the detail for a number of the period's horror films, which may not be surprising since he worked in the entertainment industry well into the 1980s. He was adviser on the 1980s film *Midnight Offerings* (1981) and was the writer and consultant for the television show *Tucker's Witch* (1982–1983). During this period, it was Huson's book that had the most obvious influence on witch films. For example, his *Vassago* diagram and the associated magical language were replicated during a ritual sequence in George Romero's film *Hungry Wives*. However, that film doesn't limit itself to Huson's work. In a later scene when the main character takes her witchcraft initiation, she is given what is commonly called the "Fivefold Kiss." This ceremony is lifted directly from Gerald Gardner's own writings as found in the *Gardnerian Book of Shadows*."[228]

It is important to note that the modern Witchcraft movement and LaVey's Satanism predominantly affected the horror film rather than fantasy narratives. As such, a new iconography formed around the construction of the satanic horror witch, including elements from modern practice, such as pentagrams and pentacles, athames or ritual knives, candles, poppets, incense, herbs, circles, dancing, and chanting. This iconography, part of which was derived from long-established association with the occult and satanic ritual, was distinctly different from that of the fantasy witch. The satanic witch doesn't wear a pointy black hat; the fantasy witch doesn't use a pentacle. While there are crossovers, the satanic horror witch maintains a different visual and narrative language, one that is fear-based with a dose of medieval Catholicism.

---

227. Paul Huson, *Mastering Witchcraft: A Practical Guide for Witches, Warlocks and Covens* (Bloomington, Indiana: iUniverse Incorporated, 2006), 36.

228. Gerald Gardner, *Gardnerian Book of Shadows*, ed. Aiden Kelly (London: Forgotten Books, 2008), 3.

The Films and Shows

This period marks the first witch film craze, defined by a noticeable and sustained increase in witch-related productions. While that is true, these films and shows do not offer the diversity of content found in earlier decades. There was only one accused woman and she appears in a made-for-television dramatic recording of Christopher Fry's play *The Lady's Not for Burning*, which aired in 1974. There are no traditional elderly folk witches or witch doctors. The period does offer a limited number of fantasy witches, most of which are derivations of the Halloween witch. They appear in children's productions, holiday specials, or unsuccessful made-for-television films such as *Winter of the Witch* (1969) or the failed remake of *Bell, Book and Candle* (1976). With that said, the period does contain several new variations on the fantasy witch constructions in an attempt to appeal to previously untapped American audiences, including *Sabrina the Teenage Witch* (1971–1974) and *The Wiz* (1978).

For the first time in history, it is the horror witch that dominates the screen, which was heralded by the release of *Rosemary's Baby* in June 1968. The exuberance and freedom to exploit untapped subject matter using sensationalized visuals and sound was fertile ground for an explosion of horror witches, particularly those that worship Satan. This witch type, in varied incarnations, remains popular across the entire period, seizing the spotlight for the first time in Hollywood history. As a result, the representation of witchcraft practice itself—the act of magic and the use of power—takes on a central narrative role and intensity as never before seen.

Despite the overall uniformity and repetition through the period, there was, in fact, a slight shift in the timing of products offered. The satanic horror vamp dominates from 1968 through the middle of the 1970s (e.g., *Blood Sabbath*, 1972; *Necromancy*, 1972.) The teen horror witch takes over in the mid-1970s after the release of Brian De Palma's successful film *Carrie* (1976). The small number of non-horror witches span the entire period, dotting the entertainment landscape.

As an aside, there were also several famous witch-themed films released during this era, including *Witchfinder General* (1968), *The Devils* (1971), and *The Wicker Man* (1973). While they are all considered classics, and infamously so in one case, the three films were all created in the UK under a different film system and do not qualify for the study.

The Satanic Horror Witch Unleashed

In 1969, after the production code was removed, the conceptual and narrative conflation of Christian-based satanic themes, occult ritual practice, modern day Witchcraft, and other common witch tropes merged into a singular narrative identity, becoming the very recognizable horror witch film. This new product was then sensationalized further with displays of physical violence, nudity, and implied sexual perversions. This created a body of work that had never been seen previously in Hollywood's history. These horror films have few broomsticks, warty noses, and cauldrons. The satanic witch film contains its own language, using imagery understood as occult, paranormal, and satanic witchcraft.

Some of that language, as noted earlier, is taken directly from the modern Witchcraft movement, while some comes from the infamous *Malleus Maleficarum*, from Aleister Crowley's writings, or even from Freemasonry. Instead of black dresses and pointy hats, satanic witches are recognized by their nudity, heavy makeup, medieval monk-like hooded robes, or even a visual normalcy off-set by odd behavior as seen in *Rosemary's Baby*. Instead of wands and crystal balls, these witches wield knives, tarot cards, and candles. Instead of cats and flying monkeys, they are surrounded by coven members, snakes, and ghosts. Instead of performing love spells and looking for ruby slippers, their work is marked by death, sex, and the worship of Lucifer.

Most horror witch films produced during this period were low-budget exploitation films and in some cases straight-up pornography (e.g., *The Witchmaker*, 1969; *Sex Rituals of the Occult*, 1970; *Psyched by the 4D Witch*, 1973). These films, particularly the early ones, are heavily packed with gratuitous nudity and are short on suspense, violence, or gore. The scare factor, or even creep factor, is low. In terms of cinematic storytelling, Polanski's *Rosemary's Baby* (1968) and Brian De Palma's *Carrie* (1976) both stand out as anomalies in that respect. The majority of the 1970s witch horror films are more a joyful romp through society's forbidden pleasures and unspoken realms than anything else.

It is important to note that some of the period's horror films use the word "witch" in the title or in advertising but don't actually contain concrete or identifiable witch themes, characters, or plotlines. This occurs in other genres as well, particularly science fiction (e.g., *Escape to Witch Mountain*, 1975). In the case of horror, the films capitalize on the cultural connection being made between witches and themes of violence or sex to promote their exploitative works. Such films might include stories of non-occult related ritualistic violence (e.g., *Warlock Moon*, 1973), unconventional sexual activity (e.g., *Psyched by the 4D Witch*, 1973), or psychological trauma (e.g., *The Witch Who Came from the Sea*, 1976). In many of these films, the word "witch" is either never used at all or it is only used a few times as a slur. These films capitalize on the tantalizing forbidden nature of witchcraft to draw attention to a scenario involving trauma, crime, or what was considered to be aberrant behavior.

With the horror film developing as it did, it is not surprising that the satanic horror witch, an iteration of the wild woman, emerged in full and became the dominant construction. Over this period, that construction only deviates slightly, with a few basic variations depending on the film's narrative. Generally speaking, the films themselves move from classic occult coven narratives (e.g., *Necromancy*, 1972) through stories of satanic possession (e.g., *Daughters of Satan*, 1972) to those of female empowerment (e.g., *Carrie*). Within that scope, there are two main types of female witches presented: the vamp witch and the young wild woman.

Wild Women and Horror Vamps

The vamp witch, as already noted, is the mature wild woman who is well-versed in her own power, beauty, and sexuality. In previous decades, she manifested in several genres such as fantasy animation (e.g., *Sleeping Beauty*, 1959), romantic comedy (e.g., *Bell, Book and Candle*, 1958), and early horror (e.g., *The Undead*, 1957). In this period, she exists predominantly as a full-fledged horror monster with few exceptions (e.g., *Hungry Wives*, 1973). In these films, the vamp witch is either married or single and presents as either a bored housewife (e.g., *Hungry Wives*), a resurrected witch once burned at the stake (e.g., *Mark of the Witch*, 1970), or a satanic coven priestess (e.g., *Blood Sabbath*, 1972).

The Bored Housewife

The vamp witch's personal mission is to hold on to her perceived power, symbolized by physical beauty and sexuality. This theme is most pronounced in George Romero's 1973 film *Hungry Wives*, originally titled *Jack's Wife*. While the film is categorized as horror, it is more a dramatic study on female agency and gender negotiations in modern suburbia than anything else. Romero himself said, "It isn't really [horror]. It deals with the occult peripherally."[229] The film also includes a more nuanced understanding of counterculture and the Witchcraft movement than any other horror witch film of the period.

Romero wrote the script himself after researching modern Witchcraft for another project and imagined it as a reflection of second wave feminism. The film opens by painting a picture of the main character, Joan, as a depressed and bored suburban housewife. She suffers from recurring nightmares about her age, and she fights with her college-age daughter. Her husband is abusive and inattentive, and her social club is boringly average. Through her friend Shirley, Joan is introduced to witchcraft, which then becomes a path to self-preservation and empowerment. Reading from a witchcraft book, Shirley says, "The religion offers, further, a retreat for emotional

---

229. Tony Williams, ed., *George A. Romero: Interviews* (Jackson, MS: University Press of Mississippi, 2011), 37.

women, repressed women, masculine women and those suffering from personal dis-appointment or nervous maladjustment." Shirley then adds, "Christ, what other kind of women are there? No wonder this stuff's getting so damn popular."

Jan White as Joan Mitchell, a bored suburban housewife, performs her first witchcraft spell that changes her fate and empowers her life in Hungry Wives *(1973), also released as* Season of the Witch. *[Source: Anchor Bay /Photofest. Copyright: © Anchor Bay]*

After she begins to practice witchcraft, Joan visually changes appearance. Through-out most of the film, she presents as conservative with her hair tied back in a simple fashion, or homely and unkempt. Her clothes are dark and nondescript. She reflects what Greg, her young lover, calls, "middle-class morality." Even when Joan dresses up, her makeup is understated, and her facial expressions remain morose. In the film's final scene, after her extramarital affair with Greg and her witchcraft initiation, Joan teases her hair high and wears dramatic makeup. With lips upturned, she tells Shirley, "I'm a witch."

Visually and narratively, Joan takes the exact opposite route as Gillian Holroyd of *Bell, Book and Candle;* she goes from "humdrum" to vamp. Although the film ends with her looking somewhat uneasy about her claim, Joan moves from a point of powerlessness to a point of power through sexual liberation and witchcraft. As such, the film is a product of its time and comes the closest to a true feminist witch narrative, a unique model for the period.

In addition to its feminist underpinnings, Romero's film also depicts witchcraft as a genuine practice through Marion Hamilton, a local tarot reader and witch. At the end of the film, Hamilton, who physically appears as an average contemporary woman, initiates Joan into her coven through a ritual that is based on modern Witchcraft practice in action and words. Interestingly, the ritual scene is intercut with the shooting death of Joan's husband. Close-up shots of his blood body are interspersed with the religious ritual knife waving in front of Joan's naked body. Through that sequence, Joan is literally and metaphorically freed from her abusive marriage and from her powerless existence.

Romero's film was made with a small crew and equally small budget. It was unsuccessful at the time, criticized for being too "wordy."[230] In a 2010 interview, the film's star, Jan White, said that Romero had written a "fairly pornographic" script in order to attract investors, but he never had any intention of filming in that way.[231] However, producers insisted on marketing the film as soft-core pornography, which is suggested by the film's title: *Hungry Wives*. Romero told film critic Tony Williams that he didn't understand the name or the ads, and later added, "there's nothing [pornographic] in it."[232] After the success of Romero's 1978 film *Dawn of the Dead*, *Hungry Wives* was re-released as *Season of the Witch* with no better success. Despite its difficulties, Romero's low-budget witch film provides a unique construction of witchcraft and witches that is not replicated again for nearly a decade or beyond, whether it be the themes of self-empowerment (e.g., *The Craft*, 1996) or the bored housewife narrative (e.g., *Witches' Brew*, 1980; *The Witches of Eastwick*, 1987).

Ghost Witches and the Priestess

The other two forms of 1970s horror vamps are the ghost witch and coven priestess. Unlike the bored housewife, these two witches are both antagonists, offering little depth of character or social commentary within their own personal narrative constructions. They are simply transgressive wild women, practicing an evil art form to gain control of a man, to get revenge, or to maintain youthful beauty. Ghost witches were typically women who were once hung or burned for the practice of witchcraft, whether or not they actually did. Coven leaders are priestesses and teachers within a small witchcraft community.

---

230. Williams, ed., *George A. Romero: Interviews*, 38.

231. Gavin Schmidtt, trans., "Interview with Jan White, star of *Season of the Witch*," *Killer Interviews*, http://killerinterviews.com.

232. Williams, ed., *George A. Romero: Interviews*, 38.

The ghost witch appears in the revenge narrative, one that capitalizes on the viewers' collective understanding of the Salem mythos and other witch-hunting history, and that tells the story of a woman scorned. Visually speaking, ghost witches appear in several different forms: in flashback (e.g., *Mark of the Witch*), as a spirit (e.g., *Night of Dark Shadows*, 1971), as images in paintings (e.g., *Daughters of Satan*), or as a possession (e.g., *Mark of the Witch*). In some films, multiple constructions are used. For example, in *Daughters of Satan*, the film's three witches are first shown in flashback performing a ritual beating of another woman. As is typical of early 1970s satanic ritual scenes, the characters are partly naked, and the coven leader takes pleasure in the violent acts. Back in present day, the magical triad appears in an enchanted painting that represents them being burned at the stake. The plot begins again when the witches leave the painting and come to possess three modern women in order to enact revenge on their accuser's descendent.

In the films that incorporate possession, the ghost witch typically enters the body of the film's young heroine (e.g., *Mark of the Witch*, *Daughters of Satan*). When that happens, the unsuspecting heroine transitions from an innocent and often demure woman to a wild, aggressive vamp witch. For example, in *Mark of the Witch*, Jill, a studious college student, is possessed by a ghost witch who was alive in the 1600s. During a party, Jill accidently summons her when testing a magic ritual. Before the possession, Jill is polite and controlled in behavior. She dresses conservatively in mostly pastel blues with her dark hair tied back. After the witch takes over, Jill's vocal tones are lower and more dramatic in cadence. She wears black; her hair is down and her breasts partially exposed. Jill's sense of agency and control, albeit through satanic possession, is symbolized by the sexualization of her body and a freedom of movement and it coincides with the typical depiction of a threatening feminine power.

The same visual cues are found in the final horror witch construction: the satanic coven leader or high priestesses, which is exactly what the ghost possessing Jill claims to be in *Mark of the Witch*. The coven leader as horror vamp witch appears in a number of different films including *Blood Sabbath* (1972), *Daughters of Satan* (1972), *Simon, King of the Witches* (1971), and *Blood Orgy of the She Devils* (1973). The coven leader's stock appearance is similar to that of Jill's after possession. Her hair is either dramatically styled or wildly down, and her makeup is exaggerated. She wears large jewelry and dresses in bold reds, purples, or blacks. Her breasts are often exposed, which is a cue pointing to her wild, nonconformist, and uncontrolled nature. The coven leader performs witchcraft rituals, works within a group, often teaches other young witches, and seeks to destroy or seduce an unsuspecting young male character.

Blood Sabbath's Alotta typifies this character. In comparing her with the older vamp witch Livia from Roger Corman's *The Undead* (1957), it is easy to see the extremes in representation that occurred during this period. While both characters are satanic witches who are hyper-sexualized, independent, and aggressive, they are different in construction due to censorship, narrative structure, and the sociopolitical climate. The older character, Livia, reflects the Hollywood femme fatale trope mixed with the fantasy witch. She is more a 1950s pinup girl than a practitioner of modern occultism. Although she has sold her soul to the Devil, Livia works alone and is closer in construction to Disney's Wicked Queen than any 1970s horror high priestess. Furthermore, Livia would not be considered deviant by 1970s counterculture standards. Corman's vamp witch was crafted within the limits of the Production Code and within a horror narrative that is more fantasy than paranormal reality.

Like Livia, Alotta also seeks the attention of the film's male protagonist; however, she is wrapped in the period's occult language and imagery. She is not alone. Alotta leads a coven of naked female witches. She is the horror vamp in a post-Code, low-budget film that does not contain a fantasy element. The witchcraft themes, violence, and sexual aspects of the plot are heavily exploited. Where Livia's quest is to presumably win the romantic love of Pendragon, Alotta's quest is the sexual conquest of David in service of the Devil. Livia tricks. Alotta kills. Livia transforms into cat. Alotta holds blood sacrifice rituals. The older censored satanic witch Livia is a mere shadow of the vamp witch that was offered during the 1970s.

The Threat of the Vamp Witch

The horror film's witch, specifically the priestess, does not provide any openings for moral ambiguity. She is evil and defined clearly as such by her support or enactment of criminal acts against a male character. In *Blood Sabbath*, Alotta kills a priest. In *Blood Orgy of the She Devils*, Mara murders random young men and conducts rituals in which her students, dancing and half-naked, kill their chosen male victim. The transgressive behavior of past vamp witches, such as Livia, Jennifer, or Gillian, was limited to the seduction of one man. The danger was contained to one narrative thread between two characters. In these contemporary horror films, the posed danger is not only to a man singled out by the witch, but also to society as the witches show no remorse, treat murder as ritualized activity, and teach other women to do the same. In these films, the danger is no longer containable, making the witch a looming threat to society.

As was evident in *Rosemary's Baby*, these early 1970s horror witch films do not contain underlying conservative-based warning messages regarding the practice of witchcraft and other occult activities. Their purpose is far simpler. They are reactionary exploitation films that springboard off a climate of experimentation and change bred by sociopolitical instability. While the witches are the bad guys, they are rarely assimilated or even offered redemption. They don't always die, either. The rush of horror witch films in the early 1970s simply capitalize on a wave of cinematic sensationalism for cheap thrills and ticket sales. Like *Rosemary's Baby*, they also expressed the contemporary social fear that an underground, home-born threat was pervasive in American society. These witches were not invaders; they were our neighbors.

Teen Horror Witch

The vamp witch, in all forms, dominates the early part of the period, eventually giving way to the young wild woman as a witch, typified by films like Brian De Palma's *Carrie* (1976) and its television movie spinoffs (e.g., *The Spell*, 1977; *The Initiation of Sarah*, 1978) as well as Wes Craven's *Summer of Fear* (1978). Such films capitalized on the newly established teen horror market, which was fueled by the popularity of slasher films such as *Texas Chainsaw Massacre* (1974) and *Halloween* (1978). In teen witch horror films, the main character typically operates on the periphery of a social sphere due to an oddity about her appearance (e.g., weight, plain-looking, meek in behavior) or her lived experience (e.g., new girl, orphan, abused child). For example, in *Carrie*, the title character is presented as shy, insecure, and homely, wearing no makeup and baggy clothing. She is socially ostracized due to her behavior and the effects of her mother's religious extremism.

These films typically set up an antagonistic environment during the opening scene through the use of poignant visuals illustrating the main character's social inadequacies. For example, in *The Spell*, a single shot composition is used to delineate the difference; Rita wears a full gym suit while her classmates are in shorts and t-shirts or leotards. In *Summer of Fear*, also called *Stranger in Our House*, the witch has a distinct southern accent and wears dresses rather than "blue jeans."

Director Brian De Palma provides the most striking example of this type of opening in *Carrie*. He first tracks through a crowded girls' high school locker room at waist or mid-level. The camera acting as voyeur floats through the rows of lockers as the girls laugh, talk, primp, and spare no modesty for the viewer. The camera's eye finally comes to rest in the shower, where Carrie stands alone under the water, cleaning her body. The film then cuts to close-ups of her skin and follows her hands as they move across it. The tempo slows sensually as it explores what seems to be a very private moment.

This nearly erotic opening sequence makes the sudden and unexpected appearance of blood, along with the following chaos in the locker room, just as jarring for the viewer as it is for Carrie herself. Naked, wet, and bleeding, Carrie frantically enters the group space, where she is mocked by the other girls. Frightened and cowering, she presents as a scared animal trapped in the corner by hunters.

De Palma's locker room sequence exemplifies another feature of the teen witch horror film. Every time horror's young wild woman attempts to enter the film's presentation of normalcy, whether visually or narratively, she immediately gets pulled out and is defined as a monster. This is only reinforced by her practice of witchcraft or her innate power. Carrie was showering peacefully when she got her period; both are normal events. But the scene immediately turns abusive, chaotic, and ugly.

The Teen Girl as Monster

The teen horror witch is an extreme version of the young wild woman. She is not simply transgressive; she is defined as a metaphoric or literal monster. Like the horror vamp, she does not simply disobey social rules; she is a true threat to society. Her monstrous nature is found both in her biological possession of magic, making her nonhuman, and in how she uses or misuses her power against men, family, and society.

Most of the period teen witch horror films were made-for-television movies, with few exceptions such as *Carrie*. They are plot-focused and revolve classically around adolescent female empowerment gone wrong. They thrive on a female coming of age story and a typical high school narrative based on the interplay between the misfits and the cool kids. While these themes span the genres, horror takes the tension further, making the adolescent witch a danger to herself and to society.

Due to this fact, she typically must die by accidental fire, which is a witch film narrative trope. However, the teen witch is still just that—a young girl. Therefore, she is never purposefully burned. She dies by accident or by her own mistake. Society's hands are kept clean from the murder of a child, even if she is an evil one. This is a similar narrative device found in Disney's *Snow White and the Seven Dwarfs* in which the Wicked Queen accidentally runs off a cliff. Nobody killed her. A good character can never commit murder.

Similar to classic fairy tales, teen witch horrors often contain the otherwise elusive mother-daughter dynamic. In several films, the young witch doesn't die until she has enacted revenge on a hostile or inept mother figure. Carrie kills her abusive mother before they are both killed by the house fire. Sarah dies while killing a satanic vamp witch, who presents as her mother. In *Summer of Fear*, Julia attempts to kill not only her aunt but also her cousin. Often the mother turns out to be as ethically problematic as the evil daughter. In those cases, the familial battles are not good versus evil, but rather a fight for dominance.

More often than not, the teen horror witch is in high school and still maturing in all ways. She exists in that dangerous state of liminality that was so revered in the silent era. Allegorically speaking, her magical power parallels her sexuality and the coming of age. Her battle is as much with herself as it is with family and society. This is a very common adolescent struggle and a theme found in many teen films. However, the horror film makes that battle literal and the teen witch only becomes the monster due to her difficulty negotiating the boundaries of her own power and controlling her emotional resources. Her outcast status drives the teen witch toward that narcissistic level of desire and the engagement in what is deemed unhealthy activity. Like Jess-Belle, she moves past the possibility of a redemption rescue and a happy ending. The teen horror witch becomes the horror monster when she crosses a line from a simple wild girl to a social threat, and as such, she must die. Some die tragically like Jess-Belle (e.g., *The Initiation of Sarah*) and others die after committing mass murder (e.g., *Carrie*).

There is one exception to the rule. In Wes Craven's *Summer of Fear*, Julia, in true horror style, survives her burning to continue the reign of terror. However, his film was not a Carrie spin-off like many of the others. Craven's film doesn't provide sympathetic shots of the teen witch struggling with her reality or clumsily managing her powers. She just arrives, a meek and conservative teen with a country accent. As the film moves on, Julia's developing powers are paralleled by a change in appearance as she goes from a conservative prep school girl to a vamp in black lingerie. Craven's teen witch is a crossover. While the character treatment is more like that of *Blood Sabbath*'s Alotta, the film plays out like a teen horror film complete with a male professor expert, boyfriend, and down-to-earth heroine. However, the narrative provides no internal moral counterpoint to Julia's actions; she is pure evil and in the end survives her fiery death, suggesting that evil is always lurking.

A Closer Look: *Carrie*

Based on Stephen King's novel of the same name, De Palma's *Carrie* is the most iconic of the teen witch horror films and stands out among them because, along with being a critical and box office success, the film negotiates themes that most of the others do not even touch. In an essay titled "Ragtime: the Horror of Growing Up Female," Serafina Kent Bathrick writes, "De Palma's own attitude informs the very structure and imagery of the film—by sexualizing and mystifying this dread dualism of destruction tied to women's reproductive power, he invites us to enjoy it as a spectacle and a travesty of growing up female."[233] Bathrick's point is visually illustrated perfectly in the locker room scene mentioned earlier. The camera relishes in the visuals depicting a sequence in which Carrie faces not only getting her period but also being socially ostracized—two markers of "growing up female." The *Carrie* spin-offs never slow down to indulge in this theme, even if it is suggested in the film's plot structure.

Bathrick likens the treatment of Carrie to the treatment of women as witches in medieval times. She posits that a woman's biological existence and the perceived magical powers associated with it were feared. While Bathrick applies her theory to all fe-

---

233. Serafina Kent Bathrick, "Ragtime: The Horror of Growing Up Female," *Jump Cut* 14 (1977): 9.

male characters' struggles with sexuality and physicality, her remarks about witchcraft and Carrie are pertinent to this study. Her allegorical presentation also mirrors other critical works and conversations about a witch's power in films throughout cinematic history, such as Diana Anselmo-Sequeira's discussion of "apparitional girlhood" and mysticism in silent film, Gaylyn Studlar's theories on the child-woman and Mary Pickford films, or Barbara Creed's seminal work on the "monstrous-feminine." These three cases and others throughout this study demonstrate that witchcraft is more often than not a stand-in for female sexuality and power, being something engaging, empowering, enticing, and also intensely fear provoking. In Carrie's case, it is the liminal state of the teen girl as she moves from child to woman, an unknown state where she loses her prized innocence and gains the fearsome power of female sexuality.

In "magical gift" narratives, Bathrick's allegory is expressed most literally because the power is internal to the character and arrives unexpectedly, such as in *Carrie* or older productions like *Alcoa Presents: One Step Beyond*'s "Make Me Not a Witch" (1959) or *Spitfire* (1934). It is important to recognize, however, that neither Trigger nor Amy are adolescents moving into a state of womanhood, nor are they characters in a teen horror film in which the female body and sexuality are center to the narrative. That difference is critical to character construction. Amy is a scared child. Trigger is a recluse who doesn't want to fit in. While witchcraft still defines their powers, it is not linked to sexuality, but rather to gender expression and personal agency.

Carrie, by contrast, is a lonely, shy teen who just wants to be normal and is, quite literally, coming of age as depicted in the opening shower scene. While in silent films the mystical or special power was linked to coming of age and the fragility of the adolescent, it was external to her (e.g., *Mysteries of Myra*, 1916). In *Carrie* and the other teen horror films, the dangerous power is as much a part of the teens' beingness as her fragility. The danger is not external to her. Therefore, Carrie exists as both victim and monster, both child and woman. In her essay "Woman as Witch: *Carrie*," Barbara Creed recognizes the duality of her personality, saying Carrie is "a divided personality. On the one hand she is a painfully shy, withdrawn, child-like girl who just wants to be 'normal' like every other teenager, while on the other hand she has the power of telekinesis which enables her to transform into an avenging female fury."[234]

While most of the period's horror witch films do create a tug-of-war between the sensual and the horrific, De Palma takes the tensions deeper, investigating the reasons for Carrie's condition, adding both a religious and social layer to his narrative. Carrie is a victim of her mother's religious zealotry, who is also constructed as a monster as shown through her oppression and abuse of Carrie. Interestingly, the film

---

234. Creed, *The Monstrous-Feminine*, 78.

doesn't present an easy moral solution and ultimately has no hero. Innocent people are killed alongside the cruel, and the few who do survive live forever with nightmares. With that said, *Carrie* is as much a social commentary investigating the social traps associated with womanhood, the demonization of a woman's body, and the extremes of social engagement. The film's intersection between witchcraft and horror is only implied rather than overt due to those themes. Although brilliant in execution, *Carrie* remains a witch film only marginally.

Narrative Construction in 1970s Horror

The various forms of female horror witches appear in three different narrative models: the coven next door, revenge of the witch, and the teenage monster film. In all three of these popular horror witch narratives, the source of an individual or coven's power is presumed or stated to be Satan. These films present a tension between something familiar that is then tinged with something marked as dangerous or evil: young girls with kinetic powers, quaint towns run by necromancers, grandmother figures who corrupt children, sexually alluring women who kill men. The enticing or the normal is twisted and repackaged with something disturbing. That is the essence of horror; it forces the viewer to confront and negotiate that duality.

The Coven Next Door

Crowhaven Farm (1970) typifies the coven-next-door theme, which dominated the early part of the period and provided the widest opening for sensationalized occult practice. Other films with this structure include *The Witchmaker* (1969), *Black Noon* (1971), *The Touch of Satan* (1971), *The Brotherhood of Satan* (1971), *Daughters of Satan* (1972), *Blood Sabbath* (1972), *Necromancy* (1972), *Satan's School for Girls* (1973), *Blood Orgy of the She Devils* (1973), and *Satan's Cheerleaders* (1977). The popular television show *Starsky and Hutch* explored this theme in a 1978 episode called "Satan's Witches." In these films, a protagonist moves into a new home or visits an area within close proximity to a satanic coven made up of individuals who otherwise read as normal. The markings of satanic practice appear gradually through odd behaviors and the discovery of pentagrams, candles, chanting, or altar space.

This horror narrative runs directly counter to the "witch as invader" scenario found in films like *Weird Woman* (1944). In those older films, the invader is the magical character who disrupts normalcy. Notably, these films were produced predominantly in the 1940s when the country was fearful of foreign influence. Contrary to that, the 1970s invasion films posit the non-magical protagonist as the invader. These films tell the story of normalcy disrupting a magical world defined as a satanic coven.

It is not surprising that such narratives were popular during a period of social upheaval, war, and political instability.

In most of the coven-based films, an innocent couple together discovers the occult group, and the young wife is eventually tormented either into illness, as in *Black Noon*, or into participation, as in *Necromancy*. In two of the period's films, however, the innocent victim is a single man who accidently stumbles upon the coven and becomes its target (i.e., *Blood Sabbath*, *Touch of Satan*). In those cases, a young, restless witch attracts the attention of the unsuspecting hero, and in return, becomes seduced herself, giving the film a contemporary and non-comical *I Married a Witch* theme. Additionally, in the few films in which a woman comes across the coven alone, the leaders are predominantly men and the coven operates almost like a harem (e.g., *Satan's School for Girls*, *Satan's Cheerleaders*). In *Satan's School for Girls*, Satan himself is the coven leader.

In the coven-next-door narrative model, film endings are variable, but often the extremes of practice survive, providing an unresolved conclusion (e.g., *Necromancy*, *Brotherhood of Satan*), which suggests the possibility of evil continuing in the world. The good don't always survive; or better yet, the evil doesn't always die or can't die due to immortality. At the end of *Black Noon*, the immortal coven of witches drive past the town sign, which reads the town's name, "San Melas." Backwards, as shown in the truck's mirror, the sign reads "*Salem.*"

Revenge of the Witch and the Teen Monster

The theme of witch immortality, which helps define the horror witch as a monster, is also the centerpiece of the second most common witch narrative construction: the revenge of the witch. In these films, a ghost witch is resurrected to enact revenge on the descendants of her killers, or to reconnect with her lover. For example, in *Daughters of Satan*, the three resurrected witches seek revenge against their executioner's descendent, James Robertson (Tom Selleck). In the film *Mark of the Witch*, a resurrected high priestess is determined to reunite with her former coven mate and lover who has been reborn as a university professor. Films with this scenario include *Daughters of Satan*, *Mark of the Witch*, *Night of Dark Shadows*, *Crowhaven Farm*, and *Beyond Evil*.

As with the coven-next-door narrative, the revenge of the witch typically opens with a couple accidently encountering something from the past that invokes the spirit of the witch. In *Daughters of Satan* for example, the hero purchases a painting that is enchanted with the spirits of three witches. These revenge narratives are similar in nature to any story about hauntings. They rely more heavily on the paranormal concepts of ghosts and spirits than on transgressive behaviors, occult ritual, and satanic witchcraft. Most have a gothic sensibility, which is readily apparent in the visuals, and are tied to a medieval or Salem witch hunt story. While the revenge narrative was not as prevalent as the coven-next-door, it does eventually take center stage in 1999 and beyond after the break-out success of indie film *The Blair Witch Project* (1999).

The third and final construction is the teen monster narrative, as discussed in detail earlier. Some of these scenarios focus on witchcraft as the distinguishing evil power, (e.g., *Summer of Fear*) and some feature a nondescript psychic power (e.g., *Initiation of Sarah*). The teen monster narrative is simply a teen outcast film dressed in a horror witch aesthetic. This narrative became increasingly popular after *Carrie's* success and it continued to remain popular through the early 1980s, eventually dying off.

Magical Men of 1970s Horror

Although female witches always dominate witch films, the number of magical men continued to increase during this period chiefly due to the popularity of satanic and occult themes. Two types of characters dominate: the male witch and the occultist. The male witch is constructed specifically as a religion-based mystical magician. He appears in just one film: *Simon, King of the Witches*. The second character is the occultist, who appeared in past decades (e.g., *House of the Black Death*), and is typically found in satanic-based horror films, such as *Necromancy*, *Brotherhood of Satan*, *Satan's School for Girls*, and *Satan's Cheerleaders*.

The Male Witch

The 1971 low-budget film *Simon, King of the Witches* is an anomaly for witch films, because the magical work is framed as a deity-centered religion. Furthermore, Simon's power is not defined as satanic in origin, but rather a combination of natural inclination and magical education. With that said, as with most witch films, the narrative is a negotiation of power in relation to society. In this case, it's a masculine-based dance, which involves the quest for power over the presented culture and not a negotiation of power through it. *Simon, King of the Witches* is very much a story of one man's fight to be the alpha male and define his masculinity. At one point, Simon looks out over the ocean and says, "All powers of the gods will be mine."

Like many horror films, the opening shots are dark and stormy. Within minutes, Simon breaks the proverbial fourth wall, speaking directly to the camera to explain that he is a "warlock" and one of the "few true magicians." In doing so, Simon is both verbally claiming his power over society as well as enforcing it on the viewer through direct address. However, the visuals of the opening scene do not correspond to that powerful assertion, because Simon is water-logged and presents as a vagrant. Throughout the film, Simon is consistently attempting to prove his divine worth despite his meager existence.

Simon, King of the Witches is a notable film in its representation of witchcraft as a whole. It is one of the first narratives that ties religion so deeply to magical practice without a satanic element. Simon's magic involves Egyptian gods and not Lucifer. Additionally, the film borrows from the modern Witchcraft movement through its presentation of magical ceremony as something deeply sacred. Finally, in the middle of the film, Simon stumbles upon a witchcraft ritual led by a stereotypical horror vamp priestess. She tells him, "We the Wicca worship the queen of the night." This is the first mainstream American witch film to include the term Wicca, a name used for the religious practice of Witchcraft as first coined by British Witch Gerald Gardner.

After witnessing the ceremony, Simon mocks Wicca as "not real magic," which is a product of the film's misogynistic sensibility as well as Simon's own mission to be king. The film's male universe, as well as the anti-hero's quest for power, have no need for well-constructed, strong female magical characters. Throughout the narrative, Simon uses and disposes of women for sexual pleasure, magical power, and financial gain.

However, in the end, Simon loses his quest and is killed on the streets during a storm in shots that are similar to those at the film's opening scene. Before stabbing him, two young junkies push him down onto the wet street, and yell, "Everything has gone wrong, man." As the two run away, one says, "We needed him." Allegorically speaking, the film parallels the country's own social crisis as it loses faith in its leaders, searches for its identity through renegotiations of gender, and mimics the idea of a lost quest for ultimate dominance.

The Occultist

While the male witch is a rarity, the occultist is not. However, like the male witch, the occultist is also working to establish and maintain power over a community, a society, or in the case of the film *Necromancy*, death. When in ritual settings, the occultist is typically adorned in monk-like robes with an oversized hood, wearing a large gold pendant. Where satanic female witches often work alone, occultists almost always work within a group and are most readily found in the coven-next-door narrative. They make promises, host social events, and give gifts to their followers. In *Necromancy*, Mr. Cato (Orson Welles), provides jobs, a place to live, and entertainment for his neighbors. In *Brotherhood of Satan*, Doc Duncan provides everlasting life to his followers.

Legendary actor Orson Welles stars as Mr. Cato, the leader of a
Satanic coven of witches, in the 1972 horror film Necromancy.
[Source: Cinema Releasing Corporation /Photofest.
© Cinema Releasing Corporation]

In *Satan's School for Girls* and *Satan's Cheerleaders*, the occultist facilitates the gifting of mystical power to himself and others through the stereotypical narrative of a virginal sacrifice. This sacrifice, whether death or sex, is based on a typical misogynistic theme that permeates horror films and is often found at the center of the rites performed by a male-led coven. In *Necromancy's* opening scene, a group of witches, first robed and then naked, circles around a young blonde woman whose breasts are fully exposed. A robed male leader approaches her for an initiation rite, caressing her breasts. The scene is relevant only as a descriptor, presenting the coven as socially transgressive and evil through what appears to be a violation of the young woman.

It is important to note that the magical man can also take on the form of Satan himself. However, in many of those occult-based films, such as Richard Donner's *The Omen* (1976), the narratives focus predominantly on demonology and other similar elements of evil more than they do on witchcraft practice as an identifier. Male magical characters that fit this study will continue to remain minimal in comparison to the overwhelming number of female witches.

Fantasy Witches and Halloween

When moving beyond the horror genre into fantasy, the witch becomes, as she always has been, just a witch. All satanic connections are gone. In the 1970s, the Halloween fantasy witch appeared more frequently than in any past decades, even if the genre did not dominate. This can be attributed to an increase in television programming supported by increased demand, technological improvements, and the coming of cable. Those changes paved the way for more children's programming, animation, and holiday specials. The popular October holiday, which was slowly evolving into the start of the illustrious holiday season, began to earn its own television specials themed exclusively around witches.

Animated Halloween Witches

Producers of children's television animation, which had found a weekly home on the networks every Saturday morning, provided witch-inspired versions of their standard fare, either to celebrate Halloween or not, such as *Tijuana Toads*, "Croakus Pocus" (1971), *Sabrina the Teenage Witch* (1971–1974), or *Scooby-Doo*, "To Switch a Witch" (1978). In all cases, the animated witch remained constant in her simplified visual construction. Even decades after she was first created, she is still the same recognizable female figure with an elongated nose and chin, warts, unkempt hair, a pointed hat, a long dark draping dress, and often green skin. Warner Brothers was one step ahead of most studios in that respect, because it could still rely on its well-known character: Witch Hazel. In the 1970s animated *Sabrina* series, it is Sabrina's two aunties, Hilda and Zelda, that draw from this iconography; Sabrina does not.

The Hanna-Barbera cartoon series *Scooby-Doo*, which was an animated spoof of the horror genre, added a notable historical touch to its witch construction in order to offer a moderate scare factor for its young audience. Unlike other animated shows, *Scooby-Doo* witches tend to wear purple, have human-colored light skin, with hats and shoes adorned with Puritan-inspired buckles. This historical cue links witches to Salem, providing a modicum of realism to the character and situation. The *Scooby-Doo* narratives mimic the period's horror witch films in that they capitalized on the revenge narrative, which lent itself to the show's paranormal sensibility.

Live Action Halloween Witches

The decade's Halloween witches were not limited to animation. The iconic character could also be found in live-action television, including *Winter of the Witch* (1969), *H. R. Pufnstuf* (1969–1970), and *The Paul Lynde Halloween Special* (1976). These productions presented the same classic Halloween witch character only in a live-action format. *The Winter of the Witch* offers a slight twist on the narrative, in that the character itself does not reflect the two-dimensionality of her outward appearance. She looks like the classic witch but is defiant in her action, not as a woman but as a witch. In both cases, the witch questions her purpose and identity.

Winter of the Witch is based on Wende and Harry Devlin's children's book *Old Black Witch!* first published in 1963. The film was produced for children by *Parents Magazine Incorporated* and was well received. *Winter of the Witch* tells the heart-warming story of a single mother and child who move into an abandoned house where an old witch lives. That may sound like the beginning of a horror film; however, it isn't. The witch befriends the boy, telling him about her past escapades frightening people. She laments the changes in society, saying "The world's full of evil nowadays. People don't need witches anymore."

While the film grapples with society's loss of innocence and simplicity, allegorically through the construction of this Halloween icon, it also offers hope. The boy discovers a new job for the old witch. She makes blueberry pancakes that restore people's happiness. At the end of the film, the witch says, "People need something to believe in," and that hope is in "the goodness of the pancakes." Whether or not the magically laced blueberry pancakes reflect the prevalent "Lucy in the Sky with Diamonds" drug culture can be left up for debate; however, the film does contain an overt political commentary uncommon to children's fantasy witch productions. The theme of loss and hope mirrors a society turned over on itself and lost in its own identity. While some filmmakers and animators did attempt to deconstruct the classic figure, moving her beyond the expected caricature, the majority of Halloween fantasy witches remained two dimensional and classic in form.

Margaret Hamilton and the Continuing Influence of *The Wizard of Oz*

The influence of MGM's *Wizard of Oz* and, more specifically, the popularity of the Wicked Witch of the West continued to exert influence on American culture, moving beyond the codification of cinematic witches and into reality. In other words, actress Margaret Hamilton, who played MGM's classic character, was hired to appear as herself or as a Wicked Witch in a variety of television programs. For example, in Paul

Lynde's 1976 Halloween special, she appears as a guest on the show, but eventually takes on her classic role for a campy skit about a witches' beauty pageant. Additionally, Hamilton was hired to appear in two of the decade's most popular children's television shows: *Mr. Rogers' Neighborhood* and *Sesame Street*.

Mr. Rogers' Neighborhood

Mr. Rogers' Neighborhood, which launched as a series in 1968, aired an episode on May 14, 1975, in which Hamilton visits Mr. Rogers at his home. The goal of the program was to demystify the character of the witch and to explain to children "why you shouldn't be afraid." Hamilton, as herself, tries on the costume in a slow unthreatening manner, typical of Rogers's programming. There are no special effects or sensationalized elements to even suggest that the witch is real. Rogers tells the camera, "You know, witches are make-believe. They're pretend."

After it aired, episode 1453 sparked protests from the growing Witchcraft movement. In interviews over the years, famed Salem witch Laurie Cabot has publicly complained about Rogers's incorrect statement that "witches don't exist." She referenced her distaste with the episode in 1988, when she was interviewed about the creation of a Witchcraft anti-defamation league called "Witches League for Public Awareness." In the article, Cabot is quoted as saying, "It was also things like Mr. Rogers saying on his children's show: 'You don't have to be afraid of witches, because there aren't any.' What a wonderful thing for our children to watch." [235]

Mr. Rogers' Neighborhood's presentation of the witch as a product of children's fiction is not surprising considering that Rogers graduated as a minister from the Pittsburgh Theological Seminary in 1962. Although he never practiced, his theological interests suggest a leaning toward a conservative Christian family value system that would reject the notion of the witch as real. But more importantly, Rogers's passion was to provide a comfortable, safe viewing space that projected a nonhostile, supportive atmosphere for children. The show was nearly an oasis in a culture gone wild.

Sesame Street

In February 1976, *Sesame Street* took a totally different approach in bringing Hamilton on set. In episode 0847, which aired February 10, Hamilton appears not as herself but as the classic witch. According to Children's Television Network archives, the now infamous episode features the Wicked Witch losing her broom on Sesame Street. The story

---

235. Ken Franckling, "Witches Work to Counter Bad Image," *Lodi-News Sentinel*, October 26, 1988, 13.

then follows her attempts to retrieve it. With the exception of Big Bird and Oscar the Grouch, the inhabitants of Sesame Street are visibly frightened of Hamilton's character.

Like the earlier *Mr. Rogers' Neighborhood* episode, *Sesame Street* received complaints. But this time letters came not only from modern Witches, concerned about the perpetuation of stereotypes and fairy tale imagery, but from a diversity of parents. The show was deemed too scary for young children. In a memo dated April 4, 1976, Sesame Street researcher Anna Herrera noted that further testing had been done on the program to witness what the letters had suggested. But the tests proved otherwise. However, in the memo, Herrera notes that episode 0847 was the "first to have received this large amount of mail (with negative comments); all within a very short period of time." [236] As such Herrera recommended that the show never be re-run, and it has not been released to the public in any form since that point.

Oz Adaptations

In addition to Hamilton's live appearances, there were two new adaptations of Baum's classic story: *The Wonderful Land of Oz* (1969) and *The Wiz* (1978). The latter movie became a landmark cultural event and will be discussed in a separate section. The earlier film, *The Wonderful Land of Oz*, was a low-budget children's production produced and directed by Barry Mahon, who was better known for his work in sexploitation films. While Mahon attempted to stay close to the tale found in Baum's second book *The Marvelous Land of Oz*, Mahon's film is generally considered to be one of the least sophisticated Oz adaptation attempts. It was poorly received and quickly forgotten until it was re-released on DVD in 2001.[237]

Despite his narrative proximity to the original, Mahon's witch Mombi looks far more like a classic Halloween witch than the old Victorian clown witches found in the original turn-of-the-century drawings. She is dressed all in black and has elongated facial features with dark recessed eyes. Her voice is scratchy and aged. Mahon's Mombi is yet another reflection of many years of developing cinematic witch construction and another example of the hardening of iconography surrounding the Oz characters.

---

236. Anna Herrera, Internal Memorandum, April 4, 1976; source: Children's Televisions Workshop papers, Special Collections, University of Maryland, College Park, Maryland.

237. Paul Simpson, *A Brief Guide to Oz: 75 Years Going Over the Rainbow* (London: Constable & Robinson Ltd., 2013), 106.

The Teen Fantasy Witch

While the Halloween witch was the dominant fantasy construction of the era, it was not the only one. Just as the last period saw the birth of the goodly child witch, this period saw the birth of the teen fantasy witch, a construction that is not entirely different from that in the horror film. Both characters move about the narrative attempting to negotiate social pressures and emerging sexuality. However, unlike teen horror witch films, the teen fantasy narratives don't waste time sourcing her magic; she is not a wild woman. The power exists as a fantastical wish-fulfillment detail for the female viewer, giving her an opportunity to imagine herself with that control. The narratives provide a fantasy escape for teens struggling with similar issues. The most notable teen witches found during this period are Tabitha and Sabrina.

Produced by Columbia Pictures, *Tabitha* was a spin-off of the popular show *Bewitched*, which had gone off the air in 1972. The new show, which aired in 1977, shared the escapades of Samantha and Darren Stephens's now grown-up children: Tabitha and Adam. However, the sitcom was unable to recreate the popularity of its predecessor. A review published in the *Warsaw Times-Union* sums viewer response in one sentence, "It sadly lacks the magic of '*Bewitched*.'"[238] Only thirteen episodes, including the unaired pilot, were ever produced. Some reviewers believed that *Tabitha* failed due to a lack of believability in its connection to the original, while others attributed its failings to poor and erratic scheduling by ABC.[239] Either way, *Tabitha* was not destined for fame.

A Closer Look: *Sabrina the Teenage Witch*

During that same time frame, another young witch did become a hit: Sabrina. Since her creation in the early 1960s, Archie Comics' *Sabrina the Teenage Witch* has emerged as one of the most successful witch franchises in American culture. Originally created by George Gladir and Dan DeCarlo, *Sabrina* appeared as the lead story for *Archie's Mad House* Issue #22, released in October 1962. Within that issue, she describes herself as a "modern witch," who believes "life should be a ball."[240] Sabrina further explains what it means to be a witch within the *Archie* universe. Interestingly, those rules include not being able to "fall in love" without losing her magical powers; this concept mirrors the rules found in *I Married a Witch* (1942) and *Bell, Book and Candle* (1958).

---

238. Joan Hanauer, "NBC Looks at America's Most Unreported Crime—Incest," *Warsaw Times Union*, May 5, 1977, 6.

239. Bob Leszczak, *Single Season Sitcoms, 1948–1979: A Complete Guide* (Jefferson, NC: McFarland Publishing. 2012), 178.

240. Dan DeCarlo and George Gladir, *Archie's Mad House, Issue #22* (Archie Comic Publications Inc: 1962), 29.

The original comic book Sabrina visually recalls actress Marilyn Monroe, and she behaves as a playful trickster reminiscent of Jennifer in *I Married a Witch*. When Gladir and DeCarlo created the character, they never imagined that she would be popular and were quoted as saying, "I think we both envisioned it as a one-shot and were surprised when fans asked for more." [241] The two men were even more surprised when, in 1970, CBS picked up *Sabrina* as an animated program for their Saturday morning lineup. The original show was called *Sabrina and the Groovie Goolies*, which was eventually changed to *Sabrina the Teenage Witch*. The program aired on CBS through 1974.

Sabrina's original appearance with its pinup sex appeal as well as her impish nature were altered in order to serve a broader children's television audience. The new animated Sabrina is kind, helpful, and plays the role of a good friend. Her compassionate nature worries her aunties Hilda and Zelda, who were constructed as classic Halloween witches with purple robes and pointy hats. The two older women serve as foils to Sabrina's goodness, playing the role of the morally ambiguous tricksters.

It is important to note that Sabrina herself is only a "half-witch," similar to Honey Halfwitch. She fits the mold of a typical teenager who wants to fit in to conventional human society. Where the comic Sabrina was characterized as a young Jennifer, the cartoon Sabrina is closer in nature to Samantha of *Bewitched*. And, like Samantha and other past witches, Sabrina gave female viewers an opportunity to align themselves with a character whose innate power was not deemed sinful or crazy. Through the character of Sabrina, young girls could indulge in what could be termed "wishcraft," or the fantasy of manifesting their own wishes in a world that regularly suppresses their ability to do so. This fact alone explains her long-lasting popularity.

The original CBS cartoon went off the air in 1974, but that was not the end for Sabrina. The station re-ran thirteen episodes from 1977–1978 under the title *Sabrina, Super Witch*. The episodes were part of *The New Archie and Sabrina Hour*, but they did not receive the same fanfare as the earlier show. Then, in 1996, Sabrina got a new boost when she was reimagined in a live-action version during a period of time that saw an upswing in witch film popularity and the birth of a new "girl power" feminist movement.

Fantasy's "New Black Magic"

Another new development in witch character construction came by way of Broadway. In 1978, Hollywood released a film version of the Tony Award-winning all-black musical *The Wiz*, which was a modern adaptation of Baum's classic tale. Unfortunately, the film did not live up to the standards set by the successful musical. It was

---

241. Scott Shaw, *Archie's Mad House No. 22*, Oddball Comics, April 2, 2007.

considered an expensive flop, despite its all-star cast, which included Michael Jackson, Lena Horne, Nipsey Russell, Mabel King, Diana Ross, and Richard Pryor, and celebrated director Sydney Lumet.

In his book *Toms, Coons, Mulattoes, Mammies, and Bucks*, film historian Donald Bogle laments, "The sad irony was that the decade, which had opened by revealing to the industry that there *was* a black audience, closed with the industry believing that the black film and black audiences were both dead."[242] Bogle blames the film's failure on poor direction and acting performances and faulty screenwriting. He suggests that the film could have been "dripping with rich ethnic juices," but it wasn't.[243] He was not alone in that analysis. In 1977, film critic Pauline Kael said the film had a "stagnant atmosphere" and it looked "rushed and cheap."[244] In an interview, director Sidney Lumet told reporters that "it was a disaster."[245]

Although *The Wiz* was largely a disappointment, the film is a landmark in the study of American cinematic witches. For the first time in a major Hollywood release, Black witches appear without the stereotypical framework of "othering." In other words, *The Wiz*'s witches are not confined to constructions involving "Voodoo" or any other practice codified in that way, nor are they inhabitants of Africa or "the islands." These witches aren't constructed within a racist colonial-based ideology that labels them as "backwards" or "natives." Similarly, the film did not present its witches solely as iterations of MGM's characters. *The Wiz* exists as a fantasy film that attempts to explore an authentic Black American cultural experience, and its witches reflect that mission.

Changing Representation

The witches in *The Wiz* were not the first Black witches in mainstream American productions outside of the Tituba character trope. Black actresses were hired to play coven members in several early 1970s films, such as in *Blood Sabbath*. In these films, the all-female groups typically contain at least one woman with darker skin. However, these characters have little to no impact on the narrative and are more indicative of the early 1970s progressive entrance into the exploitation experience. The presence of a black or brown body reads as "wild," emphasizing the transgressive and even

---

242. Bogle, *Toms, Coons, Mulattoes, Mammies, and Bucks*, 266.

243. Bogle, *Toms, Coons, Mulattoes, Mammies, and Bucks*, 265.

244. Pauline Kael, "Review of '*The Wiz*,'" *The New Yorker*, October 30, 1978, 139.

245. Chris Nashawaty, "Sidney Lumet: How He Saw His Oscar-Nominated Films," *Entertainment Weekly*, updated April 9, 2011, https://ew.com/gallery/sidney-lumet-how-he-saw-his-oscar-nominated-films/?slide=345132.

dangerous nature of the coven. Black characters are completely absent from the non-witchcraft portions of these films. The films' use of the black or brown body is, as in the past, based on a racist ideology that defines such figures as inherently sexual and wild. By adding these actors into the depictions of witchcraft ritual, the occult experience is intensified for an all-white audience.

Later in the decade, the failed sitcom *Tabitha* aired one episode called "The New Black Magic," which centered on a visit from Tabitha's sexually aggressive and morally skewed Black friend named Portia. Similar to the early horror films, the episode focused on Portia's sexual promiscuity and intent to corrupt others. The title is a play on words, suggesting that the evil magic, also called black magic, is the magic of Black witches.

Generally speaking, the female body has always been a defining aspect of witch construction in some form, whether it be skin color, facial structures, hair texture, or exposed breasts. In a society that is coming to terms with its diversity, racism, and gender imbalances, and an industry that suddenly realized it had a paying Black audience, it is not surprising that Black witches began to appear. However, the construction was still limited and constrained by an underlying cultural bigotry. Therefore, *The Wiz* presented an entirely new possibility, demonstrating not only female empowerment in its own terms but also reflecting the cultural vibrancy and struggles present in the Black American experience.

The Witches of *The Wiz*

It is important to note that *The Wiz* is not a remake of the MGM film. It is wholly based on the original books, containing all three of Baum's witches, who are named Miss One (Thelma Carpenter), Evillene (Mabel King), and Glinda (Lena Horne). The first two witches, Miss One and Evillene, are modern, urban modifications of the classic clown witch: one evil and one not. Miss One is a comical crone figure designed as a magical bag lady with layers of clothing in blues and purples. She has a variety of assorted items hanging on her belt, and she parades around an urban play yard. Focusing on numbers, Miss One explains Oz to Dorothy, and adds that "her magic doesn't amount to much." She is simply the caretaker of the munchkins. Like many other past witches, Miss One is defined as good by her soft colors, low-level magic, and care of others.

Played by Mabel King, Evillene, the wicked witch of the musical film The Wiz, *sits on her throne commanding flying monkeys and a legion of factory workers (1978). [Source: Universal /Photofest. Copyright: © Universal Pictures]*

Evillene, on the other hand, is the evil adaptation of the clown witch. She is a sweatshop owner who doesn't want "bad news." Her dress, which is predominantly reds and orange, looks like the candy house of a *Hansel and Gretel* fairytale. Her over-adornment makes her appear deformed, almost like a horror version of the classic Hollywood mammy. Considering the collective experience of Black America, it is not at all surprising that the show's evil character operates a sweatshop, forcing its inhabitants to work under adverse conditions. She is the big bad boss, the slave owner, and even the over-culture that oppresses marginalized populations.

Finally, Glinda the Good is defined as a star and she appears only at the end of the film. Dressed in silver and blue, Glinda descends from above and stands before a dark blue background. She is defined as a celestial figure with an angelic appearance similar to most constructions of this character. Horne delivers a powerful performance, which is only dampened by poor framing and the campy floating star babies. However, her message is one of inspiration and almost spiritual in nature as she empowers Dorothy by saying "believe in yourself." This remains one of the most moving moments in the film.

Despite its progressive nature, *The Wiz*'s witch character constructions incorporate one traditional ideological concept: ugly is bad and beautiful is good. Miss One says of the dead bad witch, "This chick put the ug in ugly," and later calls Evillene "her uglier sister." In addition, the film uses the traditional construct that celestial-bound magic is heavenly, from God and therefore good. The earth-bound witches, Evillene and Evilmean, are bad. Both good witches are bathed in blues while the evil character is surrounded by oranges and reds. This polarity is not unique to *The Wiz*, but it is reflective of the narrative's Christian underpinnings.

While the witches may appear less magical to an average American viewer due to the lack of readily identifiable witch iconography and few displays of magical power, all three characters have a strong narrative presence that overshadows the film's male figures. This reflects the themes found in the original books that were largely absent from the MGM film. *The Wiz*'s witches and the non-magical women of the film stand tall and strong, which ties into the musical's themes. Unlike its predecessor, *The Wiz* is about community connection, knowing where you belong, who you are inside, and who your people are.

The exact role *The Wiz* had in dealing a death blow to the all-Black feature film is unclear. However, as Bogle suggests, *The Wiz*'s failure may have caused Hollywood to back down from producing such films for quite a number of years. Regardless, Lumet's film was indeed a missed opportunity considering the wide success of the Broadway show and the contemporary social climate. While in the moment *The Wiz* may not have helped in the quest to end racial inequalities within the entertainment industry or society at large, it is a notable landmark for the introduction of Black witches free of the constraints formed by a deeply embedded racist ideology that underscored much of Hollywood's language and history.

Conclusion

By 1978, the interest in witch-centered material was beginning to wane to a large extent. The witch craze was over. However, before it ended, the construction of the witch had been forever changed by the period's unique negotiations of her varied constructions. Along with fully embracing the satanic witch film, there were several new characters that emerged due to a broadening awareness of audience demographics and expanding viewership through cable television. Despite the increase in witch films, there was little character diversity across genres and types, as was seen in the previous two decades. The fantasy-based Halloween witch and the satanic horror witch dominate with little variation.

There were several anomalies on television; however, they were mostly inconsequential. These included the failed attempt to remake *Bell, Book and Candle* (1976), which is no longer available to view, and an adaptation of Christopher Fry's play *The Lady's Not for Burning*. This latter production was a filmed play, for the most part, and not true cinema. In addition, there were anomalies within the popular genres such as *Winter of the Witch*, *The Wiz*, and *Hungry Wives*. While most of these films were not successful at the box office or on the television, they exemplified ideological shifts in a changing world.

At the same time, the period produced two of the most famous teenage witches: Sabrina and Carrie. While Sabrina would not realize her full potential until the 1990s, this is where she began. *Carrie*, by contrast, was immediately successful and inspired a number of spin-offs that birthed the first wave of teen witch horror films following on the heels of the popular teen slasher (e.g., *Texas Chainsaw Massacre*, 1974; *Halloween*, 1978). Going forward into the socially conservative decade of the 1980s, the contributions of this period, specifically regarding horror witches, were not completely lost. They remained etched into Hollywood film language and show up again in force during the next cinematic witch craze.

Chapter 8: Filmography

The Wonderful Land of Oz	1969	Berry Mahon
Winter of the Witch	1969	Gerald Herman
Scooby-Doo, Where Are You! "Which Witch Is Which?"	1969	Joe Ruby, Ken Spears
The Witchmaker	1969	William O. Brown
H. R. Pufnstuf	1969–1970	Marty Krofft, Sid Krofft (creators)
Crowhaven Farm	1970	Walter Grauman
Mark of the Witch	1970	Thomas W. Moore
Sex Rituals of the Occult	1970	Robert Caramico
Simon, King of the Witches	1971	Bruce Kessler
The Touch of Satan	1971	Don Henderson
Black Noon	1971	Bernard L. Kowalski
Sabrina the Teenage Witch	1971	Hal Southerland
The Brotherhood of Satan	1971	Bernard McEveety
Tijuana Toads, "Croakus Pocus"	1971	Arthur Davis
Night of Dark Shadows	1971	Dan Curtis
Necromancy, or The Witching	1972	Bert I. Gordon
Blood Sabbath	1972	B. Murphy
Daughters of Satan	1972	Hollingsworth Morse
Hungry Wives	1973	George Romero
Psyched by the 4D Witch	1973	Victor Luminera

Blood Orgy of the She Devils	1973	Ted Mikels
Satan's School for Girls	1973	David Lowell Rich
Warlock Moon	1973	William Herbert
The Lady's Not for Burning	1974	Joseph Hardy
Mr. Rogers' Neighborhood, 1453	1975	Bill Moates
The Witch Who Came from the Sea	1976	Matt Cimber
Bell, Book and Candle	1976	Hy Averback
Carrie	1976	Brian De Palma
The Paul Lynde Halloween Special	1976	Sid Smith
Sabrina, Super Witch	1977–1978	Hal Southerland
Sesame Street, 0847	1976	Robert Myhrum
The Spell	1977	Lee Philips
Tabitha	1977–1978	Jerry Mayer
Satan's Cheerleaders	1977	Greydon Clark
The Initiation of Sarah	1978	Robert Day
Summer of Fear	1978	Wes Craven
Starsky and Hutch, "Satan's Witches"	1978	Nicholas Sgarro
The Wiz	1978	Sidney Lumet
Scooby-Doo, "To Switch a Witch"	1978	Joe Ruby, Ken Spears (creators)

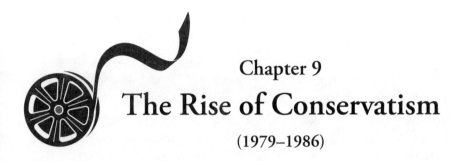

Chapter 9

The Rise of Conservatism

(1979–1986)

As the 1970s culture of experimentation subsided and the country was no longer at war, society shifted again through the disco era and an economic downturn into the 1980s, which gave rise to a new brand of Christian fundamentalism and political conservatism. Historian Cameron Addis notes that the "liberal wave," which had started decades ago during the Progressive Era had run out of steam by the mid-1970s. The landslide election of conservative Ronald Reagan with his promise to "make America great again," was the outcome of that social pendulum swinging back to the right.[246] In addition, part of this overarching trend was a distinct rise in a modern fundamentalist Christian movement. In 1979, Jerri Falwell founded the Moral Majority, which worked closely with and within right wing politics. And in 1977, James Dobson launched Focus on the Family.

With regard to witch films, the ramification of this conservative shift is not fully evident in narrative cinema and television until the late 1980s. Similar to other decades, cultural shifts are not necessarily amplified in cinematic expression as they happen. There is often a delay. For example, it wasn't until the early 1970s that films and shows had been fully enveloped by the progressive changes of the 1960s. Despite that fact, there is always subtle evidence of change as it occurs. In this case, the popularity of witch films had died down by the start of the era and, paralleling the national

---

246. Cameron Addis, "Conservative Resurgence," History Hub, accessed March 1, 2020, http://sites
.austincc.edu/caddis/conservative-resurgence/.

climate, the film industry was moving away from progressive and inventive cinema styles and sensational content.

The Growing Modern Witchcraft Movement

Growing alongside but far outside the new brand of Christian fundamentalism was the modern Witchcraft movement. As noted in the last chapter, two of the most influential books on American Witchcraft were published in 1979, including *Drawing Down the Moon* by NPR journalist Margot Adler and *The Spiral Dance* by environmentalist and Reclaiming founder Starhawk. In addition, by the early 1980s, popular Witchcraft author Scott Cunningham began publishing material supporting the solitary practice of Witchcraft as a religion. Finally, adding to the growing number of Pagan and Witchcraft organizations, Isaac Bonewits successfully launched Ár nDraíocht Féin: A Druid Fellowship, which would become a national organization supporting Druids, clergy, and followers. Despite the end of the cultural revolution that helped to birth and support the modern Witchcraft movement, the community continued to expand. In fact, in 1986, a US court, for the first time, formally recognized Wicca as a religion in the landmark case *Dettmer v. Landon*.[247]

The Influence on Entertainment

While the movement's influence on the horror witch remained embedded in traditional cinematic language, there were a few attempts to echo the idea that witchcraft could be a religion. For example, in the *B. J. and the Bear* episode "B. J. and the Witch" (1980), Deidre the witch says, "It's because you don't understand it. It's the oldest faith in the world." Deidre is described as a "white witch" and healer. Like the herbal healers of the silent era, Deidre is a woman who lives alone in a small cottage. However, unlike those wild women, she expresses her practice in positive terms with no narrative suggestions of insanity or fantasy. The source of her power is not from Satan, a Christian God, or insanity. It is "the oldest faith." Unfortunately, Deidre suffers the same fate as many of her predecessors. She is burned, although the show does intimate that she could still be alive. "B. J. and the Witch" is progressive on the one hand, reflecting the growing presence of modern Witchcraft, but traditional on the other, bringing with it the rising tide of Christian fundamentalism.

A more direct connection between the modern practice of Witchcraft and Hollywood came by way of author Paul Huson, whose 1970 book *Mastering Witchcraft* was used in many screenplays as a stand-in for magic, as noted in the last chapter. During this era, Huson is also credited with creating and writing the short-lived television show *Tucker's Witch* (1982–1983), a detective series that followed husband and wife

---

247. *Dettmer v. Landon*, 799 F.2d 929 (4th Cir. 1986).

team Rick and Amanda Tucker as they solved cases in California. Amanda is a third-generation psychic and witch, a character detail that is never framed as evil or derogatory. However, at the same time, the show did regularly suggest that Amanda was incompetent and a bit crazy, which is more a commentary on gender politics than on the ethics of witchcraft practice.

While these new representations are limited, they do demonstrate that subtle shifts were being made in the cultural understanding of the modern practice. Unfortunately, as the period moves on, the growing moral panic begins to take aim at modern Witches and other occult practitioners. As portrayed in the *B. J. and the Bear* episode, society struggles with accepting the presence of Witchcraft even when solely defined as a form of herbalism and natural healing. By 1987, more and more films and television choose to depict the latter.

The Films and Shows

The movement toward social stability and conservatism, both culturally and artistically, along with the introduction of new media, cable, and home video, brought with it an increase in adaptations, witch-related fantasy, and long-beloved witch characters. The films feature a host of well-established stories, characters, and settings. This repetition coincided with the ideological concept of "making America great again" and a return to what was perceived to be normalcy.

Collectively speaking, the witch character moved from the state of being a symbol of the cultural rebel, whether evil or not, back to the role of the inconsequential magical woman or conventional archetype. While the horror trends and sensationalism of the last decade still lingered in the early part of the decade, such as in the horror film *Midnight Offerings* (1981), they did not dominate again until Satanic Panic takes hold of Hollywood.

Epic fantasy adventures captivated audiences with their unique presentation of sorcery and magic (e.g., *Conan the Barbarian*, 1982; *The Beastmaster*, 1982) along with fairy tales and adaptations. Not surprisingly, this period also saw the first narrative film since the 1930s to retell Salem's story in a historical context (i.e., *Three Sovereigns for Sarah*, 1985), and it saw the return of the wild woman with a special gift from God. This was largely a transition period between two witch film popularity waves. It began after an aggressive era of witch exploitation and then ends as the cultural backlash against the occult reaches a fever pitch.

Horror Leftovers

Despite the declining interest in witch films, the late 1970s did produce a few horror films that were related to the older 1970s models. These included *Midnight Offerings*

(1981), *Beyond Evil* (1980), *Burned at the Stake* (1982), and *The Devonsville Terror* (1983). Three of these 1970s-style films share the concept of witchcraft as legacy and heritage. Whether it is a biological anomaly, such as in *Midnight Offerings*, or an ancestral relationship, as in *Burned at the Stake* and *Devonsville Terror*, the story revolves around a familial connection to witchcraft that eventually goes wrong. In three of the films, including *Devonsville Terror*, *Beyond Evil*, and *Burned at the Stake*, the narrative focuses on a resurrected ghost witch or witches. In *Beyond Evil*, the ghost witch haunts an old house recently purchased by a young couple. In *Burned at the Stake*, Salem's Ann Putnam attempts to inhabit the body of a modern-day school-age girl, Loreena. In *Devonsville Terror*, three women who unknowingly are reincarnated witches return to the town in which their former selves were burned.

While at school, Vivian (Melissa Sue Anderson), a powerful and
troubled teenage witch, confronts another teen witch Robin (Mary Beth
McDonough) in the made-for-television horror film Midnight Offerings *(1981).*
[Source: ABC/PhotoFest. Copyright: © ABC]

These films were low budget or, in the case of *Midnight Offerings*, made for television. All are residuals from the past decade. However, two offer a slight twist on typical themes and are worth noting. *Midnight Offerings* was the last of the teen witch horror films of the era. It captures similar themes found in the earlier works such as *Carrie* (1976) and its television spin-offs. Unlike its predecessors, *Midnight Offerings* includes a taste of modern Witchcraft. The second film worth noting is *Devonsville Terror*. While on the surface the plot tells the tale of good people moving into an evil town, the film's narrative is more eloquent than that, or tries to be. It has a powerfully feminist undercurrent that does not appear in most early 1970s low-budget horror films. It pays tribute to second wave feminism and reflects the late 1970s surge in powerful female characters.

A Closer Look: *Midnight Offerings*

Midnight Offerings, which was released in 1981, is the last teen witch horror of its kind following the witch craze of the earlier decade. While thematically the film was inspired by the popularity of *Carrie*, similar to *The Spell* (1977) or *The Initiation of Sarah* (1978), *Midnight Offerings* has a different moral approach than the others. In this case, the witch construction is split into good and evil. Vivian, the main character, is the evil witch who uses power and sexuality to control men, friends, parents, and teachers. She is clearly depicted as a satanic witch, recalling the imagery and language used in the early 1970s horror witch films, including words from Huson's book *Mastering Witchcraft*. For example, Vivian recites "By Barabbas, by Satanas," which are both terms found in his book.

Opposing her is Robin, who is the typical outcast "new girl" and, as it turns out, a good witch. She is visually introduced as the outcast in the same way as past films. The camera shows her alone on-screen, isolating her from the shots of groups of kids. Additionally, to set her apart, Robin has long, light-colored hair and a hopeful smile, which contrasts Vivan's short dark hair and striking light-colored eyes. While Robin is called a witch, her power is not linked to satanic ritual. Robin helps friends, loves her father, doesn't kill, and is never sexualized. She is the classic girl next door.

Unlike *Carrie*, the film's tension is neither between society and the witch nor between aspects of one's self. In *Midnight Offerings*, the battle is between biological witches, whether that be Vivian and Robin or Vivian and her witch mother. It is notable that this film depicts the rare magical mother-daughter relationship. Even more rare, the mother is the one who is good and the teen is not. Together with Robin, the mother battles Vivian in a fight to the death. In the end, the mother sacrifices herself to stop her daughter's evil. Like most witches, the two die classically by fire. *Midnight Offerings* is a predecessor to the 1996 cult classic *The Craft*.

The film's narrative develops a strong polarity of good and evil. The mother, who is neither sexualized nor seeking anything for her own gain, operates in a natural maternal role. She is often seen in the kitchen or the home space. The outcast girl, already a sympathetic figure from the start, is often shown helping others. The concept of magic in these cases is naturalized as part of their biology and normalized as part of and within socially acceptable roles in terms of gender and age. The mother cooks dinner and the teen is a good friend.

The contrast is Vivian, a popular girl at school who has dark hair and almost supernatural eyes. While her magic is also naturally achieved, Vivian's practice includes ritualistic and occult elements, unlike the other two. Her biological power isn't enough; she wants more. Wild women typically step beyond acceptability, which establishes their role as the antagonist. In this case, that transgression is not simply witchcraft alone; it is witchcraft with occult ritual. This shift in representation coincides with society's attempts to renegotiate both the moral boundaries surrounding Witchcraft and the power shifts with regard to gender roles. It is not bad for a woman, or a witch, to have her own intrinsic power, but it is morally reprehensible for a woman or witch to seek power beyond what is naturally acquired.

A Closer Look: *Devonsville Terror*

In 1983, Ulli Lommel's *Devonsville Terror* makes use of the accused woman construction in its feminist-inspired horror narrative. As noted earlier, it still retains many common elements found within the witch films of the 1970s, including small towns, three-hundred-year-old legends, rituals, and new visitors. Additionally, *Devonsville Terror* reflects the previous period's attempts to embed a feminist ethic and female-focused spirituality into the witch narrative, similar to what was found in *Hungry Wives* (1973).

In *Devonsville Terror*, three career women arrive in a small New England town that has a witch-killing history and, as a result, is cursed. As is typical for many horror witch films, the narrative opens with a seventeenth century flashback containing mobs, fire, and death. Then the film flashes forward to present day when three career-focused, politically progressive women arrive in the small town. Monica is a radio show host who promotes women's empowerment; Chris is an environmental scientist; Jenny is a schoolteacher who explains that "God could be a woman." However, none of them are witches, other than possibly being the reincarnation of the original three women killed, who may or may not have been witches themselves. Despite that fact, the film does have an abruptly bizarre supernatural ending in which Jenny suddenly gains magical powers and kills off all the men.

While not a polished film, *Devonsville Terror* offers a loosely constructed commentary on contemporary gender politics. The male characters want to rid themselves of the progressive women. They are portrayed as murderous, lecherous, and gang-like, and are often shown gathered around a dinner table discussing their plans. The one woman present for these meetings is frequently told to "shut up." Unlike most horror witch films, it is the men who are evil humans, and the town's witches are just trying to survive. As noted, *Devonsville Terror* reflects the broader trend toward expressing a feminist ethos that was often found in the films of the earlier decade. However, it is an anomaly for the 1980s.

Witch-Lite and Bored Women

There were two other notable films that retained elements from 1970s expressions of witchcraft: *The Halloween That Almost Wasn't* (1979) and *Witches' Brew* (1980). Like *Devonsville Terror*, these two films were both produced at the beginning of the period and, therefore, were naturally influenced by former trends. Both films are comedy and capitalized on the concept that women are bored or unsatisfied with daily life. The former was a made-for-television holiday special and the second is a cinematic adaptation of the novel *Conjure Wife*.

A Closer Look: *Witches' Brew*

Witches' Brew (1980) is the third adaptation of Fritz Leiber's popular novel first published in 1943. The previous films included *Weird Woman* (1944) and the British film *Burn, Witch, Burn* (1962), originally titled *Night of the Eagle*. *Conjure Wife*'s plot centers on a professor who discovers that he is married to a woman who practices magic. In the case of *Weird Woman*, the magic was a South Seas religion. In *Night of the Eagle*, the wife practices Obeah after spending years in Jamaica. In *Witches' Brew*, the wife learns witchcraft from a local, older American woman played by Lana Turner in her last film role. In this case, the foreign element is gone, and the magic is purely American made. In fact, the film is nothing like the 1944 version.

Witches' Brew was an attempt to spoof the horror genre, including its fascination with witchcraft. The film contains ritual and séance, a witchcraft-practicing matriarch or priestess, and a coven of what could be defined as bored housewives. While *Witches' Brew* includes many 1970s tropes and adapts a well-known story, it is the "bored housewife" theme that is worth noting. George Romero capitalized on this concept in his 1973 film *Hungry Wives*. In both films, suburban housewives seek out a witch, constructed as a priestess figure, to teach them witchcraft. This theme coincides with the idea that a woman, when left alone, is vulnerable to the mystical. It parallels the silent era's notion of adolescent liminality, even if these women are beyond their teen years.

The bored housewife could also be considered a symbolic version of the biblical Eve, who is seduced into eating an apple by a mystical force defined as the Devil. In all cases, the theme suggests that the danger of female power is still present even after marriage. However, the conclusion of the bored housewife film is not necessarily as predictable as one might expect. *Hungry Wives* turned the concept on its head with its feminist revisionism. Even if it's not read as such, Romero's film implies that Joan is better off being a witch than she was a wife. In that case, the film's symbolic biblical Eve eats the apple, sleeps with Satan, kills her husband, and walks off into the promised land with a new sense of self. In that sense, Joan is perhaps the Bible's Lilith.

Witches' Brew, while playing off the bored housewives aesthetic, has none of the underlying feminist contemplations found in the earlier film. In *Hungry Wives*, Joan seeks out a witch to save herself; in *Witches' Brew*, the women seek out a witch, Vivian, to advance their husbands' career objectives, and they fail. In this case, Eve eats the apple, is punished for doing so, and is forced to return home to her husband.

With that said, the film's comedic proscenium allows for a comic ending during which Margret (Teri Garr) uses magic, once again, to assist her husband. There is a *Bewitched* sensibility about the last scene that resolves with the same conclusion as *Midnight Offerings*. A woman or witch's power is acceptable provided she stays in her lane. *Witches' Brew* was not successful and largely panned by critics. Like *Midnight Offerings* or *Devonsville Terror*, it was one of the last witchcraft films released that still clung to either a genre or subject matter that's popularity had ended several years earlier.

A Closer Look: *The Halloween That Almost Wasn't*

In 1979, ABC aired a children's holiday special with a distinctly feminist theme. *The Halloween That Almost Wasn't* stars a classic and very conventional Halloween witch (Mariette Hartley) who is unsatisfied with her role within the cultural status quo of monster society. The entire narrative spoofs classic horror texts and, in doing so, challenges gender-based social convention. As the story goes, Winnie no longer wants to participate in the annual October holiday, which is solely orchestrated by Dracula. She's tired of taking orders, of being less respected than Dracula and unloved, of being the "ugly girl" and the butt of all the jokes. Winnie no longer wants to be the witch.

Dracula and the rest of the male monsters eventually realize that Halloween will not occur if the witch, who is the only female character, does not ride across the moon. She is the pinnacle of their entire existence and purpose. They bend to her conditions and she finally agrees, saying, "A girl can change her mind." In the end, the witch realizes that she is needed as she is. She doesn't need to change. The position of the female character as essential to this male-dominant monster universe interjects an awareness of the contemporary feminist movement into a children's holiday special. In addition to confronting patriarchal systems, the film also champions the otherwise marginalized members of society for their own essential roles. The "ugly girl" is needed just as she is.

While the majority of Halloween fantasy witches, including the classic Wicked Witch of the West, remain two-dimensional, some filmmakers reimagined the character within a contemporary cultural context. The 1969 children's special *Winter of the Witch* provided commentary on the war and a growing social insecurity. *The Halloween That Almost Wasn't* explored gender roles and the authenticity of personal identity. It also broke through the conventional ideology surrounding a woman's appearance as it relates to female power.

Witches in Children's Entertainment

While *The Halloween That Almost Wasn't* offered a new look at a classic character, most productions of the period did not follow suit. Americans continued their love affair with the largely two-dimensional, unexamined classic Halloween witch. The beloved character appears in several different forms to entertain or sometimes scare young children. With the popularity of Saturday morning cartoons, animation was the main source for these characters. The witch appears in holiday-inspired episodes of popular shows such as *Casper Saves Halloween* (1979), *The Smurfs'* "All Hallows Eve" (1983) and "The Littlest Witch" (1983), and *Super Friends'* "The Planet of Oz" (1979) and "The Witch's Arcade" (1981). Studios such as Disney produced holiday specials such as *Haunted Halloween* (1982), *Halloween Treat* (1982), and *A Disney Halloween* (1983), and NBC aired the animated movie *The Great Bear Scare* (1983).

A Closer Look: *The Trouble with Miss Switch*

In most of these productions, the witch is a secondary character or villain. However, one notable animated children's film places witchcraft center stage. Released in 1980, *The Trouble with Miss Switch* is a cinematic adaptation of the popular 1971 children's book by Barbara Brooks Wallace. The film originally aired on ABC in two parts. It tells the story of a schoolteacher who, as the children discover, is really a witch. While that might sound like the makings of a horror film, this schoolteacher is good.

As with other productions released in the early part of the decade, *The Trouble with Miss Switch* challenges viewer assumptions about witchcraft and the witch in general.

The film contains two Halloween witches—a young adult woman and a crone. The former is a teacher, who is tall and thin with long black hair. When in the classroom, she appears as a severe school marm with her hair in a bun. But as a witch, her hair flows freely and her appearance nearly mimics *The Addams Family*'s Morticia. The old crone, by contrast, has gray hair and elongated facial features. She is the film's antagonist. As such, the narrative incorporates the classic fairy-tale-based notion that ugly and old is bad and young and beautiful is good.

Despite relying on classic witch tropes, *The Trouble with Miss Switch* offered a progressive attitude toward the idea of magical practice. As seen in other films of the era, the concept of witchcraft, allegorically a woman's power, was being renegotiated. The boundaries of good magic and bad magic were being reset. In the case of this film, animators gave children a powerful and intelligent female role model in the form of a classic witch, complete with a pointy hat, black cloaks, and long hair. The film also encouraged learning through the embodiment of a creative and accessible teacher, a role that is often reserved for magical nannies like Mary Poppins. This concept is repeated in the 1990s animated series *The Magic School Bus* with Miss Frizzle, who reads as a magical nanny or by extension a would-be clown witch.

Mister Rogers' Neighborhood in a Changing Climate

While the progressive movements of the 1970s did influence productions as late as 1981, the conservative social shifts were increasingly evident as the decade moved on. The changing attitude toward witchcraft is found in, for example, the third installation of the *Halloween* trilogy released in 1982. The film's popular antagonist, Mike Myers, is absent. Instead, the antagonists are killing children to resurrect an ancient form of witchcraft. The film was panned, and the franchise returned to Myers-driven narratives in 1986, but *Halloween III* is a precursor to the coming storm of witch films that reflect a growing moral panic.

The shifting attitude is also evident through an examination of the re-airing of *Mister Rogers' Neighborhood*'s 1970s Margaret Hamilton episodes (1453, 1454). When comparing parent reception between the original airing in 1975 to those received in 1986, the changing climate becomes all too evident. In 1975, the Fred Rogers Company received few complaints about Hamilton's appearance. However, in 1986, parent letters poured into local PBS stations and to Rogers himself. The majority of these complaints quoted Christian scripture, referenced Dr. James Dobson's evangelical work, and some even noted that "instances of Witchcraft were on the rise" citing news reports of ritual child abuse.[248]

---

248. Correspondence to Fred Rogers, 1986; source: Fred Rogers Center Archives, Latrobe, Pennsylvania.

The 1986 airing was near the end of this period as the Satanic Panic was taking hold of American society on a national scale. The panic produced a real and palpable fear that was just beginning to spiral out of control from sensationalized news reports and television shows to affect observable everyday behaviors, including reactions to fictional representations of witchcraft.

To further illustrate this ideological shift, the large number of letters sent to the Children's Television Network (CTW) in response to Hamilton's 1976 appearance on *Sesame Street* do not contain religious rhetoric. Although there were enough objections to have the show banned, religion was not the reason for the objections. In those letters, parents were predominantly concerned about the episode being "frightening," with little to no mention of Satanism or scripture.

By contrast, the 1986 letters to Rogers were overwhelmingly religion-based and primarily concerned with the show giving platform to satanic ideas. This comparison is not perfect due to potential differences in the viewer demographics. However, CTW never re-aired its Hamilton episode to allow for a direct comparison. Regardless, the language found in the 1986 complaints to Rogers's show provides evidence of the change in society's engagement with witchcraft. For the first time in American entertainment history, the practice of witchcraft was considered real, for both better and worse.

A Fantasy and Fairy Tales Revival

While fantasy-based stories containing witches were nearly absent from the last period, the 1980s saw a revival in epic fantasy and literary adaptations. Several filmed theater productions of Shakespeare's *Macbeth* aired on television between 1981–1983, most of which were produced in the UK. Shelley Duvall produced and starred in the award-winning *Faerie Tale Theatre*, a series that aired on the newly launched cable television station Showtime. In addition, classic stories were often found embedded within other narratives such as in the animated show *The Hugga Bunch* (1985) or in Dolly Parton's holiday special *A Smoky Mountain Christmas* (1986). It is also notable that, during this period, a joint British-American production resurrected, once again, the Oz stories in the live action film *Return to Oz* (1985). The film stars Fairuza Balk as Dorothy. Balk would later go on to become the star of the 1996 film *The Craft*.

Fairy Tales Mashup

Modelling on the period's popular comedy-horror genre, the fantasy film *Troll* relies on a viewer's knowledge of fairy tales to build its own original narrative. In this film, a troll is set free in a contemporary apartment complex and commences with turning the residents into fairy tale characters and the apartment building into a magical forest. The young protagonist, notably named Harry Potter Jr., is the only one left to stop the troll.

During his quest, Harry discovers that his neighbor, Eunice St. Clair (June Lockhart), is a witch. Eunice is a typical elderly fantasy crone who helps the male protagonist in his quest. While she is a fantasy witch, she is not a Halloween witch. Eunice is a cross between Vivian in *Witches' Brew* and a classic magical nanny, such as Miss Price (Angela Lansbury) in the joint British-American film *Bedknobs and Broomsticks* (1971). Narratively she functions as a moral compass with a male coming-of-age story. While the film is notable, *Troll* was largely an attempt to bank on the success of other similar films such as *Gremlins* (1984). It was largely panned and has no relation to the later *Troll* sequels.

Epic Fantasy

While literary adaptations and fairy tale derivatives experienced a revival, epic fantasy was the dominant form of the genre. Often labeled "sword and sorcery" due to its content, epic fantasy was revived in the early 1980s after a relative twenty-year hiatus. Sword and sorcery films focus specifically on combat and magic with medieval-inspired art direction that recalls the Arthurian legend or J. R. R. Tolkien's *Lord of the Rings*. Like traditional westerns, sword and sorcery films center on stories about men and their quests. Generally, a young man must overcome the death of a father figure to challenge a false father and take his rightful place in society. This is the typical male coming-of-age story and one that defines masculinity in terms of warriors, conquerors, and kings. This narrative structure relegates women to secondary roles as sexual props, obstacles, mothers, or inspirations.

In terms of witches and witchcraft, the female magical characters function very traditionally and do not reflect any of the progressive changes that had been made in witch construction up to this point. If nothing else, the female witches recall the characters in Shakespeare's *Macbeth* or classic fairy tales. They are often amoral magical servants (e.g., *The Beastmaster*, 1982), fantasy crones (e.g., *Troll*, 1986; *The Dark Crystal*, 1982), or evil seductresses (e.g., *Conan the Barbarian*, 1982). Any male witches are either elderly wizards (e.g., *Dragonslayer*, 1981) or fantasy magicians (e.g., *The Beastmaster*, 1982). The structure is traditional and, in many ways, conforms to Production Code representations of witchcraft and magical practice.

In consideration of sociopolitical currents, it is not surprising that these films demonstrate a traditional Christian moral structure, which is further evident through the depiction of magic in relation to character construction. For example, in *Conan the Barbarian*, the witch is a seductress and evil fantasy vamp. The male magician is a sidekick and buffoon, and the male occultist literally appears as a snake. In the end, both the vamp and the occultist die. The male magician is Asian and constructed as a magical other. He is permitted to live. Both the characters and their narrative roles are traditional in execution.

Similarly, in *The Beastmaster*, a triad of witches appear in the opening sequence as happens in Shakespeare's *Macbeth*. The three deformed, elderly women stand over a cauldron acting as seers for a fantasy magician. Shortly after this scrying scene, one of the witches performs a magic spell to steal a baby out of a pregnant woman's body and then ritually attempts to kill the child. In this scene, the single fantasy crone is defined as the mythical Baba Yaga who harms unsuspecting children or the wood-land witch of *Hansel and Gretel*. While *The Beastmaster* witches do look more like disfigured monsters than old women, they read as archetypal fantasy crones.

During this period, sword and sorcery films had reached a new level of popu-larity and all contain some form of magic and epic quest, even if there is no witch. Other such films include *Legend* (1985), *Ladyhawke* (1985), Disney's animated film *The Black Cauldron* (1985), and *Labyrinth* (1986). It was during this period that the British film *Excalibur* (1981) was released, starring Helen Mirren as Morgana who is a sorceress and witch. And in 1984, the popular German-produced film *The Never-Ending Story* hit the big screen. Science fiction had its own version of these narratives from the *Star Wars* franchise to films like *The Last Starfighter* (1984).

A Closer Look: *The Dark Crystal*

Famed Muppets innovator Jim Henson was involved partially with several of the already mentioned productions (e.g., *Labyrinth*, the *Star Wars* franchise, *NeverEnd-ing Story*). His creativity and his Muppets lent themselves to the fantastical worlds that were being developed. However, his own film *The Dark Crystal* (1982) also falls neatly into the category of sword and sorcery films due to its look and its narrative, which contains a classic male coming-of-age story. As the story begins, a young male Gelfling named Jen loses his guardian; as a result, he sets off on a journey to rid the world of evil. During that journey, he meets a girl, many helpful creatures, a few mys-tical shamans, and a witch named Aughra.

Aughra is a classic fantasy crone, narratively similar in function to Eunice St. Clair in *Troll*. She lives alone and has wrinkled features with a mop of gray hair. However, Aughra, like the rest of Henson's characters, was modeled on the artistry of fantasy illustrator Brian Froud. Therefore, Aughra is not a human witch. Her body and face are distortions of human features in the unique way Froud creates his fairy beings. Despite her appearance, she is never demonized and therefore she is not the symbolic monstrous-feminine. Nobody in the *Dark Crystal* universe is human so there is no juxtaposition to create such a metaphoric characterization. She is recognized solely as a nonthreatening forest witch. As such, Aughra is the classic amoral fantasy crone who holds secret information, barters for magic, and tests the morality of the hero.

Unlike the period's other sword and sorcery films, *The Dark Crystal* handles the polarity of good and evil as two sides of the same coin rather than two forces locked in perpetual combat. Jen's purpose is not to destroy evil but to bring it into balance with good. Defined as two tribes, good and evil together can heal the crystal and heal the world. Within a typical sword and sorcery narrative, Henson embedded a unique, almost Zen, spiritual or philosophical moral construct. *The Dark Crystal* stood alone in this presentation of magic and morality during this era.

As noted, most sword and sorcery narratives chose a more traditional route, reflecting the emergent social conservatism with its harsh binary moral structures. These films, while aggressively powerful in their ability to absorb viewers into their world, were dogmatic in their approach to ethics, gender roles, and magic. Good is good; bad is bad. The boundaries are defined by traditional Production-Code Hollywood language. Women can only have magic if they are useless old crones in the wood. Men can only have magic if they are old and wise or an emasculated, comedic "other." All offending forms must be destroyed.

The Return of the Accused Woman

Not only did fantasy return but so did the classic witch as an accused woman. During this period, she makes her return in several films, but most notably in the PBS special *Three Sovereigns for Sarah*. The last significant film containing an accused woman was Victor Fleming's *Joan of Arc* (1948), although an accused woman backstory can be found buried in a few later horror films (e.g., *The Undead*, 1957) and in several ghost witch films (e.g., *Daughters of Satan*, 1972; *Devonsville Terror*, 1983).

In 1985, PBS aired a three-hour mini-series called *Three Sovereigns for Sarah*, loosely based on the book *Salem Possessed* by history professor Stephen Nissenbaum and Paul Boyer. Financed by the National Endowment for the Humanities the series was filmed in authentic locations throughout the Boston area and reportedly built its script with actual Salem trial transcripts. It is largely considered one of the best adaptations of the city's historic events. When a *New York Times* reporter asked the show's star Vanessa Redgrave about the broadcast's "contemporary significance," Redgrave replied, "There is still a tremendous amount of mystical demagoguery around." [249]

---

249. Fox Butterfield, "Television; The Witches of Salem Get a New Hearing," review of *Three Sovereigns for Sarah*, by Philip Leacock, *The New York Times*, October 28, 1984.

Redgrave plays Sarah Cloyce, one of the many women accused of witchcraft in the small Salem village. Unlike the 1937 film *The Maid of Salem*, *Three Sovereigns for Sarah* blames the Puritans' social system and its believers for the moral panic. Sarah tells a trio of judges, "It was not Providence that cursed us but our own precious kind." Preacher Samuel Parris is portrayed as an overzealous and hostile figure; the villagers are depicted as greedy; the young accusatory girls are shown as unethical and dangerously immature. This is a marked change from the 1937 narrative, which blamed jealousy, drunkenness, child's play, and misunderstandings.

Additionally, *Three Sovereigns for Sarah* does not end comfortably, but rather leaves a question of justice. Surrounded by men, including her nephew and three judges, a disfigured and aged Sarah tells her tale with the only goal being to clear her dead sisters' names from the accusation of witchcraft. At the end of the film, the judges inform her that they cannot clear any names without full investigations. However, they give her three sovereigns: one for each of her two hanged sisters and one for herself. It is a symbol of the state's apology.

Donald Symington and Vanessa Redgrave star as Peter and Sarah Cloyce in the American Playhouse special Three Sovereigns for Sarah *(1985).*
[Source: Richard B. Trask. Copyright: © Richard B. Trask]

The film provides no fanfare or celebration for the gesture. It plods through this point with the same slow sobriety as the rest of the film. The muddy visuals are unrelenting. Sarah goes off to die; the victims are left unforgiven. *Three Sovereigns for*

Sarah does not offer repentance or a bright future. It leaves the viewer wondering if there is any difference between those men who precipitated the trials and the judges hearing Sarah's case. Their gesture appears empty; and the film makes no attempt to visually correct for that, leaving the viewer as frustrated with the results as Sarah.

Three Sovereigns for Sarah continues to be shown to students of American history and is lauded for its tone and accuracy. Although it is not the most famous adaptation of Salem's legacy, it is largely one of the few that explores the depth of personal pain heaped on the community, specifically women. Despite its marked criticism of the establishment, it is also notable that it was the first Salem story produced outright in decades, returning to the concept that conservative and stable social periods revive an interest in stories about us, our history, and our people.

It is also notable that the accused woman is developing a new level of character depth that releases her from her traditional role of narrative pawn in a discussion on the benefits of reason. In contemporary stories, the accused woman is not offered redemption through a happy marital ending, such as in *Devonsville Terror*, nor is she saved from death, torture, or rape, as in the 1991 film *The Pit and the Pendulum*, nor is she vindicated by the government as in *Three Sovereigns for Sarah*. It is her victim-hood, rather than her misstep, that is at the center of the modern narrative, which forces the viewer to confront the powerless state of women in relation to patriarchal oppression. At the end of *Devonsville Terror*, the lone surviving woman of an accused trio, Jenny, kills the group of murderous men. At the end of *Three Sovereigns for Sarah*, the lone surviving woman of an accused trio, Sarah, becomes the catalyst for an investigation into the witch trials. Despite these shows of agency and oppression, such narratives were anomalies overall. With that said, these films do demonstrate how cultural meaning, despite changes in society, continues to build on itself and past ideologies do not completely disappear from the collective mindset.

Wild Woman, God, and *Resurrection*

When Hollywood shifted away from the censorship code in 1968, the industry was launched into a new era that consequently invited religion more directly into its witch constructions. This first came by way of the satanic-based horror film. Then, as the upheaval of the 1970s was put to rest, religious expression shifted from explorations of the socially transgressive to what the PCA might have considered "correct thinking." As seen in the sword and sorcery films, there was a revival of a clearly defined good and evil based on Christian values. In silent film terms, the "new woman" was once again being replaced by the "true woman."

While the early 1970s horror films also defined witchcraft as evil within religious terms, these same films provoked and upended normative structures by providing an alternative, which was based in an exploited reality. Gender norms were often transgressed, power structures were questioned, and evil wasn't always the loser on the battlefield. With the return of conservatism and the fundamentalist Christian movement, the structures were put back in place, including a strong sense of positive religiosity defined by a love of God and Christian-based culture. This is a world where good always wins. Magical practice, witchcraft, or wizardry were once again relegated back to evil or superstitious whimsy.

A Closer Look: *Resurrection*

The film *Resurrection* (1980) is demonstrative of the growing appeal of religion-based films or what some reviewers called "woo" movies. As one *New York Times* writer opens her review: "*Resurrection* is a movie about faith, and one that must be taken on faith. It's a little bit mad. But it has the courage of its conviction, and a beauty and persuasiveness that help keep the doubts at bay."[250] Directed by Daniel Petrie and written by Lewis John Carolino, *Resurrection* (1980) tells the story of Edna Mae, who finds herself with healing powers after surviving a car crash. When she finally accepts and adjusts to her gift, Edna Mae (Ellen Burstyn) uses it to help locals, resulting in her being both loved and feared. Like other films about faith healing, *Resurrection* is often considered a witch film due to the presence of power and the fear and accusations it causes.

In many ways, *Resurrection* recalls the 1934 film *Spitfire*. In the two films, the heroine is gifted with a power to heal through the laying on of hands. However, *Resurrection* is more than just a plot-focused story about a wild woman and her path to redemption, as in the past. The film is a contemplation on faith through the questioning of the source of Edna Mae's power and, allegorically speaking, the source of a woman's power. Is it of God, the Devil, the universe, or just a scientific phenomenon?

Spitfire never questions the divine source of Trigger's power, even when the town does. The viewer spends ample time alone with the heroine, witnessing her sincerity and devotion to God and her deceased father. While the villagers only see the rough and tumble wild woman, the viewer is privy to Trigger's internal conversations, paralleled by the film's art direction. Trigger is sympathetic. She believes in God and, therefore, her power must be of God, regardless of the town labeling her a witch. Unlike Trigger, Edna Mae is never directly called a witch. In addition, she had long been accepted into her local community before her power arrives. In other words, Edna Mae was never an outcast. Her transgression is not poor social behavior but the power itself, and that is where the film is focused. What is this power?

---

250. Janet Maslin, "'Resurrection' Has the Manner of a Fairy Tale," *New York Times*, November 7, 1980, https://www.nytimes.com/1980/11/07/archives/resurrection-has-the-manner-of-a-fairy-tale.html.

In award-winning film **Resurrection** *(1980), Edna Mae uses her*
newly discovered powers to cure and heal her friends and neighbors.
Shown: Madeleine Sherwood (far left background), Ellen Burstyn (as Edna).
[Source: Universal Pictures /Photofest, © Universal Pictures]

Within the framework of witch narratives, Edna Mae is a wild woman who moves from a "true woman" accepted by her town to a "new woman" who is misunderstood within society. Even with its theologically suggestive title, the film never offers a definitive answer to the question of Edna Mae's power. The script even poses that question directly, forcing the characters and viewers to accept the answer given by the heroine: "Does it matter?"

Despite differences in their stories, both Trigger and Edna Mae are forced, by the end of the film, into a solitary existence. We don't know what happens to Trigger; she walks off into the sunset alone with only a promise that she would return. By contrast, we do know what happens to Edna Mae. She buys a gas station, talks about two-headed snakes, raises dogs, and heals sick little boys that happen to come along. Edna Mae changes from the young wild woman witch to the elderly folk witch living a liminal existence. In that way, Edna Mae's character arc offers a new twist on the wild woman character construction and unique moment in narrative witch history. However, the woman as witch still has to make a sacrifice to keep her magic. She cannot have power and community, and that is the story of the folk witch.

At the same time, the film focuses on Edna and not on character action. Like the period's accused women stories, this film derives its strength from revealing the witch's character, her oppression, her persecution, and eventually her own choice to leave it all behind. It also models the trend in renegotiating the acceptable boundaries of magical practice in wake of the growing acceptance of its reality as a religion or spiritual practice. What is this power? When is it good and when is it bad?

The Spiritual Lessons of *Resurrection*

The producers first intended *Resurrection* to be a Christian-friendly film with spiritual tones that would appeal to the growing religious sector. The film was originally released solely across the Bible Belt and other areas considered to be Christian strongholds, but it only received a lukewarm reception. While the film is about faith, the film does not offer the expected biblical conclusions. Quite the opposite, the film expresses a spiritual universality that is unique to magical films. In other words, the "woo" is not uniquely Christian. Realizing their mistake, the film's producers distributed the film nationwide with a positive result. *Resurrection* eventually received two Academy Award nominations.

According to production files, the director and actress Ellen Burstyn attended healing centers to study for her role as Edna Mae.[251] Famed spiritual healer Rosayln Bruyere was hired as a consultant on the set. Moreover, Burstyn herself was a personal student of religion and spirituality, which she confesses in her autobiography *Lessons in Becoming Myself*. In a 2017 interview with Belief.net, Burstyn explains the freedom she found when first learning about world religions. Rather than claiming one way, she felt free to say: "I am a spirit opening to the truth that lives in all of these religions," and she adds this "brings you into a place where you see that the differences are in the dogma, and the essence is very, very similar. The truth is there spread out and speaking."[252]

---

251. Production Notes; source: *Resurrection* Production Files, Margaret Herrick Library, Academy of Motion Picture Arts and Sciences, Beverly Hills, California.

252. "Ellen Burstyn's True Face," Beliefnet, June 7, 2017, https://www.beliefnet.com/entertainment/celebrities/ellen-burstyns-true-face.aspx.

In her book, Burstyn credits her time filming *Resurrection* as one of her most important spiritual experiences. During film, she was studying Sufism and she brings that experience to her interpretation of her character. She writes, "[M]y intention with *Resurrection* was to bring into the public's consciousness the image of the feminine, the sacred feminine, complete with her sexuality, her healing powers, and her message that God/Goddess manifests in human beings as love." [253] Burstyn's spiritual beliefs manifest in the tone and direction of the film, creating a magical witch character that is more about spiritual connectivity through power than manipulation of power.

Conclusion

The period opens just after the end of the first wave of witch film popularity. The early years saw the most concentrated number of witch films, many of which retained some of the iconography, themes, and language of the progressive 1970s, such as *Resurrection* and *Devonsville Terror*. As society's pendulum was swinging away from the radical movements of the past and into a political conservatism, there was marked decrease in the number of witches and the types. As such, the period does not produce any landmark witch films, but it does demonstrate once again how times of conservatism, socioeconomic stability, and increased industry competition brings back reliable genres, such as fantasy as well as classic witch character constructions.

As the period goes on and the number of witch films decrease, the progressive concepts found in witch films are also mostly abandoned. By the mid-1980s, a significant shift had occurred in the American spectator's relationship to witchcraft. This is most clearly evidenced in the comparison of reactions to Margaret Hamilton's appearance in *Mr. Rogers' Neighborhood*. Witchcraft was no longer considered a silly pastime, a superstition, a backwards practice, or something hippies practiced in the park. Witchcraft was real. This renegotiation of meaning was evident both in the narratives that employ good and bad witches and in the projection of witchcraft as pure evil or complete superstition. The latter constructions appear predominantly during the more progressive early period, while the former constructions dominate the end of the period with the rise of Satanic Panic.

---

253. Ellen Burstyn, *Lessons in Becoming Myself* (London: Riverhead Books, 2007), 350.

Chapter 9: Filmography

The Halloween That Almost Wasn't	1979	Bruce Bilson
Super Friends, "Planet of Oz"	1979	Oscar Defau
Casper Saves Halloween	1979	Carl Urbano and Chris Cuddington
The Trouble with Miss Switch	1980	Charles A. Nichols
Beyond Evil	1980	Herb Freed
Witches' Brew	1980	Richard Shorr
B. J. and the Bear, "B. J. and the Witch"	1980	Charles R. Rondeau
Resurrection	1980	Daniel Petrie
Dragonslayer	1981	Matthew Robbins
Midnight Offerings	1981	Rod Holcomb
Super Friends, "The Witch's Arcade"	1981	George Gordon et al.
Disney's Halloween Treat	1982	Clyde Geronimi et al.
Macbeth	1982	Kirk Browning
Burned at the Stake	1982	Bert I. Gordon
Tucker's Witch	1982– 1983	Paul Huson and William Bast (creators)
Beastmaster	1982	Don Coscarelli
Halloween III: Season of the Witch	1982	Tommy Lee Wallace
Conan the Barbarian	1982	John Milius

The Dark Crystal	1982	Jim Henson, Frank Oz
Disney's Haunted Halloween	1983	William Robert Yates
Faerie Tale Theatre, "Rapunzel"	1983	Gilbert Cates
Smurfs, "All Hallows' Eve"	1983	Oscar Dufau et al.
Smurfs, "The Littlest Witch"	1983	Oscar Dufau et al.
The Great Bear Scare	1983	Hal Mason
Tales from the Darkside	1983–1988	(Multiple)
Something Wicked This Way Comes	1983	Jack Clayton
The Devonsville Terror	1983	Ulli Lommel
The Hugga Bunch	1985	Gus Jekel
Three Sovereigns for Sarah	1985	Philip Leacock
Return to Oz	1985	Walter Murch
Troll	1986	John Carl Buechler
Deadtime Stories	1986	Jeffrey Delman
A Smoky Mountain Christmas	1986	Henry Winkler

Chapter 10

The Satanic Panic

(1987–1998)

In 1983, accusations were made against owners and childcare workers at the Mc-Martin Preschool in Manhattan Beach, California. They were accused of ritual child abuse, including sodomy, rape, and other forms of molestation. Stories circulated of animal sacrifice, secret tunnels, blood drinking, and the placing of pentagrams on children's bottoms. In 1984, 384 McMartin preschool children of the 400 interviewed were diagnosed as having been sexually abused. Arrests were made. Despite all early doubts as to the credibility of the children's testimonies and the legitimacy of various reports, the McMartin trial continued for seven years, becoming the most expensive and longest running criminal trial in American history.[254]

The McMartin case marked the beginning of what eventually became known as the Satanic Panic—a culturally based fear that fed off an underlying concern about satanic-based ritual child abuse and thrived in the sociopolitical conservatism of the Reagan era. During this period, modern Witches formed legal support organizations such as The Witches League for Public Awareness founded by Laurie Cabot and Lady Liberty League founded by Selena Fox in order to protect themselves from growing religious bigotry. They partnered with law enforcement and media, working to distinguish their religion from the misconceptions perpetuated by the panic. Even when

---

254. Linder, Doug, "The McMartin Preschool Abuse Trial: A Commentary," Faculty website, University of Missouri-Kansas City, 2003, http://law2.umkc.edu/faculty/projects/ftrials/mcmartin /mcmartinaccount.html.

the McMartin case was settled in 1990 with no evidence of wrongdoing, the damage had already been done. A fear of Satanism, witchcraft, and child corruption were embedded in the psyche of contemporary Americans.

In addition to the moral panic, the conservative movement also brought with it a push against any advancements that had been made by and for women in earlier decades. Journalist Susan Faludi focuses on this point in her award-winning book *Backlash: The Undeclared War Against American Women*, which is an unapologetic critique of the overt and micro-aggressive attacks on progressive cultural movements, specifically feminism and gender equality. In the opening chapter, she argues, "The word may be that women have been 'liberated,' but women themselves seem to feel otherwise." [255] Her words are eventually echoed by feminist critics of the 1990s "girl power" movement that was built on the idea that the gender war had been won.

While the infamous McMartin case ended in 1990, it took several years for any significant public or official renunciation of satanic-based conspiracy theories that fueled the panic. In 1992, the FBI, led by Kenneth V. Lanning, published a document that discredited the presence of ritualized and organized satanic crimes against children. Then, over the next few years, other public figures followed suit. Most notably, in December 1995, famed talk show host Geraldo Rivera apologized for his part in perpetuating the fear through his popular shows.

Despite the damage and lingering residual fears, society did begin to shift away from its intense suspicion of witchcraft back to the quasi-acceptance found in the early 1980s. Similarly, the backlash against women receded, allowing the growth of a reactionary post-feminist movement that promoted "girl power," as previously mentioned. In films, this change is realized quite abruptly in 1996 with a dramatic shift in the presentation of witches. This unusually swift pivot can only be attributed to the residual influence of past progressive movements, demonstrating once again how society's story builds on itself one block at a time.

The Films and Shows

Due to the onset of the panic and its subsequent retreat, the trajectory of witchcraft representations during the period is clear cut. Before this period begins, witches had retired back to a relative state of being either inconsequential or conventional in construction. As the social fear spread, witch films began to reflect the panic, moving witches into a new place of empowerment and legitimacy, if only negative in nature.

---

255. Susan Faludi, *Backlash: The Undeclared War Against American Women* (New York: Doubleday, 1991), xiv.

The period begins in 1987 as witches start to fill the screen once again, launching the second witch popularity wave nearly twenty years after the first. Witch productions increased quickly in number, and their focus was predominantly satanic-based witchcraft (e.g., *Witches of Eastwick*, 1987; *Witchcraft*, 1988) or a fantastic form of the monstrous-feminine (e.g., *Wicked Stepmother*, 1989; *Hocus Pocus*, 1993). Alongside horror, many of the films were light comedy or family based (e.g., *Hello Again*, 1987; *Teen Witch*, 1989; *The Witching of Ben Wagner*, 1987). Although these lighter films do not always overtly express the rising cultural fears of the occult, they do help build the cultural momentum and reflect a society grappling with notions of witchcraft and women's power.

The panic's influence on all witch productions is evident through its repetition of traditional witch constructions, all designed with a new contemporary aesthetic. For example, there was a preponderance of hyper-sexualized vamps (e.g., *Witchcraft II: The Temptress*, 1989), evil fantasy witches (e.g., *The Little Mermaid*, 1989), and child-eating witches (e.g., *To Save a Child*, 1991). These films not only defined witchcraft as a satanic evil, but they also, allegorically, demonized the independent woman or the "new woman." They champion traditional gender roles, supporting Faludi's claims about a backlash.

This point is only reinforced by the fact that there was a notable decrease in male witches during the era, despite an increase in witch films overall. This is an important point because during the 1970s witch film craze there was a sizeable increase in male magical figures alongside female witches. During that period, it was social structures that were being constructed as evil, and that included all genders. By contrast, in this period the evil is defined almost entirely by a single transgressive woman.

As the panic died down and the grip of social conservatism loosened, satanic-specific witch narratives mostly disappeared, giving rise to a new breed of empowered Hollywood witches as magical teenagers (e.g., *The Craft*; *Sabrina, the Teenage Witch*, 1996). This trajectory parallels the earlier decade's witch cycle in which coven and priestess horror is followed almost exclusively by teen horror. Just as *Carrie* (1976) marked the shift in the 1970s, *The Craft* (1996) does the same exactly twenty years later. However, unlike the older teen witch films, the 1990s witch productions, both on television and in cinema, offered increasingly positive representations of witchcraft as forms of female identity and empowerment. The wild woman as a teen is no longer the victim-monster. She becomes the hero and witchcraft is her weapon. The witch, who begins the period as inconsequential, survives the Satanic Panic backlash and arrives in the end as the empowered adolescent girl.

Animation and the Halloween Witch

Once again, despite cultural shifts, the depiction of the witch within animation changes little. American audiences continued their love affair with the classic green-faced Halloween witch, whether she was embedded in holiday-inspired films or not. Examples include Tim Burton's film *The Nightmare Before Christmas* (1993), the television movie *Scooby-Doo and the Ghoul School* (1988), as well as the cartoon episodes *The New Adventures of Mighty Mouse*, "Witch Tricks" (1988), *The Real Ghostbusters*, "If I Were a Witch Man" (1989), *The Sylvester & Tweety Mysteries*, "Autumn's Leaving" (1996), and *Witches in Stitches* (1997). In 1990, DiC Entertainment launched a short-lived animated series based on MGM's film *The Wizard of Oz* and that included the classic witches.

With that said, several animated cartoons did attempt to handle the classic Halloween witch with more nuance. In some cases, she is self-reflexive in narrative pitch (e.g., *Animaniacs*, "Witch One/Macbeth," 1994), while in other cases, she provokes discussions on the ethical use of magic (e.g., *Aladdin*, "Strike Up the Sand," 1994). This change in character complexity is due to several key factors, including the renewed interest in witch popularity, an increase in the consumption of animated content by older audiences, an increasingly media-savvy viewership, and a postmodern sensibility that sought to challenge viewers by breaking apart narratives.

A Closer Look: *The Simpsons*

One of the best examples of animation's artistic evolution is found in Matt Groening's *The Simpsons*. In its first airing in 1989, *The Simpsons* was designed as a typical family sitcom complete with a mother, father, and three kids. However, through its satirical style and writing, the show, episode after episode, subverts what we know about family life, social convention, and cultural dynamics. Consistently over its long run, *The Simpsons* has offered a critical look at American culture, sparing nothing and no one, and that includes witchcraft. At the end of this period in 1997 after society's fears had largely quelled, *The Simpsons* aired "Easy Bake Coven," which dishes up a host of witchcraft iconography and transitional narratives to mock the dying moral panic.

"Easy Bake Coven" was part of that year's Halloween special. It begins as a parody of Arthur Miller's play *The Crucible*, which coincidentally had just been released as a live-action film for the first time in history. The episode opens like a horror film with red title letters against a dark, gray sky and leafless tree. The famous cartoon family is found living in the seventeenth century town of Sprynge-Field. The show then goes on to parody the classic Salem narrative, using many of the elements from its well-known mythos, including burnings, bonnets, buckles, accusations, town meetings, and deep Christian piety. As the show progresses, the writers mock the witch panic, equating it with religious zealotry and ideological fascism. In the opening scene, Flanders remarks after a public burning, "Well, that's seventy-five witches we've processed. That oughta show God whose side we're on."

Eventually, Marge Simpson is accused of witchcraft and a trial ensues. But here's where *The Simpsons*'s writers take the story for a spin. After Marge jumps off the cliff to her presumed death, she rises, flying on a broomstick. Her classic yellow skin is now green; her tall blue hair is now black. Marge has become the iconic animated Halloween witch. But the writers did not stop there in their encapsulation of the American witch narrative. Marge flies from the mock Salem village toward a rocky crag where her two sisters, also dressed as iconic Halloween witches, are stirring a cauldron.

When Marge arrives, the three witches stand together over the cauldron, and viewers suddenly find themselves in Shakespeare's play *Macbeth*. At this point, they leave the cave, searching for edible children, and the show migrates again to *Hansel and Gretel*, recalling the fear of the recent panic. But it doesn't end there, the final twist on this referential cultural journey lands the three green witches at the Flanders house, where the mother offers them treats in place of the children. The witches accept. The show ends with an explanation on how the Halloween tradition of "trick or treat" was born. As is typical of the series, *The Simpsons*'s "Easy Bake Coven" played off the viewer's cultural literacy to subvert what we know about contemporary social dynamics toward the creation of an entirely different narrative.

Return of the Animated Vamp

While the animation industry as a whole was expanding its reach to serve new audiences, Walt Disney Studios still remained the biggest name in full-length animated features. However, their market share noticeably decreased due to surging competition and a decade of lackluster releases. To revive the studio, Disney CEO Michael Eisner turned to past success and that meant the classic princess formula. Looking for a big win, Disney released *The Little Mermaid* (1989) based on Hans Christian Andersen's work "Den Lille Havfrue" published in 1837. The film was an immediate success and Disney was once again on top. Not only did the film contain a contemporary spunky princess, a Broadway soundtrack, and famous voice actors, but it also included a monstrous witch: Ursula.

As with past films, animators only used the original fairy tale as inspiration. Consequently, Andersen's Sea Witch is distinctly different from Disney's Ursula. Although described in terms of darkness and fear, the literary Sea Witch is a classic amoral fantasy hag who lives outside of society. She warns the little mermaid that her wish to be human is unwise, but as a woman of business, the witch performs the spell anyway for a price. She has no other role in Andersen's story. As was done with both *Snow White and the Seven Dwarfs* (1937) and *Sleeping Beauty* (1959), Disney condensed the original tale's complex moral structure and then expanded out using the Sea Witch as the main antagonist. The result is defined almost completely by a simple, binary understanding of good and evil with the adolescent princess as good and the vamp witch as evil.

At first glance, Ursula appears to be a classic Disney witch who, like Maleficent, has been ostracized from the kingdom. Her coloring is even similar to the older witches, including blacks, purples, and touches of bright red. However, Ursula is quite different from her predecessors in appearance and action. She is not obsessed with physical beauty or enacting revenge. Ursula ultimately wants to rule the kingdom. Her end game is world domination, which presents her more like a magical man than a fantasy witch.

In addition, Ursula is an octopus, a literal monster who reads as an aggressive, overweight woman wearing bright red lipstick. Like the older witches, Ursula is both woman and monster, bad mother and vamp witch. However, her natural state is the monstrous one. The Wicked Queen is always human. Maleficent, who appears human most of the time, changes into a dragon only at the end. Ursula is always the monster who only uses a human form temporarily to enact her will. When the spell is broken, she returns to her natural monstrous state. Historian Elizabeth Bell notes in her essay "Somatexts at the Disney Shop," Ursula's "tentacles physically manifest the enveloping, consumptive sexuality of the deadly woman."[256]

As mentioned earlier, Ursula has little interest in her own body image, yet she understands feminine power and how it works within gender politics, and she bestows this wisdom on Ariel, the young mermaid. For example, she tells Ariel to use her body language because the men on land "don't like a lot of chatter." The Wicked Queen and Maleficent never engage in this type of discourse. In fact, they rarely engage directly with the heroine at all, other than from a distance or as a looming, mystical threat.

Ursula's goal is not Ariel's destruction, as is the case in the other films. She needs the girl as a weapon to take over the kingdom. In order to trap her, Ursula employs her own understanding of adolescent sexuality, taking advantage of Ariel's naturally occurring transition to womanhood. Ursula forces that change along, symbolized by her giving the mermaid legs. Then, she sends Ariel off to "get her man." Rather than focus on her own body, Ursula uses that of a young girl in her quest for power. As such, Ursula's sexual prowess is contained solely in her knowledge of female agency as it operates successfully within the patriarchy.

---

256. Bell, "Somatexts at the Disney Shop," 117.

It is often noted that Ursula was modeled on the famous drag queen Divine, and this reading is not at all difficult to see when looking at the character's visual design and her performance in "Poor Unfortunate Souls." In the essay "Where Do the Mermaids Stand?" Laura Sells observes:

> Ursula stages a camp drag show about being a woman in the white male system, beginning 'backstage' with hair mousse and lipstick. She shimmies and wiggles in an exaggerated style while her eels swirl around her, forming a feather boa. This performance is a masquerade, a drag show starring Ursula as the ironic figure.[257]

Sells goes on to argue that this characterization adds to the destabilization of gender, making Ursula more threatening. As noted earlier, Ursula's goal is more in line with that of a magical man, which is supported by this nonbinary gender construction.

As such, Ursula exists as the foremost evil for the conservative establishment. She is an empowered female character, embracing a gender construction often seen as abhorrent. She uses feminine sexual power, as allowed in conventional gender play, against the patriarchy in order to bring it down. She is the bad mother and monstrous-feminine packaged in a nontraditional gender expression. As a result, Ursula is ultimately doomed, dying violently, impaled by a ship's mast as the symbolic giant phallus. The patriarchy wins, the fairy tale narrative is realized, and the young woman, now aware of her sexuality and its power, is safely contained by a prince husband, becoming "part of his world." Disney, once again, created a traditional cinematic story that fit neatly into contemporary America of the 1980s.

Literary Adaptations: Dark Fantasy

Disney was not the only studio to return to classic stories. The witch film revival brought with it other adaptations, from fairy tales to well-known literature. The representation of these witches, whether crones or vamps, took on a new level of intensity in expression similar to the Disney film. Many of these adaptations are intermingled with true horror, creating a twisted look at the old story (e.g., *Pumpkinhead*, 1988; *Rumpelstiltskin*, 1995; *Snow White: A Tale of Terror*, 1997). Such adaptations are often labeled "dark fantasy."

While dark fantasy was not dominant during the era, it did dot the landscape simply due to the rise in witch films. In these narratives, the witch does not wholly

---

257. Laura Sells, "Where Do the Mermaids Stand?" in *From Mouse to Mermaid: The Politics of Film, Gender, and Culture*, ed. Elizabeth Bell et al. (Bloomington: Indiana University Press, 1995), 182.

convert to a typical horror witch, but rather, she becomes the most extreme version of her fantasy self. Filmmakers played off the most terrifying aspects of the witch including her physical appearance defined by age or deformity, her wanton use of female sexuality, the iconography of death, a fascination with creatures of the dark (e.g., owls, rats, snakes, bats), and of course magic.

A Closer Look: *Pumpkinhead*

Released in 1988, the live action horror film *Pumpkinhead* is loosely based on Nathaniel Hawthorne's *Feathertop*. Directed by Stan Winston, *Pumpkinhead* the film is not a faithful retelling of Hawthorne's story but rather a derivative of its cultural legacy. In the original story, the crone is wronged by society. In the movie, it is Ed Harley, the film's tragic hero, who is wronged. This is the first time the story was adapted since the 1961 musical version. Unlike that adaptation and earlier ones, Winston's *Pumpkinhead* manages to capture the moral essence of Hawthorne's story, including the desire for revenge and the ethical responsibility to family, self, and community.

Haggis the witch (Florence Schauffler) carries the body of tragic hero
Ed Harley (Lance Henriksen) into a graveyard in Pumpkinhead *(1988).*
[Source: United Artists/Photofest. © United Artists]

Pumpkinhead is often categorized as dark fantasy, predominantly due to the presence of the witch and mystical monster. However, on its simplest level, *Pumpkinhead* is purely a classic teen slasher film and thematically it is a moral tale baked within Christian guideposts. Rather than resting on the sensationalized juxtaposition of teenage sexuality and a murderous bloodletting, the film engages with the dutiful concept: "Be careful what you wish for." This disallows the narrative to settle into a binary ethical structure, which is more typical for the average horror film. In witch film terms, *Pumpkinhead* is less dark fantasy and more horror's answer to the western drama.

Pumpkinhead begins with a group of reckless teens accidently killing a young boy, after which his father, Ed Harley, engages a witch's magic to enact revenge. The crone calls up the murderous monster, who picks off the teens one by one. In the end, the narrative allows the viewer to empathize with the remaining two teens who do show remorse for the accident and with Harley as he redeems himself in death. Like Hawthorne's scarecrow who refuses to live falsely as a man and ends his monstrous life, Harley does the same, committing suicide when he realizes his own humanity is tied to the monster.

As for the film's elderly folk witch, she lives alone deep in the mountains, playing the role of the feared Baba Yaga. She is the old wild woman of the western drama distorted by the horror setting. "She can't help you," Ed Harley is told by a neighbor. "All she can do is take you straight to hell." When the witch scene begins, her woodland cabin is dark and bathed in red light and shadow. The witch is predominantly shown in silhouette close-ups, accentuating the lines of her aged skin, the unnatural length of her fingers and nails, and the gnarly kinks in her hair. Later in the graveyard as she raises the monstrous Pumpkinhead, the witch is shown covered in rags. Mice, spiders, and owls further decorate the sequence. Visually speaking, the witch is a fantasy crone.

Because the witch's role in the narrative transmutes the story from a simple slasher film not only into dark fantasy but also into a moral tale, religion takes on a more significant role. "God is the only thing that can stop what's out there, Kim," says one of the teens after Pumpkinhead has killed his first victim. While the witch herself is framed as part of the mystical mountain world and warns about the ramifications of revenge, she is also marked as damned in a Christian sense. Her magic is sourced. After realizing the depth of the horror that he has unleashed, Harley goes back to the witch, who explains she can do nothing to stop the murders. "God damn you," Harley yells at the witch. "He already has," she responds.

Despite this theological connection, the witch is not the antagonizing satanic evil, rather she exists as a moral compass for Harley as is common for the elderly folk witch. Her function is truly liminal in that her existence is dangerous but accepted as existing. In that way, she is like the wild wood or the cemetery. She lives in a space between evil and good, dead and alive, just and unjust. In this role, the witch can either be the pathway to goodness or to the dark side of the psyche. Her construction and her warning mirror that of Granny Hart from *The Twilight Zone*'s "Jess-Belle" (1963): "Be careful what you ask for."

Despite the complexities, Christian ethical structure, and its celebrated literary source, *Pumpkinhead* received only moderate reception. However, it has since picked up a cult following and has inspired several television and direct-to-video sequels, none of which capture the nuances present in the original. While *Rumpelstiltskin* (1995) or *Snow White: A Tale of Terror* (1998) are more classic examples of the dark fantasy genre, *Pumpkinhead* remains one of the period's most powerful and classic representations of horror's elderly folk witch (Florence Schauffler) in an adaptive tale. Like her predecessors, she demonstrates in extreme terms how this character construction can have little screen time but significantly alter the film's trajectory. The witch offers the viewer the tools by which to judge the protagonist, and then the film's narrative follows through as a literal enactment of that judging. In *Pumpkinhead*, the crone's customer makes a poor choice and is ultimately punished through a redemptive death. In that way, the film provides a moral lesson reminiscent of the film's literary origins.

Literary Adaptations: The Accused Woman

Hawthorne's work was not the only classic story adapted during this period. Arthur Miller's *The Crucible* found its way to the silver screen for the first time since its publication in 1953. Often said to be an allegory for 1950s McCarthyism and the Red Scare, it is not surprising that a play warning of the dangers of moral panic was adapted during this era. Despite being Miller's most produced work, *The Crucible* was not brought to the silver screen until 1996. After the film's release, *New York Times* journalist Victor Navasky asked Miller about the relationship between his work, the film, and the political climate. Miller responded:

> I have had immense confidence in the applicability of the play to almost any time, the reason being it's dealing with a paranoid situation. But that situation doesn't depend on any particular political or sociological development. I wrote it blind to the world. The enemy is within, and within stays within, and we can't get out of within.[258]

---

258. Victor Navasky, "The Demons of Salem, With Us Still," *The New York Times*, September 8, 1996, https://www.nytimes.com/1996/09/08/movies/the-demons-of-salem-with-us-still.html.

Navasky himself did make the connection, saying: "A case in point: The nation-wide rash of child molestation trials in which children have charged daycare center workers with unspeakable crimes." [259] The public made the connection as well. Navasky adds that Miller had already received mail "pressing that analogy." [260]

The Crucible, which was released after the FBI's statement condemning the panic, is a direct critique of the decade's insanity just as Miller's play was originally meant to be. However, not all accused woman films or those simply playing off Salem's legacy make strong social statements. In fact, most do not. For example, the live-action-comedy *Love at Stake* (1987) is a parody of Salem's famous history. During the trial scene, Dr. Joyce Brothers appears in a cameo to testify as to what is really going on in Salem. She describes the town's chaos as a "case of mass hysteria brought on by repressive religious doctrine, which in turn stifles individual sexual expression." In some ways this could be considered a critique, but the timing is wrong, and it fits in with a number of other contemporary witch-related comedies that parody common witchcraft narratives to capitalize on the growing interest in witch films.

The accused woman narrative appears in only a small number of films during this period, spanning several genres. *Love at Stake* is a sex comedy; *The Simpsons*'s "Easy Bake Coven" (1997) is an animated sitcom. In 1998, *Dangerous Beauty*, a biopic drama, tells the story of the famous Venetian courtesan Veronica Franco. In this film, Veronica, an accused woman, is labeled a witch due to transgressive behavior defined by her sharp wit, intelligence, knowledge, and her job as a courtesan. The story is the same, regardless of genre.

A Closer Look: *The Pit and the Pendulum*

In the horror genre, the accused woman narrative is intensified through sensational-ism and other extremes as is the case with *The Pit and the Pendulum* (1991), another literary adaptation. Inspired by Edgar Allan Poe's short story of the same name, "The Pit and the Pendulum" tells the tale of a young baker's wife imprisoned for the prac-tice of witchcraft due to her outspoken nature. *Pit and the Pendulum* is one of many films inspired by Poe's original story; however, those other adaptations and the origi-nal tale do not contain a narrative thread pertaining to witchcraft. This theme was added to the 1991 film to capitalize on contemporary cultural interests and to provide a basis for the film's sexual component. *The Pit and the Pendulum* is as much a graph-ic and deeply evocative portrayal of the Grand Inquisitor's sadistic nature, which in-cludes a forbidden sexual lust for Maria, as it is the story of an accused woman.

---

259. Navasky, "The Demons of Salem."
260. Navasky, "The Demons of Salem."

Unlike historical dramas like *The Crucible*, horror can cross-purpose their depiction of the witch by offering a potentially true magical component within its fantastical structures. *The Pit and the Pendulum*, for example, introduces such an element containing a subtextual Joan of Arc story. While Maria is the classic accused woman, she evolves, by choice, into a wild woman. Maria hears voices and although the film intimates this detail in early scenes, it is not presented wholesale until Maria meets Esmerelda, another female prisoner accused of witchcraft.

Esmerelda is the classic elderly folk witch. She offers Maria a spiritual path away from the pain of physical torture and into the bliss of witchcraft. This is a typical relationship between the crone and young wild woman. Just as *The Twilight Zone*'s Granny Hart showed Jess-Belle the path to becoming a witch, Esmerelda shows Maria. However, *The Pit and the Pendulum* provides a more nuanced understanding of both traditional religion and witchcraft. *The Twilight Zone* episode's morality was binary with Christianity painted as good and witchcraft as evil. Granny Hart is described as someone who sold her soul. By contrast, when Esmerelda introduces herself, she says that she is a witch, adding, "I don't ride brooms through the hours and kiss the Devil's cock. I am a midwife. I grow herbs and try to heal the sick as best I can."

The Pit and the Pendulum disposes with the biblically derived negative concept of the crone witch and embraces her as a healer, offering her sympathy. It shows Esmerelda falling victim not to the church as a whole, but to the sadistic horrors of the Grand Inquisitor, who himself flouts church doctrine and even kills a Catholic bishop. Witchcraft is not evil in this film, but a natural pathway. This construction parallels the earlier period's attempts to renegotiate the boundaries of good and bad magic. *The Pit and the Pendulum* not only vindicates the crone witch but also vindicates the female witch as a mystic, giving way to the vilification of not religious doctrine but the sexually repressed and sadistic individual man.

While the introduction of the witch into Poe's story was propelled by the growing interest in witch films, filmmakers embedded a transitional feminist subplot in which the accused woman, instead of relying on the redemptive rescue, turns to witchcraft to save herself. With the help of an older woman, she transitions to the wild woman, a purposefully transgressive, powerful female. Although Maria's husband does show up at the end, it is Maria and her powerful magic that save her from the evils of one man's power-hungry psychosis.

The Horror Witch Reborn

Both dark fantasy and stories of the accused woman found only limited popularity during this period, showing up simply because fairy tales and trial films are typical narratives for the witch. Hawthorne, Poe, the Grimm Brothers, and Miller are names often associated with stories of the occult, witchcraft, and the macabre. Therefore, it is not surprising that their works were adapted during the second wave of witch film popularity. It is even less surprising that, with few exceptions, they were adapted through the lens of horror given the social climate.

Outside of adaptation, the horror genre produced a sizable body of original work beginning in the late 1980s and increasing over time. Along with this revived interest in true witch horror came a new character—a contemporary vamp witch who was neither the 1970s coven leader nor the follower of a satanic religion. This period's vamp witch generally works alone or in a trio of women. Like Ursula and the dark fantasy witches, she is intense in depiction and, in most cases, she feeds off a defined evil source for power and beauty. Along with that construction, there were a few horror folk witches (e.g., *Black Magic Woman*, 1991) and a few films with covens (e.g., *To Save a Child*, 1991).

For the most part, the period's horror witch films avoid feminist themes and all associations to modern Witchcraft practice. The genre increasingly captures the misogynistic narratives more typical to horror in general, including the objectification of nude female bodies, prolonged captivity and the abuse of female characters by male aggressors, and magic as pure evil. To better understand the nature of the period's horror witch construction, the films can be divided into two main categories based on underlying themes: "sex and Satan" and "save the child."

With only one exception, the period's horror films fit into those categories. The film *Bay Coven* (1987) offers a narrative more typical to older witch films. It depicts a coven-next-door scenario in which a young couple move into a town run by satanic witches. In the 1970s, this theme reflected a population concerned with the presence of an underlying systemic evil in all society rather than a localized evil present in a single-family unit or within a single wild woman. For that reason, films with themes like *Bay Coven* weren't prominent.

The Horror Witch: Sex and Satan

As shown in previous chapters, cinematic witches are commonly defined by the physical body, whether that be elongated noses with warts or exposed breasts. In satanic-based horror, the characterization is typically focused on the latter, which is part of the hyper-sexualization of the vamp witch. As the witch film cycle picked up in the late 1980s, there was a noticeable increase in the gratuitous displays of female nudity and depictions of sexuality as linked to satanic activity. Aided by wardrobe and makeup, the camera spent focused time on the physicality of the film's witch, linking her magical power to her sexual prowess. For example, in *Witchcraft II: The Temptress*

(1989), William Adams (born William Spanner) walks by his witch neighbor, Delores, on his way home from high school. She is standing on a ladder painting her house wearing black lingerie and high heels. When William spots her, the camera pans slowly across her backside in close-up. Delores is a horror vamp witch who is defined by a hyper-realized sexuality that codifies her as evil.

While the 1970s vamp witches were constructed similarly, the older horror films do not make the witch's sexuality central to the story. Rather, it was only a character detail. The camera's eye does not caress their bodies or explore their nudity any further, because those films were more interested in the entire transgressive community experience rather than the actions of one witch. In the 1980s, the satanic vamp witch is on her own, as she was prior to 1968, and she is a threat to only a single man. The exploration of Delores's backside is not entirely unlike the spell scene in *Bell, Book and Candle* in which Gillian is facing away from the camera wearing an open-back dress. In her book, Susan Faludi observed that Hollywood's complicity in the media backlash against women was the perpetuation of narratives in which "unwed women shrink to sniveling spinsters or inflate to fire-breathing she-devils."[261] The vamp witch is Faludi's she-devil.

Visually speaking, the period's horror vamp often does attempt to blend into the film's contemporary environment. However, when she does stand out, she typically wears reds and blacks. Her home is filled with an overabundance of candles, pentacles, and Baphomet images. As the film builds its horror, the vamp's sexual fortitude is commonly juxtaposed to sensationalized shots of objects that evoke disgust, darkness, the macabre, and a witchcraft mythos. Through that visual comparison, these witch films elicit both desire and repulsion at the same time, creating a horror response that draws from a place where extremes meet.

In *Black Magic Woman* (1991), for example, the male hero, after being seduced by presumed-witch Cassandra, wakes in his bed to find his white sheets covered in blood, eggs, and snakes. In *Black Magic* (1992), Alex Gage is slowly seduced by Lillian through a narrative process that is continually being challenged by stories and images of death, frogs, crows, and other witch imagery. In these films, sexual fantasy and desire becomes the man's undoing, which is linked to the grotesque and monstrous as defined by the woman as witch. Other films that contain this construction include *Spellbinder* (1988), *Seduced by Evil* (1994), and *Serpent's Lair* (1995).

During this same period of time, a number of independent filmmakers joined the witch craze, making low-budget horror-inspired films for the direct-to-video market. They capitalized on the salacious occult themes that were attached to the sexuality

---

261. Faludi, *Backlash*, xi.

of the vamp witch. It is important to note that most of those productions were designated as erotic horror and most are considered soft porn. These include *The Coven* (1993), *The Coven 2* (1993), *The Temptress* (1995), *Sorceress* (1995), *Witch Academy* (1995), and some of the films in the *Witchcraft* franchise (e.g., *The Temptress*, 1989; *Judgement Hour*, 1995). The levels of eroticism vary.

This is a notable point because the vamp witch character is easily translatable into the erotic environment due to the construction's focus on body, beauty, and sexuality. After a filmmaker drops the story and any narrative nuances, all that is left is an objectified, socially transgressive woman. However, it is important to remember that witch narratives had long been used in erotic films or "nudies" (e.g., *The Naked Witch*, 1967; *Sex Rituals of the Occult*, 1970). The filmmakers of the 1980s were not inventing something new, just adding a visual intensity that was not present in earlier decades, which parallels the increase in intensity within the period's non-erotic witch films, such as in *Pumpkinhead* (1988) and *The Little Mermaid* (1989).

A Closer Look: *The Witches of Eastwick*

The Witches of Eastwick (1987), based on John Updike's 1984 best-selling novel of the same name, is a border film that exists just before the witch film craze moves into full swing, and it embraces the "sex and Satan" theme quite literally. While more of a dark comedy than pure horror, *The Witches of Eastwick* tells the story of three restless women who turn to witchcraft to fulfill their needs. When the original book was published, Updike was celebrated for his expression of female empowerment thriving within patriarchal structures. At the same time, he was criticized for the book's depiction of misogyny and the treatment of unattached women as evil witches.

The film version of Updike's story is quite different from his novel. While the novel focuses on the archetypical female witch trio as willing participants in a magical craft, the film does not. It's trio, played by Cher, Susan Sarandon, and Michelle Pfeiffer, only accidently comes by magic over wine and wishful thinking. Updike's trio know that they are not "a bent rib, as the infamous *Malleus Maleficarum* had it." [262] By contrast, the film's women become exactly that, which reflects the ideology that a woman's power and social position can only be attained through men. In the case of a witch, that man is Satan. In this film, the transactional exchange between woman and man or witch and Satan is quite literal. The women are only empowered through sexual acquiescence.

---

262. John Updike, *The Witches of Eastwick* (New York: Ballantine Books, 1984), 14.

In The Witches of Eastwick *(1987), three local women, Alex, Jane,
and Sukie, use magic to rid the town of Darryl Van Horne, who turns
out to be the devil. Shown left to right: Cher, Susan Sarandon, and Michelle Pfeiffer.
[Source: Warner Brothers/Photofest. © Warner Brothers]*

Similar to the novel, the film's trio are victims of society, divorce, infidelity, and objectification. However, unlike in the novel, the film's witches are never freed from that state of victimhood. While their satanic-based witchcraft at first seems to free them, the same magic eventually becomes a trap. After they meet Satan, known as Darryl Van Horne (Jack Nicholson), their appearances become less ordinary and haggard. Their hair gets bigger; their clothes get tighter. The trio eventually agrees to participate in a polyamorous relationship, a scene which includes images of them wearing lingerie on silk bed sheets. In one respect, *The Witches of Eastwick* is a *Pygmalion* tale with the Devil as teacher.

If the 1983 film *Devonsville Terror* offers a story warning against the perversions of man, *The Witches of Eastwick* warns against the susceptibility of women to be seduced into evil. However, that reading is far too simple. *The Witches of Eastwick* does attempt to retain some of Updike's original feminist themes. As already noted, the film, like the novel, opens with the women constructed as victims of men and society. Additionally, the bewitched women aren't completely powerless; they do eventually use magic on their own to rid the town of Satan, which gives way to the film's most famous scene in which Van Horne delivers a monologue on women and God.

After saving the town, the happy trio of witches retain Van Horne's mansion, remaining as wildly adorned and artistically inspired as they were before Satan's death. However, the women are still trapped as victims. They gave up their personal powers but retained the one element that is acceptable to the male gaze: their beauty. This is emphasized in the final moments of the film when Van Horne appears on the television. They are still in his home, being watched. It is important to note that Updike's book was published in 1984 coming out of a progressive decade that generally supported contemplations on women's independence. By contrast, the film was produced in the late 1980s, embracing a typical misogynistic horror aesthetic and reflecting what Faludi would posit as evidence of the cultural backlash against women.

The Horror Witch: Save the Child

In "sex and Satan" narratives, the fear revolves around uncontained female sexuality signified by the satanic vamp witch. In other narratives, the exploited fear, which partially emanates from the fairy tale motif, is the loss, defilement, or corruption of the child. This *Hansel and Gretel*-inspired theme, if you will, was particularly relevant to an era that harbored a moral panic concerning ritual child abuse. The "save the child" scenario typically revolves around a non-magical mother needing to protect a child of any age from a witchcraft coven or Satan himself, although there are variations such as in the *X-Files* episode "Die Hand Die Verletzt" (1995). While this endangerment narrative was found in films prior to 1988 (e.g., *Rosemary's Baby*, *Beastmaster*, *Troll*, *Something Wicked this Way Comes*), it became more prominent during the Satanic Panic.

As an example, *Witchcraft* (1988) opens with quick close-up shots of a young mother giving birth to a child, who she then must protect throughout the rest of the film. Deemed unfit to care for the child by her husband, the young mother wades through the narrative as if in a dream, unaware of the evils around her but frightened by her suspicions. Her elderly mother-in-law, dressed in dark, severe, and near-gothic clothing, takes over childcare. At the end, it is revealed that this grandmother is a three-hundred-year-old satanic witch who wants to raise the baby to be the coven's leader. In the very last shot, after the witches are killed, the mother sits exhausted holding her child as white smoke surrounds her. She appears angelic, even Madonna-like. The juxtaposition of this imagery against the previous satanic iconography offers the entire film a transcendental moment of redemption.

While "sex and Satan" films present evil invading normalcy such as in *The Witches of Eastwick*, "save the child" films works like a coven-next-door narrative with the normal accidentally encountering the satanic. In many of them, there is an evil mother-in-law witch or priestess. When the priestess is a crone, she is not sexualized and is often portrayed as a gothic immortal or undead monster (e.g., *To Save a Child*, 1991; *Spell*, 2020). Interestingly, in the film *Witchcraft*, the son turns out to be the mother's three-hundred-year-old witch lover, which adds an Oedipal tone to the film's end reveal, making Satanic practice that much more disturbing to the viewer.

Another similar film is the 1991 made for television movie aptly titled *To Save a Child*. Originally called *The Craft*, the film tells the story of Isabella who gives birth to a child halfway through the story. When she becomes suspicious of her in-law's activities, she turns to a former professor. He says, "You may not believe in pagan religions, but they exist anyway." Just as with the mother in *Witchcraft*, Isabella escapes the coven's clutches with the help of a secondary male character, in this case a Native American man who signifies freedom, wisdom, and Americana. However, before that escape, and in an ironic reversal of classic imagery, a mob of witches carrying lit torches chase her out of town.

Interestingly, *To Save a Child* is one of the first films to generate a successful protest campaign from the growing modern Witchcraft community. In 1990, ABC began its plans for a mini-series called *The Craft*. After word reached Pagan community leaders, they took up a letter writing campaign, urging modern Witches to write to ABC executives with their concerns. An article published in the Spring 1991 issue of *Circle Network News* reads, "ABC would not consider airing a pilot or series with this type of plot about Jews, Roman Catholics, African-American Baptists, or other mainstream religious groups."[263] The writer goes on to say that the film is likely to "fuel hate-crimes against Wiccans and other Pagans. It puts the entire movement at risk."[264] The letter writing campaign was successful and by the summer of that year, ABC had cancelled production. However, the pilot had already been filmed; it was renamed *To Save a Child* and released that fall as a prime-time movie.

In *To Save a Child* and *Witchcraft*, the endangerment theme is the narrative's centerpiece. However, that is not always the case; the theme is sometimes used as a plot device within a broader story. For example, in the film *Warlock* (1989), the title character discovers a boy alone on a playground. Church bells ring in the distance and the Warlock asks the boy why he isn't attending Sunday service. The child explains that

---

263. "Act Now to Uphold Religious Freedom for Wiccans," *Circle Network News*, Spring 1991, 5

264. "Act Now to Uphold Religious Freedom for Wiccans," *Circle Network News*, Spring 1991, 5.

his dad doesn't believe. The conversation continues with the boy asking why the man wasn't in church. The Warlock answers:

> "Witches can't set foot on church grounds."
> The boy responds, "Witches are girls."
> "Some are men."
> "So where's your broomstick? Witches need broomsticks to fly.
> Didn't you never see *The Wizard of Oz*?"
> The Warlock responds, "I need no broomstick to fly."

As the viewer then discovers, witches fly by using a brew made from the fat of an unbaptized adolescent male. In the next scene, the boy has disappeared, and the Warlock is shown flying.

However, *Warlock* is an anomaly. The "save the child" horror theme typically involves a coven and often juxtaposes an older female witch serving as "bad mother" with the non-magical heroine as "good mother." In *To Save a Child*, the "good" mother accidently encounters a satanic ritual being performed by her mother-in-law. In a series of fast, distorted close-ups, the older woman appears to be kneeling naked before a smoking hole in the ground. Her straggly gray hair falls at her back as she invokes "the dark one." When caught the woman turns and appears for a single moment as a beast, reminiscent of classic fairy-tale transformations.

While the "save the child" theme was mostly absent from 1970s witch films, it was prominent during this period when viewers feared that it could be reality. Taking this idea one step further, these narratives focus on what is perceived to be the destruction of the nuclear family, subtly placing blame on women. They codify a collective social anxiety concerning the placement of young children in day care settings, which became a substitute family space as women pursued careers. Like the day care center, the film's coven becomes a false family. The narratives posit that the working mother chose poorly and, as a result, must accept her traditional role and save the innocent child victim from the evils of the false family.

Witchcraft and the Family

Horror was not the only genre in which the fear of ritual child abuse was expressed. This was a recurrent theme in films created as family entertainment. These children-friendly productions express the possibility that witchcraft exists as a lurking social danger, which most typically plays out in comedic versions of the horror genre's "save the child" scenario. The most well-known of these films are *The Witches* (1990) and *Hocus Pocus* (1993), both of which use a classic Halloween aesthetic to produce a quasi-horror narrative centered on child-hating witches. Other similar films include the Olson twins' vehicle *Double, Double, Toil and Trouble* (1993) and Disney's *The Witching of Ben Wagner* (1987).

A Closer Look: *The Witches* and *Hocus Pocus*

In 1990, Muppets creator Jim Henson released a film adaptation of Roald Dahl's novel *The Witches*. The film was directed by Nicolas Roeg and was a joint British-American production, which technically disqualifies it from the study. However, it is important to note the film's presence in the American witch film canon due to its lasting imprint on American culture and its relationship to the 1993 Disney film *Hocus Pocus*. In short, the film tells the story of a coven of female witches, defined as demons, who hate children and who seek to trap them and turn them into mice.

After its release, *The Witches* received only moderate reviews and ultimately failed at the box office. In August 1990, *New York Times* reviewer Caryn James wrote, "*The Witches* resembles a brilliantly told bedtime story, though the teller of this children's tale may well be the slightly cracked relative who can't judge when scary stories become nightmares."[265] Dahl himself called it "utterly appalling."[266] As a result, he refused to release another one of his books for film adaptation. Despite underperforming, Anjelica Huston's portrayal of the Grand High Witch has since garnered the film a cult following, and she is considered one of the most recognizable cinematic witches. Her character was constructed to be a goth-like vamp that recalls Morticia Addams, a character Huston played only one year later in the reboot of *The Addams Family*. However, the Grand High Witch is also a monster, as shown when she removes her wig and mask.

Released three years later, Disney's film *Hocus Pocus* followed a similar pattern in that it performed poorly at the box office and was criticized for being overly buoyant, messy, and not able to find its key audience. *New York Times* reviewer Janet Maslin called the film an "unholy mess" and went on to observe that the film was "aimed squarely at the Nowheresville between juvenile and adult audiences."[267] Despite the

---

265. Caryn James, "When the Ladies Take Off Their Wigs, Head for Home. Fast," *The New York Times*, August 24, 1990, https://www.nytimes.com/1990/08/24/movies/review-film-when-the-ladies-take -off-their-wigs-head-for-home-fast.html.

266. Tom Bishop, "Willy Wonka's Everlasting Film Plot," *BBC News*, July 11, 2005, http://news.bbc .co.uk/2/hi/entertainment/4660873.stm.

267. Janet Maslin. "Bette Midler, Queen Witch in Heavy Makeup." *The New York Times*, July 16 1993, https://www.nytimes.com/1993/07/16/movies/review-film-bette-midler-queen-witch-in-heavy -makeup.html.

poor showing, *Hocus Pocus* has also garnered a cult following due to its outrageous witches, more specifically Bette Midler's portrayal of Winifred Sanderson.

The three Sanderson sisters are yet another example of the Hollywood magical trio. In this case, the comical threesome, played by Midler, Sarah Jessica Parker, and Kathy Najimy, are contemporary forms of the Victorian clown witch. The Sanderson's costumes, including makeup, hair, and clothing, are bursting with wild colors that recall a Renaissance Festival comedic entertainment extravaganza. Their appearances support their wild behavior, from the way they walk, talk, giggle, and fall over each other. Moreover, the Sanderson sisters are three-hundred-year-old Salem witches, who are resurrected only when a virgin lights "the black flame candle." In order to stay alive, they must suck the souls of the town's children. Virgins, candles, spiderwebs, spells, mummies, graveyards, black cats, and the death of children are all tossed about as the film progresses toward a conclusion. The film is a wild basket of cinematic fantasy witchcraft delights.

As noted earlier, *The Witches* and *Hocus Pocus* were both released at the beginning of the witch cycle and during the height of the moral panic. They both portray the idea that children are in mortal danger due to a lurking evil presence, which is defined as the unattached and empowered middle-aged women. Bucking that trend to some degree was *Double, Double, Toil and Trouble*, which does attempt to nuance its presentation of witchcraft. Cloris Leachman plays twin sisters, each of whom embody good and bad magic. The good witch wears lace-adorned white clothing, while the bad sister has a typical gothic appearance. This evokes the Hollywood convention of the good witch as angel or nanny and the bad witch as demonic monster. In either case, the threat is waged at children.

Teen Magic: Outcasts and Weirdos

The "save the child" theme rarely concerns teenagers and, even more specifically, girls. However, teen girls had their own witchcraft narrative that capitalized on the intersection of witchcraft, female adolescence, and teen culture. They span several genres, including the rom-com, fantasy, and of course horror. Regardless of the genre, the teen girl exists in a liminal space somewhere between childhood and adulthood, as in past decades. The discovery of magic is her allegorical coming of age and the discovery of her unique female identity and power. That newfound sexuality and her dying innocence are both holy grails in that sense—a fleeting something to protect or contain before she becomes dangerous.[268]

---

268. Diana Anselmo-Sequeira, "Apparitional Girlhood: Material Ephemerality and the Historiography of Female Adolescence in Early American Film," 25.

As in the 1970s, the teen witch horror films rise in popularity as the horror vamp witch films decline. Examples of such films include *The Craft* (1996) or *I've Been Waiting for You* (1998) and an episode of the television show *The Outer Limits*, "The Choice" (1995). However, those films and shows were not the first to indulge in the topic of teen witchcraft during the period. In 1989, a romantic comedy titled *Teen Witch* told the classic story of an unpopular high school girl who discovers her magical power on her sixteenth birthday. It is the *Carrie* story without the horror, the interpersonal complexity, sophisticated storytelling, and violent death.

Unlike Brian De Palma's classic film *Carrie* (1976), *Teen Witch* is plot driven and lacks cinematic depth. It uses witchcraft simply as a narrative device to give Louise, the awkward girl, a pathway to popularity. Once empowered, Louise's clothes go from baggy to tight and from drab to colorful. She is envied by girls and wanted by boys. During the final dance scene, she abandons her magic completely, as symbolized by an amulet, in favor of love and friendship. The film posits this decision as the correct moral choice because it frames her use of magic as a sign of selfish narcissism. In other words, the morality of the film counsels against her becoming the vamp. Although she does reject magic, she retains her fabulous transformation, similar to *The Witches of Eastwick*. As such, *Teen Witch* is another *Pygmalion* story with witchcraft as the professor.

To reiterate, *Teen Witch* is not a horror film. It is a classic 1980s high school movie with an infusion of magic and fantasy. Its presentation of magic as teen wishcraft fits with the lighter witchcraft fare produced at the start of the period before the full weight of the Satanic Panic overtook narratives. Additionally, the film provides a family friendly alternative to the horror films, containing the same classic narrative that demonstrates the need to contain feminine power.

A Closer Look: *The Craft*

The Craft (1996), by contrast, is a true marker of the period's teen witch cinematic aesthetic. Directed by Andrew Fleming, *The Craft* was released at the height of witch film popularity and is a teen horror film in every respect. Its narrative centers on four misfit girls (i.e., Rochelle, Nancy, Sarah, and Bonnie) seeking empowerment through magic. Although it contains many canned horror tropes and has a campy ending, the film handled the subjects of witchcraft and female empowerment differently than prior horror films as well as other past teen witch films; this fact alone led to its cult success.

The Craft explores the plight of four outcast girls and their process of becoming witches. It does not dwell on conventional transgressions, such as drinking alcohol, sex, smoking, theft, or divisive appearances. Rather the film introduces the girls as victims. It presents Nancy's (Fairuza Balk) abusive family life, Bonnie's (Neve Campbell) extensive physical scarring, and Rochelle's (Rachel True) daily exposure to racism. The film invests enough of its visual minutes within their victimhood to permit the viewer to develop empathy for their transformative experience. We want them to be free, and magic becomes the path to that freedom, as was the case with Joan in *Hungry Wives* (1973).

Four outcast teens find their power through magic in the breakout film
The Craft *(1996), starring (left to right) Robin Tunney as Sarah, Fairuza*
Balk as Nancy, Rachel True as Rochelle, and Neve Campbell as Bonnie.
[Source: Columbia Pictures/Photofest. © Columbia Pictures]

The girls' witchcraft practice is not considered a transgressive activity or even satanic, but rather something deeply spiritual that provides them with both strength and safety. For example, the first ritual scene under the tree is well-lit and takes place during the day in an idyllic setting. By presenting the process as spiritual rather than satanic, the film further allows the viewer to align with the misfits. Near the end of that ritual sequence, after the camera enjoys a sweeping pan of the girls' faces, butterflies fill the air creating a mystical fairy tale moment. The metaphysical component of the narrative is unique for horror witch films in this period (e.g., *Witchhouse*, 1999).

In addition, the film offers a positive magical mother figure in the bookstore owner, who is constructed as a non-comical New Age witch, a contemporary manifestation of the wild woman. This character acts as a spiritual and emotional guide, assisting Sarah (Robin Tunney) and connecting her to her dead mother, another witch. Through this character connection, witchcraft is further framed as natural and a woman's birthright, passed from mother to daughter. This is quite different from the 1970s teen horror films that placed the magical daughter in direct opposition with the mother figure, ending in a fierce battle to the fiery death (e.g., *Carrie*, 1976; *Midnight Offerings*, 1981).

Despite these unique elements, *The Craft* eventually begins to shift in tone as the girls become drunk on their newfound power and are released through magic from the visual traps of victimhood. While justice seems to be served, the film steps in as moral judge, saying, "Be careful what you wish for." In the second major ritual scene, the girls are on the beach at night. As they perform the ceremony, the shot sequence increases in speed; the camera circles in 360-degree pans, and a storm kicks up in the background. Unlike the peaceful daytime scene, this ritual scene is darker, chaotic, and tense, all of which suggest satanic practice at least by visual standards. This sequence is an important narrative turning point because it opens the door for Nancy to become the film's villain.

Although *The Craft's* magic is never specifically defined as satanic, the film was released in 1996 and is a crossover production that still retained society's lingering fear of Satanism. That element is juxtaposed with the exploration of witchcraft as a positive spiritual force. As such, the film reflects a society once again renegotiating its understanding of witchcraft and female power. Where are the boundaries between good and bad magic? When does it become a transgressive act? As such, the film's focus is less concerned with the girls' embrace of power and more invested in the girls' search for the limitations of that power. The narrative allows them to accept a healthy, natural witchcraft and then dance at the borders of true transgression with only marginal ramifications. That is, until Nancy chooses to go too far.

To help create this nuance in the representation of magic specifically, *The Craft's* producers employed Pat Devin, a modern Witch and Dianic Elder Priestess, as a technical adviser from the start of production. In a 1998 article, Devin wrote:

> The first version of the script that I read I considered pretty encouraging for the genre. There was no mention of Satan, aside from the line about if God and the Devil were playing football, Manon would be the stadium: more Gnostic than Wiccan, but a great line.[269]

---

269. John Brightshadow Yohalum, "An Interview With Pat Devin: Consultant for '*The Craft*,'" Covenant of the Goddess newsletter, March 1998, http://wychwoodacastlebetweentheworlds.com/interview WithPatDevin.htm.

While she did not love every aspect of the final film, Devin said, "I decided to try to get as much truth into what was, after all, a teenage date spooky movie, as I could. I knew the results would not be perfect."[270] The realistic details, which were noticeable to Wiccan viewers, included the invocations of the elements and phrases like "Hail to the guardians of the watchtower of the west." In fact, *The Craft* was the first witch film since *Midnight Offerings* (1981) to make a real attempt to employ aspects of modern practice, and the first one to do so within a reasonably correct context.

While *The Craft* did include details that made witchcraft more relatable and helped to define the girls' spirituality, the film also clung to conventional horror tropes. For example, Nancy, as the antagonist, is the only one who drinks, demonstrates promiscuity, steals, and dresses in a goth style. Although she is as much a victim as the others, the film slowly builds on her deprivation, which is accented by her non-conventional style. It is interesting to note this characterization follows a Hollywood pattern that frames the antagonist witch teen with a severe look, whether that be goth or otherwise (e.g., *Midnight Offerings*). Her appearance is visually juxtaposed to that of the good girl with her mousy brown hair and nondescript, culturally normative clothing.

Although *The Craft* is as campy as other teen witch films, it stands out as an important transitional film due to its depth of characterization and nuanced approach to witchcraft. While in many respects Fleming's film embodies the ethic of the moral panic, including the fear of unbridled feminine power as symbolized by wild nature, sexuality, and magic, it does walk a line, creating a bridge to an entirely different possibility. Nancy, as the antagonist, appears to die; but she is the only one, which leaves the redemptive other three free to live with magic without assimilation or punishment.

After 1996, most teen witch horror films made the traditional connections between witchcraft and Satanism, avoiding *The Craft*'s nuanced approach, including dead witch stories and rituals to invoke demons. Despite that fact, they also increasingly included language from modern Witchcraft practice just as *The Craft* did, although not as artfully. For example, in Christopher Leitch's teen slasher *I've Been Waiting for You*, Sarah, a psychic young witch, uses a common Wiccan chant to trick others. This chant is a prayer to the goddess Hecate and was written in 1995 by Wiccan Katlyn Breene. Although the made-for-TV movie was not popular, it demonstrates the influence of *The Craft* as well as the growing trend in distinguishing Wicca from other forms of magic. The language of modern Witchcraft was helping Hollywood to define the elusive boundaries between good and bad magic.

---

270. Yohalum, "An Interview With Pat Devin."

Beyond Othering: Black Witch Magic

As noted earlier, *The Craft* was a border film that embraced aspects of the panic but also offered a progressive attitude toward witchcraft and a sympathetic view of the adolescent girl as outsider. Woven into that narrative is the story of Rochelle, a teenage American girl ostracized simply for being Black. As with its depiction of magic, *The Craft* addresses race and bigotry in a way that had not been done before, allowing the Black witch, as a wild woman, the space to stand in her identity and in her power as a witch.

Despite the 1970's nominal introduction of a Black witch absent racially derived characterizations common in earlier years, the 1980s did not follow suit. As historian Donald Bogle noted, "The sad irony was that the decade, which had opened by revealing to the industry that there *was* a black audience, closed with the industry believing that the black film and black audiences were both dead."[271] In the 1980s, people of color do appear as witches but once again are trapped in the role of "the magical other." Actress Pam Grier, for example, played the witch in *Something Wicked This Way Comes*, but her role was limited, and her character read as exotic. Her darker skin tone codified the character as nonnormative, playing into the creepy travelling circus environment. Later in the decade, Nicaraguan actress Barbara Carrera played the vamp witch in both *Wicked Stepmother* and *Love at Stake*. Similarly, Apollonia Kotero, who is of Mexican descent, played the witch in *Black Magic Woman* (1991). With their striking appearances and accents, these three actresses read as foreign or "not us" as defined by the average viewer, which contributes to the evil vamp witch's hyper-sensationalized character. It also legitimizes their use of magic, as in the past. Their existence is both exotic and forbidden, something that creates desire and repulsion.

In a slightly different construction, the H. P. Lovecraft-inspired *Cast a Deadly Spell* (1991) and *Witch Hunt* (1994) contain a middle-aged Black woman named Hyppolyta Laveau Kropotkin, played by both Arnetia Walker and Sheryl Lee Ralph, respectively. In these made-for-television films, Hyppolyta, also spelled Hypolite or Hypolyta, is a licensed witch and a priestess living in an American world in which "everyone practices magic." She is an anomaly, in that respect, and the only independent female character in either film. At the same time, Hyppolyta is a secondary character who anchors the hero's journey to reality. Similarly, the 1996 film *The Crucible* offers an updated version of Tituba (Charlayne Woodard) who is more sympathetic, human, younger, and narratively prominent than past depictions (e.g., *Maid of Salem*, 1937), but she is still a secondary character and narrative pawn. That role and her otherness are rooted in the stories told about Salem's famous trials.

---

271. Bogle, *Toms, Coons, Mulattoes, Mammies, and Bucks*, 266.

While Hippolyta and Woodard's Tituba are steps forward in representation, it isn't until *The Craft* that a Black American witch appears with any textual significance in her own right. Rochelle (Rachel True) is one of the four victimized teen witches and she is depicted as a typical American teen without the past codifications of otherness. At the same time, it does not present her through a colorblind filter, in that it acknowledges a real lived experience for contemporary Black teenagers. Rochelle's personal trauma and the one that leads her to witchcraft is defined by openly racist attacks from other students.

While Rochelle's presence is a landmark in terms of witch constructions, her character development was undercut, or overcut as it were, having family scenes removed from the final movie. In the end, filmmakers did not present her story as thoroughly as the other three. In a 2016 article, a blogger at the *Graveyard Shift Sisters* laments this point, saying that she, as a nerdy Black teen in 1996, needed more Rochelle. She writes, "Rochelle's score to settle was not explored and displayed enough with the emotional weight it carried. It was played as superficial comeuppance for Laura's racial intolerance."[272] The full weight of the conflict within Rochelle and the reasons for her being the outcast were only grazed, leaving many teen girls, specifically those that identified with her, unsatisfied.

In her book *True Heart Intuitive Tarot*, actress Rachel True, who played Rochelle, expresses a similar dissatisfaction with Black witches found on screen. She wrote, "Most black characters I saw in popular movies at the time were not indicative of my personal experience… The archetypes are well recognizable."[273] She goes on to say that these archetypical roles, such as the "hood girl" or the first family member to go to college, helped to "solidify the idea in white American minds that all black people were leading hard scrabble lower-class lives."[274] This statement is supported by a history in which there were decades of few, if any, positive representations of witches being women of color and particularly American women of color.

True goes on to say that her "experience of isolated blackness made it easy to connect with Rochelle."[275] Prior to the film, she was already personally involved in magic and mystical arts; she therefore found it is easy to identify with a character who finds her internal power through magic. However, mirroring the reactions of fans who

---

272. "20 Years of The Craft: Why We Needed More of Rochelle," *Graveyard Shift Sisters* (blog), http://www.graveyardshiftsisters.com/2016/11/20-years-of-craft-why-we-needed-more-of.html.

273. Rachel True, *True Heart Intuitive Tarot, Guidebook and Deck* (Boston: Houghton Mifflin Harcourt, 2020), 80.

274. True, *True Heart*, 80.

275. True, *True Heart*, 80.

wanted more, True notes that she was often slighted during publicity events and undercut in promotional material. While the film was about all four girls, she got the least attention on-screen as well as in the creative process, as she has said. True wrote: "Hollywood is still Hollywood," acknowledging that race and gender still play significant roles, often as obstacles, in the industry.[276]

While Rochelle's construction was far from perfect, she remains the first prominent Black witch to be found in teen witch horror films, and she stands alone as such in the period. Additionally, Rochelle is the first prominent Black American witch to stand as a positive character at the center of the narrative, free from the shackles of racist codification, sexualization, and overt othering.

Teen Magic and Girl Power

As the panic finally ebbed and horrific tales of vamp witches disappeared, teen witchery was mainly what remained. Witch productions dramatically shifted, in an almost whiplash fashion, away from moral fearmongering to the exploration of teen empowerment and the normalization of witchcraft. As noted earlier, 1996 was the watershed year with *The Craft* and *The Crucible* as clear markers that the panic was over. It was also in that year that the industry brought back an old favorite after an eighteen-year hiatus. In her live-action debut, Sabrina returned to the screen in a Showtime movie simply called *Sabrina, the Teenage Witch* starring Melissa Joan Hart. The following fall, ABC began airing a sitcom of the same name, heralding what some theorists have labeled "prime-time feminism."[277]

After the success of *Sabrina, the Teenage Witch* (1996) and *The Craft* (1996), the industry jumped on fantasy teen narratives including two successful witch-related television series: *Buffy the Vampire Slayer* (1997–2003) and *Charmed* (1998–2006). Unlike *Sabrina*, the two shows were a mix of fantasy and horror that combine teen angst with magic and heroism. While both shows build clear lines between good and evil as in most horror- and fantasy-inspired narratives, the witch is now on the side of good. Evil is defined by an amoral human, a satanic-like monster, a ghoul, a vampire, or similar. Together with *The Craft* and *Sabrina, the Teenage Witch*, these productions helped to redefine the identity of the witch in American entertainment. Each one has its own unique place in the representation of witchcraft, including explorations of identity, sexuality, personal power, and one's place in community.

---

276. True, *True Heart*, 96.

277. Sarah Projansky and Leah R. Vande Berg, "Sabrina, the Teenage…?: Girls, Witches, Mortals, and the Limitations of Prime-Time Feminism," *Fantasy Girls: Gender in the New Universe of Science Fiction and Fantasy Television*, ed. Elyce Rae Helford (Lanham, MD: Rowman & Littlefield Publishers, Inc., 2000), 13.

A Closer Look: *Sabrina, the Teenage Witch*

Sabrina was given a contemporary look, along with her two witchy aunts and their talking cat, Salem. The comic book character's original sassy sexuality was abandoned completely for a '90s casual girl-next-door trendy teen aesthetic, and her aunts were redesigned as modern suburban women. The new franchise was a success. The show ran until 2003, generating spin-offs such as *Sabrina Goes to Rome* (1998), *Sabrina, Down Under* (1999), Canada's *Sabrina: The Animated Series* (1999–2000), *Sabrina the Teenage Witch in Friends Forever* (2002), and the jointly produced series *Sabrina: Secrets of a Teenage Witch* (2013–2014). She also made crossover appearances on other ABC sitcoms such as in season five's *Boy Meets World* episode "The Witches of Pennbrook" (1997).

Although Sabrina moved into a contemporary setting, the show retained many fantasy narrative witch tropes, such as discovering her power at the age of sixteen, black cats, and witches as non-mortals. Magic, in this case, is simply a function of wishcraft, similar to the show's 1970s animated predecessor and the film *Teen Witch* (1989). Magic is almost entirely in service to the whims of teenage love, angst, frustration, and more. The aunties are no different, performing magic, similar to Samantha, in service to their adult and parenting lives. It was a sitcom for tweens and teens that allowed young viewers to fixate on the possibility of their own internal power, and it was at the center of what became labeled the post-feminist "girl power" movement.

Sabrina's magic is unsourced. Like Samantha or Morticia, she and her aunties are fantasy witches despite the realistic environment. Unlike the 1989 film *Teen Witch*, the *Sabrina* franchise makes no moral judgment on the use of that magic. Although aimed at a younger audience, the sitcom was to the 1990s what *Bewitched* was to the 1960s. Sabrina spends her days negotiating life as a witch living in a mortal world. *Sabrina* and its spin-offs are the first in a line of contemporary witch-related television shows that engage with magic and normalize it in ways that hadn't been done since *Bewitched* or *The Addams Family*. Even so, Sabrina and her aunts aren't trying to break their witchy habit; nor are they created to appear as outsiders in their magic.

Girl Power, Witchcraft, and Post Feminism

Before looking at *Charmed* and *Buffy the Vampire Slayer*, it is important to examine the "girl power" cultural movement that emerged in the 1990s and how it was expressed through these shows. The term "girl power" is largely attributed to the punk music scene and it was spread through 1990s pop music groups like the Spice Girls.

Embracing the term "girl" as a signifier of a youthful and independent femininity, the movement's ideology is defined as a brand of third wave feminism that seized upon the remnants of earlier movements to define the power of the young woman.

However, the emphasis behind the "girl power" movement is distinct from its feminist foremothers. The new movement was proudly apolitical, for the most part, and embraced a personal approach to gender identification rather than community based. In other words, what defines a girl is whatever she wants. She can be anything. The movement rejected past feminist ideologies in favor of a "we are who we are" mantra. Historians Sarah Projansky and Leah R. Vande Berg note that television productions drew "on [the second wave feminist] ideals of equality, inclusion, and 'free' choice to define a contemporary moment in which women have achieved various feminist goals and thus in which feminist activism is supposedly no longer necessary." [278] Ironically, the movement approached gender politics with the same notion as the 1980s: liberation had already been won.

With equality achieved, girls could move on to focus on self-making and the exploration of personal power. Projansky and Vande Berg go on to define this new movement as post feminism. Sociologist Jessica K. Taft adds that the movement's reactionary attitude "implies that Girl Power is softer, sexier, less active than feminism, and that Girl Power gives feminism a 'kick up the arse' by emphasizing beauty and appearance" over political structures and society's accepted gender constructs. [279] As Taft notes, "Magazines and advertisements aimed at girls use the discourse of Girl Power in a way that reflects the ideologies of individualism and personal responsibility." [280]

While the movement did have a significant positive influence on the cinematic representation of young women, feminist scholars are quick to point out that it also had notable limitations. The stripping away of the sociopolitical elements from the movement voids its power, giving its adherents a complacency toward gender inequalities still present. Calling the movement anti-feminist, Taft goes further, noting that "girl power" assumed a white, suburban middle-class aesthetic that "ignores the substantial contributions of Black, [Latina], non-Western, and queer feminists, and erases their claims about the intersectionality of race, class, gender, sexuality, nation, and ability." [281] In this reading, the movement is not only seen as exclusive, but also as another tool of the conservative patriarchy with its own limits and rules. In other words, "girl power" is a false ideology meant to convince women that the war is won

---

278. Projansky and Vande Berg, "Sabrina, the Teenage…?," 15.

279. Jessica K. Taft, "Girl Power Politics: Pop-Culture Barriers and Organizational Resistance," *All About the Girl: Culture, Power, and Identity*, ed. Anita Harris (New York: Routledge, 2004), 71.

280. Taft, "Girl Power Politics," 71.

281. Taft, "Girl Power Politics," 73.

and that they can fully engage with their power or in self-making but only within certain definable social boundaries; in this case, the realms of beauty and fashion.

In academic discourse, *Sabrina, the Teenage Witch* is often one of the examples of this post-feminist "girl power" ideology. Considering witchcraft is most often an allegory of women's power, this should come as no surprise. The movement gained momentum as the panic ended while supernatural subjects, including witchcraft, were still popular, and it also explains why the teen witch films did not follow the 1970s trend and stick strictly to stories of the monstrous teen girl. While *Carrie* (1976) produced a string of horror films similar in structure and theme, *The Craft* spawned few if any. What it did do was inspire teen viewers to explore witchcraft as a radical form of self-making and it contributed to the growing cultural exploration of "girl power" along with *Sabrina*, *Charmed*, and *Buffy the Vampire Slayer*.

In these shows, magic, if you will, is the witch's natural state, one that she needs to embrace and explore. There are options now; girls can be anything, whether that be vampire slayers, witches, Wiccans, lesbians, and even heroes. However, a girl also needs to know the limits and boundaries of this new self-making. Magic, allegorically a woman's power, is now acceptable; however, it still must be contained within appropriate socially defined structures. Even if the goalposts have moved, there are still goalposts. Ironically, this shift in representation makes the radical nature of witchcraft transgressive only relational not literal. When the wild woman is acceptable, she ceases to be the wild woman.

A Closer Look: *Charmed*

In 1998, the WB network launched the show *Charmed* (1998–2006), which followed the lives of the Halliwell sisters who discover that they are hereditary witches. Its first episode was titled "Something Wicca This Way Comes," demonstrating the rising consciousness of the modern Witchcraft movement. Creator Constance M. Burge explained in an interview that the WB wanted a companion show to the newly successful *Buffy the Vampire Slayer* that would focus on witches. Burge said, "I didn't know anything about witches at the time, although I had a lot of preconceived ideas and notions."[282] After a "fairly significant" amount of research, Burge successfully pitched the show, pulling from mythology, history, and her own family history.

Throughout most of its eight seasons, *Charmed* has its women using witchcraft, or allegorically their personal power, to defend against masculine demonic forces. That

---

282. Ed Gross, "'Charmed' Creator Spills Best-Kept Show Secrets in a Recovered Interview (EXCLU-SIVE)," *In Touch Weekly*, February 16, 2018, https://www.intouchweekly.com/posts/charmed-cast-secrets-154161/.

is the basis of the show's feminist ethic. However, not only are the women powerful warriors, but they are also attractive, sexy, and fashionable. They are a combination of the young vamp witch and the girl next door. They are part Morticia and part Samantha, and they are primary examples of the "girl power" movement.

Although the Halliwells recall the classic witchcraft trope of a trio of powerful witches, they defy the original concept modeled on Shakespeare's weird sisters. While they are defined as wild women who come together to wield magic, they are not crones nor are they morally ambiguous. As suggested by Burge and noted by historian Karin Beeler, the show did embrace classic witchcraft iconography, old stories, and mythology; however, it simultaneously rejected or challenged the feminist order, which is symbolically represented by the sisters' battles with elderly female monsters, controlling forces, or traditional expectations.[283] Using a young, conventionally attractive wild women trio as a replacement for the crone trio is another way in which the show normalized witchcraft and promoted the new movement.

However, *Charmed* is less a definitive feminist or even an anti-feminist script and more of a working contemplation of a woman's power within a structured society, including her own learned behaviors. One of the common tensions found in *Charmed* is the sisters' relationship between magic and men, a theme that has followed the witch since her early days of cinema. Can a woman be in love and be a witch? Historian Cariona Miller asserts that the "fun and boys" theme creates "a problem for a fully feminist reading" of *Charmed*, along with the women's often insistence that they are tired of being witches.[284] Power is difficult and comes with a price as it always has for the woman. The Halliwell sisters struggle with both throughout. With power comes responsibilities, challenges, sacrifice, and struggle. Whereas older films made the decision for the woman as witch by giving her two options—death or marriage, *Charmed* allows for these discussions, both the conventional and the progressive. As with the girls of *The Craft*, the sisters are in search of the new social boundaries in which they can wield their power safely.

A Closer Look: *Buffy the Vampire Slayer*

A similar dynamic is found in another successful WB fantasy television series: *Buffy the Vampire Slayer* produced by Joss Whedon. The show was a take-off from a film

---

283. Karin Beeler, "Old Myths, New Powers: Images of Second-Wave and Third-Wave Feminism in *Charmed*," in *Investigating Charmed: The Magic Power of TV*, ed. Karin Beeler and Stan Beeler (London: I. B. Tauris, 2007), 102.

284. Catriona Miller, "I Just Want to be Normal Again: Power and Gender in Charmed," in *Investigating Charmed: The Magic Power of TV*, ed. Karin Beeler and Stan Beeler (London: I. B. Taurus, 2007), 73.

of the same name that was released in 1992. Like the Halliwell sisters, Buffy's friend Willow Rosenburg becomes increasingly aware of her inherent magical ability and eventually hones that skill, calling herself a witch. As Willow grows in knowledge and power, she pushes boundaries, questioning her role, ethics, and her identity.

Unlike in *Charmed* or *Sabrina*, *Buffy*'s witchcraft-centered conversation is limited to a single character and her development over the series' run from 1997–2003. Willow's fears, weaknesses, and vulnerability are showcased throughout the seasons, making her relatable as the nerd, the teen outcast, and the witch. While Willow's character construction begins the series similar to *The Craft*'s Sarah, a sideshow good girl, Willow then moves into a construction more similar to Nancy as she negotiates her magical power, pushing past the boundaries and discerning right from wrong.

Much has been written about Willow in relation to the dynamic moral complexity set forth by the entire show. While the show employed various fantasy conventions associated with classic monster archetypes, it also challenged binary constructions, allowing for gray areas including redemption and apology. Willow's dive into witchcraft is one of those challenges, as was the writers' choice to have her fall in love with another witch Tara Maclay, making them one of the first positive representations of a lesbian couple on prime-time television.

As such, Willow is considered one of the most interesting *Buffy* characters, because her arc is so dramatic, going from a shy nerdy teen in love with a male werewolf to a powerful witch in a healthy relationship with another woman. However, it is also important to note that, while these strides in representation were made, the presence of a witch in the *Buffy* text is linked entirely to the show's monster movie premise. Ultimately what Whedon did was create a mashup of film tropes, religion, and a social reality in order to enhance the relatability of an otherwise completely fantastical premise.

Within that mashup, Whedon included elements found in modern Witchcraft practice, going so far as to use the term Wicca in a spiritual or religious sense. In one of the most popular fourth season episodes called "Hush," Willow attends a Wiccan student meeting and is unimpressed, calling the group a bunch of "wanna blessed-bes," referring to the common Wiccan expression "Blessed Be." Then she goes on to say, "You know, nowadays every girl with a henna tattoo and a spice rack thinks she's a sister of the Dark Ones." This second statement is reflective of the "girl power" movement's influence on the popularity of modern Witchcraft among teens at the time.

Witch-Lite: Hotel Rooms, Bookstores, Crystal Balls

The trajectory of witch constructions from the uncontrollable, transgressive wild woman to a self-empowered, heroic witch is also evident in the period's lighter fare. These "witch-lite" films, if you will, follow the same pattern emerging in the late 1980s, hitting a stride by the early 1990s, and then slowly converting from stock Halloween constructions (e.g., *Wicked Stepmother*, 1989; *Love at Stake*, 1987) to more contemporary, relatable characters (e.g., *Sabrina, the Teenage Witch*, 1996). Comedy, as in the past, acts as a convenient and safe place to tell fantastical witch stories with freedom and absurdity without invoking fear or moral outrage. Some of these films and shows are farces that openly mock cinematic witch tropes, the moral panic, horror conventions, and even the reality of modern Witchcraft (e.g., *Love at Stake*; *Four Rooms*, 1994). Others provide a space for the rarely seen contemporary clown witch, who takes the form of a new-hippie fortune teller or bookstore owner (e.g., *Teen Witch*; *Hello Again*, 1990).

The Sex Comedy

Both *Love at Stake* (1987) and *Four Rooms* (1995) are farcical R-rated sex comedies that mock the hyper-realized vamp witch construction, including her appearance, overt displays of sexuality, and the need to toy with men. *Elvira: Mistress of the Dark* (1988) is yet another example. The 1987 film *Love at Stake* is a Salem-based narrative with not only an accused woman but also a classic horror vamp named Faith Stewart (Barbara Carrera). Using a classic narrative structure, Faith seduces hero Miles Campbell for amusement and uses magic to force the villagers to accuse the heroine of witchcraft. This is the basic premise, for example, behind Corman's *The Undead* (1957). However, Faith is not the film's true antagonist; she turns out to be a stereotypical amoral fairy tale crone, a fact that reveals itself at the end. She is the plot provocateur and a moral compass.

In 1995 film *Four Rooms*, the opening story segment, titled "The Missing Ingredient," begins with an all-female coven of witches arriving in a single hotel room where they will resurrect their lost goddess. However, one coven member, a virgin witch aptly named Eva, was unable to bring her assigned spell ingredient: semen. She is then charged with seducing an unsuspecting male bellhop in order to procure that ingredient. Unlike *Love at Stake*, *Four Rooms* plays off several different caricatures associated with modern subcultures and progressive movements, including the angst-ridden teen, the lesbian, the dominatrix, the goth, the neo-hippie, the virgin, and the New Ager.

While *Love at Stake* bounces its comedy off historical mythology, moral panic, and film tropes, *Four Rooms* takes its cues from cultural trends. The coven's witchcraft is not associated with Satan but rather Goddess worship, reflecting an awareness of the emerging Pagan movement, even making use of Wiccan phrases such as "so mote it be." However, the segment is more about the absurdity inherent in the experience of one bellhop than it is about accurate representation of Witchcraft, women's power, feminism, sexuality, or agency.

The Rom-Com

The period's romantic comedies also found their way into the witch cycle, mocking not the vamp witch but rather portraying the metaphysical bookstore owner (e.g., *Hello Again*, 1987) or the fortune teller (e.g., *Teen Witch*). Both are contemporary forms of the wild woman folk witch with the shop or tarot parlor as the suburban reconstruction of the witch's cabin, filled with herbs, books, and occult knowledge. The owner is typically a crone or middle-aged woman who serves as mystic and keeper of knowledge. While this modern construction does appear in horror films (e.g., *Warlock, Black Magic Woman, Rumpelstiltskin, The Craft*), the romantic comedies use the character to mock the construction in a similar way that *Comin' Round the Mountain* (1951) did with its folk witch. Comedy disarms her of any perceived danger, turning her existence into a fantastical absurdity.

For example, in the 1987 film *Hello Again*, Miss Zelda (Judith Ivey) is a red-haired metaphysical bookstore owner who talks about "transmigrating souls" and ancient witchcraft wisdom. She is a wild woman version of the contemporary clown witch, recalling fantasy witches like *Bell, Book and Candle*'s Aunt Queenie or *Bewitched*'s Endora. Miss Zelda, however, wears a pentacle, reads tarot, and goes to "see a man about a unicorn." In that way, she is a parody of the modern New Age practitioner. In *Teen Witch*, the role of eccentric wisdom-keeper goes to Madame Serena (Zelda Rubinstein), an older witch who guides Louise in her discovery of magic. She is a modern version of the eldery folk witch who instructs the adolescent girl. Filmmakers undoubtedly used Rubinstein due to her unique physical stature and her well-known performance as a medium in Steven Spielberg's film *Poltergeist* (1982).

A Closer Look: *Practical Magic*

One of the most enduring witch-related rom-coms was produced at the end of the period: *Practical Magic* (1998). This one film packs a host of recognizable cinematic witch characters, including the accused woman, the vamp witch, the witch next door, the elderly aunties as contemporary clown witches, and even the classic Halloween witch. Based on Alice Hoffman's 1995 *New York Times* best-selling novel of the same name, *Practical Magic* is a fantasy film set in contemporary society, like *Bell, Book and Candle* (1958), portraying the orphaned Owens sisters (Sandra Bullock, Nicole Kidman), who come to live with their two aunts (Stockard Channing, Dianne Wiest). The young witches grow up honing their skills, dealing with local bigotry, falling in and out of love, and raising their own children. Largely a romantic comedy, the film's universe is completely a woman's world, focusing on issues typically assigned to that realm including physical abuse, love, loss, motherhood, healthcare, natural healing, and magic.

Sister witches Sally and Gillian Owens debate their chosen
lifestyles in the 1998 film Practical Magic, *starring*
(left to right) Sandra Bullock and Nicole Kidman.
[Source: ABC/Photofest © ABC]

As with many witch films, all the adult women are unwed. The elderly aunts are contemporary fantasy crones and serve as replacement mothers, similar to what is found in *Sabrina* and even *The Craft*. Sally and Ginny Owens are their grown nieces who struggle with romantic relationships, as do the women in *Charmed*. Ginny is a comedic version of the fantasy vamp, who is wild and attractive. She is Jennifer of *I Married a Witch* (1942), accepting of witchcraft and using it to her advantage. By contrast, Sally is the responsible sister who wants to be normal, like Gillian of

Bell, Book and Candle. However, Sally is unique in that she is a mother and businesswoman with no vamp-like attributes other than her age. This is one of the ways in which *Practical Magic* veers from cinematic convention. The film contains an unsexualized, middle-aged single mother witch as its heroine and makes no attempt to correct for that point.

Like other witch productions of the late 1990s, including *Charmed* and the film *Dangerous Beauty* (1998), *Practical Magic* presents options for the empowered woman. Sally finds love at the end; Ginny doesn't. The narrative allows women the freedom of choice: to practice magic or not; to be a victim or not; to live alone or in relationship. Girls can be anything. The narrative explores the gray areas in one's choices rather than presenting a binary moral system with no direction to go, as was the case for Gillian in *Bell, Book and Candle* or Edna Mae in *Resurrection* (1980). The film not only asks questions about the use of one's magic, but it flat out sets its own rules. The women demonstrate that although magical ability is genetic, it doesn't have to be practiced. Women don't have to be married, and witches can run businesses and volunteer in the classroom. There are options in self-making, but there are also boundaries.

As mentioned earlier, the film frames witchcraft as a biologically granted gift, similar to other attributes like artistic ability. However, it is also the practical work of women. This is evident in the ritual scene during which an evil spirit is exorcised from Ginny's body. Film director Griffin Dunne forced the viewer into the scene, paralleling the aunts' inclusion of non-magical women in the ceremony. Although it may first appear to be a satanic ritual with its candles and broomsticks, the situation is disarmed by imposing symbols of normalcy into the shots. When the group of non-magical women enter, they form a circle with brooms around Ginny who is writhing at the center. A shot from above shows that the circle of brooms contains a few contemporary varieties made of plastic, not only classic witch's brooms. This visual alone parallels the film's name: *Practical Magic*. Witchcraft is just another mundane activity that some people do.

Another example is Sally's apothecary store. Painted in stark white and framed with bright open windows, the store looks more like a trendy Rodeo Drive bath and body shop than a witch's herbal emporium. The elderly folk witch's cabin or the dusty metaphysical shop has been normalized, upgraded, and run through a post-feminist aesthetic. Both the ritual and shop examples demonstrate how the film conflates viewer expectations with a contemporary romantic story and thereby disarms witchcraft entirely. It pulls back the macabre curtain on witchcraft, revealing everyday human beings—not monsters, not immortals, not satanic covens. Witchcraft, once again, is normalized and made practical. It is just what these women as witches do.

Through the representation of the witch in this way, the film not only explores definitions of femininity, but also themes of social diversity and the acceptance of self and others. *Practical Magic* presents a familiar reality that frames witches as productive members of a diverse community. It does this by declawing witchcraft to create accessibility, familiarity, and a social permanence, which is exemplified by statements such as, "See. They are just like us." In this way, the entire film also could be read as a reincorporation narrative, but not of wild women into traditional gender roles. Rather, it is the assimilation of witchcraft itself into mainstream society, paralleling the depoliticization of the feminist script. Both actions defang something once considered dangerous and transgressive.

Practical Magic was largely unsuccessful, although it has since gained a cult following for its upbeat and open expression of witchcraft. Anecdotally, Dunne was convinced that the film's failure was due to a curse placed on production by a witch consultant. The consultant reportedly wanted a percentage of the film's profits rather than a consulting fee and the producers would not agree. In an interview, Dunne claims the witch told the producers, "I'm going to put a curse on you. I'm putting a curse on this movie," and then later in another phone call, the woman slipped "into tongues."[285] Dunne said he was frightened, and the lawyers eventually paid her off and she was off the production. Whether or not this account is correct is unclear; however, Dunne maintains the film was cursed.[286]

The Normalization of Witchcraft

Before moving into the next period, it is important to look briefly at Chris Carter's popular television show *The X-Files*. While largely an American production, the show was actually jointly made with Canada, a fact that disqualifies it from the study. However, two of the episodes are exceptionally indicative of the social changes that appeared in the mid-1990s with regard to witchcraft representation in film and television in the US. Always progressive, the X-Files writers often gave voice to prevailing trends and, in this case, they sought to calm fears about satanic crimes and, subsequently, brought awareness to modern Witchcraft practice. Like *The Craft* and *The Crucible*, several *X-Files* episodes offer a narrative that draws the viewer in through the fears lingering from the panic and then qualifies it, provides context, and offers exceptions.

---

285. Lila Shapiro, "*Practical Magic* Got Cursed by an Actual Witch. Is that Why it Bombed?" Vulture, Vox Media Network, October 26, 2017, https://www.vulture.com/2017/10/practical-magic-griffin -dunne-witch-curse.html.

286. Shapiro, "*Practical Magic* Got Cursed."

In the 1995 episode "Die Hand Die Verletzt," (translation: the hand that wounds), FBI agents Mulder and Skully investigate a teen ritual murder. Typical of the show, the opening scene offers the viewer a firsthand look into the crime and the mysticism. In this case, four teens are in the woods at night attempting a satanic ritual. Their antics summon the Devil who then goes on a killing spree to punish members of a local satanic cult. Right from its first moments, the episode capitalizes on contemporary horror trends, which involved sex, Satan, blood sacrifice, and children. In fact, the school itself is named Crowley High School after the famed occultist Aleister Crowley. However, the show makes a unique distinction regarding the supernatural. During the investigation, Mulder tells the ever-skeptical Scully that Wiccans are nonviolent. He says, "Even the Church of Satan has denounced violence. Witchcraft wouldn't account for this." After noting that the FBI had rejected the premise as well, Scully refers to the "crap that is on Geraldo and on television." Despite its supernatural basis, the show made distinctions between types of witchcraft that the horror films did not.

The X-Files is one of the first narrative television shows to mention Wicca within an ethical structure that suggests it's a positive practice. This happens again in a 1996 episode "Sanguinarium," but they go further. There are no children and schools in "Sanguinarium." The evil character is a single occultist—a plastic surgeon who kills patients as offerings to keep himself successful and young. It is unusual for a male occultist to operate solely for vanity; however, that is the case here. In addition, the episode contains a female nurse who happens to be a witch. The show's good witch versus bad witch theme provides the opportunity for Mulder to instruct Scully and the viewer about modern Witchcraft, Wicca, and healing practices. Again, the narrative is developing moral boundaries for magical practice. The show also lectures on the uses of pentacles, mentions the celebratory sabbats, and the use of the five magical elements.

By 1996, the language of modern Witchcraft was increasingly evident in narrative storytelling, even in satanic horror or paranormal suspense. Together with the "girl power" movement, increased visibility of the modern Pagan movement, and a strong post-feminist ethic that spawned pro-magic narratives from *The Craft* to *Practical Magic*, *The X-Files* was attempting to normalize, domesticate, or make witchcraft tame within a framework or boundaries that could be understood by contemporary Americans or, at least, by white middle-class American standards. This normalization provided a source of empowerment for young viewers who were searching for their own identity after emerging from the Reagan era and the panic. But these attempts at normalization dismissed one key aspect of the witch: she is by nature a rebel that breaks boundaries and cannot fit at the center of normalcy for long.

Conclusion

Witches entered the period as inconsequential secondary characters but quickly moved center stage as a reflection of society's Satanic Panic and the backlash against women. This launched the second witch popularity wave in American film and television. Across genres, witches, predominantly female, were routinely portrayed as child killers or abductors, seductresses, and dangerous ritualists. Some were demons while others were three-hundred-year-old witches looking for immortality. Still other witches moved from town to town destroying men's lives through sex and seduction.

As the panic subsided, witch films shifted, quite abruptly, to an expression of third wave feminism labeled as "girl power." The witch craze shifted focus to mostly teen films and expression of magic as wishcraft or heroic power. By the end of the period, magic was no longer inherently evil but rather just a tool in a woman's arsenal and defining factor of who she could be. In these later films, witchcraft is redefined as something normal, natural, and good, but only when it remains within the ethical and cultural limits and boundaries as defined most typically by middle-class, white, suburban America. As long as girls, or witches, play by the rules, she can be whatever she wants to be.

Chapter 10: Filmography

The Witches of Eastwick	1987	George Miller
Hello Again	1987	Frank Perry
Love at Stake	1987	John Moffitt
Bay Coven	1987	Carl Schenkel
Witching of Ben Wagner	1987	Paul Annett
Pumpkinhead	1988	Stan Winston
Spellbinder	1988	Janet Greek
Elvira: Mistress of the Dark	1988	James Spignorelli
Scooby-Doo and the Ghoul School	1988	Charles Nichols
The New Adventures of Mighty Mouse, "Witch Tricks"	1988	Eddie Fitzgerald
Witchcraft	1988	Rob Spera
The Real Ghostbusters, "If I Were a Witch Man"	1989	Will Meugniot
Warlock	1989	Steve Miner
Witchcraft II: The Temptress	1989	Mark Woods
Teen Witch	1989	Dorian Walker
The Little Mermaid	1989	Ron Clements, John Musker
Wicked Stepmother	1989	Larry Cohen
Witchtrap	1989	Kevin Tenney
The Witches	1990	Nicolas Roeg
The Wizard of Oz (TV)	1990	Andy Heyward, prod.

Black Magic Woman	1991	Deryn Warren
The Butcher's Wife	1991	Terry Hughes
Cast a Deadly Spell	1991	Martin Campbell
The Pit and the Pendulum	1991	Stuart Gordon
The Doors	1991	Oliver Stone
To Save a Child	1991	Robert Lieberman
Black Magic	1992	Daniel Taplitz
Death Becomes Her	1992	Robert Zemeckis
Double, Double, Toil Trouble	1993	Stuart Margolin
Hocus Pocus	1993	Kenny Ortega
The Nightmare Before Christmas	1993	Henry Selick
Witch Hunt	1994	Paul Schrader
Seduced by Evil	1994	Tony Wharmby
Animaniacs, "Witch One/ Macbeth"	1994	Michael Gerard, Jon McClenahan, Rusty Mills
Aladdin, "Strike Up the Sand"	1994	Alan Zaslove
Xena: Warrior Princess	1995– 2001	Robert Tapert, creator
The X-Files, "Die Hand Die Verletzt"	1995	Kim Manners
Four Rooms, "The Missing Ingredient"	1995	Allison Anders et al.
Rumpelstiltskin	1995	Mark Jones
Serpent's Lair	1995	Jeffrey Reiner

The Temptress	1995	Lawrence Lanoff
The Sorceress	1995	Jim Wynorski
Witch Academy	1995	Fred Olen Ray
The Outer Limits, "The Choice"	1995	Mark Sobel
The Sylvester & Tweety Mysteries, "Autumn's Leaving"	1996	Karl Toerge
The X-Files, "Sanguinarium"	1996	Kim Manners
The Craft	1996	Andrew Fleming
The Crucible	1996	Nicholas Hytner
Sabrina, the Teenage Witch	1996	Tibor Takács
Sabrina, the Teenage Witch	1996–2003	Jonathan Schmock, Nell Scovell, creator
Buffy the Vampire Slayer	1997–2003	Joss Whedon, creator
Witches in Stitches	1997	Russ Harris, Jerry Reynolds
The Simpsons, "Easy Bake Coven"	1997	Mark Kirkland
Snow White: A Tale of Terror	1997	Michael Cohn
Boy Meets World, "Witches of Pennbrook"	1997	Alan Myerson
Sabrina Goes to Rome	1998	Tibor Takács
Dangerous Beauty	1998	Marshall Herskovitz
I've Been Waiting for You	1998	Christopher Leitch
Practical Magic	1998	Griffin Dunne
Casper Meets Wendy	1998	Sean McNamara

Halloweentown	1998	Duwayne Dunham
Lucinda's Spell	1998	Jon Jacobs
Charmed	1998–2006	Constance M. Burge

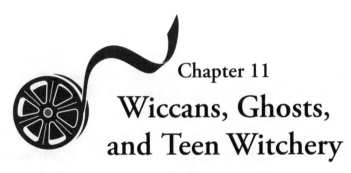

Chapter 11

Wiccans, Ghosts, and Teen Witchery

(1999–2010)

As the millennium came and went, American society was transforming with the compelling presence of digital culture. The internet and other similar technology allowed for an increase in visual narrative entertainment due to the removal of many traditional production barriers, including availability of recording equipment, the ease of media manipulation, and access to growing distribution channels and to viewers. With the eventual birth of social media and digital streaming services such as YouTube and Netflix, there was a steady flow of new productions from conventional studios as well as independent and even amateur projects.

While digital media in all forms created excitement, growth, and opportunity, the period was also marked by waves of sociopolitical turmoil. In 2000, the tech bubble burst with a corresponding stock market crash, thereby ending America's honeymoon with the new tech industry. In 2001, the US faced the unthinkable when terrorists hijacked four planes, killing nearly three thousand people in New York City, Washington, DC, and Pennsylvania. Those attacks led to a second Gulf War and aggressive changes in public security. Several years later, the American economy took another hit when the housing bubble burst, creating the banking crisis of 2007–2008. While the period was relatively stable overall, the digital revolution coupled with these tragic events fed an underlying communal uncertainty.

Teen Viewers and Teen Witchery

Within that environment, the entertainment industry as a whole was focusing a sizable portion of their marketing on youth audiences. As noted by historian Timothy Shary, Hollywood began directing its focus on teen viewers in the late 1970s. The trend continued into the 1980s across genres and subject matter, and then expanded again by the mid-1990s.[287] In 1997, as Shary notes, Teen Research Unlimited, a demographic tracking organization, reported that "going to the movies" had become the most popular activity among younger generations. The entertainment industry was successful in their marketing efforts, which continued into the 2000s.[288]

The reason for this general shift in marketing focus can be attributed to several factors, including disposable income and free time, an appeal to the "consumptive parents of tomorrow," and a filmmaker's enjoyment in reliving their own lost youth.[289] Additionally, contemporary youth audiences were not constrained by traditional modes of entertainment and viewing habits, such as trips to the movies, prescribed content, or prime time hours. They easily and naturally embraced the 24-7 on-demand stream of whatever digital content was offered, and producers were ready to feed that insatiable need.

Shary's observations are modeled in the period's witch productions. The majority, regardless of genre, are aimed at younger audiences, predominantly tweenies to mid-twenties, which parallels the industry trend. Shary writes, "[Youth films] are imbued with a unique cultural significance: they question our evolving identities from youth to adulthood while simultaneously shaping and maintaining those identities."[290] At the heart of the Hollywood witch narrative, from its very beginnings, is the search for identity independent of convention, and in many cases, the negotiation of emerging personal power during adolescence. Films about discovering and containing magic would naturally coincide with the expansion of teen-focused productions, and that is just what happened.

Films

Fantasy and the supernatural were the dominant genres during this period from epic quests to fairy tales to true horror. Stories of ghosts, monsters, mythical beasts, vampires, zombies, and of course, witches filled the screens. (e.g., *True Blood*, 2008; *Vam-*

---

287. Timothy Shary, *Generation Multiplex: The Image of Youth in Contemporary American Cinema* (Austin: University of Texas Press, 2002), 6–10.

288. Shary, *Generation Multiplex*, 10.

289. Shary, *Generation Multiplex*, 1.

290. Shary, *Generation Multiplex*, 11.

pire Diaries, 2009; *The Walking Dead*, 2010). Fueled by the success of 1990s shows like *Buffy the Vampire Slayer*, *Charmed*, and *Sabrina*, as well as *The Blair Witch Project* (1999) and the *Harry Potter* film franchise, witch films and shows were dominated by narratives specifically involving teens and young adults. While there are a few traditional witches such as the fantasy crone and some anomalies such as the accused woman in *The Gift* (2000), the modern Witch (e.g., *JAG*, "The Witches of Gulfport," 2000), or the satanic vamp (*Witches' Night*, 2007), the trends remain squarely centered on teen witchery, from hauntings to enchanted children.

Despite the continued high visibility of witchcraft narratives, witches were not the center point of the growing cultural fascination with all things magical. The second wave of witch popularity ended in 1998, and the third wave does not begin in earnest again until 2011. To clarify, the period's high visibility of witchcraft narratives is not due to the character's popularity but rather an overall increase in production and distribution, the success of a few witch-centered projects, as noted, and the general cultural love affair with the supernatural. The witch couldn't escape being seen, even if she is not the focus.

Generally speaking, the period's witchcraft-focused films are concerned primarily with exploring or connecting to one's identity (e.g., *Twitches*, 2005) or kicking the past to the curb, as expressed in the post-feminist "girl power" agenda of the 1990s (e.g., *The Blair Witch Project*, 1999). The latter concept also reflects a contemporary postmodern sensibility in which original meaning is dislodged from its source and subjectively repurposed unfettered by history or legacy. Witchcraft is no longer transgressive or a mark of a rebel, rather it is a teen's ticket to acceptance, to personal power, to community identity, or whatever else is needed. With few exceptions, the mark of the witch as a true radical living on the edge is eliminated. She becomes apolitical.

Before looking at productions, it is important to note the trajectory of dominant witch narratives across the period. Ghost stories dominate at the beginning after the release of *The Blair Witch Project* (1999). As time moves forward, there is a revival of epic fantasy and an unwavering interest in the enchanted child following the success of the *Harry Potter* films. Then by 2010, the fairytale begins to gain momentum, which eventually transforms into fractured tales and dark fantasy in the next period. As noted, teen witchery dots the entire era, finding expression across genres.

The Dawn of the Ghost Witch

By 1999, digital technology had already begun to transform America's media experience. Due to pliability of this readily accessible digital media, what is seen on the screen, or even in still photographs, could be called into question. Is what we are seeing real and factual? Has an image been digitally remastered, edited, or "photo-shopped? While Hollywood's films were edited to serve the narrative since the silent era, it wasn't common for the fiction filmmaking process to call attention to its own manipulation. American viewers have been trained to accept that notion, allowing themselves to be absorbed into the story and to forget the medium altogether. In 1999, two independent filmmakers Daniel Myrick and Eduardo Sánchez decided to take viewers for a new ride, and the result was the phenomenal breakout film success *The Blair Witch Project*. It received unexpected praise for its ingenuity and use of technology. According to *Fortune Magazine*, the film cost $60,000 to make, and earned $1.5 million at the box office on the first weekend while only in twenty-seven theaters.[291]

A Closer Look: *The Blair Witch Project*

The Blair Witch Project tells its story using a documentary-style structure through several claustrophobic camera lenses held by three fictitious student filmmakers as they venture into the Black Forest in search of the Blair Witch. What makes this film interesting in terms of witch construction is that there is no object. There is no witch. The character is an amalgam of thoughts, testimony, and stories compiled from legend, historical context, and presumed experience. In that way, the Blair Witch epitomizes the era's so-called postmodern experience. The object is itself gone, and all that is left is an unattached meaning that is easily manipulated, reworked, repurposed, and then expressed as subjectivity. Is she even real?

The Blair Witch's subjective construction isn't limited to the boundaries of the screen itself; she is also being constructed in the viewer's mind as a participant on the characters' legend-tripping journey. The viewer acts as voyeur, watching and absorbing alleged facts from what is presented as the characters' reality. *The Blair Witch Project*, thereby, delves into the psyche of our cultural fears, playing only off suggestions and social meaning, and taking the viewer to a place where the wild, uncontrolled, and natural exist with no rules. It is a place that author Joseph Conrad called "The Heart of Darkness," but in feminine terms, it is a lair of the most feared of all women, the Baba Yaga—the witch as destroyer.

---

291. Tim Carvell, "How *The Blair Witch Project* Built Up So Much Buzz Movie Moguldom on a Shoe-string." *Fortune* Magazine, August 16, 1999, https://money.cnn.com/magazines/fortune/fortune_archive/1999/08/16/264276/.

Joshua Leonard (as himself) looks on in surprise as the
team of student filmmakers hunt the Blair Witch.
[Source: Artisan Entertainment/Photofest. © Artisan Entertainment]

To create the sense of dread and build fear within its own purely subjective, post-modern modality, the film pits the visual text against the viewer, using the various handheld cameras internal to its narrative. The viewer is not only aware of the film-maker but also cannot escape the point-of-view framing of this technique. This creates an unsteady and claustrophobic tension that for some viewers was literally sickening. The experimental style limits visibility, paralleling the characters' viewpoints, while also creating stress, paranoia, and frustration in an attempt to build suspense and dread.

In this scenario, the witch is only a construction through suggestion and nothing more. She is a symbolic fear. However, while the film forces the viewer to build the witch themselves, it does offer cues that call upon one of the oldest and most common witch archetypes: the elderly folk witch—the wild feminine, uncontained nature, and the witch in the woods. Through a sprinkling of clues, the film builds the idea of an immortal crone witch living deep in the forest. She is the figure that is forgotten as a woman but remembered as a monster. Like the characters, viewers understand these cues enough to build the fearsome witch in their minds, while ignoring the lack of any objective evidence. In the end, the film leaves it to the viewer to decide if this story was just panic or reality. While the characters apparently do find something, the viewer is left in the dark, quite literally, as the film cuts to black.

Like *Rosemary's Baby* (1968), *The Blair Witch Project* is a marker for more than its novel use of media and marketing. In a postmodern culture with a distinct rising secularism and a deeply conflicted relationship with faith and rational thinking, the film forces the viewer to question what is real and what is only belief. For the viewer trapped in the camera's gaze, the Blair Witch is only an idea, a subjective suggestion, created from a historical tale of witch trials, newspaper reports of dead men and murdered children, testimonials of eerie sounds and odd happenings in the deep dark wood. Is she real? As a result, the Blair Witch is completely postmodern in her construction, but terribly traditional in her evocation.

Media Manipulation and *Curse of the Blair Witch*

It is important to note that *The Blair Witch Project* is not a film about a witch or about witchcraft like many films of this period. The witch is just a device. In a 1999 interview, directors Daniel Myrick and Eduardo Sánchez confirmed that very point. Myrick explained that the use of the witch was just a reason to "get three kids in the woods so [they] could fuck with them." It was what he calls "a triggering mechanism." Myrick goes on to say that "the Blair Witch legend is nothing more than local paranoia of these events that have taken place, like you know. The Devil's Triangle."[292] In that sense, the film is a story about legend-tripping, a typical American teen activity, and not about witches.

Just prior to the release of *The Blair Witch Project*, the SyFy channel aired another Myrick and Sánchez production called *Curse of the Blair Witch*, a mockumentary tie-in to the actual film. Part of the success of *The Blair Witch Project* was due to its pretense of reality. When it was first released, many viewers were not aware that it was fiction. The SyFy mockumentary supported the filmmakers' ruse by exploring the legend, giving more background information. It creates a reality by manipulating the cultural understanding of media texts in terms of what is framed as true. The mockumentary uses fictional testimony, professional analysis, and local interviews. To lend even more credibility to the SyFy feature, the directors inter-spliced footage from a fake 1971 film they titled "Mystic Experiences." It features a man who, according to Myrick, was a real Wiccan high priest.

---

292. Peg Aloi, "Blair Witch Project: An Interview with Directors," Witchvox, July 11, 1999 (site discontinued).

The Blair Witch Project was so successful that a sequel, titled *Book of Shadows: Blair Witch 2*, was released in 2000 through Lionsgate. The sequel was directed by Joe Berlinger and was unsuccessful, failing to capture the original's grit or poignancy. Hardcore fans often remark that they would simply like to forget that the second film ever happened. In addition to that sequel, the original film inspired spoofs and spin-offs, including low-budget productions such as *The Bogus Witch Project* (2000), *The Tony Blair Witch Project* (2000), *The Erotic Witch Project* (2000), *The Blair Thumb* (2001), *The Black Witch Project* (2001), and eventually a new sequel in 2016 called *The Blair Witch*. If that wasn't enough, the film's success inspired several low-budget films based on the real legend of Tennessee's Bell Witch, including *The Bell Witch Haunting* (2004), the UK-Canadian film *An American Haunting* (2005), and *Bell Witch: The Movie* (2007).

Horror and the Ghost Witch

The breakout success of *The Blair Witch Project* spawned a surge in ghost witch films that continued through the early part of this period. It wasn't the artistry, the deft use of media, or the specifics of the *Blair Witch* story that were replicated outside of the mentioned spin-offs. Rather it was the film's broader elements that captured the imagination of filmmakers. More specifically, two key elements were repeated time and time again: the dark woods and the witch as a ghost. While neither one of these elements were new to American cinematic storytelling, they had a profound revival during this period.

The first element, the "dark wood" setting, derives its origins from classic fairy tales and mythologies. Symbolically, the wild wood taps into a primal fear of the mysteries present in that unknown, uncontrollable space. In film and television, this concept is presented, for example, through the many retellings of *Hansel and Gretel* going back to the silent era. It is also captured in contemporary narratives such as in *The Woods* (2006). In witch-related stories, this basic fear of the wild is connected to magic, sexuality, and the female spirit. Orson Welles demonstrated this symbolic parallel in his 1948 adaptation of *Macbeth* where the leafless trees and rocks were often juxtaposed to the weird sisters and Lady Macbeth.

The second element, "the witch as ghost" is most typically a merging of a Salem-inspired accused woman story with a paranormal haunting (e.g., *Conjurer*, 2008). These horror plots generally explain, either visually or in dialogue, that a young woman, whether a witch or not, was once executed for some act that was perceived to be egregious to her village. She is then resurrected, most typically three-hundred years later, to haunt a particular location in order to exact revenge. These ghosts are always labeled *witches* whether they were in life, as with the Bell Witch, or whether they weren't, as with the Blair Witch.

Ghost witch horror films were produced mostly as features. In a few rare cases, the popular narrative found itself embedded in television shows (e.g., *Bones*, "The Headless Witch in the Woods," 2006). However, it is important to note that most of these films are low-budget, independent productions with few exceptions (e.g., *Book of Shadows: Blair Witch*, 2000; *Tooth Fairy*, 2006). This fact alone demonstrates that the interest in the ghost witch narrative is not demonstrative of an uptick in witch-related entertainment overall, but rather the lingering effects of the success of *The Blair Witch Project* within an expanding and decentralized filmmaking industry.

Regardless, the trend is notable, as it coincides with the underlying social uncertainties created by economic and political events as well as the digital revolution. The lurking ghost, in that way, is symbolic of a past that the youthful protagonist seeks to reject, survive, and destroy. In this reading, the ghost witch represents, for example, the radical legacy that third wave feminists kick to the curb or the objective and established meaning that postmodernism denies. The witch ghost represents the past that seeks to prevent a future. Looking more closely at the films, the ghost witch narratives fall into two main categories: the ghost witch in the woods (e.g., *The Blair Witch Project*) and the ghost witch as legend (e.g., *Tooth Fairy*).

Ghost Witch in the Woods

The films in the first category, "ghost witch in the woods," focus on a haunting in a wooded, wild, or abandoned space. They blend the classic primal fear with a paranormal haunting story, creating a witch-infused legend-tripping experience. For example, the 2006 *Bones* episode follows the *Blair Witch* theme very closely, including student filmmakers, a legend, and a murder by decapitation. Brian Andrews, the dead filmmaker's partner, says to the main characters, "Weird things happen in those woods," and later notes that "the witch [Maggie Cinders] made me do it." In narratives like this, the ghost witch exists as a plot device and is not necessarily real. It is interesting to note that the witch's name is Maggie, another cinematic witch trope.

Regardless of her magical ability, the ghost witch in the woods is always part of a three-hundred-year-old history tied to the wild space and, as such, she becomes the center point of the narrative (e.g., *Book of Shadows, The Woods*). In her backstory, the witch is constructed as an accused woman—a victim of either society or a single man's vanity. For example, in *Conjurer*, Haddie the witch gave birth to a child out of wedlock. The father had the baby killed and Haddie was executed. In the ghost witch films of the 1970s, the witch is never an accused woman; she is a dead satanic priestess (e.g., *Daughters of Satan*, 1972). While the ghost witch's backstory is that of an accused woman, the ghost witch begins the plot as a wild woman. She is no longer a victim of society but rather a disrupter of tradition and convention, and her magic is defined by her phantom status. It is a paranormal power and not specifically witchcraft.

In the "ghost witch in the woods" films, the wild setting is either the literal woods (e.g., *Wake the Witch*, 2010) or another wild setting such as a cave (e.g., any film based on the Bell Witch legend) or an abandoned cabin (e.g., *Conjurer*, 2008). That wild space is the witch's realm, and it symbolizes an unordered, emotional, and nonrational reality. By contrast, the living human world is defined by the rational, by normalcy, and it is defined as a masculine universe. This is not a new symbolic breakdown. Furthermore, it is important to recognize that in these films the wild wood or other space is not populated by a ghost woman, but by a ghost witch who is the symbolic manifestation of a woman's revenge. This is the monstrous-feminine in spirit form, unencumbered by obsessive narcissism, body image, or even the desire for power. She is pure revenge and a symbol of a violent past independent of her humanity and her objective self.

For example, in *Conjurer*, the opening sequence suggests a supernatural presence in a cabin at the back of a couple's property. The visuals include close-ups of bottles filled with liquids, snakeskins, and other natural items associated with witchcraft. This opening works similarly to those that begin in flashback depicting a witch burning. Both act as an omen and as a setup for the coming occult film. It also sets a proscenium around the wild space, defining it as dangerous and, as is typical for these films, the young husband is drawn to that haunted space. This creates a connection between the female ghost and male protagonist. As such, this wild untamed femininity, as symbolized by the witch in the woods, becomes a tension rooting itself between the couple, seducing the husband and destroying the wife, not unlike the 1970s satanic priestess films. However, in these films, the witch has no interest other than the disruption of the peace and stability.

Ghost Witch as Legend

The films that tell a ghost witch story without a wild setting incorporate a legend that tells of an accused woman who returns for revenge. While the character model remains the same in the two types of films, the setting is different. In legend films, the haunted space is a domestic realm (e.g., *Tooth Fairy*, 2006; *The Cry*, 2007). For example, in the *Tooth Fairy*, the setting is an old home. In the 2013 film *The Conjuring*, the haunted space is a doll and an old house and, more specifically, the basement, cupboards, and other dark areas. While these aren't untamed spaces, they are all related to domesticity. The ghost witch's lair is that which is defined by traditional feminine social roles. As is typical across all witch films, the female magical character either seeks to defend, disrupt, or obsess over the aspects of social engagement that are assigned to the woman (e.g., love, beauty, home, childhood).

Whether set in a domestic sphere or not, filmmakers rarely show the ghost witch outside of a flashback. However, unlike those films set in the wild wood, legend-based films always depict the witch as a reality. These narratives are never psychological suspense thrillers with alleged hauntings; rather they are clearly paranormal horror films with a definitive ghost witch who sometimes appears in an ephemeral form. For example, in *The Conjuring*, the ghost's soft white image is seen floating in the bedroom.

It is interesting to note that one of these legend films focuses on the retelling of the tooth fairy story, which ties into a later trend in which filmmakers renegotiate well-known narratives (e.g., *Snow White and the Huntsman*, 2012). During this period, the joint US-Australian film *Darkness Falls* (2003) did the same thing to the popular childhood tale. In both films, the tooth fairy returns to kill children after they lose their last baby tooth. This is a significant point, because the plot capitalizes very subtly on the fairy tale trope characterizing the witch as a disrupter of childhood adolescence. For example, in *Darkness Falls*, the tooth fairy first visits Kyle after he loses his last tooth and experiences his first kiss. Her hauntings destroy his ability to function in society as an adult. The witch disrupts the normal progress of adolescence and natural maturation.

Overall, ghost witch films, regardless of setting, rely heavily on established witchcraft tropes and a collective understanding of witchcraft lore and legend to reach their viewers. Because the witch does not physically exist, she must evoke meaning and fear through extratextual symbolism and suggestion. In a postmodern period seeking to reject the past, the ghost witch can represent everything from the skeletons in society's collective closet to feminine rage. She is the past that haunts, preying on a basic human fear of the unknown, unfettered emotion, and the wild.

The Undead Vamp Witch

The other type of horror witch narrative that was popular during the early part of the period involves a returning witch rather than a haunting. Like ghost witches, the returning witch may also be seeking revenge for a wrongful death or she may be looking to perpetuate her immortality. However, in contrast to ghost witches, returning witches do have actual bodies and are constructed as evil in both flashback and present day. This is an important distinction, because the contemporary ghost witch's backstory creates room for viewer empathy, even if the ghost is the villain. However, that is not the case for the returning witch. She is not blameless, and her magical practice is punctuated by either overt or suggested satanic practice. Returning witch productions include *Ghost Game* (2004), *Witches' Night* (2007), *Witches of the Caribbean* (2005), *Smallville*'s episode "Spell" (2004), *Manhater* (2005), and *The Woods* (2006). The returning witch narrative was prevalent in the early 1970s when witch horror films boomed, such as in the *Mark of the Witch* (1971) and *Daughters of Satan* (1972). Like those older films, the contemporary narratives rely on satanic tropes, rituals, and vamp witches.

A Closer Look: *Witches' Night*

In the indie film *Witches' Night*, director Paul Traynor attempts to capture a 1970s retro horror style. He incorporated ritual dancing, nudity, gender play, Satan, and a level of sexuality that was far more typical for that earlier era, when occult films were marketed more to adults than teens. In an interview Traynor said,

> To me, the 70's were the real heyday of horror, and those are the films we hoped to emulate. [...] So many horror movies today are completely dehumanizing—that's neither scary nor interesting for me. I like the slow burn; a simmering sense of dread that ultimately overflows and floods your body with bad toxins ...[293]

Using these elements outside of the context of the early 1970s sexual revolution, Traynor's film could have easily developed into a male sexual fantasy and gore fest, like many similar witch horror films of the period (e.g., *The Witch's Sabbath*, 2005). However, Traynor managed to undercut the narrative with a feminist theme or at least attempted to do so with expressions of contemporary gender politics. For example, one of the four young men mentions seeing an old woman in the woods. The lead witch mocks him asking if he was scared. After some banter, she challenges him, saying, "What? Is that the deal? Young women are easy and old women are scary?"

---

293. Hay Moon Pictures, "*Witches Night*: Directed and Written by Paul Traynor," press kit, July 31, 2007, http://witchesnight.com/press.html (page on site discontinued).

Young witches convince an unsuspecting camper to participate in a satanic ritual in
Witches' Night *(2007), starring as the witches (left to right) Meghan Jones as June,*
Lauren Ryland as Eva (center, on altar), and Stephanie Cantu as Gretchen.
[Source: Publicity Stills/Hay Moon Media]

It turns out that the women around the campfire are in fact the immortal vamp witches and ultimately the undead villains. The lead witch says to a group of men, "That's what we're all looking for, right? Immortality." However, Traynor crosses a line with their construction, making it difficult to know who is worse: the oppressor or the oppressed. The men of this film are not without fault, often expressing a violent level of misogyny. They boast things like "women are evil and unpredictable" and call independent women assorted names such as "cunts," "dykes," and "queer." The only survivor is the one man who was jilted at the altar. Unlike his friends, he maintains a respect for women throughout the film, and he lives.

While Traynor models the 1970s horror aesthetic, his film reflects a decidedly contemporary theme regarding gender, leaving room for some empathy for the witches. He walks a line between sensationalism, contemporary themes, and witch-craft cinematic tropes. Traynor acknowledged this nuanced construction, saying, "The women in *Witches' Night* are a little more enigmatic, more sexy and subtle. Although they do engage in many of your classic witch behaviors. […] The movie has satanic rituals, spellcasting, shape-shifting, dismemberment, Sapphic orgies. All the favorites." [294]

The undead vamp witch was not the dominant witch construction during the era and appears more readily in independent, low-budget films, pornography, or other

---

294. Hay Moon Pictures, "*Witches Night*: Directed and Written by Paul Traynor," press kit, July 31, 2007, http://witchesnight.com/press.html (page on site discontinued).

contemporary "schlock," as filmmaker Larry Buchanan might have said. *Witches' Night* stands out in that respect. However, together the ghost witch and undead vamp witch dominate the period's constructions.

Teen Witchcraft in Horror

A third subgenre within the period's supernatural horror films focused on coven magic, supernatural powers, or fitting into community (e.g., *Birth Rite*, 2003; *Witches of the Caribbean*, 2005; *The Initiation of Sarah*, 2006). Unlike the ghost witch and undead vamp films, these films were entirely marketed to teen audiences with no exception and were either made for television or went straight to DVD. Several of the late 1990s productions still reflect the Satanic Panic narratives such as *Witchhouse* (1999) and the *Silk Stalkings'* episode "It's the Great Pumpkin, Harry" (1999). However, all these films and shows, in one way or another, attempt to captivate viewers by recalling other successful teen horror narratives, such as *The Rage: Carrie 2* (1999) or *The Covenant* (2006).

Paying tribute to *The Craft*, David DeCoteau's film *Witches of the Caribbean* tells the story of a makeshift teen coven that forms at an island home for troubled teens. In fact, after performing their first ritual on a beach, the teens change from beach attire to a goth look. In a slow motion long shot, the four walk toward the camera in a single line, mirroring the famous image of the girls from *The Craft*. The similarities would not have been lost on contemporary viewers.

Two of the period's teen horror films are adaptations of 1970s teen horror films: *Satan's School for Girls* (2000) and *The Initiation of Sarah* (2006). *Satan's School for Girls* looked to celebrity power to bring an audience. The film stars actress Shannon Doherty who was, at the time, playing one of the Halliwell sisters in *Charmed*. As a point of nostalgia, filmmakers also brought back Kate Jackson who appeared in the original 1973 film. Similarly, filmmakers gave *The Initiation of Sarah* a contemporary face lift. The new film included more witchcraft, occult, and fantasy lore than its predecessor, playing off the popularity of epic fantasy. Actress Morgan Fairchild, who starred in the original 1978 version, returned to play the Goodwin girls' evil mother.

While many of the ghost and undead vamp horror films were marketed to teens, traditional school-based teen witch horror was limited. Witchcraft as a potentially realistic practice was no longer a cultural focus point. There was a split in representation. Magic, and consequently witchcraft, was either a viable nonthreatening religious practice, as seen in television law and police shows (e.g., *The Mentalist*, "Red Rum," 2009), or it was wielded by a host of magical characters, not just witches, who inhabit a greater supernatural and mystical universe (e.g., *Supernatural*, 2005–2020). With this change and divergence in representation of magic, teen witch horror absent the supernatural or paranormal was limited. However, together with the ghost witch and undead vamp films, these teen witch horror films do contribute to the bulk of the witch films found in the period.

Warlocks and Boy Wizards

It is impossible to talk about witches from this era without mentioning *Harry Potter*. Based on a series of books written by J. K. Rowling, the first film, *Harry Potter and the Sorcerer's Stone*, was released by Warner Brothers in 2001 and starred Daniel Radcliffe, Emma Watson, and Rupert Grint. The success of the first film led to a movie franchise lasting through 2011 with eight films covering all seven of Rowling's novels. The entire package, including spin-offs, theme parks, a stage play, and merchandising, has since become one of the most successful pop culture franchises worldwide.[295]

While the franchise's influence is unmistakable, the *Potter* films are not US films, which disqualifies them for this study. Although Warner Brothers produced and distributed them and there were American crew members, the *Potter* films were predominantly made and supported by the British film industry and are about a distinctly British world. As noted by author Emma Bell in *Directory of World Cinema: Britain*, "*Harry Potter* draws on recognizable and exportable aspects of Britishness to construct the sense of place and culture of its two worlds," muggle and magical. Bell goes on to offer examples on how the various details in the film reflect the current politics, social structures, and cultural mythologies specific to the region.[296]

However, just like any successful entertainment franchise, the *Harry Potter* films had a ripple effect on American culture, inspiring other similar productions. Not only was the *Potter* franchise one of the reasons that witch characters maintained a high level of visibility during this period, but it also spawned a plethora of male witch characters across genres for the first time in decades. In the 1960s and 1970s, the large number of male witches were predominantly occult magicians, wizards, and satanic leaders. These characters all but died out during the panic, leaving only variations on the transgressive and monstrous women with few exceptions (e.g., *Warlock*, 1989; *To Save a Child*, 1991). After the panic, witchcraft become entirely symbolic of the post-feminist "girl power" in which there was even less room for boys and men. The *Harry Potter* franchise changed this.

---

295. Marc Bernardin, "The 25 Most Powerful Film Franchises in Hollywood … and Why They Matter More than Movie Stars," *Los Angeles Times*, California Times, July 17, 2016, http://www.latimes .com/entertainment/movies/la-ca-mn-25-most-powerful-franchises-20160524-snap-story.html.

296. Emma Bell and Neil Mitchell, eds. *Directory of World Cinema: Britain* (Bristol, UK: Intellect Publishing, 2012), 13.

While the *Potter* films do capture teen-focused themes and even issues addressed in "girl power" witch productions through Hermione Granger, the films' main focus is not a young woman's adolescent struggle with self but a classic male hero saga. In that world, witchcraft, as it were, is no longer relegated to the transgressive women, rather it defines a child's place in society. "Where do I belong?" is the main question in these narratives, and magic is the element that connects the teen to their answers. The success of Rowling's books and eventually the films influenced other teen-centered witchcraft productions such as the *Halloweentown* film franchise (1998–2006), *Wizards of Waverly Place* (2007–2012), and the film *Twitches* (2005).

The *Harry Potter* franchise is ultimately an anomaly in its construction of witches and operates more as epic fantasy and a boy's coming-of-age story than a traditional witchcraft-based film. In fact, it is rare for a male witch to exist at the center of a witchcraft narrative regardless of narrative direction (e.g., *Simon, King of the Witches*, 1971; *Warlock*, 1989). More typically, male witches populate stories in which there is a community or family of witches, such as *Wizards of Waverly Place* or *Bewitched* (2005). In this period, Hollywood's male witch serves primarily one main function: create a normalcy within the cinematic universe through the establishment of family, legacy, or community, depending on the narrative's needs. Men exist in the real world, so they must exist in the magical world. In fact, this has been the primary role of the non-evil male witch for decades. Through comedy, he authenticates the female character's familial existence (e.g., *I Married a Witch*, 1942; *Bewitched*, 1964–1972) and normalizes the witching world from the viewer's perspective.

A Closer Look: *The Covenant*

In the 2006 *The Covenant*, filmmakers attempted to appeal to contemporary teen audiences hungry for supernatural stories by breaking the gender barriers in witchcraft films within a conventional narrative. *The Covenant* tells the story of four male adolescent witches and their allegorical coming into manhood through magic. At its essence, *The Covenant* is *Harry Potter* meets *Twilight*. In *The Covenant*, magic is the business of men and men only. Directed by Renny Harlin, *The Covenant* begins like many of the supernatural witchcraft stories with a flashback three-hundred years to Salem's Puritan past and then through the credits displays a montage of occult imagery mixed with old photos and writing, landscape shots, and a contemporary scene of teens dancing at a party.

*Caleb (Steven Strait), Tyler (Chace Crawford), Chase (Sebastian
Stan), and Pogue (Taylor Kitsch) perform a ritual to stop a rogue
witch from destroying them in the 2006 film* The Covenant.
[Source: Sony Pictures/Photofest. © Sony Pictures Photographer: Jonathan Wenk]

The Covenant then goes on to tell the story of the sons of Ipswitch: Caleb, Tyler, Reid, and Pogue, four witches who have inherited a magical legacy of their ancestors. While their power comes to them slowly, it matures at age eighteen, at which they fully come into their magic. The allegorical age of maturity for the girl is sixteen, at which she finds love and learns of her power; for the boy, the age of maturation is eighteen. *The Covenant*'s narrative supports this theme when Caleb's father bestows his own power onto Caleb in order to help his son fight the villain, another eighteen-year-old male witch. As a result, Caleb wins the battle to become the most powerful witch and, symbolically speaking, the alpha male.

Despite its title and the use of something called *The Book of Damnation*, the film does not go any further in its religious rhetoric. These are simply cues used as throwaways to link the film to a conventional concept of witchcraft, such as the pentacle in the film's logo or its use of Salem-based lore. The opening sequence makes this point clear, stating, "No one knows how the Power came to be. Not even *The Book of Damnation* records its beginning. But those who mastered it have always been hunted." Therefore, the boys and their magic are not evil, despite some of their antics. The four boys have an innate, inherited gift. These are both important indicators of the period's witch construction overall. With a few exceptions, witchcraft, even when represented in contemporary settings, has lost, once again, its religious connections left from the Satanic Panic and is increasingly constructed as a natural power rather than a ritualized one.

The Covenant was not well received by critics and performed moderately at the box office. As noted, filmmakers were aiming at a teen population who had become fascinated with all things supernatural. *The Covenant*'s sons of Ipswitch seem, at times, more like a glossy boyband than witchcraft practitioners, and the film feels more like a vampire saga than a Salem-based fantasy. Outside of those failings, *The Covenant* does pose the question of whether the male coming of age story, although more typically embedded in the epic fantasy, could ever work within the typical framework of the Salem story that is relegated to women. Do viewer expectations and culturally dependent understandings of historical witchcraft prevent that possibility? Was *The Covenant*'s failure in any way due to the inability to break codified norms and fit a well-established narrative into a new format that is typically ascribed to another gender?

Teen Witchery and the Enchanted Child

Teen-focused narratives were not limited to supernatural horror. Teen witchery could be found in lighter family fare on television and on the big screen. Before going further, it is important to note that the concept of the teen audience ranges from preteens or tweenies, ages nine to twelve, through young adults in their mid-twenties. The exact range varies from study to study, with the broadest being from age nine to twenty-four.[297] And it's this range that applies best to witch productions considering both the target audience and the age of the characters. For example, *Twitches* (2005), a film popular with tweens, tells the story of twenty-one-year-old women. While youth horror, such as *Witches of the Caribbean* (2005), was decidedly aimed at the older sector of this demographic, family-friendly genres contained witch-centered productions that appealed specifically to preteens (e.g., *Twitches*, 2005; *Wizards of Waverly Place*, 2007–2012).

Lighter teen witch fare began to emerge by 2005, and despite the popularity of some productions, they never overtake the popularity of the darker narratives. Most non-horror teen witchery films or shows were produced in the wake of other popular witchcraft-related productions, predominantly *Sabrina, the Teenage Witch*, the *Harry Potter* books and films, and epic fantasy films (e.g., *The Lion, the Witch and the Wardrobe*, 2005). These witch-lite productions offered wishcraft narratives and enchanted

---

297. Shary, *Generation Multiplex*, 17–18.

realms (e.g., *Wizards of Waverly Place*, 2007–2012; *Twitches*, 2005; the *Halloweentown* franchise).

The bulk of the productions, however, were largely unsuccessful spin-offs and sequels to 1990s productions, not unlike witch-related horror. For example, there were several animated shows released that reimagined Sabrina's story for younger children, including *Sabrina, the Animated Series* (1999–2000) and *Sabrina's Secret Life* (2003–2004). Similarly, Disney Channel produced three sequels to its popular film *Halloweentown* (1998), including *Halloweentown II: Kalabar's Revenge* (2001), *Halloweentown High* (2004), and *Return to Halloweentown* (2006). None of these films saw the success of the original.

Attempting to capitalize on the popularity of supernatural teen fantasy, Disney produced a new adaptation of *The Wizard of Oz* (2005) starring Jim Henson's Muppets and popular singer Ashanti as Dorothy Gale. And, although not for kids, Columbia Pictures released a derivative of *Bewitched* (2005) starring Nicole Kidman and Will Ferrell. Neither were successful, once again demonstrating that witchcraft was not a box office draw. By the end of the period, Disney got it right with two new takes on teen witchery and the enchanted child: *Wizards of Waverly Place* (2007–2012) and *Twitches* (2005) and *Twitches Too* (2007).

In all of these contemporary teen witch narratives, the witch is not an outcast, as in *Teen Witch* (1989) or *The Craft* (1996). The productions are not focused on the negotiation of magical boundaries or the acceptance of one's natural power. The teens are in search of their true identity. Where in the past the witch, such as Gillian or Samantha, seeks to reject her magical self in favor of normalcy, or a later witch, such as Willow or Rochelle, embraces her "weirdo" status symbolic of a post-feminist "girl power," these contemporary witches are seeking to fit in to both conventional society and magical society. In broader terms, these productions offer the young wild woman a new solution. She can acknowledge her power and her identity and live successfully between all words. A choice does not have to be made. This is, in part, a reflection of society's growing push to embrace a type of multiculturism.

A Closer Look: *Twitches*

The Disney Channel original film *Twitches* is a good example of both supernatural teen witchery and the enchanted child themes. Released in 2005, *Twitches* tells the story of twin girls who unexpectedly find each other after being separated at birth. The film is an adaption of a young adult book series of the same name. The two young women, who turn out to be witches, were played by Disney Channel stars Tia

Mowry and Tamera Mowry. The sisters became popular in the 1990s when starring in the popular Disney Channel show *Sister, Sister*, which had a similar basic plot. According to a 2005 *USA Today* article, *Twitches* drew 21.5 million viewers alone in its first four airings. The film popularity, which inspired the sequel *Twitches Too* (2007), stems not only from the supernatural subject matter but also a dedicated tween audience, which the Disney Channel had been nurturing since the late 1990s.[298]

Like many other enchanted child theme narratives, the twin witches, Alexandra and Camryn, discover their power after a rather normal childhood. They accidentally bump into each other on their twenty-first birthday and discover that they are magical twins. From that point on, the two girls are compelled into an epic battle of good and evil, in which the fate of the magical world is at stake. In this way, the film recalls the *Potter* series. However, *Twitches* not only clears up its quest in one movie, but it also steers clear of traditional witchcraft tropes and darker themes. For example, the iconography includes castles and clouds, magical amulets, moons, stars, and suns. The girls' magical names are derived from Greek deities: Artemis and Apolla. The aesthetic might be labeled New Age fantasy.

Twitches is less about them embracing witchcraft per se and more about women discovering and embracing identities and finding acceptance within multiple worlds. In fact, *Twitches* is as much a classic Disney princess film as it is a movie about witchcraft. The women must come to terms with both their magical power and their status as Artemis and Apolla, the princesses of Coventry. *Twitches* is largely a safe, made-for-television modern fairy tale with a New Age flavor and a predictable plotline that teaches right behavior and champions kindness.

Multiculturism and the Black Witch

While *Twitches* and its 2007 sequel *Twitches Too* remain popular within Disney's tween audiences, the films are notable for one final reason. Its witches are Black women. As noted by actress Tia Mowry in a 2019 Facebook live video, this was a calculated Disney Channel decision because the witches in the original books were not. Driving that casting choice was most likely the Mowry sisters' previous Disney Channel popularity and the similarities between the book series's plot and the *Sister, Sister*

---

298. Gary Levin, "Disney Finds a Place for Tweens: It's Not a Mickey Mouse Network Anymore," *USA Today*, updated October 27, 2005, https://usatoday30.usatoday.com/life/television/news/2005-10-26-disney_x.htm.

show. This fit seemed natural. In her video, Mowry said it "was really, really cool" that Disney adapted the story to include African American witches.[299]

In doing so, Disney took the representation of the Black witch a step further than previous representations. While *The Craft*'s Rochelle was depicted as a typical American girl, she was not the film's focus and had little to no backstory other than the racist attacks that defined her outsider status. Alex and Camryn are also defined as typical Americans, but they are the film's fairy tale heroines with full backstories, families, parents, friends, and relationships. The twin fantasy witches and their magic are completely normalized, making them highly relatable to the young American viewer.

In the popular Disney Channel movie Twitches, *Tamera Mowry and Tia Mowry play twin witches who only first discover each other and their magical power on their twenty-first birthday. [Source: Disney Channel/Photofest. © Disney Channel]*

Taking that a step further and using sociocultural language, the show is color-blind. The women's race has no bearing on the narrative or their characterization. This detail is symptomatic of the period's larger ideological disengagement with the

---

299. Tia Mowry, "Recreating My Sister, Sister & Twitches Hair Styles," Tia Mowry's Quick Fix, Facebook, June 7, 2019, https://www.facebook.com/TiaMowrysQuickFix/videos /1869331016499731/?__so__=serp_videos_tab.

past. Like the "girl power" agenda, the period's multicultural movement rejected historical politization and promoted a softer side of cultural diversity that was founded on the concept that racial equity had been achieved. While the use of Black actors as American witches absent any form of "othering" is certainly a notable achievement, the color-blind construction of the witches ignores not only cultural history and heritage but also contemporary reality and lived experience.

The casting and the treatment of race, or lack thereof, fit the Disney Channel trend in attempting to diversify their casts to better represent America's youth and appeal to broader audiences. As noted, Disney's adaptation of *The Muppets' Wizard of Oz* stars Ashanti as Dorothy Gale, Queen Latifah as Aunt Em, and David Alan Grier as Uncle Henry. In 2009, Disney Animation Studios released its first princess film starring a Black heroine: *The Princess and the Frog*, as well as a Voodoo priestess playing the role of fairy godmother and witch. While these representations are far from perfect, they exemplify a shifting representational landscape for the Black witch. The trend continues into the next decade.

Wicca and Religious Freedom on Television

Although teen narratives and fantasy dominate witch productions, other constructions did appear. Most notably, the increasing visibility of the modern Witchcraft and Pagan movements was significantly affecting the representation of Witchcraft on television. Law- and crime-based series dove directly into the subject within stories framed as the viewer's reality (e.g., *JAG*, *Boston Legal*, *The Mentalist*, *X-Files*, and *CSI: Crime Scene Investigation*). Within their formulaic narratives, these shows pushed the boundaries of social dialogue by offering minority thought and eclectic subcultures within the safe framework of a trusted, social orthodoxy: police and law enforcement. To that end, no matter what the narrative depicted as real, a viewer knows that the good guys will right the wrongs, expose corruption, and explain any oddities found. In this way, the shows normalized and even legitimized witchcraft within the viewer's universe, not unlike *Practical Magic* (1998).

In a 2000 *JAG* episode called "The Witches of Gulfport" (2000) and a *Boston Legal* episode called "Witches of Mass Destruction" (2005), religious freedom takes center stage with cases involving Wiccan practitioners. In *JAG*, a Wiccan priest is accused of sexual harassment. In *Boston Legal*, a Wiccan couple and a Christian couple come together to sue an elementary school over its Halloween celebration. The Christian couple claims the school event is satanic; the Wiccan couple claims it is derogatory. In both shows, witchcraft as Wicca is defined as a legitimate religion, and the witches, in both cases, are constructed as typical American citizens with constitutional rights to practice. The shows' writers did, in fact, consult to varying degrees with Wiccan practitioners, although not in any official recorded capacity.

In a 2009 *The Mentalist* episode "Red Rum," the witch is part of a murder investigation—one that includes the discovery of ritual paraphernalia commonly attributed to satanic practice. The episode plays first with what the viewer expects of witchcraft, and then says, "well, you were wrong," a theme found more prominently in the next period in shows like *CSI*, "The Book of Shadows" (2014). These representations not only enforce the normalization of witchcraft, they also take the concept further by "[moving] popular discourse away from the simple point that 'Witchcraft is real' or 'Wicca is Witchcraft' to 'Wicca is one of many religions.'"[300]

Despite the advancements in representation, these television series also feed off traditional Halloween tropes to relieve tension through comedy. *Boston Legal's* episode, for example, uses the MGM "Wicked Witch" musical theme throughout the show, and the Wiccan case is the lighthearted storyline for the episode. In *The Mentalist*, two of the investigators are perpetually bantering about the reality or unreality of witchcraft and superstition. While these shows demonstrate a social awareness of modern Witches, the fictional-based tropes and centuries-old ideology continue to float around mingling and often confusing the message.

A Closer Look: *The Simpsons*, "Rednecks and Broomsticks"

In the 2009 episode titled "Rednecks and Broomsticks," *The Simpsons* once again challenged contemporary perceptions of modern Witchcraft practice by turning a traditional narrative on its head. Named after the 1971 film *Bedknobs and Broomsticks*, "Rednecks and Broomsticks" takes liberties to poke and prod contemporary society, forcing it to look at itself through a satiric tone. During the 2000 US Comedy Arts Festival, *Simpsons* creator Matt Groening told attendees that his secret motto is "To entertain and to subvert."[301] He goes on to express what becomes gospel, so to speak, for the period:

> It's not so much trying to change the minds of people who are already set in their ways [meaning adults], it's to point out to children that a lot of rules that they're told by authorities who do not have their best interests at heart. If we can point out that teachers, politi-

---

300. Heather Greene, "Review: CBS' CSI and 'The Book of Shadows,'" *The Wild Hunt*, October 22, 2014, https://wildhunt.org/2014/10/review-cbs-csi-and-the-book-of-shadows.html.

301. Nick Griffiths, "America's First Family," *The Times Magazine* 5, no. 16 (April 15, 2000): 25, 27–28, https://www.simpsonsarchive.com/other/articles/firstfamily.html.

cal leaders, your parents, or your peers may be foolish, that's a good lesson. Think for yourself. [302]

That is exactly what he and the show's writers did with "Rednecks and Broomsticks."

The show begins with father Homer Simpson befriending a group of moonshine-brewing "rednecks" as his daughter Lisa discovers three young women practicing Wicca in the woods. The brief interactions between Lisa and the women present one of the most accurate depictions of modern Witchcraft on television. In their very first encounter, the witches are dressed in robes commonly used in modern practice. They tell Lisa that they are Wiccan:

> "You mean witches," Lisa responds.
> "Technically, but we're not into broomsticks or pointy hats."
> "We cast spells."
> "And they work."

The women call themselves "The Sisters of the Elements," and they worship nature and the goddess. The group uses language derived from Wiccan rituals, including the derivative phrase, "perfect faith, perfect love." While the animators constructed the women as social outsiders through socially coded imagery such as a goth style or tattoos, the trio is never mocked through the show's tone. They are only mocked by the other characters. In fact, in the end, it is the trio of witches who represent stable reality as compared to Springfield's zany population. One of the witches even mentions having an Ivy League education. The question ponders who the "weirdos" are.

The episode is emblematic of Groening's style. He subverts not only society's understanding of Wicca, but also the entire witchcraft trial narrative. The three young women are accused of blinding the townspeople and are subsequently arrested and taken to court. As it turns out, the affliction was poetically caused by the rednecks' moonshine and not the witches' magic. It is the establishment's status quo that is "foolish," not the witches. The show closes with the song "Season of the Witch" by Donovan.

Although more common in live-action television productions, *The Simpsons* was not the only animated show to engage with the reality or unreality of witchcraft. For example, in the animated film *Scooby-Doo and the Witch's Ghost* (1999), the gang meet up with practicing Wiccans to solve a witchcraft mystery. The witches make up

---

302. Griffiths, "America's First Family."

a pop-rock trio called the Hex Girls. They are constructed as vamp witches with vampire fangs, light skin, and goth-inspired attire. They reflect the "girl power" movement and could be witch-derivatives of the Spice Girls or *Charmed*'s Halliwell sisters. While Groening's stinging social criticism is not present in the *Scooby-Doo* film, the inclusion of Wicca and the distinctions made are notable for the long-running series that got its start in the 1970s as a kids' twist on paranormal horror.

The Classic Fantasy Crone in Animation

Outside of *The Simpsons*, *Scooby-Doo*, and any other representational changes in the period, the animated witch, once again, changed the least. Due to the increase in distribution channels, older cartoons were run in syndication for a new generation of viewers (e.g., *The Tom and Jerry Show*, 2014; *Mickey's House of Villains*, 2001; *Looney Tunes: Stranger than Fiction*, 2003). The classic Halloween-inspired witch could also be found in newly created animated feature films and cartoons (e.g., *Bartok the Magnificent*, 1999; The *Shrek* franchise; *Spooky Bats and Scaredy Cats*, 2009; *The Simpsons*, "I've Grown A Costume on Your Face," 2005). Popular children's shows capitalized on this recognizable witch figure for their October holiday episodes (e.g., *Dora the Explorer*, Disney's *Jake and the Never Land Pirates*, *Ultimate Spider-Man*, *Ben 10*, *Teen Titans Go!)*. The classic green-skinned elderly witch with the pointy hat was everywhere, feeding off iconic lore.

Then, as the interest in fairy-tale-based narratives increased, Disney returned, once again, to its classic princess formula with both *Tangled* (2010) and *Princess and the Frog* (2009). However, with the period's mostly positive depictions of magic, Disney did not incorporate its classic, monstrous crone or vamp witch into either film. *Tangled*'s villain is an evil adoptive mother, and the antagonist in *Princess and the Frog* is a New Orleans Voodoo priest. However, the latter film also contains a notable and unusual fantasy crone: Mama Odie.

Set in New Orleans, *Princess and the Frog*'s narrative was inspired by the Grimm Brothers' fairy tale "The Frog Prince," a story that does not contain a witch or any other magical person. However, Disney expanded, as it always does, on the short moral tale to suit its purposes. The film was reimagined in 1920s New Orleans and offered American audiences the first Disney Black princess film. The production coincided with Disney's attempt to expand its audience, as noted earlier, by appealing to a growing multicultural social movement. In its reworking of the story, Disney writers added several magical figures, including Mama Odie, a fantasy crone living alone in her cottage in Louisiana's bayou. She is the classic witch who lives an outcast's life on the borders of acceptable society.

Mama Odie is short in stature and depicted with exaggerated features, like many animated crones. Her home is filled with eccentricities and other items that are emblematic of witchcraft. And like other elderly fantasy witches, Mama Odie serves as a moral compass for the main characters. She performs magic for a price and offers a spell that ultimately teaches an ethical lesson and assists a poor girl in becoming a princess. Mama Odie is both classic fantasy crone as well as magical fairy godmother, and she does this despite any cultural and racial implications in her overall construction. While Mama Odie is certainly unique in the canon of Disney characters and animated crones in general, she is not a stretch in the studio's attempt to progressively depict the elderly magical woman. Disney simply overlaid the traditional model of the fantasy crone, whether it be Mad Madam Mim or Witch Hazel, and put her within a new, previously untapped culture and ethnic setting, paralleling what Disney did with the entire film.

Conclusion

By 1999, the second wave of witchcraft film popularity was over and new representations of witchcraft were on the horizon. The following years were dominated by ghost witches, undead vamps, and teen horror witches. At the same time, young witches populated lighter fare, inspired by the success of the *Harry Potter* franchise and the larger interest in epic fantasy. However, unlike the earlier decades, the detour did not focus on outcast adolescents embracing the dark arts. These teen witches wonder who they are and where they belong. They eventually accept their existence, live within it, and find their place comfortably in both the human and fantasy worlds. They live between.

In addition, the period saw an increased awareness of modern Witchcraft as a religious practice and a viable spiritual option. Unlike the 1970s in which modern Witchcraft language was used to enforce the concept of satanic ritual, these contemporary productions, even horror, used the language of modern Witchcraft to distinguish between destructive magic and spiritual magic. The boundaries between the two were regularly clarified through the language of a lived magical reality, despite the ever-increasing movement of productions into fantasy and despite the coming of the third witchcraft popularity wave. Witchcraft as a real and lived modern religious and occult practice had become a viable source of power for the wild woman witch.

Chapter 11: Filmography

The Rage: Carrie 2	1999	Katt Shea
Sabrina, Down Under	1999	Kenneth Koch
Witchhouse	1999	Jack Reed
The Blair Witch Project	1999	Eduardo Sanchez, Daniel. Myrick
Curse of the Blair Witch	1999	E. Sanchez, D. Myrick
Scooby-Doo and the Witch's Ghost	1999	Jim Stenstrum
Bartok the Magnificent	1999	Don Bluth, Gary Goldman
Silk Stalkings, "It's the Great Pumpkin, Harry"	1999	Chris Potter
Book of Shadows: Blair Witch 2	2000	Joe Berlinger
The Bogus Witch Project	2000	Victor Kargan et al.
The Tony Blair Witch Project	2000	Michael A. Martinez
The Erotic Witch Project	2000	John Bacchus
JAG, "The Witches of Gulfport"	2000	Tony Warmby
The Gift	2000	Sam Raimi
Satan's School for Girls	2000	Christopher Leitch
The Mists of Avalon	2001	Uli Edel
The Blair Thumb	2002	Steve Oedekerk (creator)
Halloweentown II: Kalabar's Revenge	2001	Mary Lambert

Mickey's House of Villains	2001	Jamie, Mitchell et al.
Shrek	2001	Andrew Adamson, Vicky Jenson
The Black Witch Project	2001	Velli
Sabrina the Teenage Witch in Friends Forever	2002	Scott Heming
Darkness Falls	2003	Jonathan Liebesman
Birth Rite	2003	Devin Hamilton
Tales from the Grave	2003	Stephanie Beaton
Looney Tunes: Stranger than Fiction	2003	Steve Belfer
Darkness Falls	2003	Jonathan Liebesman
The Bell Witch Haunting	2004	Ric White
Halloweentown High	2004	Mark A. Z. Dippè
Shrek 2	2004	Andrew Adamson, Kelly Asbury, Conrad Vernon
Ghost Game	2004	Joe Knee
Smallville, "Spell"	2004	Jeannot Szwarc
An American Haunting	2005	Courtney Solomon
The Witch's Sabbath	2005	Jeff Leroy
Bewitched	2005	Nora Ephron
Boston Legal, "Witches of Mass Destruction"	2005	James Bagdonas

The Muppets' Wizard of Oz	2005	Kirk R. Thatcher
Supernatural	2005–2020	Eric Kripke (creator)
Twitches	2005	Stuart Gillard
Manhater	2005	Anthony Doublin
Witches of The Caribbean	2005	David DeCoteau
The Simpsons, "I've Grown A Costume on Your Face"	2005	David Silverman (as Godzilla vs. Silverman)
Bones, "The Headless Witch in the Woods"	2006	Tony Wharmby
The Initiation of Sarah	2006	Stuart Gillard
Return to Halloweentown	2006	David Jackson
The Covenant	2006	Renny Harlin
The Woods	2006	Lucky McKee
The Tooth Fairy	2006	Chuck Bowman
Shrek the Third	2007	Chris Miller, Raman Hui
The Cry	2007	Bernadine Santistevan
Witches' Night	2007	Paul Traynor
Twitches Too	2007	Stuart Gillard
Bell Witch: The Movie	2007	Shane Marr
Wizards of Waverly Place	2007–2012	Todd J. Greenwald (creator)

Conjurer	2008	Clint Hutchison
The Simpsons, "Rednecks and Broomsticks"	2009	David Silverman
Drag Me to Hell	2009	Sam Raimi
The Mentalist, "Red Rum"	2009	Dean White
The Princess and the Frog	2009	Ron Clements, John Musker
Spooky Bats and Scaredy Cats	2009	Nathan Smith, Christopher Robin Miller
The Sorcerer's Apprentice	2010	Jon Turteltaub
Tangled	2010	Nathan Greno, Byron Howard
Wake the Witch	2010	Dorothy Booraem
Bones, "The Witch in the Wardrobe"	2010	François Velle
Shrek Forever After	2010	Mike Mitchell

Chapter 12
A New Witch Order
(2011–2020)

By 2010, the US saw the emergence of a contemporary civil rights movement, with rising tensions surrounding systemic racism, sexism, transphobia, religious bigotry, and the like. Climate change and GMOs were the buzzwords of the day, as global concerns for environmental protection added to an already present subcultural anxiety over reports of growing neo-Nazism and exclusionary nationalism. The period saw the birth of the Black Lives Matter and #MeToo movements. Over the following nine years, American society underwent a cultural war between a tightening political conservatism and the progressive movements that were symbolized, in part, by the election of America's first Black president, Barack Obama. Eventually spilling out into the streets in marches and protests, the sociopolitical tensions further destabilized the country, leading to the rise of a new populist movement, Trumpism, and the online conspiracy cult QAnon. As the period comes to close, the year 2020 only brought further turmoil in the form of a highly contentious presidential election and a global pandemic.

Since the dissolving of Hollywood's Production Code Administration in 1968, the narrative witch found herself at the center of cultural interest during periods in which social tensions were heightened. For example, she experienced a boom in the late 1960s and early 1970s during the Vietnam War and a cultural revolution. She then found herself center stage twenty years later in the late 1980s and early 1990s at the height of the Satanic Panic. Once again, about twenty years after that, there is a renewed interest in the witch and her stories. Considering the period's sociopolitical landscape, this should not be a surprise.

The Post-Postmodern

In describing the era, academics often use the term "post-postmodern," a term that defines a society in search for a concrete reality or a stabilizing factor. It is a seeking for something lost, for something sacred, or for a re-enchantment of a world that lost its meaning. As noted in the last chapter, the postmodern aesthetic rejects any established center or a connection with the past, suggesting that we can create our reality through an amalgam of choices, and that we are not and should not be bound to any history or finite culturally derived mythos. We take what we want and leave the rest. For example, the 1990s "girl power" ideology, for better and worse, rejected its feminist origins just as the multicultural movement distanced itself from past or current racial politics. By contrast, the post-postmodern aesthetic seeks a re-grounding, a search for an essential center, a connection with what was. It looks for new inspiration in old formats. This might be described as a type of communal search for nostalgic meaning.

In *Chronicles of Love & Resentment*, author Eric Gans discusses post-postmodernism in terms of narrative-based heroism. He writes that in earlier periods there was a common moral hero, defined as the underdog overcoming and winning. The defined morality imposed upon him was crafted through a Christian understanding. In the past, the witch could never be a moral hero, despite her position as the underdog. By traditional standards, she was a witch, meaning she is either bad, amoral, and insignificant or neutered with limited power. Bad is bad; good is good.[303] In order to be good, she had to cease to be the witch.

The delineations between bad and good begin to shift in the late 1990s into the 2000s as seen in films such as *The Craft* (1996) or *Practical Magic* (1998), both of which reset traditional moral goalposts. In those films, the witch can be good if she does good things as defined by conventional society. However, the structures themselves are not broken. Rather the witch is offered a heroic redemption through a complete rejection of her legacy and past meaning. She can remain a witch, but she needs to otherwise conform. These turn-of-the-millennium expressions of witchcraft were content in their displays of strength within that digestible, contained, or so-called "softer, sexier" context.[304] In postmodern terms, these representations took the good

---

303. Eric Gans, "Moral Heroism," *Chronicles of Love & Resentment* 237 (June 9, 2001), *Anthropoetics: The Journal of Generative Anthropology*, http://www.anthropoetics.ucla.edu/views/vw237.htm.
304. Taft, "Girl Power Politics," 71.

elements of witchcraft and discarded the rest. As such, these representations never challenged the basic structures that created the concept of the witch in the first place, nor did they question the institutions that defined morality itself. Good was still good, and bad was still bad.

It is important to note that, like any ideological movement, there is no definitive start and end date. The process is organic and fluid. While post-postmodernist ideals were evident before this era, it wasn't until the 2010s that there was an obvious directional shift toward post-postmodern themes in witchcraft-based productions. In their search for personal power and identity, these witches ponder legacy and eventually convention itself. The films don't reject standing cultural systems as one might expect, but rather they embrace them and seek to recognize their subjectivity. Gans calls this recognition an "unromantic…negotiating [of] mutual grievances."[305] In witch films, this manifests through the retelling of traditional stories, historical and fictional, from the witch's perspective as well as a recognition of a single witch's ability to be both evil and heroic. The stories collectively wonder if what we knew all along was wrong.

The Films and Shows

Throughout much of Hollywood's existence, witches were defined by genre, magical ability, motivation, or a morality imposed upon her by an external system. The accused woman, the wild woman, and the fantasy witch were easily identifiable, and there was limited crossover. During this era, these witch characterizations mix and merge more than ever before. Witches have backstories, which are invariably the tale of the accused woman, and nearly all witches are constructed as victims. Most witches are also defined by biological ability rather than ceremonial practice. In other words, witchcraft and other magical gifts are not learned or earned; it's your family heritage, your genetic makeup, and your natural state of being.

Continuing from the last decade, fantasy and horror are the most prominent genres, both alone and merged. While epic fantasy and the paranormal reigned in the last decade, this period sees the return of the fairy tale in the form of dark fantasy (e.g., *Snow White and the Huntsman*, 2012). That subgenre alone heralds the coming of a third witch film cycle. As the period ends, teen horror and teen witchery are back with a 1990s twist. The period overall is punctuated with adaptations, remakes, histories, and stories retold as American society turns to confront its own legacy and redefine its identity. What we were taught may have been wrong, and what we thought was wrong may have been right.

---

305. Gans, "Moral Heroism."

Witchcraft Evolution in Feature Animation

Animation might seem like the last place to start when examining progressive expressions of witch characters. After all, American cartoons established and supported one of the most consistently popular constructions: the Halloween witch. While that classic character still appeared in cartoon series (e.g., *The Owl House*, 2020; *Alvinnn! And the Chipmunks*, "Blabber Mouth," 2017) and Halloween specials (e.g., *Alvinnn! And the Chipmunks*, "Switch Witch," 2016) as an iconic symbol of the holiday, feature animation became more reflexive of the shifts in representation as they were happening in live-action films. Films like *ParaNorman* (2012), *Brave* (2012), and *Frozen* (2013) offered new perspectives on classic stories and iconic characters.

The stop-motion animated horror-inspired film *ParaNorman* (2012) was produced by a small Oregon-based animation studio: LAIKA. In this full-length feature film, the witch is a ghost who haunts an iconic New England tourist town named Blithe Hollow. As shown in the opening scene, the town is littered with images of the classic Halloween witch from bumper stickers that read, "My other car is a broomstick," to a statue of a hunched-back witch on the village green. In addition, the town's welcome sign depicts two smiling Puritans with a happy, green-skinned witch hanging in the gallows. The sign reads, "Welcome to Blithe Hollow: A Great Place to Hang." This is LAIKA's narrative nod to Salem, both its history and contemporary existence.

ParaNorman tells the story of a misfit boy who can speak to ghosts, one of which is the town's legendary three-hundred-year-old child ghost witch, Agatha or "Aggie." Through that relationship, Norman learns that Aggie was executed for witchcraft because she could see ghosts. Since that point, she has haunted Blithe Hollow in her demon-like green ghost form. Once Norman learns the story from the witch's perspective, the narrative offers the ghost child a direction not commonly seen: redemption. Aggie accepts his help, after which she visually changes back into a young Puritan girl with dark eyes and brown hair. Sitting quietly under a tree with Norman, Aggie sadly confesses that she just wants to be with her mommy. Through Norman's own oddity and his friendship, Aggie re-embraces her own goodness and her place in the social order.

While the film is unique in that it allows the ghost witch a heroic rescue with Norman as the white knight, it also retains a definitive Christian aesthetic and binary moral understanding of witchcraft. When Aggie finally gives up her cruelty as defined by witchcraft, she becomes human and can now "be with her mommy," which reads as heaven. The film defines "witchcraft" as both silly and evil, while the word "gift" is used to explain Norman and Aggie's ability to talk to dead people. Using traditional definitions of the witch, Aggie is an accused girl who becomes wild in ghost form. Then, through redemption, she is assimilated back into society through acceptance of her proper role as a daughter.

Similar to *ParaNorman*, Pixar's *Brave* (2012) walks a line between a traditional witch representation and something new. Based on an original story by Brenda Chapman, *Brave* contains a definite feminist theme that allows Merida, the young heroine, a chance to struggle against her non-magical mother without the moral rigidity seen in older Disney films. In terms of the film's unnamed witch, she is a stereotype who is easily recognizable with her stooped posture, elongated facial features, white hair, and spindly fingers. She lives alone in a woodland cabin containing cauldrons, crows, candles, and broomsticks. She offers both moral advice and magic for a price. She is the Scottish version of *Princess and the Frog*'s Mama Odie, who is both a fairy godmother and an amoral fantasy folk witch.

Interestingly, this fairy-tale-inspired story does not contain the typical Disney polarization between its female characters. Both the mother and the crone witch support the young woman's search for identity as she matures into adulthood. While there is tension between Merida and her mother, it is not a binary good and evil scenario; rather it is representation of the typical and contemporary mother-daughter conflict.

Notably, the story was written by a woman. In fact, Chapman was the first woman to develop a Pixar film, and Merida is the studio's first female protagonist. In 2017, Chapman said, "This was a story that I created, which came from a very personal place, as a woman and a mother."[306] Although she was removed from production early on, she said that her vision was realized. It is her imprint that allows both the heroine, the good mother, and the crone witch to exist all in one universe without conflict, redemption, assimilation, or death.

A Closer Look: *Frozen*

The biggest shift in the depiction of the animated witch occurred in Disney's film *Frozen* (2013), which is an adaptation of Hans Christian Andersen's "The Snow Queen." In 2017, the film became the "top-grossing feature animated film of all time and the fifth highest-grossing film of in history."[307] It won an Academy Award for the best animated film and the best original song, "Let it Go." Similar to *Brave*, *Frozen* boasts a female director and screenplay writer, Jennifer Lee. In 2013, her co-director Chris

---

306. Yohana Desta, "Pixar's Had a Problem with Women for Decades," *Vanity Fair*, November 22, 2017, http://vanityfair.com/hollywood/2017/11/pixar-john-lasseter-boys-club.

307. Michal Lev-Ram, "Frozen's Elsa Wins in Retail, but Anna Is the Real Leader," *Fortune*, November 6, 2014, http://fortune.com/2014/11/06/disney-frozen/.

Buck credited Lee with creating "some of the best female characters [Disney has] ever done, the most fully realized, the most three-dimensional. These aren't female characters that are put up on a pedestal; these are real, gritty, flawed females that are just human."[308]

After the film's release, it seemed that Elsa was everywhere. The name became one of the top baby names of 2014, and the following Halloween little Elsa's were on every doorstep asking for candy. This phenomenon left many wondering why the film's other heroine, Anna, was falling behind in popularity. To understand Elsa's popularity, it is important to look at her characterization within the terms of witch constructions. Elsa is the girl with a natural gift, like Joan of Arc, Carrie, Trigger, or Edna Mae. In Elsa's case, she was born with the power of ice magic. When she accidentally freezes her kingdom, Elsa is labeled a sorceress and "flees to a life of self-imposed isolation."[309] Lee offered a bit of symbolic foreshadowing when Anna walks by a painting of a woman in armor and addresses her as Joan.

Frozen then presents a complex ethical dynamic that hasn't occurred within any past Disney princess film. Both good and evil exist within Elsa; she is both the film's hero and the villain. This is at the center of *Frozen*'s inner dialogue. For example, the troll king demonstrates that magic can be used both for good or bad. Visually, he demonstrates *good magic* with blue imagery and *bad magic* with red imagery. These colors are conventionally understood cultural cues for heaven and hell or good and bad.

When Elsa reaches the top of the snowy mountain, Disney twists the paradigm again. She accepts her authentic self and her place in the world. This is visually "signified by Elsa's … change from a buttoned-up, high-collared dress to a shimmering, trailing gown with plunging necklines. As she walks out onto the balcony, hips swaying and hair flowing, Elsa demonstrates full control of her life, her magic and her sexuality. No Disney female character has ever completely owned her magical existence within the narrative and remained 'good.'"[310] Elsa is the classic princess, the heroine, and the witch, all wrapped into one. She is both the wild woman and the fantasy witch. Elsa moves willingly from maiden to womanhood completely unfettered, living in the untamed wilderness. While she has chosen freedom, she has also chosen isolation, like Edna Mae. Magic always comes with a price. Or, so we've been taught.

---

308. Tara McNamara, "Jennifer Lee, On Becoming Disney's First Female Director," *Fandango*, October 10, 2013. http://www.fandango.com/movie-news/jennifer-lee-on-becoming-disney-animations -first-female-director-742513.

309. Heather Greene, "Review: Disney's *Frozen*, A Tale of Two Princesses," *The Wild Hunt*, December 1, 2013, https://wildhunt.org/2013/12/disneys-frozen-a-tale-of-two-princesses.html.

310. Greene, "Review: Disney's *Frozen*."

Then, near the end of the film, Disney once again fractures its own paradigm, breaking the rules of cinematic witch construction. When Elsa accidentally freezes her sister's heart, the spell must be broken by an act of true love. The viewer assumes this means a fairy tale kiss by the leading man. However, distressed by what she has done, Elsa hugs her sister; Anna lives. This is Elsa's moment of redemption. She, like Anna, is saved by their sororal bond. Elsa is welcomed back into the kingdom as she is, and in the end, the witch queen does not need to sacrifice her sexual expression, her communal heritage, or her magic. Where *ParaNorman*'s Aggie must give up her power to receive redemption, Elsa does not. Moreover, like many witches of the era, the primary question is not of identity or belonging, nor fitting witchcraft into palpable mainstream structures. The question concerns how the witch can use her power within community. In the end, Elsa figures that out.

Going back to the question of why Anna was less popular than Elsa, there is an essential difference in their characterizations. While both are equally as heroic and fallible, Elsa has magic and the power of personal expression. Where Anna is cute, Elsa is glamorous and sexy. This detail alone sits at the center of fan response, and it is not surprising within a culture that is often driven by beauty and spectacle—particularly its relationship to a woman's social power. Despite any progression in the allegorical representation of female agency within this film, the allure of youth and beauty do not wane, which is a fact that is addressed directly through witch figures in live-action shows (e.g., *Game of Thrones*, 2011–2019).

Once Upon a Fractured Fairy Tale

Frozen was released during the height of the third witch craze, and its popularity is partly indicative of a renewed interest in fairy tale adaptations and similar stories. Like *Frozen*, most of the contemporary retellings are not simply regurgitations of the old tales, and unlike *Frozen*, most were not meant for younger audiences. These fairy tale adaptations are what is sometimes called "fractured," a term originally coined by Jack Zipes, award-winning professor of literature and folklore.

In an essay titled "Envisioning Ambiguity," historians Pauline Greenhill and Sidney Eve Matrix explain this concept, saying that these adaptations "unsecure the narrative integrity of the classic tales while remaining faithful to the overarching generic conventions, albeit modernized in some cases."[311] Greenhill and Matrix published their book before the witch cycle and the corresponding fairy tale films hit the market. They applied their explanation to a postmodern aesthetic, which does allow

---

311. Pauline Greenhill and Sidney Eve Matrix, eds., "Envisioning Ambiguity," introduction to *Fairy Tale Films: Visions of Ambiguity* (Logan, UT: Utah State University Press. 2010), 14.

for narrative fracturing. However, when we look at the contemporary resurgence of fractured fairy tale productions, it is the post-postmodern experience that informs them. First, the sheer volume of these films from 2010–2020, coupled with epic fantasy, children's fantasy, and the like, demonstrates the post-postmodern searching for reconnection and re-enchantment. Furthermore, in the breaking down of the story, the films challenge the overarching generic folklore conventions and re-examine the story's vital center.

There are three main types of fractured fairy tale products containing witches: the crossover narrative, the subversive, and the inspired. Each of these types reimagine the witch within the newly constructed fantasy model. First, crossover narratives intersect various fairy tales to create one big story (e.g., *Into the Woods*, 2014; *Once Upon a Time*, 2011–2018; *Grimm*, 2011–2017; *Descendants*, 2015). They can be dark and subversive or comedic. In both cases, the various tales are combined into one big single narrative plane. Secondly, the subversive tales force the viewer to look at a familiar story from a unique perspective (e.g., *Beastly*, 2011; *Maleficent*, 2014). And finally, the inspired narratives are only loosely based on traditional stories but are not necessarily telling that particular tale (e.g., *Hansel & Gretel: Witch Hunters*; *Snow White and the Huntsman*; *Hansel & Gretel Get Baked*).

The Crossover Narrative

In 2014, Steven Sondheim's Broadway musical *Into the Woods* made its film debut starring Meryl Streep as the witch. Sondheim's crossover fairy tale saga, weaving several Grimm and Perrault fairy tales together, was first seen on stage in 1987, winning three Tony awards for best original score, best book of a musical, and best leading actress. It ran for two more years before it closed but has since been produced many times for the stage, including a Broadway revival in 2002. It is not surprising that the musical was produced for the screen during the third witch cycle.

In order to unite the various fairy tale plots into one narrative, Sondheim created a new narrative based on a witch's personal quest for forgiveness and freedom. It is rare for witches to have backstories in the original fairy tales. Sondheim gave her one. She is the victim of her mother's abuse and the Baker's father. She explains that her neighbor was robbing her garden, stealing her arugula and rutabaga. Through this backstory, her actions, not her magical state, are explained, which is an important distinction. The backstory isn't about sourcing magic, it's about justifying her actions, or reframing the character's own personal narrative in order to demonstrate that what we understood to be evil was actually just a result of personal suffering. These fractured tales tear apart not only the narratives, but also the delineations of conventional morality. What is good and evil? Again, this is a theme that runs through the period alongside the witch.

Although *Into the Woods* renegotiates its witch construction, it also plays into archetypes with regard to female beauty. The witch's ugly appearance is the result of a curse placed on her by her mother after the beans were stolen. When the curse is lifted, the witch is once again young and beautiful; she is forgiven, redeemed, and free. Her blue-tinted hair is pulled up dramatically and her clothes resemble a ball gown. But she also loses her magical power. While the witch remains a moral compass throughout the rest of the play and does provide space for a progressive moral relativism, her own narrative is traditional. Age is unwanted; beauty or power both come with a price. This construct is not new (e.g., *The Undead*, 1957).

Subversive Tales

The second type of fractured fairy tale, the subversive tale, builds its entire narrative on this premise of moral relativism. These films tell a known story from another perspective. For example, in the film *Maleficent*, directed by Robert Stromberg, viewers learn the motivations behind one of Disney's most feared villains. When the film opens, Maleficent is a young fairy of the moors. She is dressed in brown clothing and has "large feathered wings that drag on the ground and tower above her head." [312] She eventually meets Stefan, an orphaned human boy lurking at the borders of her land. They become friends and fall in love, growing in both strength and influence. Stefan's lust for power eventually leads to a "violent moment of betrayal": he cuts off her wings. This moment then drives the film's plot into the classic *Sleeping Beauty* narrative including the famous "christening" scene.

Thematically, Maleficent (Angelina Jolie) is constructed as a "fallen angel." As I wrote in a past review, "Near the beginning of the film, she flies up to the clouds, faces the camera and opens her wings. This imagery recalls an angel against the sky. When Stefan performs the violent act of cutting off her wings, Maleficent is grounded." [313] He essentially rapes her and she becomes the fallen angel. This concept is mirrored visually by "the darkening of the moors and the skeleton imagery behind her throne." [314]

After this change, "hatred and vengeance consume [Maleficent] as she becomes the dark queen with all the expected iconic trappings … such as a staff, black leather

---

312. Heather Greene, "Film Review: Disney's *Maleficent*," *The Wild Hunt*, June 1, 2014, https://wildhunt .org/2014/06/review-disneys-maleficent.html.

313. Greene, "Film Review: Disney's *Maleficent*."

314. Greene, "Film Review: Disney's *Maleficent*."

cap around her horns, black clothes and a crow." [315] Through her victimization, she becomes the sexualized and vengeful vamp witch. She goes from angel to devil.

Although Maleficent is driven to revenge, she finds redemption through familial love, similar to Elsa. In this way, Disney fractures another classically embedded fairy tale theme—the "anti-mother." In this tale, "it is the 'anti-mother' or dark witch who actually cares for the child and keeps her safe. Where the fairies are tired of raising Aurora, Maleficent and the crow protect her and become her shadow guardians. In a complete reversal, the film turns the 'anti-mother,' who is typically jealous of youth, into the good or 'godmother' as Aurora says." [316]

As in *Brave* and *The Princess and the Frog*, the fairy godmother and witch are one. And like Elsa, Maleficent does not need to transform back to her pre-witch days to play this role. She remains the dark-clad, powerful gothic vamp witch. She retains her beauty, sexuality, power, and the love of a child. At the end of the film, Maleficent flies into the sky, once again "[pausing] in profile with wings outstretched which recalls the Winged Nike." [317] The world made her a witch and she won her battle in that form.

Inspired Narratives

The third and final type of fairy tale construction involves using the tales as inspiration to create a new narrative steeped in dark fantasy and horror. This trend produced films like *Snow White and the Huntsman* (2012), *Hansel & Gretel: Witch Hunters* (2013), *Mirror Mirror* (2012), *Hansel & Gretel Get Baked* (2013), and *Hansel vs. Gretel* (2015). In all cases, the witch doesn't have a backstory; she exists as the primary evil and reflects the period's depiction of witches as supernatural entities or literal monsters. In *Hansel & Gretel: Witch Hunters*, the witches are monstrous zombie-like creatures disguised as beautiful women. In *Hansel vs. Gretel*, the witches are a coven of immortal seductresses. The witch is an extreme and never what she seems, not a woman, not even a beast.

The witch as true monster was only suggested in older productions including *Twilight Zone*, "Jess-Belle" (1963), *The Little Mermaid* (1989), or in the ghost witch films of the 2000s. However, in these contemporary fairy tale productions, the monster witch's construction is taken beyond any recognizable animal form or even amorphic ghost to a literal abomination. Only twice before this period did this construction appear: *Jack the Giant Killer* (1962) and *The Witches* (1990). As with those two films,

---

315. Greene, "Film Review: Disney's *Maleficent*."

316. Greene, "Film Review: Disney's *Maleficent*."

317. Greene, "Film Review: Disney's *Maleficent*."

these contemporary characters are designed as inhuman monsters that, more often than not, can disguise themselves as human.

While many fictional witches are consistently looking to mask old age or simply remain alive, the monster witch takes this concept to an extreme. They are not simply the elderly Baba Yaga or even *Game of Thrones*' Red Witch in elderly form. These monstrous fantasy witches are nearly unrecognizable as human in visual construction and action. They offer no form of mercy, compassion, or acknowledgement of a troubled past. This narrative treatment provides the protagonists, who may or may not be themselves morally perfect, with a clear enemy. In other words, it is easier for viewers to align with the antihero when there is such a clearly monstrous villain. In a world increasingly interested in subjective experiences and moral relativism, the monstrous witch provides an acceptable opponent for even the most unlikable of characters (e.g., *Hansel & Gretel: Witch Hunters*) The morality structure of the narrative expands, providing space for protagonist wrongdoing while still allowing for a binary that champions good over evil. During this era, the monster witch is one of the few constructions that contained a simplified depiction of witchcraft as evil and, symbolically speaking, a literal representation of a woman unhinged.

The Witches of Epic Fantasy

Fairy tale adaptations were only one of the many types of fantasy narratives popular at this time. Epic fantasy, for example, continued to find audiences well into the 2010s, although it no longer held the same level of dominance as in the 2000s. Epic fantasy appeared mostly on television, including popular shows like the HBO series *Game of Thrones* (2011–2019) and the History Channel series *Vikings* (2013–2020) as well as the unsuccessful 2019 Netflix series based on Jim Henson's 1982 film *The Dark Crystal*. On the big screen, contemporary epic fantasy made witchcraft more central to the story, including films like *Season of the Witch* (2011) and *The Last Witch Hunter* (2015) as well as the superhero-based film *Suicide Squad* (2016).

As noted in the last chapter, epic fantasy as a whole tends to be a male-dominated universe that shares a hero's saga. Even with a stronger infusion of witchcraft, that doesn't change; however, as with the period's fairy tale adaptation, the construction of witchcraft in epic fantasy is far more nuanced than in past decades. *The Last Witch Hunter*, for example, uses iconography from Norse Mythology, a Viking historical aesthetic, and common witchcraft tropes to tell the tale of an immortal witch hunter who, with the help of the church, strives to keep a balance between the witch world and the human world. "Most witches are afraid of [Kaulder]," boasts the show's promo material.

In a 2015 interview, actor Vin Diesel, who plays Kaulder, explained that the film was based upon his childhood Dungeons & Dragons character.[318]

By the film's end, Kaulder must face off against the newly woken ancient witch queen who is visually depicted as uncontrolled nature. She is yet another example of the witch monster. However, she is not the only witch in the film. The rest of the witches are part of a living witch world that exists alongside humanity and plays by human rules. As with the period's dark fairy tales, the film's narrative provides the expected conventional binary between good and evil, but it has been stretched to allow for the subjective acceptance of the witch world. It does this by providing an ultimate evil in the form of the witch queen as monster. In that way, she symbolizes an extremist ideology and a common villain against which we all must come together to beat. While *The Last Witch Hunter* does include some complex themes, it is ultimately a hero sago placing the safety of the entire known world on the shoulders of one immortal white man. At the end, a young female witch tells Kaulder that there is still evil out there waiting. He asks, "Waiting for what." She answers, "A world without you … we still need you."

Unlike *The Last Witch Hunter* and other films, the television epic fantasies do not focus on witchcraft, as was the case in older sagas (e.g., *Conan the Barbarian*, 1982; *Dragonslayer*, 1981). These shows contain a single witch or other similar magical character who helps to define the magical aspects of the fantastic world. *Game of Thrones* has the Red Witch and *Vikings* has Queen Aslaug. *The Dark Crystal* has Aughra. Witches, warlocks, and wizards are expected in such an extensive magical universe.

A Closer Look: *Game of Thrones*

Many of the period's most popular epic fantasy productions, including *Vikings*, were written and produced entirely outside of the US and don't qualify for this study. However, the HBO series *Game of Thrones* was not. In fact, it is the only epic series that is wholly a US production, including its source novels. The show is an adaptation of George R. R. Martin's series A *Song of Ice and Fire*, of which the first was titled A *Game of Thrones*. Martin's story is a complex epic fantasy that weaves together a variety of narratives that tackle politics, gender play, sexuality, religion, romance, and more, all tangled in the deeply fantastic world of Westeros. More importantly,

---

318. Donna Dickens, "If It Weren't for Vin Diesel's 'D&D' Character, 'The Last Witch Hunter' Wouldn't Exist," Uproxx, OpenWeb, September 30, 2015, http://uproxx.com/hitfix/if-it-werent-for-vin -diesels-dungeons-dragons-character-the-last-witch-hunter-wouldnt-exist.

its main witch is a complex representation of a classic magical character and of the plight of contemporary womanhood.

Game of Thrones had several witch characters, including Maggy the Frog and Mirri Maz Dur. However, the most prominent and memorable witch is Melisandre (Carice van Houten). Also called the Red Witch, Melisandre's construction is complex in that it is both stereotypical and deeply subversive. She presents as both a powerful, sexualized woman who works against the establishment and an evangelical-type religious figure—the combination of which is contrary to anything that has been seen before. From a basic structural standpoint, Melisandre is a vamp witch who uses her seduction and magic to control men and to maintain her position of power. She is often dressed in dark colors, specifically rich reds that match her hair, and adorned with large jewelry. She is a seductress with powers granted to her through her god-figure, R'hllor, who may or may not be a Lucifer figure.

Since the majority of the Westeros world practices some form of polytheism, her fundamentalist beliefs in a one god are as transgressive as her vamp-like behavior. This is where the irony lies. This characterization is a reversal in the use of religion within the framework of witchcraft. Melisandre says, "Stannis does not need to beg this lord or that lord for support, the Lord of Light stands behind him." Throughout the show, she speaks of hellfire, darkness, and the binary constructs of good and evil. "If half an onion is black with rot, it's a rotten onion. A man is good or he is evil," she explains. Her language is recognized as fundamentalist in nature, paralleling it to Christian moral themes. This presents the irony, because witches typically exist as the antithesis to that religious attitude, even those horror witches devoted to Satan, and magic is traditionally the anathema of the Christian world. *Game of Thrones* throws that out and blends these constructions, creating a unique version of the witch.

However, there is another feature to Melisandre's characterization that is unusual and profoundly important in construction of female witches. In the premier episode of season six (2016), after the show had outrun Martin's original novels, Melisandre removes her iconic necklace to reveal her true self: an aged woman that resembles a classic fantasy crone. She is stooped, wrinkled, thin, and has gray straggly hair hanging off an almost bald head. The fiery vamp proves to be only a guise to maintain control in the highly political world of Westeros. Like *The Little Mermaid*'s Ursula, Melisandre as a witch understands how female seduction works within a patriarchal configuration and uses it to her own end. Ursula changes to a dark-haired young beauty in order to control Prince Eric; Melisandre does the same. The witch knows that beauty equals power.

*Carice van Houten stars as Melisandre, or the Red Witch,
in HBO's epic fantasy series* Game of Thrones *(2011–2019)*
[Source: HBO/Photofest. Copyright: © HBO]

The moment of her transformation from vamp to crone has powerful meaning beyond plot intrigue. The camera participates in Melisandre's process of becoming, resting on the private and difficult movement. In flickering candlelight, Melisandre first removes her clothing revealing a youthful naked body. Her face is pained, knowing what is to come. In close-up, she begins to remove her necklace and the camera cuts to a close-up of her dresser top. An aged hand enters the frame and places the necklace down; the camera pans up to the mirror to show a distorted image of an old woman. When the camera returns to Melisandre, she has transformed to an elderly woman of an indeterminate age.

In a review for *The Atlantic*, Megan Garber wrote, "The show that has reveled in all manner of boundary-pushing imagery, from the violent to the sexual, found a new way to shock its viewers: to present them with a woman who is at once naked and old."[319] Through that one scene, the show, allegorically speaking, forced the viewer to face a reality of the female experience—one that commits women to a life of perpetual

319. Megan Garber, "*Game of Thrones* and the Paradox of Female Beauty," *The Atlantic*, April 25, 2016, https://www.theatlantic.com/entertainment/archive/2016/04/game-of-thones-red-woman-old -ageism/479760.

struggle with the aging process. The dejected and depressed expression on Melisandre's face demonstrates her own emotional process, potentially paralleling that of a viewer's own personal experience. The show offered a profound commentary on reality as well as allowing for a rare very private moment for the cinematic witch. As the scene ends, Melisandre climbs into the bed to go to sleep, resigned to her reality.

Wizard of Oz Again and Again

If the 2000s were defined by the enchanted child and teen witchcraft, this period is defined by adaptations. From the already mentioned retellings of fairy tales to the cinematic interpretations of popular fantasy novels (e.g., *Game of Thrones*, *Beautiful Creatures*), the period's witch productions are overrun with the re-examination and execution of well-known and popular stories. Given that fact, it is not surprising that *The Wizard of Oz* was revisited multiple times and in many forms, including receiving its own fracturing. Films based on L. Frank Baum's classic included the miniseries *The Witches of Oz* (2011), *Dorothy and the Witches of Oz* (2012), *Oz the Great and Powerful* (2013), *The Legends of Oz: Dorothy's Return* (2014), *The Wiz Live!* (2015), and *Emerald City*, (2017). The Wicked Witch on her own made an appearance in ABC's successful show *Once Upon a Time* (2011–2018). These are only a few instances. Fueling the Oz frenzy was a perfect storm of cultural events, including a renewed interest in the witch, the fascination with adapting old stories, and in 2014, MGM's film celebrated its seventy-fifth anniversary. While most of the productions were made for television and received little fanfare, the century-old beloved tale was being retold, fractured, and even reimagined once again.

A Closer Look: *Oz the Great and Powerful*

Although author Gregory Maguire had already given the Wicked Witch and Glinda a backstory through his 1995 book *Wicked: The Life and Times of the Wicked Witch of the West* and its Broadway adaptation *Wicked*, the novel had yet to be adapted for the screen. In the meantime, Disney Studios jumped in, offering its own unconnected backstory for the famous villain in the 2013 film *Oz the Great and Powerful*. Not only does *Oz the Great and Powerful* attempt to explain the Wicked Witch's history but also that of Glinda and Oz, and in doing so, lands itself in a place of beautiful misogyny.

In this backstory, the Wicked Witch, named Theodora, transforms into the Wicked Witch after being rebuffed by Oz. Through that heartbreak, she becomes the manifestation of "a woman scorned." In the transformation scene, Evanora, her evil sister, hands Theodora a magic apple that will protect her heart from pain. Theodora bites the apple in a fairy tale crossover moment, and it freezes her heart, turning her into an embodiment of anger, rage, and jealousy. Both evil witches have dark hair, wield fireballs from their hands, and dress in dark, tight clothing.

The construction of Glinda is similarly traditional in its treatment of female witches. Like in the original film, she is blonde and dresses in light colors, and she can only practice magic through a wand given to her by, in this case, her father. If that wand is broken, she loses her power. By contrast, the two evil witches wield magical power from their own body. They do not need a wand. They do not need the symbolic phallus, so to speak, or a gift from a man.

The film is also punctuated with Christian theological symbols and themes. Oz's journey alone is a story of a hero's redemption. The narrative tests his ethical base through friendship, compassion, love, and the sacrifice of one's own goals for the common good. In this configuration, the blonde-haired Glinda, adorned in pure white and glitter makeup, plays the role of angel who leads Oz to goodness. It is not surprising that she floats in bubbles and produces white puffy clouds. The religion-based symbolism is similar to that in the 1939 MGM film. By contrast, Evanora is the fantasy vamp and devil who uses seduction, glamoury, and magic to achieve her selfish goals. When her younger sister is pained with jealousy, she tempts the child to evil with a poison apple—the forbidden fruit. In eating the fruit, Theodora is cast out of goodness into evil and transformed into a beast. Through rage and vengeance, she moves past the vamp stage to pure monster. While *Oz the Great and Powerful* offers the magical characters a backstory, it does so in a way that promotes the traditional mythos that has plagued the witch for centuries.

History and Horror

Just as in the past, an interest in retelling well-known fictional stories was often paired with the retelling of historical stories and popular myths. This is particularly notable in a post-postmodern America that was seeking to ground itself in its own history through a re-examination and reinterpretation. Therefore, it is not surprising to find several witch-related productions that bind their fictional horror narratives to a historical framework (e.g., Salem, 2014–2017; *American Horror Story: Coven*, 2013; *The Witch*, 2015). Doing so within the horror genre not only lends itself to the inclusion of witchcraft, but also connects it allegorically to the often-ignored horrors of America's collective story. The visual and narrative devices of cinema can make literal the fantastical fears and horrific beliefs of the past, forcing the viewer to viscerally connect to that historical moment, even if it has been highly exaggerated and sensationalized.

For example, creators Ryan Murphy and Brad Falchuk purposefully incorporated both cultural and historical elements to develop and sustain their fictional narrative in the FX horror anthology *American Horror Story*'s third season titled *Coven*. Characters such as Marie Laveau (Angela Bassett), Madame Delphine LaLaurie (Kathy Bates), and the Axeman of New Orleans (Danny Huston) are all historical figures. Additionally, the show capitalizes on the mysteries, folklore, and culture of both Salem and New Orleans, invoking history as a dark, foreboding ghost from which there is no escape. Similarly, director Robert Eggers relies not on fact but rather on an overarching historical culture and mythology to set a foreboding tone for his fictional film *The Witch* (2015).

A Closer Look: *Salem*

Like *American Horror Story: Coven*, the WGN series *Salem* relies both on fact and mythos, using horror to re-examine one of America's most famous stories. Created by Adam Simon and Brannon Braga, *Salem* (2014–2017) is set in 1692 and retells the city's legendary history with creative license. The show does not provide a deep-diving history lesson like *Three Sovereigns for Sarah* (1985); rather it uses the horror genre to capture the tense climate, thereby evoking a visceral fear, chaos, and moral uncertainty that is atypical to the average Salem story. What Simon brought forth suggests not that the show's factual history is entirely incorrect, but rather that the stories we tell may not be as clean as they seem. This ideological premise carries over in the show's depiction of witchcraft.

Right from its first episode, *Salem* suggests that no one character is without fault, not even the Christian ministers. For example, Cotton Mather is portrayed as a religious zealot and described as the "most dangerous type of fool … The kind that thinks he knows everything." [320] Mather is further demonized through a consistent show of hypocrisy. *Salem* not only depicts moral relativism, but it relishes that very ideology. In an interview, Simon remarked on this point, saying:

> In our imaginary version, Salem became in effect the witches' vengeance upon the Puritans for all the oppression they had doled out in the past in England and for their oppressive intent in the New World. I wanted to get away from the simplistic idea of the witch hunt and McCarthyism as it was handed down from *The Crucible* and look at it differently in a post-9/11 world with conspiracies on all sides including governments; where nothing was quite what it seemed and where it was possible that real attacks might be followed

---

320. Adam Simon, email to the author, July 1, 2017.

up by false flag operations aimed in all the wrong directions. A world where beliefs make reality for better and for worse.[321]

As Simon suggests, the concept carries through directly in the construction of Salem's witches, from their personal stories to their magical actions.

During the show's premier, Mary Sibley is depicted as an innocent young woman in love who becomes pregnant out of wedlock. Rather than face public shame, she turns to witchcraft in order to rid herself of the unborn child. Mary is choosing to avoid the fate of the accused woman in favor of the wild woman. Although she never becomes the accused, she is still depicted as a victim of social expectations. Her actions, deemed transgressive from a society's center point, are justified from her own subjectivity as a means of survival or rebellion against an unfair world. Unlike past narratives, the viewer is privy to her experience, making her more relatable. In this way, Salem's witches exist at the tipping point that places the viewer into the uncomfortable position of understanding the reason but disliking the means. Through them the viewer might ask, "Success at what cost?"

Like other horror witches of the period, both men and women are monstrous creatures that hide their true form with a human appearance. However, these characters are not genetically witches; they earn their power from Satan and their monstrous form is the symbolic loss of the soul. As always, power comes with a price and, in this case, it is one's humanity. Magic is not given freely, even if its evocation is understandable from the victim's standpoint. Again, that is where the show's ethical question rests: success at what cost? However, unlike past productions such as *Twilight Zone's* "Jess-Belle" (1963), *Salem* doesn't take sides.

While creators took liberties in its retelling of history, they did attempt to mimic the historical practice of folk magic as described in historical texts as well as the fear of it. Simon said that they wanted to be "true to witchcraft as we know it from both the anthropological perspective (Emma Wilby especially) and from the practitioners' perspective—in a nutshell to stop going on about whether it was real or not and assume that of course it was real."[322] As I described in a past review, "[the witches] perform magic with oils, frogs, lizards, hogs, blood and fire. They hold sabbats in the dark woods wearing beastly masks. They have familiars and understand the nuances in 'life, love, war and death.'"[323] Using the horror genre, the writers could literalize that magic and thereby evoke a viewer's strong fear and disgust response, potentially

---

321. Simon, email to the author.

322. Simon, email to the author.

323. Heather Greene, "WGN America's Salem," *The Wild Hunt*, April 24, 2014, https://wildhunt
    .org/2014/04/review-wgn-americas-salem.html.

paralleling a Puritan reaction, as noted earlier.. However, the show also juxtaposes those scenes to the contradictory or oppressive behavior and crimes of the establishment, which ultimately places the viewer in a constant uncomfortable moral uncertainty, which, as Simon suggested, was his aim.

Salem's run ended in 2017, and Simon said he was pleased with the final results. "I don't claim that I achieved all or even most of what I hoped but given that we were in a very commercial context on a very commercial network—literally one still built on commercial advertising—I believe it was both the truest and most radical depiction of witchcraft in a popular medium."[324] He is correct in terms of the representations of the witch. The depictions, while sensationalized and glossy, did attempt to capture something other than just another Salem plot positing the irrational, accused woman against a just and reasoned society. In fact, the show's importance has nothing to do with the town's historical legacy and more to do with the town's ideological imprint on American culture. What does the story mean within our culture, within cinema, and to the representation of witchcraft? Salem forces the viewer to review that question and to also consider how we tell our histories.

Beyond Othering

In the cinematic re-examining of our collective stories within a magical framework, the politics, realities, and weight of history is brought back into the representation of Black witches. As noted in the last chapter, Black witches found increased positive representation by the late 1990s and into the 2000s, primarily due to "girl power" and a growing multicultural movement. While that shift is notable, the characters were often distanced, if not wholly removed, from the politics of race and any other pertinent sociocultural legacy. As in Twitches (2005), the two Black witches were constructed to fit a generic American normalcy that ignored unique aspects of their personal racial identity. In that way, these character constructions swung the pendulum of representation to the opposite extreme from golden era constructions that embraced racial and ethnic "othering." In 2013, author and modern Witch Crystal Blanton expressed similar complaints as both actress Rachel True and the writer at the Graveyard Shift Sisters blog. Blanton said, "People of Color in the Craft have not been represented equally in television or movies unless looking at something that is

---

324. Simon, email to the author.

specifically VooDoo inspired. There are not very many People of Color playing roles in the Witchy or mystical dramas." [325]

By the middle of this era, however, representation began to change significantly. The appearance of Black witches increased, and this time, the depth of that construction expanded, reflecting the sociocultural climate that was, among other things, pushing racial discourse to the forefront of culture. As noted, these changes in representation correspond, in part, to the collective re-evaluation of America's history and renewed search for American national identity. Some of the period's most notable Black witches and magical women include Amma in *Beautiful Creatures*, Queenie and Marie Laveau in *American Horror Story: Coven*, Eloise in *Spell*, Tituba in *Salem*, Prudence and Rosalind in the *Chilling Adventures of Sabrina*, and the witches of *The Wiz Live!* (2015). In addition, this is the first period to introduce a prominent and positive Black male witch, Ambrose in *Chilling Adventures of Sabrina*. This is particularly important because Black magical men have been almost entirely characterized as witch doctors (e.g., *White Witch Doctor*, 1953) and Voodoo priests, or simply used as props decorating a satanic coven (e.g., *The Devil's Hand*, 1961). Ambrose is none of those things.

Folk Witches and Hoodoo

All of the period's notable Black female witches are constructed specifically as witches defined as such by their own American identities and dedicated narratives. They are not trapped within a foreign cultural context, codified as deviant, or used as decoration to frame the morality of the white characters. These representational shifts were not accidental. For example, in the novel *Beautiful Creatures*, the character of Amma (Viola Davis) is a maid; however, she was reimagined as a librarian in the film. Amma plays the role of the elderly folk witch, parsing out knowledge, asking moral questions, and pushing the main characters to confront themselves. In 2013, actress Viola Davis said, "I understand and I respect the book…but this is 2013, and I think that when black people are woven into the lives of characters in 2013, then I think they play other roles than maids." [326]

325. Crystal Blanton, "Column: *American Horror Story: Coven*, Witches, Television, and Diversity," *The Wild Hunt*, November 15, 2013, http://wildhunt.org/2013/11/american-horror-story-coven -witches-television-and-diversity.html.

326. Rebecca Ford, "'Beautiful Creatures' Star Viola Davis on Why Her Character Isn't a Maid in the Adaptation (Q&A)," *The Hollywood Reporter*, February 12, 2013, http://www.hollywoodreporter.com /news/beautiful-creatures-star-viola-davis-420439.

To prepare for the role, Davis spent time in New Orleans' French Quarter with tarot readers and seers. She said, "I also did a lot of research on the Yoruba tradition in Nigeria, because they do a lot of meditation and channeling." [327] It is important to note that despite Davis's personal research, Amma is not constructed as a Voodoo priestess like Marie Laveau; she is a witch, or caster as they say, like the others. However, Davis's unique cultural twist is resident in her interpretation of Amma, giving the character a nuance that was not previously captured in the representation of any Black witch.

Another new character construction is the Hoodoo witch. She is an iteration of the elderly folk witch or crone wild woman. For example, the grandmother (Octavia Spencer) in the joint UK-US adaptation of Roald Dahl's *The Witches* (2020) practices Hoodoo and is defined as a healer. She is a main protagonist and the film's heroine. In the horror film *Spell* (2020), Eloise (Loretta Devine), the primary villain, is also a Hoodoo practitioner who is also defined as a root worker and Appalachian fixer. Similarly, Rosalind (Jaz Sinclair) and her grandmother (L. Scott Caldwell) in *Chilling Adventures of Sabrina* (2018–2020) are described as seers. Hoodoo is a distinctly American form of folk magic, and in these films, characterizes the witch as American and magical within her unique cultural identity as a Black woman. Although not all Black witches fit this role, many begin to take it on whether as powerful central villain or heroine. The web series *Juju*, which began in 2019, is another example.

With that said, the representation of magic itself within these Hoodoo-based narratives, like any other production, is subjected to the general American cultural understanding of magic, witches, and women. While *Spell* is a landmark horror film, for example, with its nearly all-Black cast and its Black villainous witch, the film is classic in its use of horror devices, its witchcraft narrative, and its plot. In many ways, *Spell* is an early 1990s horror film with a classic coven-based plot in which an unsuspecting contemporary family falls victim to a backwoods coven of witches. As expected, magic is the domain of an undead, evil woman seeking to maintain her and her coven members' immortality. She is the classic elderly satanic folk witch who can't cross salt lines, and in the end, dies a witch's death by fire. The film pits folk belief, defined as irrational, wild, and country, against modernity, defined as rational, atheistic, and urban. Once again, the latter is embodied in the male hero who must save the family and the world from the witch. While he does so through his own knowledge of magic, he does not re-embrace his country roots and returns to his world of modernity. While the all-Black cast is novel and the Hoodoo witch is a new construct, the film's narrative is quite conventional for a witch horror film.

---

327. Ford, "'Beautiful Creatures' Star Viola Davis."

A Closer Look: *American Horror Story: Coven*

The changing representation of Black witches was noticeable as early as 2013 with the release of *American Horror Story: Coven*, which combined a witchcraft teen horror story with the history of New Orleans' mysticism, the reality of virulent racism, and the novelty of cinematic witchcraft. The show includes the character Queenie (Gabourey "Gabby" Sidibe) who, as author Crystal Blanton points out, was not only a Black teen but also "large-figured, dark-[skinned]," making her stand out as exceptional in multiple ways.[328] In episode two, Queenie herself points to the deficits in the media representation of witches. She says, "I grew up on white girl shit like *Charmed*, and *Sabrina, the Teenage Cracker*. I didn't know that there even were Black witches. But as it turns out, I'm an heir to Tituba. She was a house slave in Salem. She was the first to be accused of witchcraft." Queenie's comment reflects *Coven*'s dance with history and pop culture within its reflection on race.

Unlike *The Craft*'s Rochelle, Queenie speaks directly to representational issues, not waiting on magic to solve the problem. Rochelle is a product of her time, created dynamically as witchcraft in media was just beginning to take on spiritual and cultural acceptability. Queenie is the next evolution. She knows who she is and accepts it. Identity and personal self-making are no longer a focus. Queenie is not at school to learn who she is but rather to learn what to do with her power as a Black witch, literally and allegorically as a young woman in America.

Blanton asks, "What does it mean for African American and ethnic minorities to have more representation in the media as a part of the Witch culture?"[329] This issue was raised by the *Graveyard Shift Sisters* concerning Rochelle.[330] The question points to the profound meaning resident in the character of Queenie and the show's refusal to back down from conversations on race. Using American history and regional legacy, *Coven*'s narrative forces a re-evaluation of national identity and the stories about ourselves. In that way, the show exemplifies the entire period's thematic relationship to narrative witchcraft. Maybe we were wrong. Maybe the witch was right. With that in mind, it is not at all surprising to witness the emergence of a character like Queenie along with a storyline that confronts the legacy of slavery and the modern repercussions head on.

---

328. Blanton, "Column: *American Horror Story: Coven*."

329. Blanton, "Column: *American Horror Story: Coven*."

330. "20 Years of The Craft: Why We Needed More Rochelle."

*Young witch Queenie, played by Gabourey Sidibe, performs a spell with
other students in the third season of* American Horror Story *titled "Coven."*
[Source: FX Network/Photofest. © FX Network]

With that said, Queenie's construction is not perfect. As Blanton points out, she
plays into media tropes of the "angry black woman" and there is an unrelenting focus
on her weight.[331] That is an important point. While Queenie embodies a step forward
on the trajectory of witch construction, she still captures stereotypes used in the depiction of Black women. However, within the scope of this study, Queenie presents something new: a strong, dark-skinned, teen witch who does not play into the stereotypes
of beauty or agency and who is not othered through religious practice or ethnicity. She
is the new representation of the adolescent girl who embraces the forbidden mystical,
rejects conventional boundaries, and searches for her place and role in community.

Teen Witchcraft: Fantasy to Horror

The popularity of teen-based fantasy, which took center stage in the last period, showed
no signs of ending at the start of this period, although the interest was fading. Early
teen witchcraft productions were largely tied to or embedded in fantasy and the fairy
tale genre as a holdover from the last period, including the continued popularity of

---

331. Blanton, "Column: *American Horror Story: Coven.*"

vampire-inspired series such as HBO's *True Blood* (2008–2014). However, as with the past witch cycles, witchcraft-related productions dedicated to teens surged again at the end of the period as the period's dominant genres declined. While these later teen productions are fantasy inspired, they move ever closer to true horror.

Gothic Teen Fantasy: *Beautiful Creatures*

The film *Beautiful Creatures* (2013) is an example of one of the period's early teen fantasy films that drew from the vampire narrative's gothic aesthetic, playing off the popularity of productions like the Twilight Saga (2008–2012), *The Vampire Diaries* (2009–2017) and *True Blood*. While it contains some elements of horror, the film is more dark fantasy, fitting in with the fairy-tale-based witch productions popular at the time. Based on the 2009 *New York Times* best-selling book by Kami Garcia and Margaret Stohl, *Beautiful Creatures* is a love story, a saga of self-identity, and a fantasy about witchcraft in a sleepy Southern town. A restless, non-magical boy, Ethan Wate, meets Lena Duchannes, a magical girl who wants to be normal. Ethan must come to terms with her family and his love for her. And she must learn to accept her own identity, her new powers, and her journey as a witch. This story has been told before.

Directed by Richard LaGravenese, *Beautiful Creatures* received mixed reviews and is considered one of the biggest box office failures of the year. It was criticized for being overdone and clumsy in its attempt to capture the *Twilight* fans whose saga had just run its course. However, the film dances very openly with the idea of moral relativism, which is the important element of this film in terms of witch construction. Lena is about to turn sixteen, at which point she will be chosen either for good or for bad. This pending event looms over her the entire film. "What will I become?"

The film contains a number of different witches, most of whom are part of the Duchannes family. They are visually sculpted around traditional expectations on what defines a good or bad witch. Good witches, such as Emmaline (Eileen Atkins), dress in light colors and recall proper Victorian women or contemporary clown witches. By contrast, bad witches, such as Ridley (Emmy Rossum), are vamps with red hair who wear short skirts and black lace. While the film presents typical ethical binaries through these characterizations, they still exist as a viable family unit. Allegorically speaking, the group could represent any modern American dysfunctional family, and the dinner gathering could be any family reunion. That is one way the film suggests its complex moral structure. Bad and good exist within the same relatively peaceful space. The real struggle is within the young witch. Will the unnamed "power that be" choose her for good or bad? The film presents both possibilities. "Look at me, Ethan. Am I dark or light?" she asks.

When that moment of maturity arrives, the film takes an atypical turn. Lena is both good and bad, visually represented through two different color eyes. She is neither extreme. If *Beautiful Creatures* is read as an allegory for the teen's maturation into adulthood, Lena does not end up having to make choices; she can remain the wild woman and still be connected to her community. Lena controls her destiny, her growth, her sexuality, and her magic. While the storytelling is cumbersome, the film sits in an unusual place in 2013, dancing with ethical binaries and trying to rest on the idea that our actions define our morality, not any biological predisposition. The film closes as Ethan recovers from amnesia and remembers Lena, screaming out her name along the roadside. Love wins, even for the morally ambiguous young wild woman witch. Like Queenie or Disney's Elsa, Lena accepts her identity as a whole of herself and then is in the position to ask, "What now?"

Teen Horror: *Chilling Adventures of Sabrina*

Beautiful Creatures as a teen fantasy film was an anomaly in the timing of its release but is a precursor to later teen productions, some of which do away completely with the questions presented in the 2013 film and just accept subjective morality as an absolute. These later teen productions also notably turn away from dark fantasy and move closer to the horror genre. Productions include Lionsgate's *The Blair Witch*, Freeform's joint Canadian-US series *Motherland: Fort Salem* (2020–), the web series *Juju* (2019–), and independent, low budget and B-films such as *Reel Nightmare* (2017), *The Witch Files* (2018), *The Incantation* (2018), or *Loon Lake* (2019).

Perhaps the most striking witch teen production released during this period was Netflix's *Chilling Adventures of Sabrina* (2018–2020). The story is based on Roberto Aguirre-Sacasa's graphic novel inspired by Archie Comics' famous character. The sixty-year evolution of Sabrina is quite remarkable. She began as a teen fantasy vamp in comic books and then, in the 1970s, she was reimagined in children's cartoons as a friendly half-witch fumbling with her magic and humanity. By the late 1990s, Sabrina emerged as a live-action witch next door emblematic of third wave feminism and "girl power." Her magic was normalized as was done with *Bewitched* (1964–1972). Through the 2000s, even after the sitcom had run its course, various animated series emerged with Sabrina in purely symbolic form as a child witch. These characters are younger and do not resemble any of the former character's designs except for her blonde hair.

In 2018, the Sabrina story takes a dark turn into horror, paralleling the retelling of other witchcraft-related stories and histories. In this new incarnation, Sabrina (Kiernan Shipka) is still the blonde-haired half-witch who struggles to balance her mortal and magical lives. She wears contemporary teen attire, goes to high school, has a boyfriend, and participates in school clubs. She lives with her aunties, Hilda and Zelda, her cat, Salem, and her cousin, Ambrose. That is where normalcy ends.

To create a greater sense of mystery and intensity, Aguirre-Sacasa often aimed at capturing a subtle comic book style through art direction and color palette, and this is particularly evident with Sabrina. Her clothes are often made up of large, solid panels of red and black with few patterns. This becomes increasingly apparent as she more fully participates in magic and after she embraces the religious aspects of witchcraft by signing the *Book of the Beast*. After that moment, Sabrina appears on camera with a new, sexy swagger. Her hair is lighter, and her clothes are tighter. She is also wearing a dark red dress with a lace collar mimicking the costumes worn by the sexy and unpredictable trio of weird sisters. As in the past, when the witch accepts her natural power, she radiates sexuality, confidence, and an alluring beauty (e.g., *The Witches of Eastwick*, 1987; *Frozen*, 2013).

The show employs an array of classic, historical, satanic, and modern Witch iconography to build its magical comic book inspired universe. Instead of living in a brightly lit modern home like the '90s Sabrina, this contemporary Sabrina and her family live in a dark Victorian mansion, which serves as the family's funeral parlor. An old cemetery sits on the mansion's grounds. Her human friends, in a kitschy nod to modern Witchcraft, create a group called Women's Intersectional Cultural and Creative Association (WICCA) to empower female students. Additionally, a Baphomet statue sits in the lobby of Sabrina's witchcraft school. The image is a copy of one created by The Satanic Temple, an activist and religious organization based in Salem. The show was sued for using the statue without permission; however, the suit was "amicably settled" and the show continued to employ the statue.[332] These are only a few examples of recognizable iconography that decorate the show's fictional world.

Satanic Witchcraft as Religion

Included in that rich representation is the embrace of witchcraft as a true Satanic religion; however, the show does this in a way that is unexpected. Rather than Satan turning people into witches, as in *Salem* (2014–2017) and other horror films, these witches are biologically born as in most fantasy narratives, and Satan is their main deity. Based on a mix of Catholicism, Wicca, and historical European lore, Sabrina's witchcraft universe is defined specifically as a subcultural religious community com-

---

332. "Satanists 'Amicably' Settle Warner Bros Lawsuit over Chilling Adventures of Sabrina," *The Guardian*, November 21, 2018, https://www.theguardian.com/film/2018/nov/22/chilling-adventures-of -sabrina-satanists-settle-warner-bros-case.

plete with a school and temple. The show does not demonize the practice even in its depictions of human sacrifice, necromancy, and wild sex in the woods during Lupercalia. These details serve to build the show's dark comic universe, adding to the creep factor as well as providing a farcical undercurrent. *Sabrina* is as much fantasy as horror, and it makes no claims at being otherwise.

Furthermore, the presentation of this satanic-based religious experience demonstrates one of the ways the show engages in extreme subjectivity and challenges long-standing belief systems and other conventional structures of society. *Chilling Adventures of Sabrina* asks and answers: "What if witches were actually satanic worshippers? Is that necessarily bad?" While *Beautiful Creatures* also engaged in moral relativism, it did not challenge the boundaries defining moral binaries. It only concluded that a witch can embody both. The *Sabrina* show breaks the binaries entirely. This theme is observable in the construction of the characters themselves. Often an episode's main conflict is not between characters but within a character. For example, Sabrina's choice to resurrect her boyfriend's dead brother seems like a good idea until it is not. Each character struggles with similar choices, making no one witch overtly evil or good. Even Madam Satan is given a moment of relatability when she saves Sabrina. The series depicts morality as something not imposed by community but rather one of personal negotiation. In that way, *Sabrina* is a realization of *Beautiful Creatures*'s conclusion. Witchcraft or one's power is only a matter of biology; it's how that power is used in service to community that defines it as good and evil.

Return to the 1990s with a Twist

Sabrina's return is notable beyond its renegotiation of a classic story. The show was part of a trend that sought to resurrect several narrative witch texts made popular in the 1990s. These contemporary reboots existed as both nostalgic journeys for older fans and an appeal to a new generation of Witchcraft-curious teens. As in the late 1990s, modern Witchcraft was seeing a resurgence in popularity and practice among younger generations, paralleling contemporary empowerment movements. In a *Bustle* interview, author and modern Witch Pam Grossman acknowledges the trend, saying that "for some people, [witchcraft is] more about the fashion or some other aspect of the culture of witchcraft."[333] However, in many cases, the popularity leads to actual practice. Grossman speculates that social media is partly fueling the trend, allowing for easy dissemination of information and group meetings. With that said, it is not

---

333. Peg Aloi, "Witches Are Having a Moment. It Isn't the First Time," *Bustle*, July 17, 2019, https://www.bustle.com/p/waking-the-witch-author-pam-grossman-on-why-witches-are-having-such-a-huge-cultural-moment-18204873.

surprising, then, that these reboot productions, originally created during another surge in teen Witchcraft popularity, were released.

Included in the 1990s teen witch reboots are *Charmed* (2018–), *Chilling Adventures of Sabrina* (2018–2020), *The Craft: Legacy* (2020), *Blair Witch* (2016), and *The Witches* (2020). There were rumors that *Practical Magic* and even *Hocus Pocus* would be revisited. It is important to note that none of these reboots were as successful as their predecessors, with perhaps the exception of *Sabrina*, which is a reimagination, as already shown. *Blair Witch* and *The Craft: Legacy* are sequels. *Charmed* and *The Witches* are remakes.

A Closer Look: *The Craft: Legacy*

Directed by Zoe Lister-Jones, *The Craft: Legacy* had a lot riding on its release because the original film retained a strong cult following. The original not only inspired people to pursue Witchcraft but also gave voice to the "weirdos." Despite any failings, the original film is iconic in the teen horror canon, let alone witch films. Lister-Jones recognized the original's cultural power. In an interview with *Vanity Fair*, she said, "[The first film was] intersectional at a time when representation was not being prioritized in popular culture. But I wanted to take that and go further with it—to look at the ways in which the community is so much more powerful than the individual."[334]

Lister-Jones's statement expresses the general trend in the period's witch films. As seen, the explorations are less about the witch discovering her power or accepting her identity, and more about the witch negotiating her power in community. *The Craft: Legacy* spends less time than the original on the girls' personal conflicts and more on their fight against external forces in a hostile landscape. In the article Lister-Jones explains "That landscape … is one in which the leadership of the United States is brazenly and openly disrespectful to women, not to mention people of color, immigrants, and the LGBTQ community."[335] The film's sociopolitical messages, as described by Lister-Jones, are overt from character development to plot.

Three of the four witches, for example, are women of color and one of them is a trans woman. In an interview with *The Gay Times*, Zoey Luna, who plays Lourdes, said, "I think [*The Craft*'s director] found ways to incorporate my identity as a trans woman in a way that was so seamless, and not necessarily overkill. I'm very appreciative of the way that she wrote my character and included her identity without being

---

334. Valentina Valentini, "Exclusive: How Zoe Lister-Jones Reimagined *The Craft*'s Iconic Teen Witches," *Vanity Fair*, October 13, 2020, https://www.vanityfair.com/hollywood/2020/10/the-craft-legacy-remake-sequel-zoe-lister-jones.

335. Valentini, "Exclusive: How Zoe Lister-Jones Reimagined *The Craft*'s Iconic Teen Witches."

super noisy about it." [336] Lister-Jones's progressive and deliberate construction of her witch quartet is actually demonstrative of the period's 1990s reboots. For example, *Charmed*'s trio of sisters are depicted as Latina and the entire cast is more diverse than the original series. The middle sister, Mel Vera, is also lesbian. *The Witches* and *Chilling Adventures of Sabrina* are no different, as discussed earlier. These characters accept and embrace all aspects of identity, legacy, and heritage, as well as their transgressions, or—borrowing terms from *The Craft* (1996)—their "weirdo" status. Witchcraft is no longer just a symbolic representation of femininity that must be handled, but it encompasses an adolescent's whole identity, including their gender, sexuality, race, ethnicity and beyond.

Despite the diversity in characterization, *The Craft: Legacy* focuses primarily on the new girl, Lily, who moves into her mother's boyfriend's home and shortly after discovers that she's a witch. In a walk down the street, she casually accepts the other three girls' friendship and embraces magic quite quickly. She has found her community through embracing her authentic self. The other teens do not have backstories; they simply make up the community of women, or the film's magical world, if you will, and together they take on misogyny and hate quite literally. In the end, the four witches use their power to destroy her mother's evil boyfriend. Lister-Jones explains, "No shade to the original [film]—and women are allowed to be villains—but ultimately it was about women whose power was too overwhelming for them to harness and was turned on each other ... The message that I want to put into the universe is that there is no power too great for women to harness and that we always need to be wary of turning that power on each other." [337]

As with *The Craft*, modern Witches acted as consultants on the sequel to give it an air of authenticity. Lister-Jones took this work a step further than the original producers. *The Craft: Legacy* had three consultants including Pam Grossman, Bri Luna, and Aerin Fogel. Not only did these witches choreograph the rituals and offer script suggestions, but they also protected the set. Lister-Jones said, "Whatever portals we were opening ... I wanted to make sure that we were doing it with the right intentions and also closing those portals at the day's end." [338]

In terms of the representation of magic, writers removed the worship of the deity Manon as the center of witchcraft practice. Lister-Jones felt that the devotion to a male deity did not fit with her feminist text, particularly one whose villains are male

---

336. "Zoey Luna Is Inspiring a New Generation of Trans Youth with Her Character in The Craft: Legacy" *Gay Times*, October 29, 2020, https://www.gaytimes.co.uk/culture/zoey-luna-is-inspiring -a-new-generation-of-trans-youth-with-her-character-in-the-craft-legacy/.

337. Valentini, "How Zoe Lister-Jones Reimagined."

338. Valentini, "How Zoe Lister-Jones Reimagined."

abusers. In the 1996 film, the presence of Manon gave the story the connection it needed to the Satanic Panic, which changed Nancy from a natural witch to a ritualistic and even satanic witch. Lister-Jones rejected those concepts, saying, "Witchcraft has much of its roots in goddess worship, [which] was so globally essential to so many cultures and then was just really wiped out. It's 2020, and we're getting back into it." [339] Like many of the period's witch narratives, *The Craft: Legacy* seeks to ground itself in legacy and heritage while seeking out community and purpose. And that theme is satisfied further in the end when Lily, who the viewer eventually finds out is adopted, meets her birth mother, Nancy from the first film.

Love, Witchcraft, and the Wild Wood

After 2016, the witch popularity cycle began to move predictably toward teen-related fare as with past cycles. However, before doing so, two vitally different films were released, both by independent filmmakers and both labeling themselves horror: *The Witch* and *The Love Witch*. One was written and directed by a man and the other a woman. Each of the films in their own way captures and evaluates the dense iconography, methodology, and social constructions surrounding the witch as found in Hollywood. Despite their vastly different looks and approaches, they both express a similar idea: witchcraft is the chosen path of empowerment for society's victims, specifically women. It is the tool of the oppressed, demonstrating that one woman's transgression is another woman's livelihood. In doing so, they challenge the structures that have long defined our understanding of our history, society, and conventional morality.

Robert Eggers's film *The Witch*, subtitled "A New-England Folktale," won the 2015 Sundance Film Festival's directing award in the US Dramatic category and recieved critical acclaim. At the London Film Festival, the film also won the Sutherland Award for Best First Feature. Despite the praise, viewer response was mixed after it was released widely in the winter of 2016. While the film is categorized as horror, it does not match contemporary viewer expectations regarding the genre. It moves slowly, basking in the imagery. Eggers attempted to evoke the dread and desperation authentic to the period, mimicking that of the characters. The horror is resident in the same place as it is with *The Blair Witch Project* (1999): the minds of characters. One of *Salem*'s co-creators Adam Simon remarked, "I have great admiration for the film *The Witch* made a couple years after we began but which comes closer to the atmosphere I might've hoped initially to achieve in *Salem*. Eggers wasn't limited by the commercial process as the *Salem* crew was." [340]

---

339. Valentini, "How Zoe Lister-Jones Reimagined."

340. Simon, email to the author.

It is important to note that *The Witch* is categorized as a joint US-Canadian film and, as such, doesn't qualify for the study. However, it is worth noting because *The Witch* encapsulates the legacy of Hollywood's witch construction so tightly that is proves to be a good example of her construction and how contemporary social ideology relates to it. Within this one narrative, Eggers walked the viewer systematically through a host of Western witchcraft lore, including fairy tale tropes, the Baba Yaga, fear of the wild wood, the ephemeral existence of female adolescence, Satan as a goat, child endangerment, and Puritan fundamentalism. Frame by frame, this is an American witch narrative complete with accusations, suspicions, spellwork, and a missing baby.

However, Eggers didn't rest on viewer expectations just to tell another Puritan horror story. He played off the iconography to subvert the narrative, forcing the viewer to confront a single basic fear: what we believe may be wrong and what we fear may be right. Or better yet, perhaps it is what we fear that will save us from that which we believe. For example, in the end, the extreme adherence to Christian fundamentalism drives the entire family to a state of anxiety that literally kills them. Ironically, the teen girl, Thomasin, who is typically the character needing protecting, is the only survivor. She turns away from Puritan life, enters the woods, and makes a pact with Satan. Through that act of becoming the witch, she saves herself and is resurrected as an empowered woman in an ironic shot similar to an image of a rising Christ figure. Becoming the witch becomes a necessity for her and a pathway to her future. That is how the film ends. In a subversive twist, it is Satan and witchcraft who become the white knight savior, providing the adolescent girl her redemptive rescue.

Similarly, director Anna Biller attempted to subvert viewer expectations concerning witchcraft in her 2016 film *The Love Witch*. However, in contrast to Eggers's film, Biller worked with an entirely different set of American cinematic witch tropes. She tackled the lore of the vamp witch and even included elements of modern Witchcraft. Like director Paul Traynor in the film *Witches' Night*, Biller pays homage to the 1970s pulp horror films that sensationalize the female body, depict witchcraft as ritual, and explore a woman's social agency. One of her inspirations was George Romero's film *Hungry Wives* (1973), for example. However, unlike Traynor, Biller took the retro aesthetic a step further, capturing the period visually through sets, props, costumes, and coloring. She tightly packs her narrative full of witchcraft iconography to represent the vamp's universe. Her stylized visuals create a contrived almost comic book universe that Biller says reflects Elaine's distorted fantasies, which parallels the reasoning behind Eggers's visual choices.[341]

---

341. Anna Biller, email to author, May 26, 2016.

While she drew from the 1970s horror witch films, Biller did not capture the misogynist elements commonly found in those films. *The Love Witch*'s ritual scenes, for example, contain naked men and women. This is where Billers deviates in her project and expresses a contemporary sensibility. While visually graphic, these ritual sequences are not exploitative of the naked bodies or of witchcraft practice. In fact, in an interview, Biller said, "Several people in the cast who played witches were practicing witches, and I talked with them about their practices. I also lurked on internet forums and read a lot of blogs and articles and interviewed some of my friends who are witches."[342]

Elaine, a sociopathic witch played by Samantha Robinson, stirs a new potion in her eclectic California home in the indie film The Love Witch *(2016). [Source: Anna Biller © Anna Biller]*

The Love Witch tells the story of Elaine, a single woman, sociopath, and witch, living in Northern California. We meet her as she first moves into a new apartment owned by a friend and Wiccan High Priestess named Barbara. The film then follows Elaine through her negotiations of love, seduction, dating, friendship, ritual practice, and murder. Regardless of her crimes, Elaine is depicted as a victim in a male-dominated society. Her father called her stupid, crazy, and "a fatty," and her ex-husband complained about her cooking and housekeeping. She turns to witchcraft to survive, as does

---

342. Biller, email to the author, May 26, 2016.

Thomasin. She tells a police officer, "Witchcraft saved my life." This is again one of the messages echoing through this period. The thing that society most feared is the thing that saves. Taking that a step further, if witchcraft, as shown, is the symbolic representation of a woman's power, then, as Glinda said to Dorothy, we have had the power in us all along.

While Eggers's film captures a society grappling with gender constructs, religious belief, and its fear in the face of the unknown, Biller works with the more personal thematic embedded within a single witch character, including agency in the face of personal trauma and the use of feminine power within the patriarchy. "I wanted to use that imagery and combine that with the feelings of persecution I've felt as a woman, and all of the issues women have to face with self-presentation and sexual identity in a man's world," Biller said.[343] In that way, Elaine could be every cinematic witch. And together, the two films hit on the essence of the witch construction as it made its way in American cinema through the years.

Conclusion

When this period opens in 2010, the nation was contending with a second recession and was at the very beginnings of new social movements challenging established systems and ways of being. Social media had taken over as the dominant form of communication and rising extremism was lurking in the background. By 2011, a new witch cycle emerged through dark fantasy and fairy tale adaptations, both of which re-imagined beloved stories and tales. At the same time, television offered explorations of history through the horror genre, challenging the viewer to rethink the stories we tell about ourselves.

As the period moves on, dark fantasy gave way to teen films, as is typical for a witch cycle. While new material was produced, many of these productions were reboots of successful witch shows and films that were released in the 1990s. Producers were looking to revisit the connections made between those narratives and progressive teen audiences newly exploring modern Witchcraft. These 1990s reboots were given facelifts, reflecting a greater diversity as well as a deeper expression of politicized feminism reflective of the #MeToo movement.

The period saw two dominant themes. First, teen narratives expressed a desire and need for community connectivity. "What do we do with our power?" Rather than a negotiation of identity or a search for belonging, these films depict young witches searching for purpose in the world. Unlike the young wild women of the past, these witches fully embrace their wild status and refuse to compromise. These young

---

343. Biller, email to the author, May 26, 2016.

women not only reject conventional reincorporation, but they also defy othering and will not be resigned to a life in the shadows.

Those films not specifically marketed to teens root their narratives in the concept that witchcraft is the answer to trauma. Fantasy films and fractured tales made this concept the narrative center, explaining how the witch was simply a woman scorned, a victim of a society constrained by its own dogmatic inflexibility. In that respect, these witches all embody the accused woman. Instead of waiting for their redemptive rescue, they are driven to a transgressive existence. Magic, whether sourced or not, becomes her lifeline. Within both themes, the depth of character construction is no longer binary and, although there is a nostalgic movement toward resurrecting cultural heritage, what was held as truth in these narratives is regularly being questioned. As such, good and bad are possible in one character. And maybe, after all, the witch was right all along.

Chapter 12: Filmography

Beastly	2011	Daniel Barnz
Conan the Barbarian	2011	Marcus Nispel
Season of the Witch	2011	Dominic Sena
Game of Thrones	2011–2019	David Benioff, D. B. Weiss (creators)
The Good Witch's Family	2011	Craig Pryce
Grimm	2011–2017	Stephen Carpenter et al. (creators)
Suburgatory	2011–2014	Emily Kapnek (creator)
Once Upon a Time	2011–2018	Adam Horowitz et al. (creator)
ParaNorman	2012	Chris Butler, Sam Fell
Mirror Mirror	2012	Tarsem Singh
Brave	2012	Mark Andrews, Brenda Chapman
Dark Shadows	2012	Tim Burton
Dorothy and the Witches of Oz	2012	Leigh Scott
Hotel Transylvania	2012	Genndy Tartakovsky
Snow White and the Huntsman	2012	Rupert Sanders
Deadtime Stories	2012–2014	Annette Cascone et al.
American Horror Story: Coven	2013	Brian Katkin
All Cheerleaders Die	2013	Lucky McKee, Chris Silvertson

Beautiful Creatures	2013	Richard LaGravenese
Frozen	2013	Chris Buck, Jennifer Lee
Hansel & Gretel Get Baked	2013	Duane Journey
Hansel & Gretel: Witch Hunters	2013	Tommy Wirkola
The Last Keepers	2013	Maggie Greenwald
Oz the Great and Powerful	2013	Sam Raimi
Sabrina: Secrets of a Teenage Witch	2013–2014	Trevor Wall
The Conjuring	2013	James Wan
Witches of East End	2013–2014	Maggie Friedman, creator
Salem	2014–2017	Adam Simon, Brannon Braga (creators)
CSI, "The Book of Shadows"	2014	Brad Tanenbaum
Rosemary's Baby	2014	Agnieszka Holland
Into the Woods	2014	Rob Marshall
Maleficent	2014	Robert Stromberg
Melissa and Joey, "Witch Came First"	2014	Melissa Joan Hart
Return to Witch Graveyard	2014	Reuben Rox
The Legends of Oz: Dorothy's Return	2014	Will Finn, Daniel St. Pierre
Hansel vs. Gretel	2015	Ben Demaree

Tales of Halloween	2015	Darren Lynn Bousman et al.
The Witch	2015	Robert Eggers
The Last Witch Hunter	2015	Breck Eisner
The Wiz, Live!	2015	Matthew Diamond, Kenny Leon
Descendants	2015	Kenny Ortega
Blair Witch	2016	Adam Wingard
The Love Witch	2016	Anna Biller
Suicide Squad	2016	David Ayer
Alvinnn! And the Chipmunks, "Switch Witch"	2016	Janice Karman
Emerald City	2017	Matthew Arnold, Josh Friedman
Reel Nightmare	2017	Armand Petri
Alvinnn! And the Chipmunks, "Blabber Mouth"	2017	Janice Karman
Charmed	2018–	Jennie Snyder Urman, Jessica O'Toole, Amy Rardin
The Witch Files	2018	Kyle Rankin
The Incantation	2018	Jude S. Walko
Chilling Adventures of Sabrina	2018–2020	Roberto Aguirre-Sacasa (creator)

Frozen II	2019	Chris Buck, Jennifer Lee
Maleficent: Mistress of Evil	2019	Joachim Rønning
Loon Lake	2019	Ansel Faraj
Juju	2019–	Moon Ferguson (creator)
The Owl House	2020–	Dana Terrace
The Witches	2020	Robert Zemeckis
The Craft: Legacy	2020	Zoe Lister-Jones
Spell	2020	Mark Tonderai
Motherland: Fort Salem	2020–	Eliot Laurence (creator)

A Woman Unleashed:
Revisited

Going back to the beginning, the witch entered early Hollywood as an easily definable narrative character with only marginal associations to the powerfully embedded
social or religious ideology of centuries past. In an American cultural system that
placed reason above belief, the witch's symbolic value was contained within genre and
her construction limited. In those early days, she was simply a whimsical figure of
fantasy (e.g., *The Wonderful Wizard of Oz*, 1910), an old woman in the woods, or the
victim of overzealous religiosity and social greed (e.g., *Joan the Woman*, 1916).

As the film industry evolved and eventually was strangled by its own censorship
office, deeper modes of character representation seeped into the witch's construction,
and her value within narrative language expanded, although remaining within the
clear genre-based structural confines (e.g., *Spitfire*, 1934) of the earlier decades. This
shift also provided more overt depictions of the witch as the woman gone astray (e.g.,
Weird Woman, 1944). At the same time, these nuanced representations also provided
a pathway for subversive readings by a population of viewers looking for a means of
escaping their otherwise repressive social experience.

Then, as society shifted again, as the censorship code was dismantled, and as gender equality rose to the forefront of political rhetoric, the witch's role within narrative
productions changed again. She entered the horror genre in full, evoking the age-old
religious iconography that posited witchcraft as destructive and evil (e.g., *Rosemary's
Baby*, 1968). However, through the undercurrents of society and the presence of a
modern Witchcraft movement, magic as a real and viable practice slowly emerged
into the public eye, challenged the boundaries of acceptability and, in cinematic
terms, pushed to the surface a subversive relationship between the viewer and the

witch and normalized her within suburban America's standards of being (e.g., *Practical Magic*, 1998).

By 2010, a final witch cycle emerges pushing construction further, allowing the witch to challenge structures and standards rather than accepting them. By 2020, witchcraft narratives had embraced the depth and complexity of symbolic meaning possible within that single character, one that had always been present. The witch is presented as either good or evil, as both or neither. She is always transgressive, radical, and dangerous, but often necessary. Thematically, the most contemporary witch constructions return the witch to her basic form: the amoral figure who acts as moral gauge for the main characters, demonstrating that it's not the power that's evil but what we do with it. "Be careful what you wish for" is her motto.

The American viewership's love affair with fictional witches and witchcraft, whether occult or fantasy, appears to have grown over time, or at the very least become more publicly expressed. While the entirety of witch constructions do use key iconic language stemming from pre-Hollywood history (e.g., black pointed hats, brooms, full moons), the American cinematic witch archetype emerged on its own terms, perpetrated by American industry, culture, history, and sociopolitical trends. As a result, a unique language developed, which eventually formed ideological concepts unique to the American way from green skin to Salem's legacy to the inclusion of Hoodoo.

After removing excess details, the sensationalism, the fanfare, and the kitsch found in most representations, the American narrative witch is at her very essence a woman unleashed, coinciding with the age-old ideology. She is the woman who knows too much, who does too much, who exists at the borders of society to challenge or even break its boundaries. At Hollywood's start, the witch was largely ignored, then she was contained either thematically or narratively. Later, she was demonized and then respected within limits but, at the very least, heard. Finally, she is reconsidered on her own terms. These changes in representation are less reflective of the population's interest in Witchcraft and more reflective of shifting sociocultural trends regarding gender politics, religious expression, and female agency. No matter the societal standards, the witch is always the woman on the edge. Therefore, as the boundaries of social values and conduct shift, the witch naturally does as well. She is never the accepted central female figure for long, because at essence she is a radical.

Therefore, it is not difficult to understand how characters like the Wicked Witch of the West or the cast of *The Craft* (1996) invoked powerful responses in their viewership, specifically in women and girls. If the witch archetype represents the expression of unfettered, authentic femininity, in whatever form that may take, those sectors of society who feel confined by a constrictive social order or simply by the virtue of being a teenager, would gravitate to such radical modes of representation. This concept was illustrated directly in George Romero's 1973 film *Hungry Wives*.

While early films may have provided a subversive pleasure for its female viewers, later films openly invited them to entertain and embrace their power through unfettered expressions of magic (e.g., *The Love Witch*, 2016). In the case of evil witches, they often have a backstory of abuse justifying her actions and making her sympathetic and proving that her power is what can ultimately save her, her family, and even the world (e.g., *The Craft: Legacy*, 2020). As Steven Sondheim suggested in his musical *Into the Woods* (2014), maybe the witch was right after all, even if her actions were not.

However, it is important to note that while the most contemporary narratives do make progress in their expression of dynamic female agency, two entirely new themes develop: the monster witch and the woman as victim. While the older films delineate between the accused woman, the wild woman, and the fantasy witch, the later films are not quite as clear in these constructions. This development allows for the creation of an extreme evil witch devoid of any ideological nuance. This seemingly takes the character construction out of the realms of all socially based critique by making the so-called witch a physical abomination, a monstrosity of epic proportion that is undeniably nonhuman. She is the ultimate evil (e.g., *The Last Witch Hunter*, 2015).

At the same time, an increasing number of witches take on the mantle of the accused. As such, witchcraft becomes a safety net for the oppressed. She's a witch because she is damaged. Allegorically speaking, defining the powerful woman as a victim frames the woman only in terms of her disempowerment. The witch does not exist in and of herself without that trauma (e.g., *The Witch*, 2015). Her proverbial scars become the source, so to speak, of her magic. There are exceptions, of course, specifically within lighter fantasy fare (e.g., *Twitches*, 2005). However, in general, the last two periods introduce these two new extremes in witch construction: a literal manifestation of monstrous femininity devoid of all humanity and a woman only empowered by her victimhood.

There is still much room for negotiation; the story is not over. The witch's existence is so basic within human society that she will continue to shift as culture does in relation to gender politics, religiosity, sexuality, race, and the power of the individual within society. Where the narrative witch goes remains to be seen. As noted in the introduction and shown by this study, it is in fact our personal standards of normalcy that define the female rebel. How she makes us feel and how we interpret her symbolic meaning is dependent upon our own relationship to overarching culture, who we are, and what we define as progressive. It is through our own ideological experience that we recognize the witch. She is as much defined by who we are as who she is. And, as a result, the witch will always be someone who is elusive, just beyond our grasp, or perhaps even ahead of our time.

Bibliography

"20 Years of The Craft: Why We Needed More of Rochelle." *Graveyard Shift Sisters* (blog), November 16, 2016. http://www.graveyardshiftsisters.com/2016/11/20 -years-of-craft-why-we-needed-more-of.html.

"ABC Protest Update." *Circle Network News.* Summer 1991.

"Act Now to Uphold Religious Freedom for Wiccans." *Circle Network News.* Spring 1991.

Adams, Gretchen A. *The Specter of Salem: Remembering the Witch Trials in Nineteenth-Century America.* Chicago: University of Chicago Press, 2008.

Addis, Cameron. "Conservative Resurgence." History Hub. Accessed March 1, 2020. http://sites.austincc.edu/caddis/conservative-resurgence.

Adelman, Janet. "Born of Woman: Fantasies of Maternal Power in *Macbeth*." In *Shakespearean Tragedy and Gender*, edited by Madelon Sprengnether and Shirley Nelson Garner, 105–134. Bloomington: Indiana University Press, 1996.

Algeo, John. "Oz—A Notable Theosophist: L. Frank Baum." *American Theosophist* 74 (1986): 270–273. http://www.theosophical.org/publications.

Aloi, Peg. "Blair Witch Project: An Interview with Directors." Witchvox. July 11, 1999.

———. "Witches Are Having a Moment. It Isn't the First Time." *Bustle.* July 17, 2019. https://www.bustle.com/p/waking-the-witch-author-pam-grossman-on -why-witches-are-having-such-a-huge-cultural-moment-18204873.

Andersen, Hans Christian. "The Little Mermaid (Den Lille Havfrue)." Translated by Jean Hersholt. Updated September 19, 2019. Odense, Denmark: University of

Southern Denmark. First published 1837. https://andersen.sdu.dk/vaerk /hersholt/TheLittleMermaid_e.html.

Andrews, William Ressman. "The Scarecrow of Oz." Review of *His Majesty the Scarecrow*, by L. Frank Baum. *Motion Picture News*. October 24, 1914, 61.

Anselmo-Sequeira, Diana. "Apparitional Girlhood: Material Ephemerality and the Historiography of Female Adolescence in Early American Film." *Spectator* 33, no. 1 (Spring 2013): 25–35.

"*A Puritan Episode.*" Review of *A Puritan Episode*, by unknown director. *The Moving Picture News*, September 13, 1913, 27.

"At the Princess—*A Witch of Salem Town.*" Review of *A Witch of Salem Town*, by Lucius Henderson. *The Huntington Herald.* June 17, 1915.

"At the Strand." Review of *Witchcraft*, by Frank Reicher. *The Scranton Republican.* November 15, 1916, 13.

Baker, Emerson W. *A Storm of Witchcraft: The Salem Trials and The American Experience.* New York: Oxford University Press, 2015.

Barton, Jeff. "Mother Goose Gets a Makeover …" Princeton University Library Blogs. October 30, 2015. https://blogs.princeton.edu/cotsen/2015/10/mother-goose -gets-a-makeover/.

Baskette, Kirtley. "The Amazing Inside Story of How They Made 'Snow White.'" *Photoplay* 52, no. 4 (April 4, 1938): 22–23, 68–70.

Bathrick, Serafina Kent. "Ragtime: The Horror of Growing Up Female." *Jump Cut* 14 (1977): 9.

Baum, L. Frank. *Oz: The Complete Collection.* Vol. 1. New York: Aladdin, 2013.

———. *Oz: The Complete Collection.* Vol. 2. New York: Aladdin, 2013.

Bean, Jennifer M. "Introduction: Toward a Feminist Historiography of Early Cinema." In *A Feminist Reader in Early Cinema*, edited by Jennifer M. Bean and Diane Negra, 1–25. Durham: Duke University Press, 2002.

Beeler, Karin. "Old Myths, New Powers: Images of Second-Wave and Third-Wave Feminism in *Charmed.*" In *Investigating Charmed: The Magic Power of TV*, edited by Karin Beeler and Stan Beeler 101–111. London: I.B. Tauris, 2007.

Beeler, Karin, and Stan Beeler. *Investigating Charmed: The Magic Power of TV.* London: I. B. Tauris, 2007.

Bell, Elizabeth, "Somatexts at the Disney Shop." In *From Mouse to Mermaid: The Politics of Film, Gender, and Culture*, edited by Elizabeth Bell, Lynda Haas, and Laura Sells, 107–124. Bloomington: Indiana University Press, 1995.

Bell, Emma, and Neil Mitchell, eds. *Directory of World Cinema: Britain*. Bristol, UK: Intellect Publishing, 2012.

Bell, Joseph N. "TV's Witch to Watch." *Pageant*. April 1965. http://www.harpies bizarre.com/vintage-witch2watch.htm.

Bernardin, Marc. "The 25 Most Powerful Film Franchises in Hollywood … and Why They Matter More than Movie Stars." *Los Angeles Times*. California Times. June 17, 2016. https://www.latimes.com/entertainment/movies/la-ca-mn-25-most -powerful-franchises-20160524-snap-story.html.

Bernstein, Matthew. *Walter Wanger, Hollywood Independent*. Minneapolis: The University of Minnesota Press, 2000.

Bishop, Tom. "Willy Wonka's Everlasting Film Plot." *BBC News*. July 11, 2005. http:// news.bbc.co.uk/2/hi/entertainment/4660873.stm.

"*The Blackened Hills*." Review of *The Blackened Hills*, by Allan Dwan. *The Moving Picture World* 14, no. 12 (Oct.–Dec. 1912): 1232.

Blaetz, Robin. *Visions of the Maid: Joan of Arc in American Film and Culture*. Charlottesville: The University of Virginia Press, 2001.

Blanton, Crystal. "Column: *American Horror Story: Coven*, Witches, Television, and Diversity." *The Wild Hunt*. November 15, 2013. http://wildhunt.org/2013/11 /american-horror-story-coven-witches-television-and-diversity.html.

Bogdanovich, Peter. *Interviews with Orson Welles*. Internet Archive. 1969–1972, 27:12. https://archive.org/details/InterviewsWithOrsonWelles.

Bogle, Donald. *Toms, Coons, Mulattoes, Mammies, and Bucks: An Interpretive History of Blacks in American Films*. New York: Continuum, 1996.

Breene, Katlyn. "Samhain Rite for Hecate." Wisdom of Hypatia. http://wisdom ofhypatia.com, 1995. (Page discontinued.)

Buchanan, Larry. *"It Came from Hunger!" Tales of a Cinema Schlockmeister*. Columbia, SC: Larry Buchanan, 1996.

Burstyn, Ellen. *Lessons in Becoming Myself*. London: Riverhead Books, 2007.

Bush, W. Stephen. "*A Daughter of the Gods*." Review of *A Daughter of the Gods*, by Herbert Brenon. *The Moving Picture World*. November 4, 1916: 673.

Butterfield, Fox. "Television; The Witches of Salem Get a New Hearing." Review of *Three Sovereigns for Sarah*, by Philip Leacock. *The New York Times*, October 28, 1984.

Cantu, Maya. "John Van Druten Biographical Program Note, London Wall, Mint Theater Company." *Academia* (February 2014): 5–7. https://www.academia .edu/5279265/John_Van_Druten_Biographical_Program_Note_London_Wall _Mint_Theater_Company.

Card, James. *Seductive Cinema: The Art of Silent Film*. New York: Alfred A. Knopf, Inc., 1994.

Carrington, Hereward. "The Strangest Man I Have Ever Known: Aleister Crowley." Edited by Michael Kolson. (Seattle: Night of Pan Books, 2011) on *Gorish* (blog), Blogger, March 8, 2015. http://gorish.blogspot.com/2015/03/the-strangest-man-i -have-ever-known.html.

Carvell, Tim. "How The Blair Witch Project Built Up So Much Buzz Movie Mogul-dom on a Shoestring." *Fortune* magazine. August 26, 1999. https://money.cnn .com/magazines/fortune/fortune_archive/1999/08/16/264276/.

Chalmers, J. P., ed. Review of *In the Days of Witchcraft* by unknown director. *The Moving Picture World* 4, no. 15 (April 10, 1909): 449.

Chalmers, J. P., and Thomas Bedding, F.R.P.S., eds., "Biograph Films, Released September 26th, 1910, *Rose O' Salem-Town*, A Story of Puritan Witchcraft." Review of *Rose of Salem-Town*, by D. W. Griffith. *The Moving Picture World* 7, no. 14 (October 1, 1910): 761.

———. "Blunder in the Moving Pictures," Review of *The House of the Seven Gables*, by J. Searle Dawley. *The Moving Picture World* 7, no. 22 (November 26, 1910): 1242.

———. "Geraldine Farrar as Joan of Arc." *The Moving Picture World* 30, no. 13 (December 30, 1916): 1944.

———. "*In the Days of Witchcraft*." Review of *In the Days of Witchcraft* by unknown director. *The Moving Picture World* 4, no. 17 (April 24, 1909): 517.

———. *Rose O' Salem-Town* Promotional Advertisement. *The Moving Picture World* 7, no. 14 (October 1, 1910): 760.

———. "*The Witches' Cavern*." Review of *The Witches' Cavern* by unknown director. *The Moving Picture World* 5, no. 20 (November 13, 1909): 695.

Clifton, Chas. *Her Hidden Children: The Rise of Wicca and Paganism in America*. Lanham, MD: AltaMira Press, 2006.

Cohen, Karl F. *Forbidden Animation: Censored Cartoons and Blacklisted Animators in America*. Jefferson, NC: McFarland & Company Inc, 2004.

Cook, David A. *A History of Narrative Film*. New York: W. W. Norton & Company, 1996.

Counter, Rosemary. "The Most Cursed Hit Movie Ever Made." Vanity Fair. June 1, 2017. https://www.vanityfair.com/hollywood/2017/06/the-most-cursed-hit-movie-ever-made-rosemarys-baby.

Creed, Barbara. *The Monstrous-Feminine: Film, Feminism, Psychoanalysis*. London: Routledge, 1993.

Crowther, Bosley. "'The Story of Three Loves,' in Technicolor, is Presented at Radio City Music Hall." Review of *The Story of Three Loves*, by Vincente Minnelli. *The New York Times*. March 6, 1953. https://www.nytimes.com/1953/03/06/archives/the-screen-in-review-the-story-of-three-loves-in-technicolor-is.html.

Dahl, Roald. *The Witches*. New York: Scholastic Incorporated, 1997.

Davis, Amy M. *Good Girls and Wicked Witches: Women in Disney's Feature Animation*. New Barnet, UK: John Libbey Publishing, 2006.

DeCarlo, Dan, and George Gladir. *Archie's Mad House, Issue #22*. Archie Comic Publications Inc: 1962.

Desta, Yohana. "Pixar's Had a Problem with Women for Decades." *Vanity Fair*. November 22, 2017. http://vanityfair.com/hollywood/2017/11/pixar-john-lasseter-boys-club

Dickens, Donna. "If It Weren't for Vin Diesel's 'D&D' Character, 'The Last Witch Hunter' Wouldn't Exist." Uproxx. OpenWeb. September 30, 2015. http://uproxx.com/hitfix/if-it-werent-for-vin-diesels-dungeons-dragons-character-the-last-witch-hunter-wouldnt-exist.

Disney, Walt. "Temperamental Dwarfs Held Up 'Snow White,' Walt Disney Reveals." *The New York World-Telegram*. January 8, 1938, 40, 48.

Doherty, Thomas. *Hollywood's Censor: Joseph I. Breen & the Production Code Administration*. New York: Columbia University Press, 2007.

"Éclair—*Feather Top*." Review of *Feathertop*, by unknown director. *The Pittsburgh Daily Post*. June 6, 1912, 36.

Edwards, Emily D. *Metaphysical Media: The Occult Experience in Popular Culture*. Carbondale: Southern Illinois University Press, 2005.

Eliot, Marc. *Walt Disney: Hollywood's Dark Prince: A Biography*. New York: Carol Publishing Group, 1993.

"Ellen Burstyn's True Face." Belief.net. June 7, 2017. https://www.beliefnet.com /entertainment/celebrities/ellen-burstyns-true-face.aspx

Everson, William K. *American Silent Film*. New York: Da Capo Press, 1998.

"Evil Witch Sweeps Sesame Street." *The Burlington Daily Times News*. February 7, 1976.

Faludi, Susan. *Backlash: The Undeclared War Against American Women*. New York: Doubleday, 1991.

Finch, Christopher. *The Art of Walt Disney: From Mickey Mouse to the Magic Kingdoms*. New York: Abrams Books, 1975.

"*Folly of Vanity*: A Study in Nudity." Review of *Folly of Vanity*, by Maurice Elvey. *Exhibitor's Trade Review*. February 14, 1925, 85.

"*Folly of Vanity*." Review of *Folly of Vanity*, by Maurice Elvey. *Motion Picture Magazine*. February–July 1925.

Ford, Rebecca. "'Beautiful Creatures' Star Viola Davis on Why Her Character Isn't a Maid in the Adaptation (Q&A)." *The Hollywood Reporter*. February 12, 2013. http://www.hollywoodreporter.com/news/beautiful-creatures-star-viola -davis-420439.

"Fox Film Corporation." Review of *Babes in the Woods*, by Chester M. Franklin and Sidney A. Franklin. *Motion Picture World*. December 22, 1917.

Franckling, Ken. "Witches Work to Counter Bad Image." *Lodi-News Sentinel*. October 26, 1988.

Gans, Eric. "Moral Heroism." *Chronicles of Love & Resentment* 237 (June 9, 2001). http://anthropoetics.ucla.edu/views/vw237/.

Garber, Megan. "*Game of Thrones* and the Paradox of Female Beauty." *The Atlantic*. April 25, 2016. https://www.theatlantic.com/entertainment/archive/2016/04 /game-of-thones-red-woman-old-ageism/479760.

Gardner, Gerald. *Gardnerian Book of Shadows*. Edited by Aiden Kelly. London: Forgotten Books, 2008.

"Geraldine Shines as *Joan of Arc*." Review of *Joan the Woman*, by Cecil B. DeMille. *The Winnipeg Tribune*. January 6, 1917.

Gibson, Marion. "Retelling Salem Stories: Gender Politics and Witches in American Culture." *European Journal of American Culture* 25, no. 2 (August 2006): 85–107. https://doi.org/10.1386/ejac.25.2.85/1.

"Grand Theater Tonight." Review of *The Witch of Salem,* by Raymond B. West. *The Indiana Gazette.* December 22, 1913, 7.

Grant, Barry Keith, and Christopher Sharrett, eds. *Planks of Reason: Essays on the Horror Film.* Revised edition. Lanham, MD: The Scarecrow Press, 1996.

Greenberg, James. *Roman Polanski: A Retrospective.* New York: Harry N. Abrams, 2013.

Greene, Heather. "Film Review: *The Witch* (2016)." *The Wild Hunt.* February 21, 2016. http://wildhunt.org/2016/02/review-robert-eggers-the-witch.html.

———. "Review: CBS' *CSI* and 'The Book of Shadows.'" *The Wild Hunt.* October 22, 2014. http://wildhunt.org/2014/10/review-cbs-csi-and-the-book-of-shadows .html.

———. "Review: Disney's *Frozen*: A Tale of Two Princesses." *The Wild Hunt.* December 1, 2013. http://wildhunt.org/2013/12/disneys-frozen-a-tale-of-two -princesses.html.

———. "Review: Disney's *Maleficent.*" *The Wild Hunt.* June 1, 2014. http://wildhunt .org/2014/06/review-disneys-maleficent.html.

———. "Review: WGN's America's *Salem.*" *The Wild Hunt.* April 24, 2014. http:// wildhunt.org/2014/04/review-wgn-americas-salem.html.

Greenhill, Pauline, and Sidney Eve Matrix, eds. "Envisioning Ambiguity." Introduction to *Fairy Tale Films: Visions of Ambiguity.* Logan, Utah: Utah State University Press, 2010.

Griffiths, Nick. "America's First Family." *The Times Magazine* 5, no. 16 (April 15, 2000): 25, 27–28. https://www.simpsonsarchive.com/other/articles/firstfamily .html.

Grimm, Jacob, and Wilhelm Grimm. "Little Snow-White." First published in *The Grimm Brothers' Children's and Household Tales.* Vol. 1–2. Germany: Dieterich, 1857. Translated by D. L. Ashliman. http://www.pitt.edu/~dash/grimm053.html.

———. "The Frog Prince or Iron Heinrich." First published in *Children's and Household Tales.* Vol. 1–2. Germany: Dieterich, 1857. Translated by D. L. Ashliman. http://www.pitt.edu/~dash/grimm001.html.

———. "The Six Swans." First published in *The Grimm Brothers' Children's and Household Tales.* Vol. 1–2. Germany: Dieterich, 1857. Translated by D. L. Ashliman. http://www.pitt.edu/~dash/grimm049.html.

Gross, Edward. "Interview Charmed: Constance Burge the Charmed One." *TV Zone* 126. Visual Imagination Ltd. April 11, 2000. https://www.visimag.com/tvzone /t126_display.htm.

Gross, Ed. "'Charmed' Creator Spills Best-Kept Show Secrets in a Recovered Interview (EXCLUSIVE)." *In Touch Weekly*. February 16, 2018. https://www.intouch weekly.com/posts/charmed-cast-secrets-154161/.

Hall, Mordaunt. "Der Letzle Mann—The Screen." Review of *Folly of Vanity*, by Maurice Elvey. *New York Times*. January 28, 1925. https://www.nytimes.com /1925/01/28/archives/the-screen.html.

Hamilton, Margaret. Introduction to *The Making of the Wizard of Oz*, by Aljean Harmetz, xix–xxiv. New York: Hyperion, 1998.

Hanauer, Joan. "NBC Looks at America's Most Unreported Crime—Incest." Review of *Tabitha*, prod. by George Yanok. *Warsaw Times Union*. May 5, 1977.

"*Hansel and Gretel.*" Review of *Hansel and Gretel*, by Alfred J. Goulding. *The Film Daily* 26, no. 6 (December 16, 1923): 12.

Hansen, Miriam. *Babel and Babylon: Spectatorship in American Silent Film*. Cambridge: Harvard University Press, 1991.

Harmetz, Aljean. *The Making of the Wizard of Oz*. New York: Hyperion, 1998.

Harty, Kevin J. *Cinema Arthuriana: Twenty Essays*. Jefferson, NC: McFarland, 2012.

Hawthorne, Nathaniel. *Feathertop: A Moralized Tale*. France: Feedbooks, 2013. http://www.feedbooks.com.

Hay Moon Pictures. "*Witches Night*: Directed and Written by Paul Traynor." Press kit. July 31, 2007. http://witchesnight.com/press.html.

Higashi, Sumiko. "The New Woman and Consumer Culture: Cecil B. DeMille's Sex Comedies." In *A Feminist Reader in Early Cinema*. Edited by Jennifer M. Bean and Diane Negra. 298–332. Durham: Duke University Press, 2002.

Hoffman, Alice. *Practical Magic*. New York: Berkley Books, 1995.

Horowitz, Mitch. *Occult America: The Secret History of How Mysticism Shaped Our Nation*. New York: Bantam Books, 2010.

Huson, Paul. *Mastering Witchcraft: A Practical Guide for Witches, Warlocks and Covens*. Bloomington, Indiana: iUniverse Incorporated, 2006.

"*In the Days of Witchcraft.*" Review of *In the Days of Witchcraft*, by unknown director. *Tyrone Daily Herald*. April 21, 1909, 4.

"*In the Days of Witchcraft* Shown in American Films." Review of *In the Days of Witchcraft*, by Fred Huntley. *The Anaconda Standard*. August 14, 1913, 8.

"*Ivanhoe.*" Review of *Ivanhoe*, by Herbert Brenon. *The Moving Picture News*. August 30, 1913, 12.

James, Caryn. "When the Ladies Take Off Their Wigs, Head for Home. Fast." Review of *The Witches* by Nicolas Roeg. *The New York Times*. August 24, 1990. https://www.nytimes.com/1990/08/24/movies/review-film-when-the-ladies-take-off-their-wigs-head-for-home-fast.html.

Jarrett, Christian. "The Lure of Horror." *The Psychologist* 24, no. 11 (November 2011): 812–815. London: The British Psychological Society. https://thepsychologist.bps.org.uk/volume-24/edition-11/lure-horror.

Kael, Pauline. "Review of 'The Wiz.'" *The New Yorker*. October 30, 1978.

Kirby, Alan. "The Death of Postmodernism and Beyond." *Philosophy Now: A Magazine of Ideas* 58 (November/December 2006). London: Philosophy Now. https://philosophynow.org/issues/58/The_Death_of_Postmodernism_And_Beyond.

"Kinemacolor does '*Feathertop*.'" Review of *Feathertop*, by unknown director. *The Moving Picture World*. April–June 1913.

Knopper, Steve. "Behind the Scenes of *The Wiz* with Michael Jackson." *Time Magazine*. December 3, 2015. https://time.com/4135018/the-wiz-michael-jackson/.

Kramer, Heinrich, and James Sprenger. *The Malleus Maleficarum*. Translated by Reverend Montague Summers. Original 1486; Translation, 1927. New York: Dover Publications, 2012.

Kristeva, Julia. *Powers of Horror: An Essay on Abjection*. Translated by Leon S. Roudiez. New York: Columbia University Press, 1982.

Krzywinska, Tanya. *A Skin for Dancing In: Possession, Witchcraft and Voodoo in Film*. Trowbridge, Wiltshire: Flicks Books, 2000.

Langer, Mark. "Animation's Early Years." UCLA Preserved Animation Website. UCLA Film & Television Archive. n.d. http://animation.library.ucla.edu/pdf/langeressay.pdf.

Lawless, Daphne. "Weird Sisters and Wild Women: The Changing Depiction of Witches in Literature, from Shakespeare to Science Fiction." Masters diss, Victoria University of Wellington, 1999.

Leiber, Fritz. *Conjure Wife*. New York: Lion Books, Inc., 1953.

"*The Leprechawn*," Review of *The Leprechawn*, by Edwin S. Porter. *The Moving Picture World*. September 26, 1908, 241.

Leszczak, Bob. *Single Season Sitcoms, 1948–1979: A Complete Guide*. Jefferson, NC: McFarland Publishing, 2012.

Lev-Ram, Michal. "Frozen's Elsa Wins in Retail, but Anna Is the Real Leader." *Fortune*. November 6, 2014. http://fortune.com/2014/11/06/disney-frozen/.

Levin, Gary. "Disney Finds a Place for Tweens: It's not a Mickey Mouse Network Anymore." *USA Today*. Updated October 27, 2005. https://usatoday30.usatoday.com/life/television/news/2005-10-26-disney_x.htm.

Linder, Doug. "The McMartin Preschool Abuse Trial: A Commentary." Faculty website, University of Missouri-Kansas City. 2003. http://law2.umkc.edu/faculty/projects/ftrials/mcmartin/mcmartinaccount.html.

"*Lord Feathertop*," Review of *Lord Feathertop*, by Edwin S. Porter. *Moving Picture World* 3, no. 23 (December 5, 1908): 458.

Lowry, Brian. "TV Review: 'Rosemary's Baby.'" Review of *Rosemary's Baby*, by Agnieszka Holland. *Variety*, May 7, 2014. https://variety.com/2014/tv/reviews/tv-review-rosemarys-baby-1201172155/.

MacKaye, Percy. *The Scarecrow: Or, The Glass of Truth; A Tragedy of the Ludicrous*. New York: MacMillan Co., 1908.

Mallory, Michael. "Which Witch is Which?" *Animation Magazine*. October 23, 2014. http://www.animationmagazine.net/top-stories/which-witch-is-which/.

Maltin, Leonard. *Of Mice and Magic: A History of American Animated Cartoons*. Revised and updated edition. New York: Plume Group, 1987.

Marks, Lee, and Ron E. Fellow. "Witches & Demons Are Among Us!" *Famous Monsters of Filmland*. July 1970, 7–21.

Marubbio, M. Elise. *Killing the Indian Maiden: Images of Native American Women in Film*. Lexington, KY: University of Kentucky Press, 2006.

Mask, Mia, ed. *Contemporary Black American Cinema: Race, Gender and Sexuality at the Movies*. New York: Routledge, 2012.

Maslin, Janet. "Bette Midler, Queen Witch in Heavy Makeup." Review of *Hocus Pocus*, by Kenny Ortega. *The New York Times*. July 16, 1993. https://www.nytimes.com/1993/07/16/movies/review-film-bette-midler-queen-witch-in-heavy-makeup.html.

———. "'Resurrection' Has the Manner of a Fairy Tale." Review of *Resurrection*, by Daniel Petrie. *The New York Times*. November 7, 1980. https://www.nytimes.com/1980/11/07/archives/resurrection-has-the-manner-of-a-fairy-tale.html.

McDonough, Jimmy. *The Ghastly One: The Sex-Gore Netherworld of Filmmaker Andy Milligan*. Chicago, IL: A Cappella Book, 2001.

McGilligan, Patrick, ed. *Backstory 2: Interviews with Screenwriters of the 1940s and 1950s.* Los Angeles: University of California Press, 1997.

"McMartin v. County of Los Angeles," 1988. Source: Justia. https://law.justia.com /cases/california/court-of-appeal/3d/202/848.html.

McNamara, Tara. "Jennifer Lee, On Becoming Disney's First Female Director." *Fandango.* October 10, 2013. http://www.fandango.com/movie-news/jennifer-lee-on -becoming-disney-animations-first-female-director-742513.

McQuade, James S. "*The Story of the Blood Red Rose.*" Review of *The Story of the Blood Red Rose,* by Colin Campbell. *The Moving Picture World* (October 17, 1914): 341.

Miller, Arthur. *The Crucible.* New York: Penguin, 1981.

Miller, Catriona. "I Just Want to be Normal Again: Power and Gender in Charmed." *Investigating Charmed: The Magic Power of TV,* edited by Karin Beeler and Stan Beeler, 67–78. London: I.B. Taurus, 2007.

Miller, Jeff. "He Introduced Abbott & Costello to Frankenstein & the Invisible Man: A Conversation with Screenwriter Robert Lees." *Filmfax.* October/January 2000.

"*The Mischievous Elf.*" Review of *The Mischievous Elf,* by unknown director. *The Moving Picture World.* December 25, 1909, 927.

Mosely, Raymond. "Perspective: The Durable Joan." *Newsweek,* December 27, 1948. Source: *Joan of Arc* Production Files, MPAA PCA records, Margaret Herrick Library, Academy of Motion Picture Arts and Sciences, Beverly Hills, California.

"*The Mountain Witch.*" Synopsis of *The Mountain Witch,* by George Melford. *Kalem Calendar,* February 1, 1913, 15.

Mowry, Tia. September 3, 2020. "Recreating My Sister, Sister & Twitches Hair Styles." Tia Mowry's Quick Fix. Facebook. June 7, 2019. https://www.facebook.com /TiaMowrysQuickFix/videos/1869331016499731/?__so__=serp_videos_tab.

Muir, John Kenneth. *An Analytical Guide to Television's One Step Beyond, 1959–1961.* Jefferson, NC: McFarland, 2001.

Naremore, James. *The Magic World of Orson Welles.* 2nd ed. Dallas, TX: Southern Methodist University Press, 1989.

Nashawaty, Chris. "Sidney Lumet: How He Saw His Oscar-Nominated Films." *Entertainment Weekly.* Updated April 4, 2011. https://ew.com/gallery/sidney-lumet -how-he-saw-his-oscar-nominated-films/?slide=345132.

Navasky, Victor. "The Demons of Salem, With Us Still." Review of *The Crucible* by Nicholas Hytner. *The New York Times.* September 8, 1996. https://www.nytimes.com/1996/09/08/movies/the-demons-of-salem-with-us-still.html.

"The New Fox Pictures." *The Moving Picture World* 33, no. 5 (August 4, 1917): 804.

O'Dell, Cary. "*Bewitched*: Rethinking a Sixties Sitcom Classic." In *Television Quarterly* 36, no. 1 (Fall 2005): 65–68. New York: The Journal of the National Academy of Television Arts and Sciences. https://worldradiohistory.com/Archive-Television-Quarterly/TVQ_2005-Fall.pdf.

O'Hara, Helen. "Did the Devil Kill Jayne Mansfield?" *The Telegraph.* May 9, 2018. https://www.telegraph.co.uk/films/0/church-satan-founder-anton-lavey-seduced-jayne-mansfield/.

Perrault, Charles. "Sleeping Beauty in the Wood." *Perrault's Fairy Tales.* Translated by A. E. Johnson. New York: Dover Publications, Inc., 1969.

Petherbridge, Deanna. *Witches & Wicked Bodies.* Edinburgh: National Galleries of Scotland in association with the British Museum, 2013.

Pilato, Herbie. *Bewitched Forever: The Immortal Companion to Televisions Most Magical Supernatural Situation Comedy.* Irving TX: Tapestry Press, 2004.

Projansky, Sarah, and Leah R. Vande Berg, "Sabrina, the Teenage …?: Girls, Witches, Mortals, and the Limitations of Prime-Time Feminism." *Fantasy Girls: Gender in the New Universe of Science Fiction and Fantasy Television*, edited by Elyce Rae Helford, 13–40. Lanham. Maryland: Rowman & Littlefield Publishers, Inc., 2000.

Purcell, Stephen. "Shakespeare on Television." *The Edinburgh Companion to Shakespeare and the Arts*, edited by Mark Thornton Burnett, Adrian Streete, and Ramona Wray, 522–540. Edinburgh: Edinburgh University Press, 2011.

Purkiss, Diane. *The Witch in History: Early Modern and Twentieth-Century Representations.* London: Routledge, 1996.

Pravadelli, Veronica. "Cinema and the Modern Woman." In *The Wiley-Blackwell History of American Film*, edited by Cynthia Lucia, Roy Grundmann, and Art Simon, 1–22. New York: Blackwell Publishing, 2012.

Radcliffe, E. B. "Is Walt's Wizardry Topped by Mervyn's Magic?" *The Cincinnati Enquirer.* August 27, 1939, 47.

Raw, Laurence. *Adapting Nathaniel Hawthorne to the Screen: Forging New Worlds.* London: Scarecrow Press, Inc, 2008.

"Recent Classifications and Guide to Current Films." The National Catholic Office for Motion Pictures 33, no. 20 (June 27, 1968).

"Recent Films Reviewed." Review of *The House of the Seven Gables*, by J. Searle Dawley. *The Nickelodeon* 4, no. 9 (November 1, 1910): 251.

"Religion Among Millennials." Pew Research Center for Religion and Public Life. February 17, 2010. http://www.pewforum.org/2010/02/17/religion-among-the -millennials/.

"Review of *The Devil Within*," by Arthur Zellner. *Wakefield News*. July 15, 1922, 6.

Review of *Puritan Passions*, by Frank Tuttle. *Oakland Tribune*. September 23, 1923, 17.

Review of *Puritan Passions*, by Frank Tuttle. *Exhibitor's Trade Review*. October 20, 1923, 991.

Review of *Puritan Passions*, by Frank Tuttle. *Exhibitor's Trade Review*, 724.

"Reviews of New Films: *The Witch*," by Van Dyke Brooke. *The New York Dramatic Mirror*. October 31, 1908, 6.

Rhodes, Gary D. *The Birth of the American Horror Film*. Edinburgh: University of Edinburgh Press, 2018.

Rogers, Katharine M. *L. Frank Baum: Creator of Oz: A Biography*. Cambridge, MA: DaCapo Press, 2002.

"*Rose O' Salem-Town*." Review of *Rose of Salem-Town*, by D. W. Griffith. *The Nickelodeon* 4, no. 7 (October 1, 1910): 201.

"*Rose O' Salem-Town*." Review of *Rose of Salem-Town*, by D. W. Griffith. *The Moving Picture World*. October 8, 1910.

Rudnick, Bret. "An Interview with Claire Stansfield." *Whoosh!* 28 (January 1999). http://whoosh.org/issue28/istansfield1.html.

Russell, Sharon. "The Witch in Film." In *Planks of Reason: Essays on the Horror Film*. Revised edition, edited by Barry Keith Grant and Christopher Sharrett, 113–125. Lanham, MD: The Scarecrow Press, 1996.

Sand, George. *La Petite Fadette*. New York: Henry Holt and Company, 1865.

"Satanists 'Amicably' Settle Warner Bros Lawsuit over Chilling Adventures of Sabrina." The Guardian. November 21, 2018. https://www.theguardian.com/film/2018 /nov/22/chilling-adventures-of-sabrina-satanists-settle-warner-bros-case.

Schatz, Thomas. *The Genius of the System: Hollywood Filmmaking in the Studio Era*. New York: Henry Holt and Company, 1988.

Schmidtt, Gavin, trans. "Interview with Jan White, star of *Season of the Witch*," *Killer Interviews*. http://killerinterviews.com.

"Screen News Here and In Hollywood." *The New York Times*. February 19, 1938, 19.

Shakespeare, William. *Macbeth*. New York: Penguin Books, 1984.

Shary, Timothy. *Generation Multiplex: The Image of Youth in Contemporary American Cinema*. Austin: University of Texas Press, 2002.

Shaw, Scott. *Archie's Mad House No. 22*. Oddball Comics. April 2, 2007.

Simpson, Paul. *A Brief Guide To Oz: 75 Years Going Over the Rainbow*. London: Constable & Robinson Ltd., 2013.

Smith, Thorne. *The Passionate Witch*. New York: Sun Dial Press, 1942.

Smoodin, Eric. *Animating Culture: Hollywood Cartoons from the Sound Era*. New Brunswick, NJ: Rutgers University Press, 1993.

Soister, John T. *American Silent Horror, Science Fiction and Fantasy Feature Films: 1913–1929*. Jefferson, NC: McFarland, 2012.

Stedman, Eric. *The Mysteries of Myra: A Serial Squadron Lost Serial Photonovel*. California: Eric Stedman, 2010.

Stephens, Mitchell. "History of Television." Mitchell Stephens Class Pages. Last Modified 2000. http://www.nyu.edu/classes/stephens.

"Stories of the Films: *Hansel and Gretel*." Review of *Hansel and Gretel*, by J. Searle Dawley. *The Motion Picture World* 5, no. 15 (October 9, 1909): 499, 501.

Studlar, Gaylyn. "Oh, 'Doll Divine': Mary Pickford, Masquerade, and the Pedophilic Gaze." In *A Feminist Reader in Early Cinema*, edited by Jennifer M. Bean and Diane Negra, 349–373. Durham: Duke University Press, 2002.

Taft, Jessica K. "Girl Power Politics: Pop-Culture Barriers and Organizational Resistance." In *All About the Girl: Culture, Power, and Identity*, edited by Anita Harris, 69–78. New York: Routledge, 2004.

Thompson, Kristin, and David Bordwell. *Film History: An Introduction*. Boston: McGraw Hill, 2003.

"Tik Tok Man of Oz." Reviews of *His Majesty the Scarecrow*, by L. Frank Baum. *Variety*, May 1913.

Tildesley, Ruth M. "Filming Children for Children: The Delightful Pursuit of Madeline Brandeis." *National Board of Review Magazine* 4, no. 10 (December 1929): 5–7.

Trask, Richard B. "Historian on the Set: The Filming of *Three Sovereigns for Sarah*." Danvers Archival Center: The Peabody Institute Library. 2014. https://www.danverslibrary.org/archive/historian-on-the-set/.

"*The Trials of Faith*," Review of *The Trials of Faith*, by unknown director. *The Moving Picture World* 14, no. 7 (November 16, 1912): 665.

True, Rachel. *True Heart Intuitive Tarot, Guidebook and Deck*. Boston: Houghton Mifflin Harcourt, 2020.

Updike, John. *The Witches of Eastwick*. New York: Ballantine Books, 1984.

Urtheil, Heather. "Producing the Princess Collection: An Historical Look at the Animation of a Disney Heroine." Emory University Film Studies Department. Atlanta, Georgia: 1998.

Van Druten, John. *Bell, Book and Candle*. New York: Dramatist Play Service, 1976.

Vatsal, Radha. "Madeline Brandeis." *Women Film Pioneers Project*. Edited by Jane Gaines, Radha Vatsal, and Monica Dall'Asta. New York: Center for Digital Research and Scholarship Columbia University Libraries, 2013. http://wfpp.cdrs.columbia.edu/pioneer/ccp-madeline-brandeis.

Welter, Barbara. "The Cult of True Womanhood: 1820–1860." *American Quarterly* 18, no. 2, part 1 (Summer, 1966): 151–174. https://doi.org/10.2307/2711179.

Williams, Tony, ed., *George A. Romero: Interviews*. Jackson, MS: University Press of Mississippi, 2011.

Wilson, Dominique Beth. "Morgan le Fay: Celtic Origins and Literary Images." *Celts in Legend and Reality: Papers from the Sixth Australian Conference of Celtic Studies*, edited by Pamela O'Neill, 343–363. Sydney: University of Sydney, 2007.

Winslade, J Lawton. "Teen Witches, Wiccans, and 'Wanna-Blessed-Be's': Pop-Culture Magic in Buffy the Vampire Slayer." *Slayage: The Online International Journal of Buffy Studies*. 2001. http://slayage.tv/essays/slayage1/winslade.htm.

"*The Wise Witch of Fairyland*," Review of *The Wise Witch of Fairyland*, unknown director, *The Moving Picture World* 11, no. 7 (February 17, 1912): 622.

"The Witch." Review of *Spitfire*, by John Cromwell. *Picture Play* 39, no. 6 (February 1934): 47.

"*Witch Girl* Shows Mary Fuller at Best." Review of *Witch Girl*, by Walter Edwin. *The Wilmington Morning Star*. November 8, 1914, 12.

"*Witch of Salem*." Review of *The Witch of Salem*, by Raymond B. West. *The Wichita Daily Times*. December 21, 1913.

"*Witch of Salem Town*." Review of *A Witch of Salem Town*, by Lucius Henderson. *Motography* 13, no. 22 (January–June 1915): 906.

"*The Witch of the Ranch*." Review of *The Witch of the Ranch*, by unknown director. *The Moving Picture World*. June 3, 1911, 1261.

"*The Witch of the Range*." Review of *The Witch of the Range*, by Allan Dwan. *Motography* 5, no. 6 (June 1911): 149.

"*The Witch of the Range*." Review of *The Witch of the Range*, by Allan Dwan. *The Moving Picture World* 8, no. 23 (June 10, 1911): 1326–1327.

"*The Witch of the Range*." Review of *The Witch of the Range*, by Allan Dwan. *The Moving Picture World*. June 24, 1911.

"*The Woman Who Did Not Care*." Review of *The Woman Who Did Not Care*, by unknown director. *The Motion Picture World*. April–June 1913.

Yohalum, John Brightshadow. "An Interview with Pat Devin: Consultant for '*The Craft*,'" Covenant of the Goddess newsletter. March 1998. http://wychwood acastlebetweentheworlds.com/interviewWithPatDevin.htm.

Archival Sources
(ordered chronologically by publication date)

Selig Polyscope. *In the Days of Witchcraft*. 1913. Promotional Flier. Source: Margaret Herrick Library, Academy of Motion Picture Arts and Sciences. Beverly Hills, California. From: www.oscars.org.

Selig Polyscope, *Witch of the Everglades*. 1915. Promotional Flier. Source: Margaret Herrick Library, Academy of Motion Picture Arts and Sciences. Beverly Hills, California. From: www.oscars.org.

James Wingate to Merian C. Cooper. October 10, 1933. Source: *Spitfire* Production Files, MPAA PCA records. Margaret Herrick Library, Academy of Motion Picture Arts and Sciences. Beverly Hills, California.

James Wingate to Merian C. Cooper. December 9, 1933. Source: *Spitfire* Production Files, MPAA PCA records. Margaret Herrick Library, Academy of Motion Picture Arts and Sciences, Beverly Hills, California.

Joseph Breen to N. P. Whitman. January 19, 1934. Source: *Joan of Arc* Production Files, MPAA PCA records. Margaret Herrick Library, Academy of Motion Picture Arts and Sciences, Beverly Hills, California.

Joseph Breen. British Film Board censorship report. February 20, 1935. Source: *Spitfire* Production Files, MPAA PCA records. Margaret Herrick Library, Academy of Motion Picture Arts and Sciences, Beverly Hills, California.

Joseph Breen to John Hammell. August 27, 1936. Source: *Maid of Salem* Production Files, MPAA PCA records. Margaret Herrick Library, Academy of Motion Picture Arts and Sciences. Beverly Hills, California.

William E. Garity to Douglas McKinnon. March 2, 1936. Source: *Snow White and the Seven Dwarfs* Production Files, MPAA PCA records. Margaret Herrick Library, Academy of Motion Picture Arts and Sciences, Beverly Hills, California.

Howard Estabrook. "*Maid of Salem*: Notes on the first draft of treatment," June 13, 1936. Source: Howard Estabrook papers. Margaret Herrick Library, Academy of Motion Picture Arts and Sciences, Beverly Hills, California.

William H. Hays. "Self-Regulation in the Motion Picture Industry," *Annual Report to the Motion Picture Producers and Distributors of American, Inc.*, March 28, 1938. Source: Core Collection Pamphlets. Margaret Herrick Library, Academy of Motion Picture Arts and Sciences, Beverly Hills, California.

Joseph Breen. British Film Board censorship report. December 8, 1939. Source: *The Wizard of Oz,* Production Files, MPAA PCA records. Margaret Herrick Library, Academy of Motion Picture Arts and Sciences, Beverly Hills, California.

Joseph Breen to Luigi Luraschi. January 14, 1942. Source: *I Married a Witch* Production Files, MPAA PCA records. Margaret Herrick Library, Academy of Motion Picture Arts and Sciences. Beverly Hills, California.

Alfred Levitt. Interoffice Communication. January 19, 1942. Source: *I Married a Witch* Memoranda, Paramount Pictures Scripts. Margaret Herrick Library, Academy of Motion Picture Arts and Sciences, Beverly Hills, California.

Joseph Breen to Luigi Luraschi. February 11, 1942. Source: *I Married a Witch* Production Files, MPAA PCA records. Margaret Herrick Library, Academy of Motion Picture Arts and Sciences, Beverly Hills, California.

Luigi Luraschi to Preston Sturges and René Clair. May 4, 1942. Source: *I Married a Witch* Production 1941–1942, Paramount Pictures Production Records. Margaret Herrick Library, Academy of Motion Picture Arts and Sciences, Beverly Hills, California.

William B. Dover to Production Code Administration. July 20, 1953. Source: *Sleeping Beauty* Production Files, MPAA PCA records. Margaret Herrick Library, Academy of Motion Picture Arts and Sciences, Beverly Hills, California.

J.A.V. Interoffice Memo for the Files. June 3, 1956. Source: *The Witch of Guadalupe* Production Films, MPAA PCA records. Margaret Herrick Library, Academy of Motion Picture Arts and Sciences, Beverly Hills, California.

Geoffrey Shurlock to Roger Corman. July 10, 1956. Source: *The Undead* Production Files, MPAA PCA records. Margaret Herrick Library, Academy of Motion Picture Arts and Sciences, Beverly Hills, California.

Geoffrey Shurlock to Harry Cohn. October 22, 1956. Source: *Bell, Book, and Candle* Production Files, MPAA PCA records. Margaret Herrick Library, Academy of Motion Picture Arts and Sciences, Beverly Hills, California.

Morris Murphy. Interoffice Memo for the files. August 14, 1967. Source: *Rosemary's Baby* Production Films, MPAA PCA records. Margaret Herrick Library, Academy of Motion Picture Arts and Sciences, Beverly Hills, California.

Morris Murphy. Interoffice Memo for the files. February 29, 1968. Source: *Rosemary's Baby* Production Films, MPAA PCA records. Margaret Herrick Library, Academy of Motion Picture Arts and Sciences, Beverly Hills, California.

Anna Herrera. Internal Memorandum. April 4, 1976. Source: Children's Televisions Workshop papers. Special Collections, University of Maryland, College Park, Maryland.

Correspondence to Fred Rogers, 1986. Source: Fred Rogers Center Archives, Latrobe, Pennsylvania

Databases, Archives, Libraries, and Similar Resources

American Film Institute Catalog: http://www.afi.com

Behind the Name: www.behindthename.com/name

Buckland Museum of Witchcraft and Magic: http://www.bucklandmuseum.org

Fred Rogers Center: http://www.fredrogerscenter.org/

Hathi Trust Digital Library: http://www.hathitrust.org

Internet Movie Database: http://www.imdb.com

Lantern: https://lantern.mediahist.org

Mary Pickford Foundation: https://marypickford.org

National Film and Sound Archive, Australia: http://www.nfsa.gov.au

National Film Preservation Foundation: http://www.filmpreservation.org

Schomburg Center for Research in Black Culture, New York Public Library Archives & Manuscripts Collection: https://www.nypl.org/locations/schomburg

Silent Film Archive: http://www.silentfilmstillarchive.com

Special Collections at Belk Library, Appalachian State University: http://www.collec-
tions.library.appstate.edu

UCLA Film & Television Archive: http://www.cinema.ucla.edu

University of Maryland Libraries. Films@UM: https://digital.lib.umd.edu/films

Utah State University Digital Folklore Commons: https://digitalcommons.usu.edu/dfp/

Wende and Harry Devlin: http://www.harryandwendedevlin.com

Art Credit List

1. Witch Film Graphic Concentric Rings Diagram (created by the author and Llewellyn art department), page 8

2. Town leaders arrive at Rose's home to arrest her (Dorothy West) and her mother (Clara T. Bracy) for the practice of witchcraft. *Rose O' Salem Town* (1910). [Source: Screengrab. Copyright: Public Domain], page 21

3. After years alone in the Everglades, Dora (Kathlyn Williams) is brought to her senses and reunited with her daughter in *The Witch of the Everglades* (1911). [Source: William Selig Papers, Margaret Herrick Library, Academy of Motion Pictures Arts & Sciences. Copyright: Public Domain], page 29

4. The Wicked Witch of the West flies above the frightened citizens of Oz in *The Wonderful Wizard of Oz* (1910). [Source: Screengrab. Copyright: Public Domain], page 34

5. Glinda the Good descends from above to offer Dorothy advice and magical help in *The Wonderful Wizard of Oz* (1910). [Source: Screengrab. Copyright: Public Domain], page 35

6. Geraldine Farrar stars as Joan of Arc in Cecil B. DeMille's 1916 film *Joan the Woman*. [Source: Library of Congress, Prints & Photographs. Copyright: Public Domain], page 46

7. Actress Mary Pickford (center) pauses for a photo on the set of *Fanchon the Cricket* (1915). [Source: Mary Pickford Foundation and the Margaret Herrick Library, Academy of Motion Pictures Arts & Sciences. Copyright: Public Domain], page 51

8. Australian actress Annette Kellerman stars in *A Daughter of the Gods* (1916), one of the first extravagant fantasy spectacles and the first film to contain a nude scene. [Source: Bain News Service, Publisher. Library of Congress, Library of Congress, Prints & Photographs. Copyright: Public Domain], page 60

9. Spiritualist Hereward Carrington designed the character of the Grand Master after legendary occultist Aleister Crowley. [Source: Ithaca Made Movies. Copyright: Public Domain], page 65

10. Myra earns the help of a woodland witch in her fight against the Black Order in episode 13 of the 1916 serial *The Mysteries of Myra*, starring Jean Sothern as Myra and an unknown actress as the witch. [Source: Ithaca Made Movies. Copyright: Public Domain], page 67

11. Famed child star Baby Peggy appeared with Buddy Williams in *Hansel and Gretel* (1923). Starring (from left to right) Johnny Fox, Buddy Williams as Hansel, and Baby Peggy as Gretel. [Source: Universal Studios/PhotoFest. Copyright: © Universal Pictures], page 78

12. Osgood Perkins stars as Dr. Nicholas and Maude Hill as the witch Goody Rickby in *Puritan Passions* (1923). [Source: Photofest. Copyright: Public Domain], page 81

13. A 1924 advertising poster for the cartoon short *Felix Brings Home the Bacon*. [Source: Soulis Auctions Copyright: Public Domain], page 88

14. Katharine Hepburn as Trigger Hicks, a young Appalachian girl with healing powers, talks to God and dreams of a better life in Paramount's film *Spitfire* (1934). [Source: RKO Radio Pictures/Photofest. Copyright: © RKO Radio Pictures], page 99

15. Claudette Colbert stars as Barbara, a Salem woman who is accused of practicing witch-craft and tried before the town in the historically inspired film *Maid of Salem* (1937). [Source: Paramount Pictures/Photofest. Copyright: © Paramount Pictures], page 102

16. Tituba, played by Madame Sul-Te-Wan, tells Goody Goode, played by Beulah Bondi, stories of magic and dancing from her homeland. [Source: Paramount Pictures/Photofest.com. Copyright: © Paramount Pictures], page 106

17. The Wicked Witch of the West drops in on Glinda and Dorothy in Munchkinland in the MGM adaptation of Baum's classic story *The Wizard of Oz* (1939); seen from left to right: Margaret Hamilton, Judy Garland, Billie Burke.[Source: MGM/Photofest. Copyright: © MGM], page 116

18. Jennifer, a young and mischievous witch, creates a love potion to toy with a man's heart in *I Married a Witch* (1942), starring Veronica Lake. [Source: United Artists /Photofest. Copyright: © United Artists], page 131

19. Anne Gwynne stars as Paula, a young wife struggling with fitting in to American society after growing up in the South Seas. [Source: Universal Pictures / Photofest. Copyright: © Universal Pictures], page 138

20. Ingrid Bergman stars in the prestige film *Joan of Arc* (1948). [Source: RKO/ Photofest. Copyright: © RKO], page 151

21. Rosina Rubylips the witch, voiced by Anna Russell, happily discovers the wandering siblings in the 1954 film *Hansel and Gretel: An Opera Fantasy*. [Source: RKO Radio Pictures/Photofest. Copyright: © RKO Radio Pictures], page 159

22. Pleading with Amanda Summers, Josh Randall explains the dire medical condition that her son faces in *Wanted: Dead or Alive*, "The Healing Woman" (1959). Starring (left to right) Virginia Gregg, Steve McQueen. [Source: CBS/ Photofest. Copyright: © CBS], page 169

23. Aunt Queenie (Elsa Lanchester), Nicky Holroyd (Jack Lemmon), and Gillian Holroyd (Kim Novak) discuss the use of magic in *Bell, Book and Candle* (1958). [Source: Columbia Pictures/Photofest. Copyright: © Columbia Pictures], page 182

24. Lt. Andre Duvalier (Jack Nicholson) confronts Katrina (Dorothy Neumann), a local witch, about her son Eric in Roger Corman's 1963 film *The Terror*. [Source: American International Pictures/Photofest. Copyright: © American International Pictures (AIP)], page 202

25. Elizabeth Montgomery as Samantha Stephens and Agnes Moorehead as Endora befuddle Darrin (Dick York) with magic in *Bewitched* (1964–1972) [Source: ABC/Photofest. Copyright: © ABC], page 207

26. Neighbor Minnie Castavet (Ruth Gordon) and her friend Laura-Louise (Patsy Kelly) visit Rosemary (Mia Farrow) and gift her a locket filled with tannis root in the 1968 horror film *Rosemary's Baby*. [Source: Paramount Pictures/Photofest. © Paramount Pictures], page 214

27. Jan White as Joan Mitchell, a bored suburban housewife, performs her first witchcraft spell that changes her fate and empowers her life in *Hungry Wives* (1973), also released as *Season of the Witch*. [Source: Anchor Bay /Photofest. Copyright: © Anchor Bay], page 228

28. Legendary actor Orson Welles stars as Mr. Cato, the leader of a Satanic coven of witches, in the 1972 horror film *Necromancy*. [Source: Cinema Releasing Corporation /Photofest. © Cinema Releasing Corporation], page 240

29. Played by Mabel King, Evillene, the wicked witch of the musical film *The Wiz*, sits on her throne commanding flying monkeys and a legion of factory workers (1978). [Source: Universal /Photofest. Copyright: © Universal Pictures], page 249

30. While at school, Vivian (Melissa Sue Anderson), a powerful and troubled teenage witch, confronts another teen witch Robin (Mary Beth McDonough) in the made-for-television horror film *Midnight Offerings* (1981). [Source: ABC/PhotoFest. Copyright: © ABC], page 258

31. Donald Symington and Vanessa Redgrave star as Peter and Sarah Cloyce in the American Playhouse special *Three Sovereigns for Sarah* (1985). [Source: Richard B. Trask. Copyright: © Richard B. Trask], page 269

32. In award-winning film *Resurrection* (1980), Edna Mae uses her newly discovered powers to cure and heal her friends and neighbors. Shown: Madeleine Sherwood (far left background), Ellen Burstyn (as Edna). [Source: Universal Pictures /Photofest, © Universal Pictures], page 272

33. Haggis the witch (Florence Schauffler) carries the body of tragic hero Ed Harley (Lance Henriksen) into a graveyard in *Pumpkinhead* (1988). [Source: United Artists/Photofest. © United Artists], page 284

34. In *The Witches of Eastwick* (1987), three local women, Alex, Jane, and Sukie, use magic to rid the town of Darryl Van Horne, who turns out to be the devil. Shown left to right: Cher, Susan Sarandon, and Michelle Pfeiffer. [Source: Warner Brothers/Photofest. © Warner Brothers], page 292

35. Four outcast teens find their power through magic in the breakout film *The Craft* (1996), starring (left to right) Robin Tunney as Sarah, Fairuza Balk as Nancy, Rachel True as Rochelle, and Neve Campbell as Bonnie. [Source: Columbia Pictures/Photofest. © Columbia Pictures], page 299

36. Sister witches Sally and Gillian Owens debate their chosen lifestyles in the 1998 film *Practical Magic*, starring (left to right) Sandra Bullock and Nicole Kidman. [Source: ABC/Photofest © ABC], page 312

37. Joshua Leonard (as himself) looks on in surprise as the team of student filmmakers hunt the Blair Witch. [Source: Artisan Entertainment/Photofest. © Artisan Entertainment], page 325

38. Young witches convince an unsuspecting camper to participate in a satanic ritual in *Witches' Night* (2007), starring as the witches (left to right) Meghan Jones as June, Lauren Ryland as Eva (center, on altar), and Stephanie Cantu as Gretchen. [Source: Publicity Stills/Hay Moon Media], page 332

39. Caleb (Steven Strait), Tyler (Chace Crawford), Chase (Sebastian Stan), and Pogue (Taylor Kitsch) perform a ritual to stop a rogue witch from destroying them in the 2006 film *The Covenant*. [Source: Sony Pictures/Photofest. © Sony Pictures Photographer: Jonathan Wenk], page 336

40. In the popular Disney Channel movie *Twitches*, Tamera Mowry and Tia Mowry play twin witches who only first discover each other and their magical power on their twenty-first birthday. [Source: Disney Channel/Photofest. © Disney Channel], page 340

41. Carice van Houten stars as Melisandre, or the Red Witch, in HBO's epic fantasy series *Game of Thrones* (2011–2019) [Source: HBO/Photofest. Copyright: © HBO], page 364

42. Young witch Queenie, played by Gabourey Sidibe, performs a spell with other students in the third season of *American Horror Story* titled "Coven." [Source: FX Network/Photofest. © FX Network], page 373

43. Elaine, a sociopathic witch played by Samantha Robinson, stirs a new potion in her eclectic California home in the indie film *The Love Witch* (2016). [Source: Anna Biller © Anna Biller], page 382

Index

D

E

F

I

O

P

V

W

To Write to the Author

If you wish to contact the author or would like more information about this book, please write to the author in care of Llewellyn Worldwide Ltd. and we will forward your request. Both the author and publisher appreciate hearing from you and learning of your enjoyment of this book and how it has helped you. Llewellyn Worldwide Ltd. cannot guarantee that every letter written to the author can be answered, but all will be forwarded. Please write to:

Heather Greene
℅ Llewellyn Worldwide
2143 Wooddale Drive
Woodbury, MN 55125-2989

Please enclose a self-addressed stamped envelope for reply,
or $1.00 to cover costs. If outside the U.S.A., enclose
an international postal reply coupon.

Many of Llewellyn's authors have websites with additional information and resources. For more information, please visit our website at http://www.llewellyn.com